T0289880

Alteryx Designer:
The Definitive Guide

Simplify and Automate Your Analytics

Joshua Burkhow

Forewords by Olivia Duane Adams and Dean Stoecker

Beijing • Boston • Farnham • Sebastopol • Tokyo

Alteryx Designer: The Definitive Guide

by Joshua Burkhow

Copyright © 2024 Joshua Burkhow. All rights reserved.

Published by O'Reilly Media, Inc., 1005 Gravenstein Highway North, Sebastopol, CA 95472.

O'Reilly books may be purchased for educational, business, or sales promotional use. Online editions are also available for most titles (*http://oreilly.com*). For more information, contact our corporate/institutional sales department: 800-998-9938 or corporate@oreilly.com.

Acquisitions Editor: Michelle Smith	**Indexer:** Sue Klefstad
Development Editor: Melissa Potter	**Interior Designer:** David Futato
Production Editor: Katherine Tozer	**Cover Designer:** Karen Montgomery
Copyeditor: Nicole Taché	**Illustrator:** Kate Dullea
Proofreader: Sonia Saruba	

November 2023:   First Edition

Revision History for the First Edition

2023-11-15:   First Release

See *http://oreilly.com/catalog/errata.csp?isbn=9781098107529* for release details.

The O'Reilly logo is a registered trademark of O'Reilly Media, Inc. *Alteryx Designer: The Definitive Guide*, the cover image, and related trade dress are trademarks of O'Reilly Media, Inc.

The views expressed in this work are those of the author, and do not represent the publisher's views. While the publisher and the author have used good faith efforts to ensure that the information and instructions contained in this work are accurate, the publisher and the author disclaim all responsibility for errors or omissions, including without limitation responsibility for damages resulting from the use of or reliance on this work. Use of the information and instructions contained in this work is at your own risk. If any code samples or other technology this work contains or describes is subject to open source licenses or the intellectual property rights of others, it is your responsibility to ensure that your use thereof complies with such licenses and/or rights.

978-1-098-10752-9

[LSI]

To Travis Craven. I started this book thinking you would be my partner in crime taking on this nearly two-year journey. You have no idea how much I miss you, your smiling face, and your passion and ability to solve analytic problems with me. You were brilliant beyond measure and left so many of us just simply in awe of your intelligence. Yet even while doing circles around us, you were every bit of a loving human, loving father, son, teammate, and most of all, my gracious friend. Not a day goes by when I don't say "Boomshakalaka!" You had such a tremendous effect on me and I will eternally be grateful to you. Rest in peace, Brother.

To Fabricio, Amielle, and Mayanna. You are my everything. You can do anything you put your minds to. You have everything within you to do something amazing in this universe.

Table of Contents

Part II.   Basics

Part VI. Alteryx Server and Analytics Cloud

Forewords

Data and the ability to question with data is now a required job skill. These data skills are no longer just for people who study information management in school. The ability to be comfortable working with data is for everyone. As professionals in digital marketing, tax, human resources, communications, engineering, medical research, finance, legal, sales…everyone needs to be comfortable and skilled to work with data. How do we know this? As one of the three people who cofounded Alteryx over 26 years ago, I have seen organizations increasingly demand data literacy from all their employees. People are taking the lead to make the best decisions based on data. In developing these skills, you are investing in yourself, your potential and in the impact, you will make every day of your life.

Joshua Burkhow is the personification of "analytics for all"! His passion and curiosity to solve problems with data was amplified when he was introduced to Alteryx Designer. He trusted his coworker who pointed him to this data analytics technology with the "rocket fuel" he needed to solve problems. He never looked back. Joshua wants you to have fun learning and knows you will be exhilarated as you build your Alteryx Designer skills. With *Alteryx Designer: The Definitive Guide*, you will simplify and automate your data analytics journey. I encourage you to get started and never stop learning!

— Olivia Duane Adams, Cofounder,
Chief Advocacy Officer, Alteryx

The great author John Nesbitt once wrote "we are drowning in a sea of data and yet starved for knowledge." With *Alteryx Designer: The Definitive Guide*, Joshua Burkhow serves up a healthy dose of knowledge that will allow you to overcome your fear of data, help you see data as the core asset of any business, and, most importantly, advance your cognitive skills across the entire continuum of analytics.

This newfound knowledge will serve you in meaningful ways. First, it will amplify your career. As a cofounder of Alteryx and its CEO for 24 years, I have seen Alteryx catapult countless careers upward and forward. This book does a terrific job at more than helping you learn the Alteryx software; it helps you improve your skills at inarguably the hardest part of analytics: knowing which question to ask. Second, with its wide range of use cases and industry best practices, this book will give your career a high degree of mobility; true analytic thinking results in profound personal, business, and societal outcomes. I have seen thousands of analysts move from industry to industry, from functional area to functional area, including being promoted from business analyst roles to leading global analytics teams at some of the world's greatest companies.

As one of the earliest Alteryx users turned Alteryx expert, ACE and global analytics thought leaders, Joshua will teach you that analytics is a social experience. Analytics is not that scary discipline conducted only by the PhDs down the hall; it is for ordinary people wanting to do extraordinary things. And this is best accomplished together.

The knowledge you gain from this book could very well change your life. Instead of living in complex VLOOKUPs, writing SQL code until you are blue in the face, or, worse, waiting for someone else to get the answer for you, you will become more curious, creative, and confident in your ability to make the data dance to tell better stories to get bigger outcomes. And the life-changing result is that you will get all of this done while getting home early and spending more time with your family and friends. Never forget that you are just like Joshua Burkhow: one of a kind!

— *Dean Stoecker, Cofounder,*
Executive Chairman, Alteryx

Preface

This book has been more than 10 years in the making. When I first started learning Alteryx Designer as a supply chain analyst, I was most often in a state of disbelief during that time. I had been working over 70 hours a week and was very proud of myself that I had the stamina to stay afloat, but I was heading straight for burnout. I knew that working harder and longer hours was not going to cut it. I was in serious need of a smarter and more efficient way of doing things.

A colleague came by my desk one day and said, "Hey, I just saw a demo of this new software and I think you might like it. You should check it out." If it had been almost anyone else I would have ignored the request because I had zero time available, but this particular colleague had a huge influence on me and I really valued what he had to say. I watched the demo of Alteryx Designer…and something clicked right away. I often joke to my friends that it was that moment when the sky broke open, white doves flew out, and I knew I'd found the answer I was looking for! It was just such a monumental moment for me.

I didn't even miss a beat; I downloaded the trial and instantly became consumed, it's even fair to say obsessed. I again was in disbelief almost the whole way. I honestly thought that I had had enough of analytics. I knew I was smart enough, but I didn't want to spend all my days sitting in frustration—I just couldn't believe that this fell in my lap.

I wrote this book for exactly that moment. I want *Alteryx Designer: The Definitive Guide* to be the book that I wish I had at that moment and felt like I was able to do anything. Back then, I didn't know what I was supposed to know or learn. I had to be very pushy and pester every Alteryx user or employee I could find.

I hope this book falls into your lap and delivers all the joy and inspiration in analytics without all the frustration and long days and nights. I know it sounds silly, but I truly believe that you can change the world for the positive with data, information, and insights. You can affect those around you. You can increase the positive impact you have on yourself.

Who This Book Is For

Three main groups of users will benefit the most from this book:

New analysts

A member of an organization or company who has taken on Alteryx as a tool of choice will typically have some analytical skills (experience of writing basic spreadsheet functions or SQL) and may have some experience in higher order analytics.

Experienced analysts

If you are migrating from existing or legacy analytical software, then this book is for you! Many times, organizations have chosen to migrate to Alteryx for the audit and documentation, flexibility, and broad capability improvements over other such tools. In this case, you will already have a good understanding of the analytic process—this book aims to help you understand the "Alteryx way" of data workflow design and creation. Many experienced analysts often complete multiple analysis projects, but are on the hook to keep running and maintaining them. If that's you, this book will help you by showing you the features and capabilities around automating workflows.

Current Alteryx users

With so many new users of Alteryx Designer today, paired with Alteryx' aggressive release calendar, I could argue that over 90% of Alteryx users can't easily keep up with all the features and functionalities in Alteryx. The current material, although great and useful, is still very segmented and disjointed and not yet comprehensive, which is why this definitive guide will give you a resource to know more about the tool you love.

How This Book Is Organized

In writing this book, I had to decide on how to organize it and what to cover. Since it is a "Definitive Guide," I wanted it to be more granular, so that over time, other authors could expand and build off of it. I worried that if I didn't cover the tools in a structured way with a good level of detail, it would be a hindrance to others later on. I hope that many other Alteryx experts will be inspired to write books on Alteryx use cases and other industry-focused applications of Alteryx and not need any level of basic detail in their books—they can simply refer to this book.

You might soon figure out that this book does not cover absolutely everything under the sun. It could easily be a 2,000 page book. Instead, I focused on the most important topics that make the biggest difference.

You will see that each chapter is focused on a specific palette of tools. Focusing on that set of tools in each chapter also makes it easier for the reader to quickly flip to the topic that they want to learn about or brush up on.

By the end of this book, I hope you will understand:

- What Alteryx Designer is and why it is important
- The fundamental tools for cleaning and preparing data for analysis within Alteryx Designer
- In-depth knowledge of all the tools and techniques offered in Alteryx Designer
- Intermediate techniques such as spatial analytics, in database, and reporting tools
- What macros and apps are and how to build them

You will be able to:

- Install, navigate, and be fully competent in the layout and functionality of Alteryx Designer
- Construct accurate, performant, reliable, and well-documented workflows that automate business processes
- Confidently deliver analytics projects using Alteryx Designer
- Understand and use tools and configuration techniques in Alteryx Designer

Conventions Used in This Book

The following typographical conventions are used in this book:

Italic
: Indicates new terms, URLs, email addresses, filenames, and file extensions.

`Constant width`
: Used for program listings, as well as within paragraphs to refer to program elements such as variable or function names, databases, data types, environment variables, statements, and keywords.

`Constant width bold`
: Shows commands or other text that should be typed literally by the user.

This element signifies a tip or suggestion.

This element signifies a general note.

This element indicates a warning or caution.

O'Reilly Online Learning

 For more than 40 years, *O'Reilly Media* has provided technology and business training, knowledge, and insight to help companies succeed.

Our unique network of experts and innovators share their knowledge and expertise through books, articles, and our online learning platform. O'Reilly's online learning platform gives you on-demand access to live training courses, in-depth learning paths, interactive coding environments, and a vast collection of text and video from O'Reilly and 200+ other publishers. For more information, visit *https://oreilly.com*.

How to Contact Us

Please address comments and questions concerning this book to the publisher:

O'Reilly Media, Inc.
1005 Gravenstein Highway North
Sebastopol, CA 95472
800-889-8969 (in the United States or Canada)
707-829-7019 (international or local)
707-829-0104 (fax)
support@oreilly.com
https://www.oreilly.com/about/contact.html

We have a web page for this book, where we list errata, examples, and any additional information. You can access this page at *https://oreil.ly/alteryx-designer-definitive-guide*.

For news and information about our books and courses, visit *https://oreilly.com*.

Find us on LinkedIn: *https://linkedin.com/company/oreilly-media*.

Follow us on Twitter: *https://twitter.com/oreillymedia*.

Watch us on YouTube: *https://youtube.com/oreillymedia*.

Acknowledgments

I have so many people to thank who made this book possible that it could easily take another book in and of itself. There are a good number of folks without whom this project simply and truly wouldn't have become the book you are reading now:

Wanda
> Thanks for your support in allowing me to pursue a long-held dream of mine. I am grateful beyond words.

Hugo Mora
> Thank you for introducing me to Alteryx. You don't realize the impact you had on me, but you were such a great teammate and teacher!

Dean, Libby, Ned
> I hope you three don't ever have a day pass that you don't realize how enormous of a positive impact you've had on millions of people and will have on so many more in the future. You have literally changed the trajectory of people's careers and in turn their lives, including mine. I will never have enough words to show my appreciation. This book simply couldn't have even been a thought without you.

Dale Frakes and Paul Jellema
> I remember how you saw my passion for Alteryx and inspired me to pursue it. I am so thankful!

My Nike, PK, PwC, and Alteryx team
> I am proud of what we were able to accomplish! You have all had such a great impact on me. I am so grateful!

Chris Williams
> Brother from another mother! Having you as a friend is beyond words. You are brilliant and such a great human. Love you tremendously!

Fellow Alteryx ACEs and Tuvy Le

I am continuously impressed by your intelligence and kindness toward the Alteryx Community. I love our chats, laughing until we cry most of the time. Each one of you continues to inspire me daily. Tuvy—thanks for giving me a chance! I love you all tons!

Last but surely not least. David Pansegrouw and Neil Allen, as well as the entire O'Reilly team that has helped me get this across the finish line. Special callout to the amazing Melissa Potter! I simply and factually could not have done this without your guidance and wisdom. I am beyond grateful for your efforts, insights, and candor while reviewing the book. This book wouldn't have been half as good without your time and care. Thanks so much for sharing your passion for Alteryx with me.

PART I

Getting Started

CHAPTER 1

Introduction to Alteryx

I love Alteryx. If you had told me 12 years ago that I was going to become so interested in Alteryx that I'd write a book about it to get *more* people interested in it, I would have probably laughed at you or thought you were making it up.

I now spend hours, every day, building workflows, helping others build workflows, scaling workflows, and helping Alteryx users and leaders around the world to realize the value of Alteryx. I have yet to get tired of helping others get started using this platform. It's so fun to see the look on people's faces as they start to "get it" and understand why many others and I find Alteryx to be an invaluable product.

In this chapter, I am going to introduce you to Alteryx Designer and even briefly introduce you to the Alteryx Analytics Cloud Platform (AACP). You will download, install, and activate Alteryx Designer on your computer. Then, you'll learn about the supportive Alteryx community, which will give you a solid foundation on which to understand the rest of the concepts we'll cover in this book. I hope you're getting excited. Alteryx is extremely fun, and working with it can not only take your career to the next level but can also change people's lives by bringing automated solutions to common problems.

Introduction to Alteryx Designer and the Alteryx Analytics Cloud Platform

Alteryx Designer is a Windows software application that gives you an intuitive, fun, and easy-to-use drag-and-drop UI to create repeatable workflow processes for analyzing and blending data, and performing advanced analytics (such as predictive, spatial, and prescriptive). You can drag "tools" from a "tool palette" onto a "canvas," and connect those tools in a process flow that produces one of three results: a workflow, an analytic app, or a macro. You can also use these processes to quickly and automatically produce results that can be easily shared with others.

Alteryx Designer is a powerful, scalable, and dynamic application that has been (and continues to be) in a state of growth, transition, and transformation as a standalone product. To classify Alteryx Designer as an exclusively standalone product, however, would not be correct. Alteryx Designer, as well as other products like Alteryx Server for on-premises and numerous analytics cloud applications, comprise the Alteryx Analytics Cloud Platform.

It's relatively safe to say that anyone working with data in the past 10 years, and specifically in the analytics field, could see that their industry and the software products that they have been using exist in a poorly defined category. Are you a business intelligence developer or a reporting analyst? Are you an analytics professional or a data scientist? Are you an AI developer or a machine learning engineer? The list goes on. These areas of focus are fairly new, and many Alteryx users recognize they are standing in some areas simultaneously. They want to better understand what category they fall in, and so a platform that could simply satisfy *all* their needs was born.

Around 2022, Alteryx released its collection of new cloud software products—encompassing the latest vision of the AACP. AACP is the collection of cloud products that are paired with the on-premises products of Alteryx Designer and Alteryx Server (see Figure 1-1).

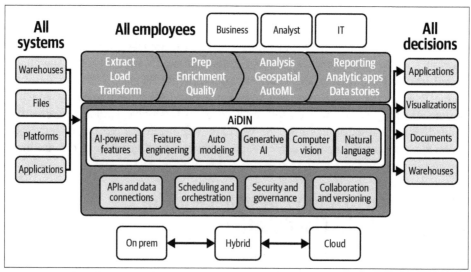

Figure 1-1. The Alteryx Analytics Cloud Platform

Let's now jump deeper into Alteryx Designer and what it has to offer as part of the AACP platform.

Figure 1-2 shows the drag-and-drop Alteryx Designer interface. Workflows are easy to build but can support highly complex and complicated processes as well.

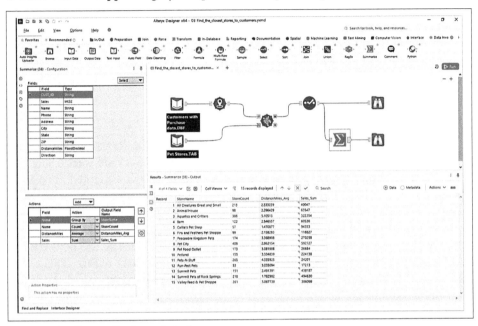

Figure 1-2. Alteryx Designer interface

Key benefits of Alteryx Designer include:

Flexibility

An extensive library of interconnected tools enables flexibility, making once difficult tasks easier. There are a number of sources that can be connected and updated via your workflows. If you want to simply clean up some poorly formatted data, then you can easily do that. But if you want to connect to a website, download a table of data, and process it further, you can do that, too.

Breadth of solutions

Designer offers a variety of workflows that can be built in order to address a wide number of use cases. This tool enables you to handle problems in many different business areas and analytics disciplines, such as Customer Success, Human Resources, Finance, Operations, Sales and Support, Marketing, and IT.

Support network

Alteryx is known to have a somewhat cult-like following—and I include myself in that group. Many Alteryx users love supporting each other on "the community" (*https://community.alteryx.com*), as we affectionately call it, and the Alteryx community now named Maveryx has won awards as well. On top of its inviting community, Alteryx as an organization has done an excellent job of providing resources and training material for its users to get started or to learn about a new category of tools and capabilities. You can quickly and easily get help from peers and expert users (or ACEs (*https://oreil.ly/_RcNu*)) any time, as well as read about the latest features of the recent releases.

It's important to pay attention to the latest versions and upgrades to see which new features are available.

Versions and Upgrades

At the time of this writing, Alteryx Designer and the other Alteryx products release on a biannual basis, with smaller fix packs released about every six weeks. The first release is usually the "major" release and subsequent releases are marked as "minor" releases, with the first minor release also referred to as the "stable" release. With Alteryx Designer being such a large piece of software with many moving parts, many users simply can't keep up with every release. It is not advisable to always be on the latest version unless you are specifically testing it. One rule many use is to try and stay "V-1" (v minus one), meaning one version behind the latest release. This allows any bugs or issues to be addressed by those testing. If you are interested in playing with the bleeding-edge updates for Alteryx Designer, I highly recommend you join the Alteryx Pilot Program (*https://oreil.ly/hZciL*). With each release, Alteryx will provide you with two main sets of information: release notes and help documentation.

Release notes (*https://oreil.ly/9dARe*) provide key information about a release, including version numbers, release dates, release type, and end-of-support dates. They also go into detail about new features as well as fixed and known issues as of that release. It is important to pay attention to these release notes closely as you can learn a lot about what that version provides you—from a new feature that might make your development much easier or provide a capability you were looking for, to knowing if a bug you are experiencing is now fixed or marked as a known issue and hopefully resolved in a future release.

Because Alteryx provides the ID number and exact version for its fixed and known issues, I have often been able to talk with Alteryx support and get more detailed information on a specific issue.

I have seen many users go through the trouble of downloading and upgrading to the latest version of Alteryx Designer only to find out the issue they are experiencing is not fixed in that release. Reviewing the release notes can save you that headache.

As someone who likely spends more time than others reading the Alteryx help documentation, I can tell you that while it is very good, it's not perfect. Help documentation can give you general guidelines, but it's not going to cover everything in painstaking detail and with screenshots of every little step. I usually go to the help documentation to get a high-level understanding of a process, but if one step isn't clear then I usually go to the community and ask for their help. Many people are willing to help and can provide that detail you need. Now, let's get you started by downloading Alteryx Designer.

Download, Install, and Activate Alteryx Designer

Downloading and installing Alteryx Designer is a relatively simple process.

Downloading Alteryx Designer

If you have a license key available, then you can get started downloading Alteryx Designer by following the steps in this section. If you don't yet have a full license and want to start a trial, then you will have that option once you have successfully installed the software. To download Alteryx Designer, take the following steps:

1. Make sure you have a computer with the minimum requirements. In particular, not having enough memory will provide a poor experience and cause you many headaches. To download Alteryx Designer (*http://downloads.alteryx.com*), you will need to have an Alteryx account, which you can create by clicking "Register here" (see Figure 1-3).

It's important to use the email address with which you have a license associated.

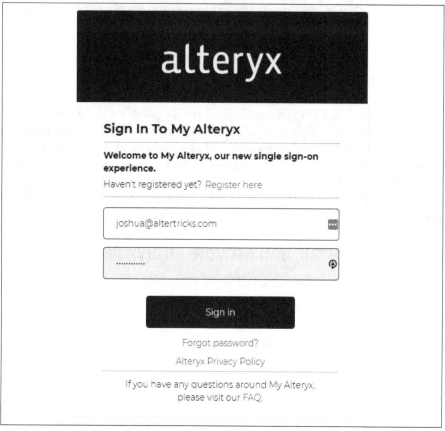

Figure 1-3. Download Alteryx Designer

2. Log in and you will see a screen like the one shown in Figure 1-4.

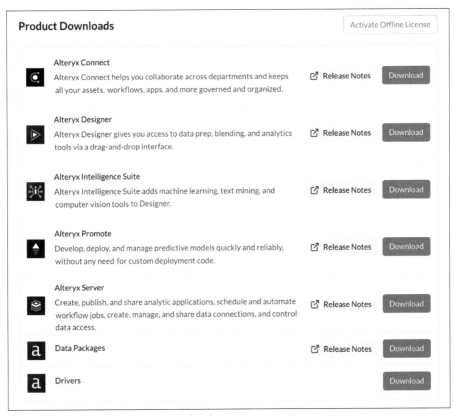

Figure 1-4. *Alteryx Product Downloads screen*

3. Click Download next to Alteryx Designer.

If you or your organization don't have licenses for the other Alteryx products, you won't see them listed for download.

4. Select the version you want to download. The latest version will be at the top (see Figure 1-5).

Figure 1-5. New or previous versions

5. Select the version you want to download and click Next. You will see a screen like the one shown in Figure 1-6 where you can download the product you need.

Alteryx provides two different installation options for Alteryx Designer: Admin version and Non-Admin version. There is no difference between the two versions when it comes to what is installed. The difference lies in *where* on your machine it gets installed. The Admin installation applies to all users on a machine and installs in the system Program Files directory at *C:\Program Files\Alteryx*. The Non-Admin installation applies only to the user who installed Alteryx and installs in the AppData folder at *C:\Users\user name\AppData\Local\Alteryx*. What this means is that you can actually install two different versions on any machine. However, it's important to note that if you have one version installed, say for example the Admin version, and you try to install another Admin version, it will remove the previously installed Admin version. Same goes for the Non-Admin version if you try to install another version.

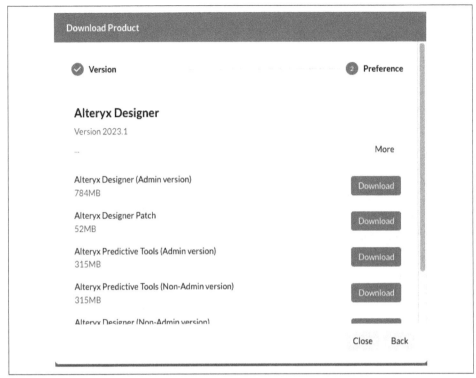

Figure 1-6. Downloads for Alteryx Designer

If you have admin access on your machine, or your organization deploys the software to your machine using the admin account, then you want to ensure you get the Admin version. However, if you want to use a different version or don't have admin rights, you can use the Non-Admin version. The following steps will demonstrate how to download and install the Admin version.

Installing or Upgrading Alteryx Designer

Installing Alteryx Designer is actually quite easy, but for new users it can be a little unclear what you should be paying close attention to for each step. The process for a new installation versus upgrading to a newer version is exactly the same. The only difference is when you are upgrading to a new version, the installer will remove the previous version prior to installing. Let's walk through the installation steps now:

1. Once you download the Admin Alteryx Designer executable file, go to the directory where they were downloaded to (this is usually the *Downloads* folder). From there, double-click the Admin Alteryx Designer *.exe*. The first screen you will see is shown in Figure 1-7.

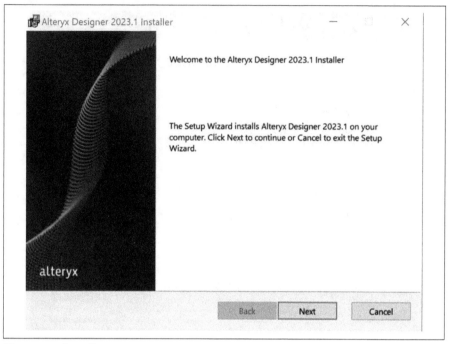

Figure 1-7. Installer screen

2. Click Next and you will see the License Terms (see Figure 1-8).

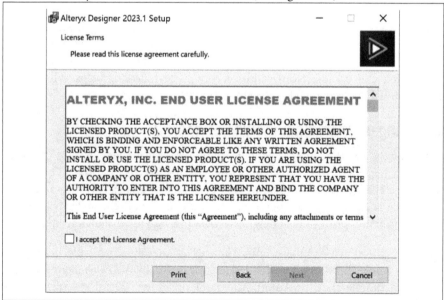

Figure 1-8. License Terms

3. Click the checkbox next to "I accept the License Agreement" and click Next. You will then see the location where the software will be installed (see Figure 1-9). You could change this, but I recommend you don't unless you have a specific reason to do so.

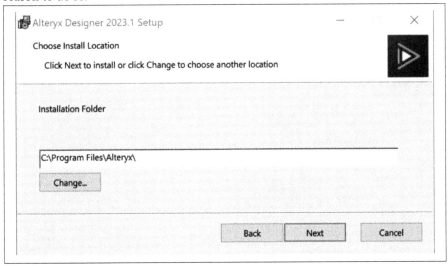

Figure 1-9. Install location

4. Click Next, and on the next screen (see Figure 1-10) click Install.

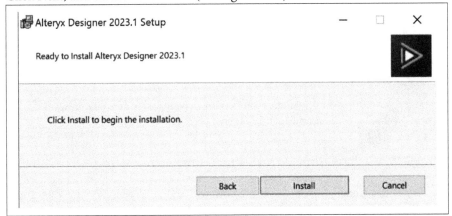

Figure 1-10. Install screen

5. Alteryx Designer will start installing. The installation process can take anywhere from 10 to 45 minutes depending on the machine you're using (see Figure 1-11).

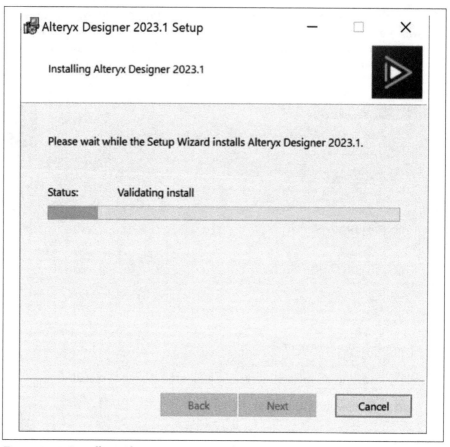

Figure 1-11. Installing Alteryx Designer

 The installation of Python dependencies can take upward of 15 minutes, so be patient.

Once the installation completes, you will see a screen like the one shown in Figure 1-12.

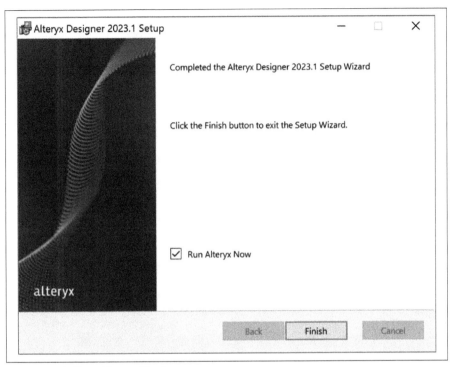

Figure 1-12. Run Alteryx Designer

6. With the box checked to Run Alteryx Now, click Finish and Alteryx Designer will open. Now it's time to activate it!

Activating Alteryx Designer

Alteryx Designer provides you with three different activation options: standard, offline, and using a license server. Most users will use the standard activation process, but if you have a scenario where the machine you are using is not connected to the internet or has traffic blocked for security reasons then you have the option to activate using an offline license. On a new installation, when you open Alteryx Designer for the first time you will see a pop-up screen that looks like the one shown in Figure 1-13.

Figure 1-13. First-time installation

Follow these steps to activate Alteryx Designer:

1. If this is not a new installation and your machine has a license already installed, nothing will change. Your license will remain the same. If you need to add a license, you can access the license manager by going to Options and selecting Manage Licenses (see Figure 1-14).

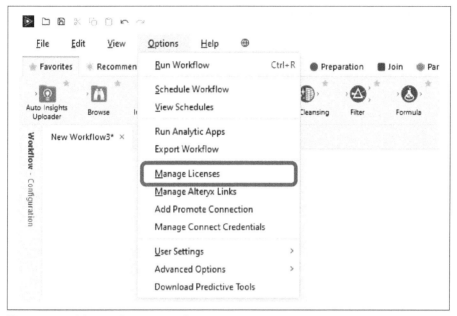

Figure 1-14. Manage Licenses in Options

2. From the Manage Licenses window, click Activate New License (see Figure 1-15).

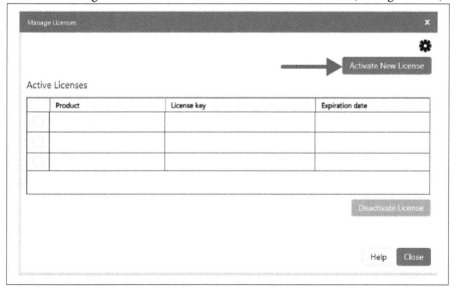

Figure 1-15. Activate New License

3. Paste in your license key(s) and click Activate (see Figure 1-16).

Figure 1-16. Alteryx Designer Activation

4. If you do not have a license key to activate at this time, you can select Start Free Trial to enter a bit of information and activate a trial key.

Congratulations! You have downloaded, installed, and activated Alteryx Designer. You are now ready to begin by getting connected with the Alteryx community to find others like you.

The Alteryx Community

As I mentioned earlier in this chapter, one of the greatest resources you have available to you as you start your Alteryx Designer journey is the industry award-winning Alteryx community site (*https://community.alteryx.com*). You will come to love and appreciate this special group of people and the extensive resources at your fingertips. I honestly had to think deeply about writing this book, since there is indeed so much amazing content and material for you through the community site. Ultimately, I wrote this book to support, extend, and improve the community to be even better than it is already.

In this section, I'll share with you some of the most important areas of the Alteryx community. The community is a huge, almost intimidating place, but I assure you that once you reach out in the discussion boards or comment on a blog post, you will start to feel welcome right away. We are a close, tight-knit group of thousands of passionate Alteryx users, and nothing makes us happier than having more friends to talk Alteryx with. Let's dive in!

Alteryx Academy

When you are first getting started with Alteryx Designer, the best resource (aside from this book) is Alteryx Academy (*https://oreil.ly/fJyyB*). Alteryx Academy is a collection of resources that is meant to help you on your journey from Alteryx novice to working Alteryx professional. There are learning paths, interactive lessons, live training sessions, videos, certifications, and (my favorite) weekly challenges.

Certifications

Alteryx offers a handful of certifications (*https://oreil.ly/6HZSw*) for all Alteryx Designer users and a handful more reserved for Alteryx Partners, which include Solution Providers, OEMs, and Technology Alliance. The four main certifications are: core, advanced, expert, and the newest certification, predictive master. In Alteryx Academy, you can find certification guides for all four of them as well as Micro-credential exams, Designer cloud exams, and Alteryx Server exams.

Discussion Boards

The discussion boards (*https://oreil.ly/c4-am*) on the Alteryx community site are one of the greatest places to not only ask questions and get help from other knowledgeable users but also find where someone may have already faced the same issue and had it resolved. Since the community has such a large user base, I would highly recommend you conduct a search of existing discussions before posting your question. It is very likely that your question has already been asked.

Knowledge

The Knowledge section (*https://oreil.ly/gbgpd*) on the Alteryx community site is another great resource for learning and getting a more in-depth view on a topic. Here, there are many articles and deep dives that you can search for by product.

Ideas

The Ideas section (*https://oreil.ly/Eqork*) is where you can see and/or post any ideas that can improve the product. If you're building a workflow and have an idea that Alteryx should implement into the product, you can write about it and have other Alteryx users vote it up. This is also a great place to see other ideas Alteryx has accepted and will be putting into a future release.

Blogs and Podcasts

The Blogs (*https://oreil.ly/3FP6-*) and Podcasts (*https://oreil.ly/1Lv-9*) sections are another great place to learn about new topics and hear from others in the Alteryx community. There are also some really great deep dives into topics like predictive analytics and advanced areas of Alteryx. Podcasts are available from major podcast apps like Google and Spotify, so you can listen to them on your next road trip!

User Groups

The User Groups section (*https://oreil.ly/44JQG*) is where you can sign up or even start a user group meetup in your area. There are more and more user groups being started every month, and it's likely that if you are in a major US city, there is one already set up in your area or perhaps you could join a virtual user group. If that's not the case, you can work with the User Groups team at Alteryx to get one set up. These groups are a great way to help other users learn more about Alteryx as well as find new friends who share similar interests.

Use Cases

The Use Cases section (*https://oreil.ly/-bhkR*) is where you can see the impact that Alteryx has had on organizations. You can get in-depth information on specific approaches that others have used to be successful—from automating PowerPoint presentations to saving a North American airline more than $1 million annually.

Alteryx Support

Alteryx provides user support for anything related to its products. While the help documentation (*https://help.alteryx.com*) is comprehensive, I highly recommend you also get familiar with the Support section (*https://oreil.ly/-niGI*) of the community—it's a great hub for any support you may need. If you are a customer, check out

Mission Control (*https://my.alteryx.com*), a one-stop-shop for support and getting started in Alteryx.

Alteryx does a reasonably good job of providing detailed information about every feature and function of Alteryx Designer. It's important to look for a circle with a question mark in it—that will provide a direct link to help documentation for the specific area you are focused on. These icons will appear in a few different places, which we will cover later in this book (see Figure 1-17).

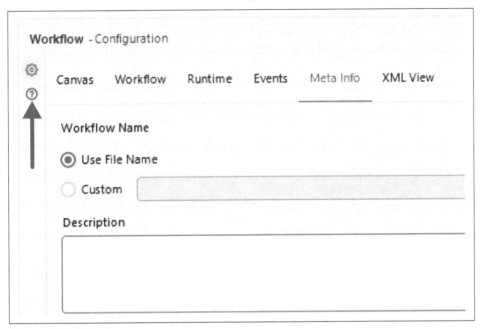

Figure 1-17. Help icon

The help icon is also available by right-clicking on a tool in the canvas (see Figure 1-18).

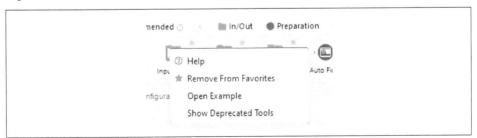

Figure 1-18. Right-click a tool in the canvas

Conclusion

In this chapter, we covered everything you need to get started with Alteryx Designer and begin to know your way around the Alteryx community. I introduced you to Alteryx Designer and the AACP platform. I talked about all the resources and help you have at your disposal. You went through a step-by-step guide to getting Alteryx downloaded, installed, and activated. Lastly, we covered the plethora of options available on the Alteryx community site for you to engage and start to learn from your peers. As with all software, there will be a lot of new things to learn and do, but remember that analytics can be very fun and exciting, and you've taken the first step toward getting there. Stick with me throughout the book and you will soon learn things that you never thought possible. In the next chapter, you will work on configuring Alteryx Designer and building the skills and knowledge you will need to create your first workflow. Let's go!

CHAPTER 2

Configuring Alteryx Designer

When you begin using Alteryx, there will likely be a point where you will hit the infamous aha moment. This is when you realize that, with Alteryx Designer, you can automate anything, you don't need to have a PhD in nuclear physics, and that it's extremely addictive and fun! You will be opened to a whole new view of your work and what can be done. In my years of conducting Alteryx training, I have had two instances where someone broke down and started to cry after the end of the class. I am fairly certain it wasn't because my training was that bad; it was because, as they stated, for the first time these users felt like they had a clear path out of a job they didn't like or an industry they weren't passionate about. This is what keeps me coming back. Witnessing, and experiencing, this aha moment is such a great feeling. I mentioned earlier that Alteryx has an almost cult-like following—as soon as you get started, you will realize why.

In this chapter, we are going to launch your Alteryx experience into orbit. You will learn how to get your environment set up and configured the way you want in order to build your first workflow. We will walk through the Alteryx Designer interface and the four main components of building a workflow. You will also be introduced to user settings that can help you as you get started—you'll become more comfortable with all the tools you have access to.

If you are completely new to the data and analytics field, I want to challenge you to push through this chapter—there will be a lot of new concepts discussed. With Alteryx, if you can get started and get the basics under your belt, then the rest will come quickly. Alteryx has a fast learning curve. You'll find that you're anxious to get into more and more as you realize this tool is not as difficult as you may have thought.

Are you ready? Buckle your seat belt, we're going to pick up speed and get going fast!

This book was written with Alteryx Designer versions 2021.3 to 2023.1. While there may be minor differences in later versions, nearly everything should be the same or very similar as you go through the examples.

The Alteryx Designer Interface

The first step is to understand the landscape of the Alteryx Designer interface. For years, I have used a simple model to help users get started. It consists of four parts that are the foundational components to building workflows in the shortest time possible: the tool palettes, canvas, configuration window, and results window.

Becoming familiar with these four components right away makes almost everything else easier to understand moving forward. These four components will translate into a four-step process that you'll walk through when you build your first workflow later in the chapter.

The Tool Palettes

First, let's get to know the tool palettes (see Figure 2-1). The tool palettes are the collections of tools that you will be using to build your workflows. They have a couple of qualities that are important to remember. First, each individual palette is specific to one area of functionality. For example, as you can see in Figure 2-1, the In/Out tool palette holds tools that allow you to bring data into or out of your workflow, while Preparation is a collection of tools that help you with cleaning or creating data. Each tool palette is both color-coded as well as shape-coded, meaning that each tool within a palette has the same icon, making it easy to remember what it's for. As we progress through this book, I will cover many of the tool palettes and the tools within them.

Figure 2-1. Tool palettes

Specific options make it easier for you to get to the tool you need. You can add the tool to your Favorites tool palette, which always stays on the far left of all the palettes. To add a tool to the Favorites palette, click the yellow star in the upper right corner of the tool. You can also right-click on the header of the tool palette and select "Pin [tool palette]" and it will hold that palette to the left so that you can quickly get to that entire collection of tools easily.

Once you get used to the colors and shapes of the tools, you can look at the work-flows you've built and recognize right away which tools are being used for specific tasks. For example, you may have mostly blue circle tools (Preparation tools), which indicates a workflow where you are doing mostly cleanup or data creation. Other workflows might show a lot of purple squares, or Joins, and you'll recognize that in those workflows you are joining a lot of data sources together. You can see in the workflow in Figure 2-2 that there are many Preparation tools, some Join tools, and even a Summary tool in use.

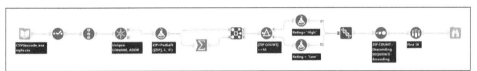

Figure 2-2. Tool colors and shapes

To use the tool palette, simply find the tool you need (which this book will help you in identifying) and drag and drop it onto the canvas, which we'll dig into next.

The Canvas

The second part of the Alteryx Designer interface, and our workflow-building process, is getting to know the canvas. The canvas is where you create your art. It's where you take tools from the palette and connect them. A clean canvas looks like Figure 2-3.

Figure 2-3. A clean canvas

The important thing to understand is that this canvas represents your workflow. Go to File > Save to save your workflow to your machine.

Three main pieces to a workflow are represented on a canvas: tools, anchors, and connections (see Figure 2-4). *Tools* are the steps in the process, *anchors* are the lime-green arrows that are the input and/or output of each tool, and *connections* are the lines between tools.

Figure 2-4. The three components of a workflow

It's important to note that failing to ensure that your tools are connected correctly can result in errors or improperly processed data.

To use the canvas, drag a tool from the tool palette (step 1) onto the canvas (step 2) (see Figure 2-5). Once you have completed that, it's time to configure the tool (step 3, which we'll discuss next).

Figure 2-5. Tool on the canvas

The Configuration Window

The third part of the interface, and our workflow-building process, is the Configuration window (see Figure 2-6). Nearly every tool that you put onto the canvas has to be configured. Although many tools have similar configuration options, nearly all of them have a different number of options you can specify. Some tools have only one item to configure, and some have close to 25. When you are getting started, it can be a little confusing to know what you need to configure and how. I'll cover almost all the tools in this book so you can always flip to a specific tool if you need a refresher on the details.

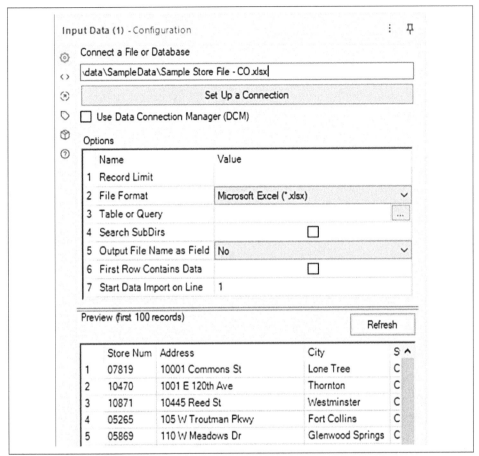

Figure 2-6. The Configuration window

The Configuration of a tool tells the Alteryx Designer engine what to do specifically or how to handle each of the tool's actions at runtime. If you select data in the Select tool (which we cover in Chapter 5), you are going to configure the tool to tell the workflow which columns you want to select. Don't worry—more on this later.

Let's move on to the fourth part of the interface, and the final step in the workflow-building process: the Results window.

The Results Window

Once you have taken a tool from the tool palette (step 1), dropped it onto the canvas (step 2), and configured it (step 3), you need to run the workflow to see the results. The Results window shows three specific items. First, it shows the data that is input or output from whatever tool anchor you selected (see Figure 2-7). Second, if you have the white canvas selected, you'll see a log of what happened during the execution of the workflow (see Figure 2-8). Third, the Results window shows you the metadata of each point in your workflow, including data types and other important information regarding the structure of your data (see Figure 2-9).

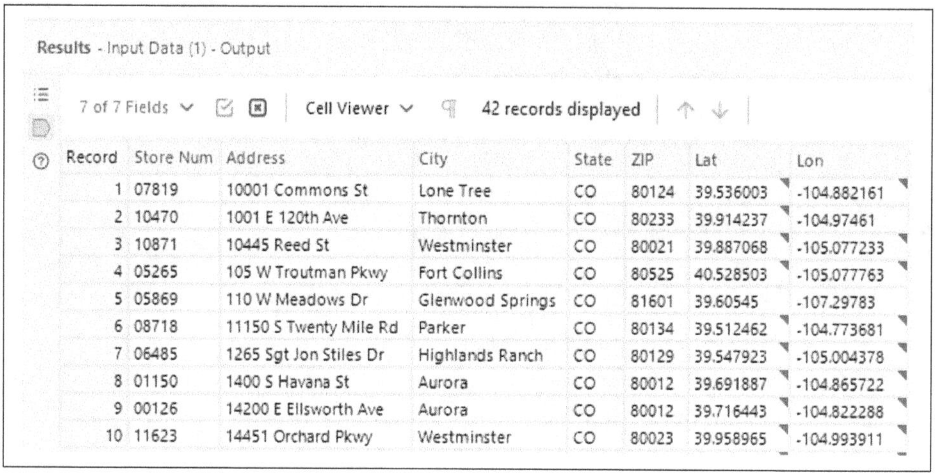

Figure 2-7. The Results window data

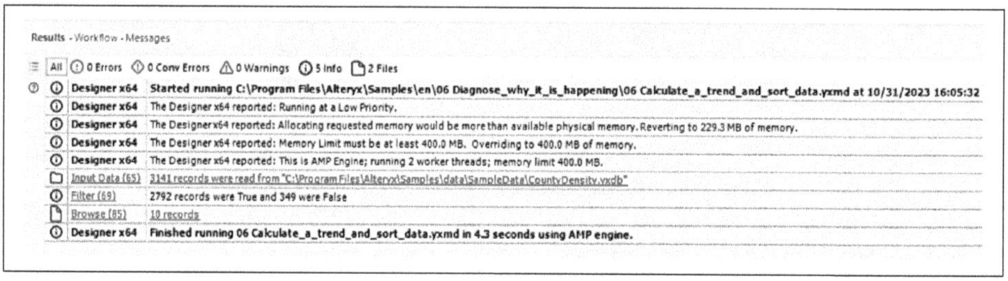

Figure 2-8. The Results window logs

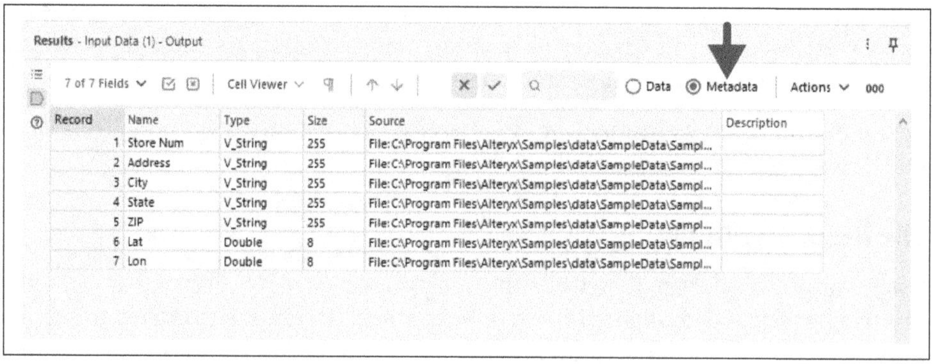

Figure 2-9. The Metadata window

The Results window is extremely important to understand. It is what you'll use to verify that the workflow you are building is correct.

Now, hopefully you can see that building workflows simply involves repeating these four steps: moving a tool from the tool palette (step 1) onto the canvas (step 2), configuring the tool (step 3) to run, and seeing the results (step 4). Once you have completed step 4, you can add another tool to the canvas and connect it to the tool you set up previously. This approach has a couple of benefits for you. First, it's a simple process. You can easily remember these four steps, and once you have done it a hundred times, it becomes ingrained in memory and you won't even need to think about it. Second, it promotes a very important design best practice—avoid putting a bunch of tools onto the canvas all at once, configuring them, and expecting they will all run appropriately. Using the four-step cycle, you will run the workflow for each additional tool you add and test it to confirm that the workflow is correct. This saves you tons of time in not having to go back and figure out what went wrong. Before we get to building your first workflow, let's touch on some important features and settings available to you in Alteryx Designer.

Important Features

One of the challenges you will face in learning Alteryx Designer is that there are so many touch points, configuration options, and features that aren't immediately obvious. I want to touch on a couple of important ones now, at the beginning of your journey, so that you can accelerate your knowledge quickly. This section covers some important features you should know right away.

Global Search

In the top right corner of Alteryx Designer is the Global Search (see Figure 2-10). This is a powerful feature that many users, including me, employ on almost every workflow. It's called a Global Search because it searches a wide variety of objects such as tools, help documentation, and community content. It also provides links to these various resources. If you search for a specific tool, let's say the Join tool, you can drag and drop that tool directly from the search results onto your canvas.

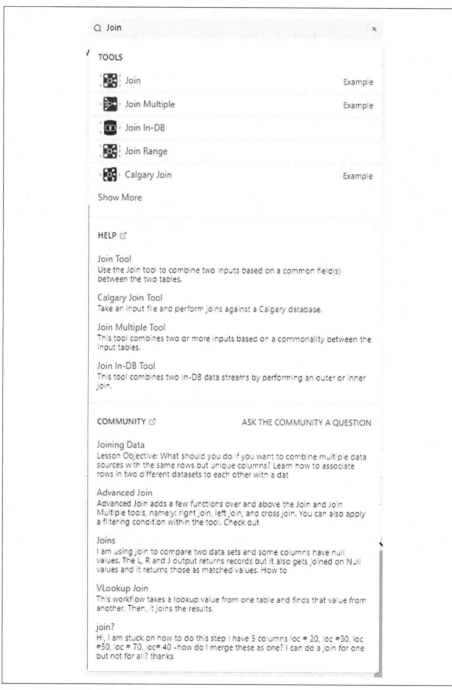

Q Join   ×

TOOLS

⊞ Join   Example

▷ Join Multiple   Example

◉ Join In-DB

⊞ Join Range

⊞ Calgary Join   Example

Show More

HELP ☐

Join Tool
Use the Join tool to combine two inputs based on a common field(s)
between the two tables.

Calgary Join Tool
Take an input file and perform joins against a Calgary database.

Join Multiple Tool
This tool combines two or more inputs based on a commonality between the
input tables.

Join In-DB Tool
This tool combines two In-DB data streams by performing an outer or inner
join.

COMMUNITY ☐   ASK THE COMMUNITY A QUESTION

Joining Data
Lesson Objective: What should you do if you want to combine multiple data
sources with the same rows but unique columns? Learn how to associate
rows in two different datasets to each other with a dat

Advanced Join
Advanced Join adds a few functions over and above the Join and Join
Multiple tools, namely: right join, left join, and cross join. You can also apply
a filtering condition within the tool. Check out

Joins
I am using join to compare two data sets and some columns have null
values. The L, R and J output returns records but it also gets joined on Null
values and it returns those as matched values. How to

VLookup Join
This workflow takes a lookup value from one table and finds that value from
another. Then, it joins the results.

join?
Hi, I am stuck on how to do this step I have 5 columns loc = 20, loc #30, loc
#50, loc # 70, loc# 40 -how do I merge these as one? I can do a join for one
but not for all? thanks

Figure 2-10. Global Search

Workflow Configuration

I briefly mentioned configuration as an important step in the process of creating a workflow. Just as there are configurations for each individual tool, there are also configurations you can set for the workflow as a whole. Navigate to the Configuration window (see Figure 2-11) by double-clicking anywhere on the canvas (not on a tool), or go to View on the menu bar and click Configuration.

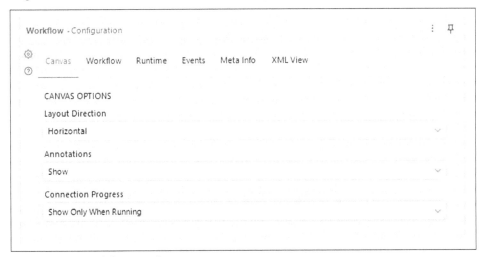

Figure 2-11. Workflow Configuration

The Workflow Configuration feature allows you to configure options that affect your entire workflow. There are five main options that are available by default—let's dig a little deeper into those.

Canvas options

The Canvas tab in the Workflow Configuration window allows you to set the layout direction of your tools on the canvas. You can also set the visibility of the annotations on your tools. Annotations are the text that is displayed beneath or above a tool. Lastly, connection progress visibility is configurable to show progress as the workflow is being completed. This is a really nice feature to enable at runtime to see the amount and size of data that is running through a particular tool.

Workflow options

The Workflow tab on the Configuration pane (see Figure 2-12) gives you a variety of valuable information. First, it shows you where your workflow is saved. It also provides clarity around what type of file you are building. For now, we are building workflows but, as we'll discuss in Chapter 13, we'll also take a look at building macros and apps. Lastly, the Workflow tab describes all the constants that are available in your workflow. Constants, while outside the scope of this book, are a powerful feature—there are three types (Engine, Question, and User) that you can tap into for various reasons.

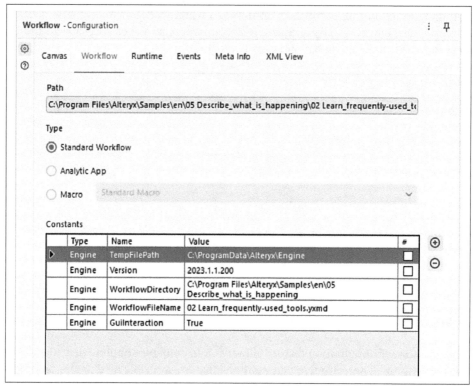

Figure 2-12. Workflow options

Runtime options

The Runtime tab in the Workflow Configuration pane (see Figure 2-13) allows you to modify how your workflow runs when you click the Run button. You can increase or decrease the memory limit that Alteryx Designer uses in the process of running your workflow. You also can change the directory where the created temp files are saved, as well as control the limit of conversion errors and set a record limit for all inputs. Lastly, you also have some nice features you can easily turn on or off as you see necessary.

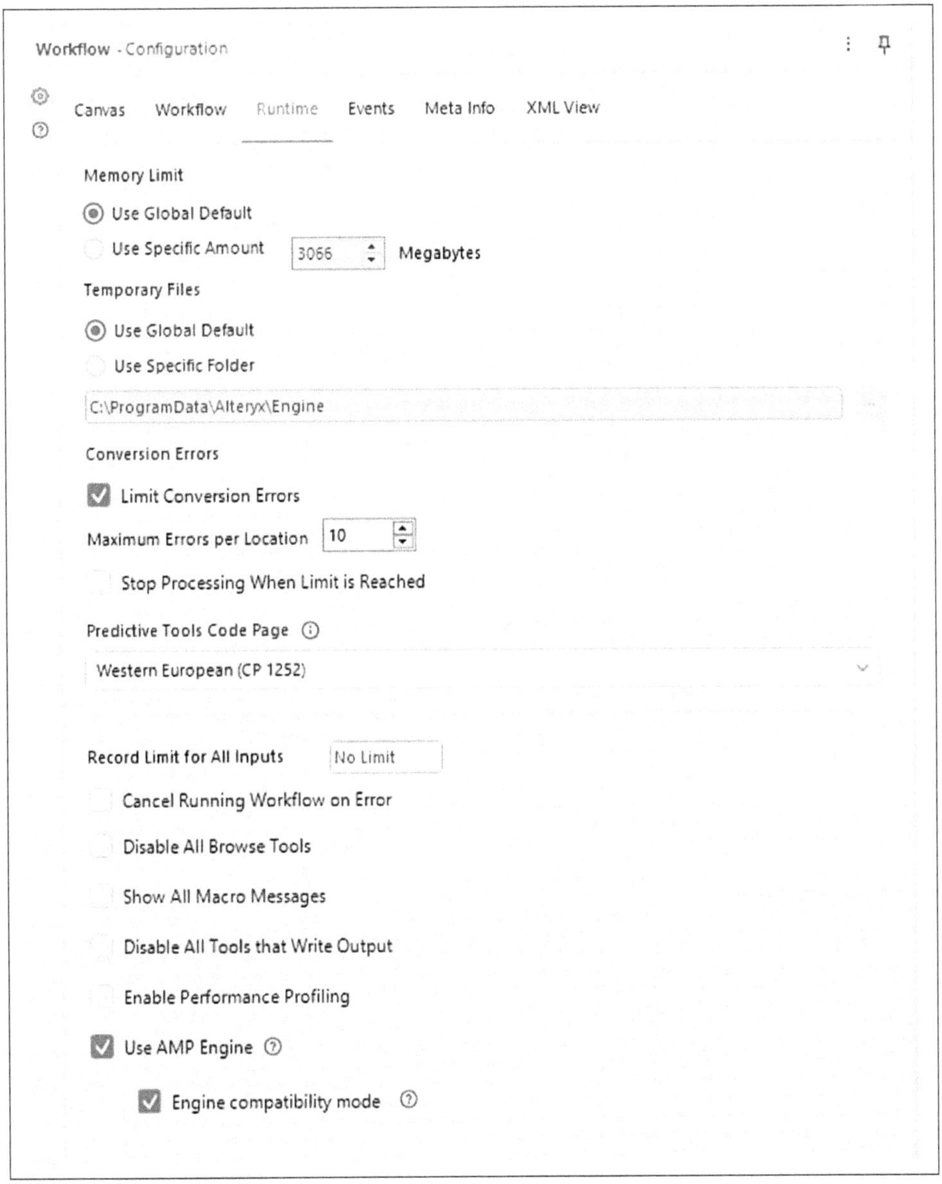

Workflow - Configuration   ⋮   📌

⚙   Canvas   Workflow   Runtime   Events   Meta Info   XML View
⑦

Memory Limit

◉ Use Global Default

○ Use Specific Amount   [3066 ↕]   Megabytes

Temporary Files

◉ Use Global Default

○ Use Specific Folder

[C:\ProgramData\Alteryx\Engine   ]

Conversion Errors

☑ Limit Conversion Errors

Maximum Errors per Location   [10   ↕]

☐ Stop Processing When Limit is Reached

Predictive Tools Code Page ⓘ

[Western European (CP 1252)   ⌄]

Record Limit for All Inputs   [No Limit   ]

☐ Cancel Running Workflow on Error

☐ Disable All Browse Tools

☐ Show All Macro Messages

☐ Disable All Tools that Write Output

☐ Enable Performance Profiling

☑ Use AMP Engine ⑦

    ☑ Engine compatibility mode ⑦

Figure 2-13. Runtime options

Events options

The Events tab in the Workflow Configuration pane (see Figure 2-14) allows you to trigger some event to happen before or after you run your workflow. For example, you can send an email to yourself when the workflow has completed.

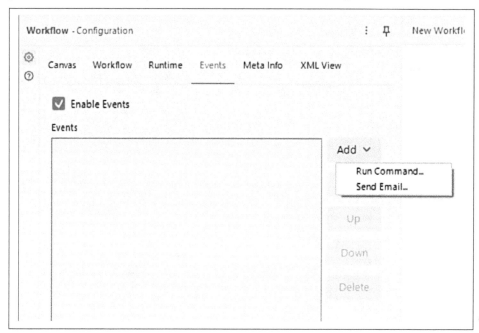

Figure 2-14. Events options

Meta Info options

The Meta Info tab on the Workflow Configuration pane (see Figure 2-15) gives you many options for describing details about your workflow. For example, you can use a different name for the workflow than what you saved, you can add a description of the workflow for others to better understand, or you can add a URL to direct users to further help documentation. The Tool Settings and Tool Palette are used when you are creating a macro. Lastly, you can ensure that the workflow is attributed to a person and/or a company.

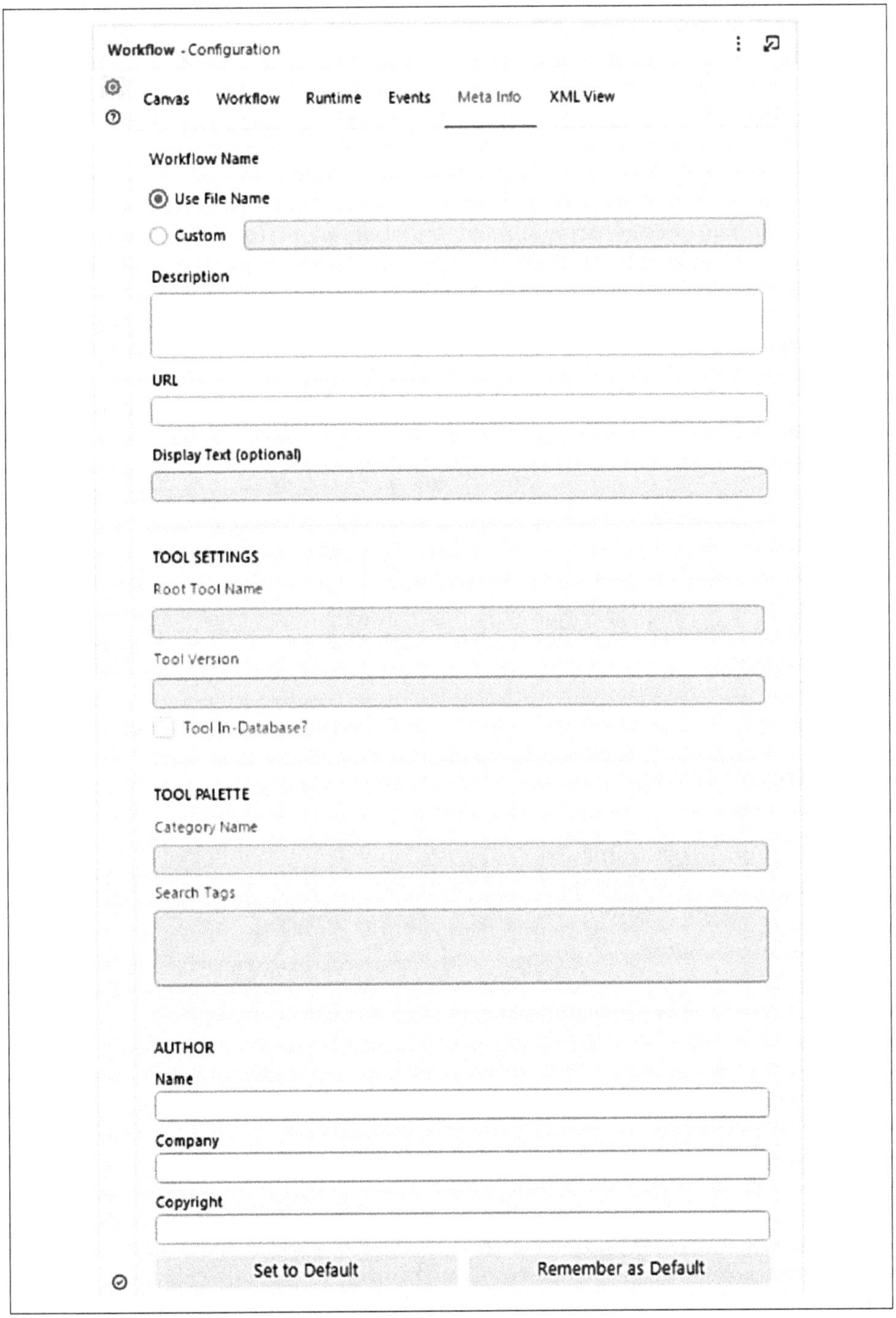

Figure 2-15. Meta Info options

These are all the options you will need to configure your workflow, but I want to make sure that you understand another important tool—user settings.

User Settings

Alteryx Designer provides a tremendous amount of user settings to control your development experience. The true power of these user settings is that they will save you from having to configure each and every workflow. Instead, you can employ user settings to make the configurations at a user level so that they apply across all workflows. The User Settings window has eight specific tabs of functionality, which I'll introduce here. You can access your user settings by going to Options > User Settings > Edit User Settings (see Figure 2-16).

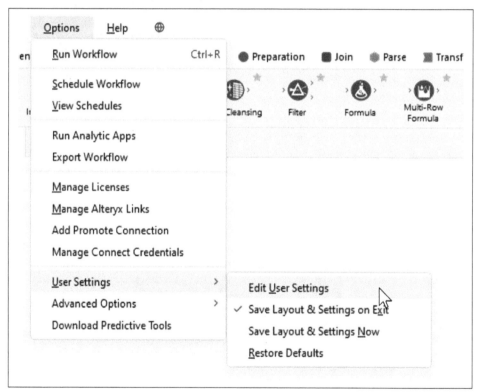

Figure 2-16. User Settings

Defaults

The Defaults tab allows you to set a global parameter on memory limit and directory, as well as a collection of features you can turn on or off as needed. To be clear, you can usually do just fine by not modifying the settings. A common configuration change that many users make is to turn off (uncheck) the "Show Start Here at startup" and "Pop up dialog at completion of workflow" options (see Figure 2-17).

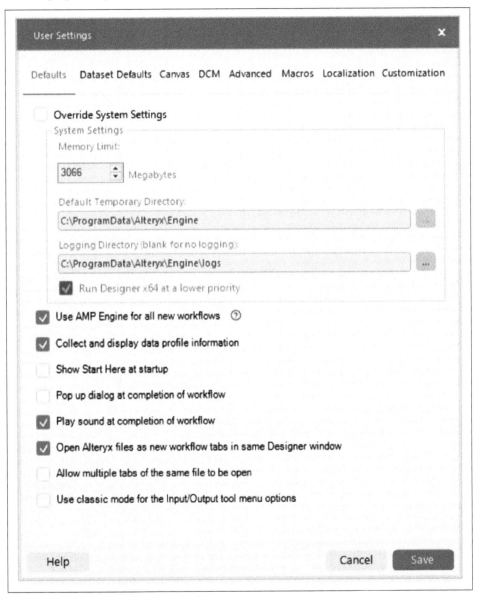

Figure 2-17. Defaults tab of User Settings

Dataset Defaults

The Dataset Defaults tab (see Figure 2-18) allows you to set the specific third-party data packages you want to use for each specific functionality.

Figure 2-18. Dataset Defaults tab of User Settings

Canvas

The Canvas tab (see Figure 2-19) allows you to change or modify anything to do with the look and feel of the canvas—from changing the background color to changing the text size and font of annotations. An important feature to turn on is "Display macro indicators on tools." I'll talk more about why this should be done in Chapter 13, when we cover macros.

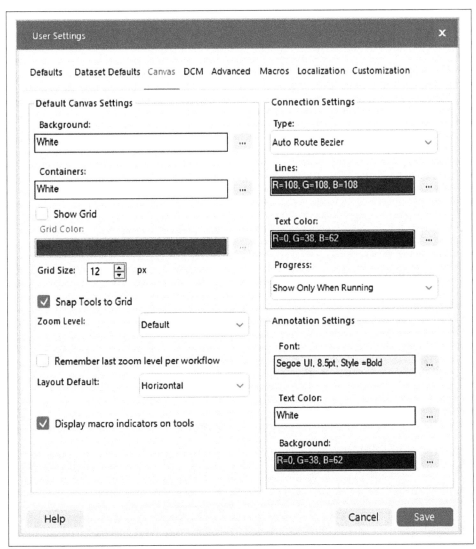

Figure 2-19. Canvas tab of User Settings

Data Connection Manager

Data Connection Manager (DCM) is a relatively new functionality that improves the way we work with database connections. I'll go into much more detail later on in this book, but for now know that you can configure user settings related to DCM (see Figure 2-20).

Figure 2-20. DCM tab of User Settings

Advanced

The Advanced tab (see Figure 2-21) has many features that you will find useful. For example, you can modify the number of times you can click Undo when you are developing workflows. You can also choose to display a number of things, such as "Display Asset Management in the Properties Window."

If you are an advanced user, I recommend turning on the "Display XML in Properties Window" feature, as it will allow you to look at the XML of the workflow if you need to do deep troubleshooting. Another important feature is Autorecover. As anyone who develops anything in software knows, the worst feeling in the world is losing your work. You can stop that from happening by ensuring you have your Autorecover settings correct. It's turned on by default, but you can modify how frequently it saves. You can also modify the memory limit per tool, as well as enable proxy settings.

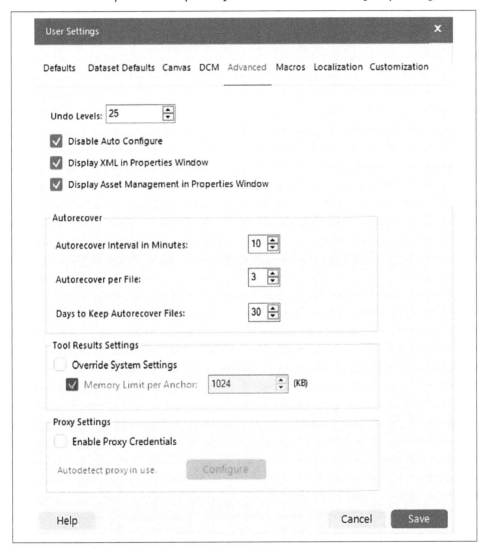

Figure 2-21. Advanced User Settings

Macros

The Macros tab on the User Settings pane (see Figure 2-22) is where you can specify a folder, either on your machine or a shared folder, to act as a repository for macros. This allows Alteryx Designer to load those and make them available each time you open and use Alteryx Designer. You can store macros in many different locations as well.

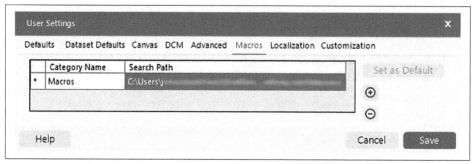

Figure 2-22. Macros tab of User Settings

Localization

The Localization tab in the User Settings pane (see Figure 2-23) allows you to change the language that is used within Alteryx as well as some key values around handling numbers, fonts, distance, and even help pages.

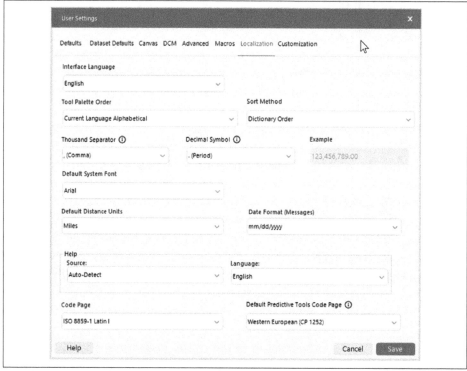

Figure 2-23. Localization tab of User Settings

Customization

The last tab in User Settings—Customization—is a new tab that was recently added to version 2023.1. It supports settings for a user to configure the Designer Theme, like setting your environment to Dark Mode. Note that as of version 2023.1, this setting is in Beta and is not fully released (see Figure 2-24).

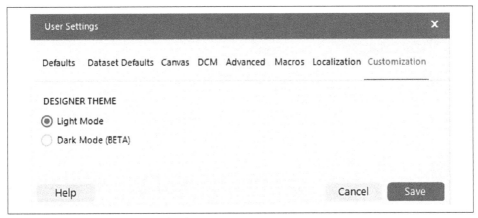

Figure 2-24. Customization tab of User Settings

You now have a high-level understanding of all the user settings you have available to you. Now, it's important for you to learn shortcuts to make your workflow building faster and more efficient.

Shortcuts

Some particularly helpful features within Alteryx are the plethora of keyboard and mouse shortcuts that you can use. Many of the more expert users will say that there are still some additional shortcuts they'd love to see in Alteryx Designer (and I agree!), but many are available today. If you set yourself up with a great keyboard and mouse, it'll make it even easier and faster for you to set up workflows. There are far too many shortcuts to cover, but I will cover a few that I find particularly useful. You can find the latest shortcuts available on the Alteryx website (*https://oreil.ly/RsVP3*).

I highly recommend the MX Master series mouse from Logitech. It has so many features and you can fully configure it to work with Alteryx, specifically. You can use one side button to run your workflow and another to open your configuration windows, all without having to drag and click every time you need it.

These shortcuts are Windows-based, since Alteryx Designer for the PC is still a Windows-native application.

Showing and hiding windows

The shortcuts in Table 2-1 help you make certain windows visible. I don't particularly like all or many of the windows open while I am building a workflow—only when I need them. If I don't need the results window at the moment, then I'd rather have it minimized in order to have the most real estate on my canvas.

Table 2-1. Shortcuts for showing and hiding windows

Action	Shortcut
Show/hide the overview window	Ctrl+Shift+V
Show/hide the results window	Ctrl+Shift+G
Show/hide the configuration window	Ctrl+Shift+C
Select the canvas	Ctrl+Shift+W
Show/hide the interface designer window	Ctrl+Shift+D

Adding a tool to the canvas

You can develop workflows in seconds by using the shortcuts in Table 2-2. Being able to add tools to the workflow without a mouse allows you to build a workflow almost entirely from a keyboard. The first thing you need to do is select the tool palette.

Table 2-2. Shortcut for adding a tool to the canvas

Action	Shortcut
Select the tool palette	Ctrl+Shift+T

Next, use the left and right arrows to navigate the different palettes. Once you get to the tab you want, you can use the down arrow to step into that palette and again use the left and right arrows to navigate through the tools in that palette. Once you pick the tool you need, hit Enter and it will be placed on the canvas. Note there are some nuances and priorities that dictate when or where the tool gets added. For example, adding a tool may depend on what tool you have currently selected, as well as whether there are multiple inputs like a Join tool.

Aligning tools

Many of us don't like having our tools haphazardly thrown around on the canvas. Curved lines drive you crazy? Not having your tools lined up feels like nails scratching a chalkboard? Me too. Table 2-3 shows the keyboard shortcuts that allow you to align a group of selected tools, whether vertically or horizontally. You can thank me later.

Table 2-3. Shortcuts to align tools

Action	Shortcut
Select all items	Ctrl+A
Deselect all selected items	Ctrl+D
Align tools horizontally	Ctrl+Shift+Hyphen
Align tools vertically	Ctrl+Shift+Plus

You can also find the same shortcuts by simply right-clicking anywhere on the canvas and selecting them from the menu.

Open, close, save, move, and run

Now for the basic shortcuts. You want to be able to open, close, save, move, and run a workflow without having to go through menus or click buttons. I got you. Table 2-4 shows how you do those things.

Table 2-4. Basic shortcuts

Action	Shortcut
Run workflow or stop workflow	Ctrl+R
Open workflow	Ctrl+O
Close workflow	Ctrl+F4
Save workflow	Ctrl+S
Save all open workflows	Ctrl+Shift+S
New workflow	Ctrl+N
Move between open workflows	Ctrl+Tab

It may take a little while to get some of these shortcuts down, but pick a few that you know you will use all the time and work with those. By far the most commonly used shortcut is Ctrl+R, to run the workflow. Let's now look at some sample workflows and data sets that are available to you.

Sample Workflows and Datasets

Some of the greatest resources you have at your fingertips are all the Sample Workflows and Sample Datasets that Alteryx Designer provides out of the box (see Figure 2-25).

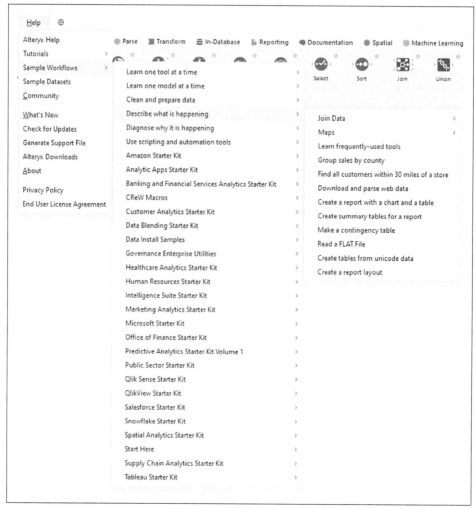

Figure 2-25. Sample Workflows

When you start out, you will most likely fall into one of two camps: you either have a use case that you think Alteryx Designer could help you with, or your team or company wants you to use Alteryx Designer to help automate some processes. Either way, these Sample Workflows and Sample Datasets will help you learn how to build workflows and use tools, as well as help you find more use cases and examples of workflows you could be building. They are such rich resources that you'll want to ensure you spend time reviewing them. You can access the Sample Workflows and Sample Datasets by going to the Help menu on the top bar.

Starter Kits

Closely related to Sample Workflows and Datasets are Starter Kits. Alteryx Starter Kits (see Figure 2-26) provide a prebuilt set of sample workflows, apps, and macros for a specific focus area.

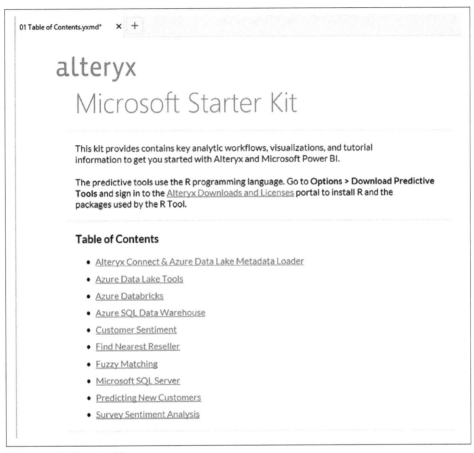

Figure 2-26. Starter Kits

As of version 2023.1, the Starter Kits available for download include:

- Alteryx Analytic Starter Kit
- Alteryx Starter Kit for Snowflake
- Alteryx Analytic Template for Amazon
- Alteryx Customer Analytics Starter Kit
- Alteryx Data Blending Starter Kit
- Alteryx Office of Finance Starter Kit

- Alteryx Public Sector Starter Kit
- Alteryx Starter Kit for Databricks
- Alteryx Starter Kit for Human Resources
- Alteryx Starter Kit for Intelligence Suite
- Alteryx Starter Kit for Marketing Analytics
- Alteryx Starter Kit for Microsoft
- Alteryx Starter Kit for Qlik
- Alteryx Starter Kit for Retail
- Alteryx Starter Kit for Salesforce
- Alteryx Starter Kit for Spatial Analytics
- Alteryx Starter Kit for Tableau
- Alteryx Supply Chain Analytics Starter Kit
- Banking and Financial Services Analytics Starter Kit
- Healthcare Analytics Starter Kit
- Predictive Analytics Starter Kit
- Enterprise Utilities

These Starter Kits have fully built workflows that show you how associated technologies work with Alteryx. For example, the Tableau Starter Kit includes a workflow that shows you how to connect Alteryx and Tableau, and also provides macros and other assets that you can use in your own workflows. I highly recommend downloading a few when you are getting started.

Favorites Tool Palette

In Alteryx Designer, you can start with the most commonly used tools as well as pick and choose which tools you want to keep close as you build workflows. The Favorites tool palette is easy to access on the far left of the tool palettes. You can "yellow star" any tool to add it to the Favorites tool palette or click the star again to remove it.

Use Favorites only for those tools that you find yourself constantly searching for. If you put everything in your Favorites, then nothing is really your favorite and you are back where you started.

Finding Help

One of the areas that I have covered briefly (and will cover a couple more times) is how to find help. Remember, if you get stuck or are not sure what a tool offers, you have plenty of options to find help—the easiest being to right-click on the tool in the palette and click Help. Alteryx Designer is designed to ensure you have access to many different help options in the application, including the help icon in the Configuration Window on the far left. When you are first getting started, I suggest you use it heavily.

Now that you understand the basics of the Alteryx Designer interface and its important features, it's time to build your first workflow.

Let's Build Your First Workflow

Now that you have Alteryx Designer set up to your preferences, it's important to start building right away. I want you to immediately put the four steps into practice and get excited to build more workflows. Let's do it! You are going to build a super quick and easy workflow that looks at store data from an Excel file.

If you don't have a blank canvas (or empty workflow) ready, do that now. You can go to File > New Workflow on the menu bar, or simply enter the shortcut Ctrl+N to open a new workflow canvas.

Step 1: Tool Palette

Remember that the first step is picking a tool from the tool palette. Find the Favorites tool palette and select the Input Data tool (see Figure 2-27).

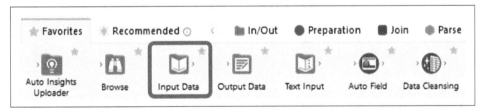

Figure 2-27. Input Data tool

Step 2: Canvas

Drag and drop or double-click the Input Data tool onto the canvas (see Figure 2-28).

Figure 2-28. Drag the tool onto the canvas

Step 3: Configure

Now you need to configure the tool. If your configuration window is not open, you can do one of the following:

- Simply double-click the tool.
- Go to View on the menu and select Configuration.
- Use the shortcut Ctrl+Alt+C.

In the Configuration menu, select "Set Up a Connection" (see Figure 2-29).

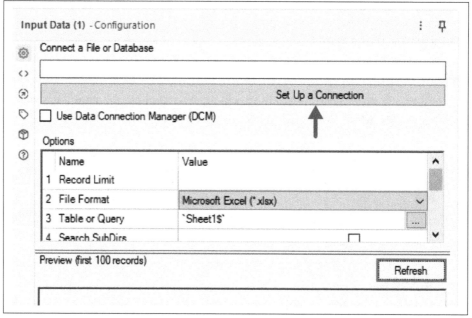

Figure 2-29. Configuration window

On the "Data connections" screen, click Files (1) on the left side and then .xlsx (2) (see Figure 2-30).

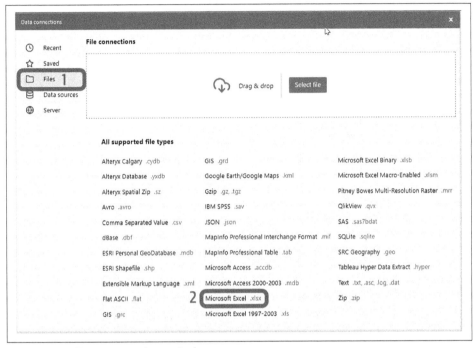

Figure 2-30. Data connections window

In the Open File window, navigate to the folder *C:\Program Files\Alteryx\Samples\data\SampleData* and select "Sample Store File - CO.xlsx" (1). You can open the file by either double-clicking on the file or by selecting it and then clicking Open (2) (see Figure 2-31).

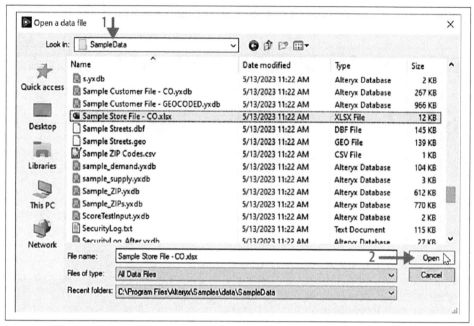

Figure 2-31. Open file

Next, tell Alteryx Designer how you want to use the Excel file. Do you want to pick a specific sheet? Select a range, or even just list out the sheets you have in the Excel workbook? In this case, I am going to select Sheet1 and click OK (see Figure 2-32).

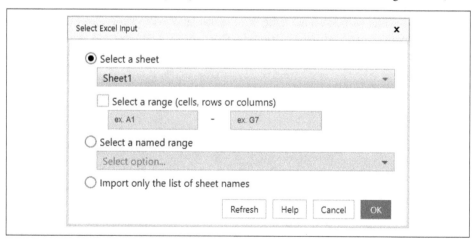

Figure 2-32. Select Excel input

Step 4: Results

Lastly, in order to view your data, you need to run the workflow. Click the blue Run button in the top right corner (see Figure 2-33).

Figure 2-33. The Run button

To see your results, click the output anchor (remember the lime green arrow) of the Input Data tool. Again, you can also go to the View menu or use the shortcut Ctrl+Alt+R in order to pull up the results panel (see Figure 2-34).

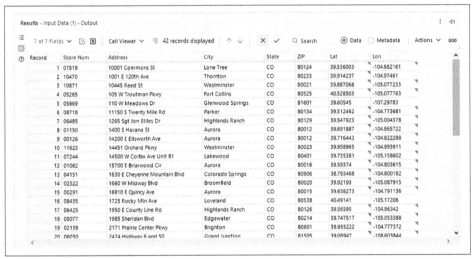

Record	Store Num	Address	City	State	ZIP	Lat	Lon
1	07819	10001 Commons St	Lone Tree	CO	80124	39.536003	-104.882161
2	10470	1001 E 120th Ave	Thornton	CO	80233	39.914237	-104.97461
3	10871	10445 Reed St	Westminster	CO	80021	39.887068	-105.077233
4	05265	105 W Troutman Pkwy	Fort Collins	CO	80525	40.528503	-105.077763
5	05869	110 W Meadows Dr	Glenwood Springs	CO	81601	39.60545	-107.29783
6	08718	11150 S Twenty Mile Rd	Parker	CO	80134	39.512462	-104.773681
7	06485	1265 Sgt Jon Stiles Dr	Highlands Ranch	CO	80129	39.547923	-105.004378
8	01150	1400 S Havana St	Aurora	CO	80012	39.691887	-104.865722
9	00126	14200 E Ellsworth Ave	Aurora	CO	80012	39.716443	-104.822288
10	11623	14451 Orchard Pkwy	Westminster	CO	80023	39.958965	-104.993911
11	07244	14500 W Colfax Ave Unit B1	Lakewood	CO	80401	39.735381	-105.158602
12	01062	15700 E Briarwood Cir	Aurora	CO	80016	39.59374	-104.803615
13	04151	1630 E Cheyenne Mountain Blvd	Colorado Springs	CO	80906	38.793468	-104.800192
14	02322	1660 W Midway Blvd	Broomfield	CO	80020	39.92193	-105.087915
15	00291	16910 E Quincy Ave	Aurora	CO	80015	39.638273	-104.791136
16	08435	1725 Rocky Mtn Ave	Loveland	CO	80538	40.49141	-105.17206
17	06425	1950 E County Line Rd	Highlands Ranch	CO	80126	39.56595	-104.96342
18	05077	1985 Sheridan Blvd	Edgewater	CO	80214	39.747517	-105.053388
19	02138	2171 Prairie Center Pkwy	Brighton	CO	80601	39.955222	-104.777372
20	06030	2474 Highway 6 and 50	Grand Junction	CO	81505	39.08947	-108.603844

Figure 2-34. The Results window

Practice Using Three Common Tools: Filter, Select, Browse

I realize you haven't yet learned how to use all the tools, but we're going to do three very easy, common tasks so you can start to see the value of Alteryx Designer. We will cover these tools in detail in later chapters.

First, you are going to filter your data. Go to your Global Search text box in the top right corner and type **Filter**. From there, click it and drag and drop the Filter tool onto your canvas. Place it close to the Input Data tool so that it is connected to the Input anchor (see Figure 2-35).

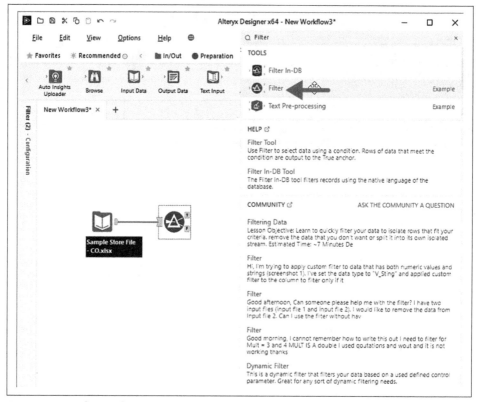

Figure 2-35. Filter tool

Now that you've added Filter from our tool palette (step 1) to our canvas (step 2), you need to configure the tool (step 3). Configure your Filter tool to show only those records where the city is "Broomfield." You can do this by first selecting the field City in the first drop-down, keeping the middle drop-down automatically set to Equals, and typing **Broomfield** in the text box, as shown in Figure 2-36.

Figure 2-36. Filter configuration

Now you've done steps 1, 2, and 3. Do you remember step 4? Right! Run the workflow and view results. Run your workflow to make sure that the data looks the way you expect. Run the workflow and click the output anchor of the Filter tool (T Output) and then look at your results window. You'll see that your data only shows records that have city values of Broomfield (see Figure 2-37).

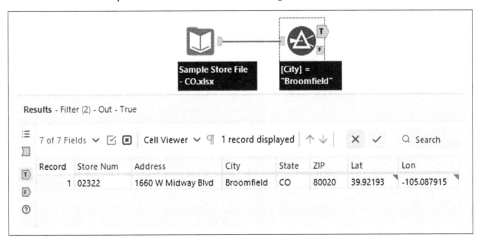

Figure 2-37. Filtered records

Oh, now that's interesting. I only see one record. And you don't need those Lat and Lon fields. Let's get rid of those two columns. You can easily do that by using the Select tool.

Again, we are following the same four-step process. Go to the Global Search and type **Select**. Drop the Select tool (step 1) onto the canvas (step 2) and connect it to the T Output anchor of the Filter tool (see Figure 2-38).

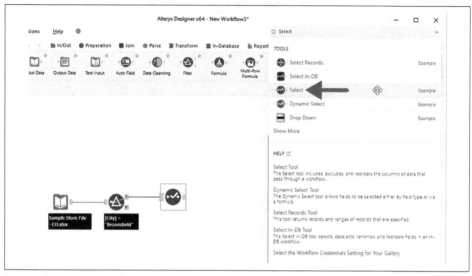

Figure 2-38. Select tool

Now, move on to step 3. Configure the Select tool by simply unchecking those two Lat and Lon fields (see Figure 2-39).

	Field	Type	Size	Rename	Description
☑	Store Num	V_String	255		
☑	Address	V_String	255		
☑	City	V_String	255		
☑	State	V_String	255		
☑	ZIP	V_String	255		
☐	Lat	Double	8		
☐	Lon	Double	8		
☑	*Unknown	Unknown	0		Dynamic or Unknown Fields

Figure 2-39. Select tool configuration

Back to step 4: run the workflow and you'll see that, viola, those two fields are no longer there (see Figure 2-40).

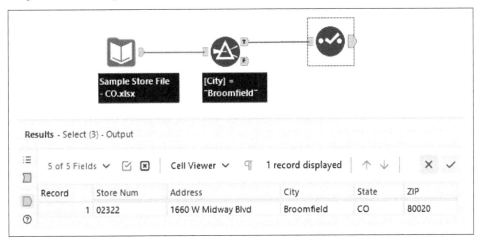

Figure 2-40. Select tool results

The last tool we are going to throw into the mix is the Browse tool. We use this a lot in building workflows, and I like it because it's easy to configure—it has no configuration! For this part, I want you to do something slightly different. I want you to right-click on the Select tool you just added and then scroll down the menu to Add Browse After. This is a cool trick to add the Browse tool rather than dragging and dropping it (see Figure 2-41).

You'll see that if you click the Browse tool to configure it, there will be a message to run the workflow. Again, there is no configuration for a Browse tool. You can now run the workflow (step 4) and see the results.

Figure 2-41. Adding the Browse tool

Congratulations! You just built your first workflow that connected to an Excel sheet in an Excel workbook, filtered your data, and even removed fields you didn't need. Now you have a clear four-step model for building any workflow going forward. Don't worry, I am going to get into many more tools and workflows, so stick with me and let's have some fun.

Conclusion

In this chapter, you've learned the underlying mechanics and configurations for building a workflow and the four key steps we all use to build efficient and effective workflows. You've learned about the important User Settings, and how to use shortcuts and some key resources like Sample Workflows and Sample Datasets, as well as Starter Kits and the Favorites tool palette. You also built your first workflow!

Remember, you can get valuable help by going to the Alteryx community site and posting a question or reading the discussions. There are thousands of other users who would love to help answer questions as you embark on your Alteryx journey. In the next chapter, you are going to put what you learned in this chapter into practice and understand how to get data into Alteryx Designer.

PART II

Basics

CHAPTER 3

Getting Data into Alteryx Designer

In this chapter, we are going to start getting deeper into the tools and functionalities of Alteryx Designer. You are going to learn how to connect Alteryx Designer to all sorts of data, from simple files to database connections and more. Although Alteryx Designer is flexible and powerful, it needs data, so the better you are at getting connected to data the more Alteryx can help!

We are going to cover the In/Out tool palette that will give you tools to not only bring data into Alteryx but also view results and output data to any file type you need. This will be a fundamental step to learn as we go deeper into Alteryx Designer and start to manipulate the data you bring in.

 Once we start to revisit specific items that have already been introduced, I am going to assume you understand the steps involved. You are going to get more knowledgeable and I will get less verbose as we move through each item. For example, I will go from "Drag and drop this tool, configure option A, option B, option C…" to just saying "Connect to this Excel sheet," as I expect you have caught on to what those steps are. This allows you to dig deeper into Alteryx as you get further into this book.

In/Out Tool Palette

The In/Out tool palette is a core set of tools that you will use every time you are building your workflows (see Figure 3-1). As a reminder, a tool palette is a collection of similar tools that you will use to build your workflows.

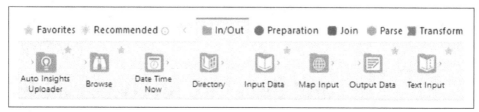

Figure 3-1. In/Out tool palette

You will always know which tools belong to the In/Out palette—they are green and have a tab folder icon:

Before we get into more detail about the individual tools, I want to ensure you have some basic foundational knowledge around why we want to use these In/Out tools in the first place. The first thing you need to think about is data sources—specifically, data source types.

Types of Data Sources

When you think about using Alteryx Designer to connect to data, there are really four main types of sources I want you to think about: files, databases, Gallery (Alteryx Server), and APIs and connectors.

We will cover connecting to files and databases in this chapter. We will not cover connecting to Gallery or API sources, as that's outside the scope of this book. For now, let's discover the ways you can connect to files and databases, which will cover 90–100% of your use cases.

The Input Data Tool

The Input Data tool is likely to be your single most-used tool:

It is a powerful tool that allows you to connect to many data sources, including files and databases. There are many configuration options available for each file or database you connect to, which will help ensure you not only connect to an authenticated source but that you pull the exact data you want.

Working with Files

A key benefit of using Alteryx is the breadth of file types that it can connect to natively (see Figure 3-2).

All supported file types		
Alteryx Calgary .cydb	GIS .grd	Microsoft Excel Binary .xlsb
Alteryx Database .yxdb	Google Earth/Google Maps .kml	Microsoft Excel Macro-Enabled .xlsm
Alteryx Spatial Zip .sz	Gzip .gz, .tgz	Pitney Bowes Multi-Resolution Raster .mrr
Avro .avro	IBM SPSS .sav	QlikView .qvx
Comma Separated Value .csv	JSON .json	SAS .sas7bdat
dBase .dbf	MapInfo Professional Interchange Format .mif	SQLite .sqlite
ESRI Personal GeoDatabase .mdb	MapInfo Professional Table .tab	SRC Geography .geo
ESRI Shapefile .shp	Microsoft Access .accdb	Tableau Hyper Data Extract .hyper
Extensible Markup Language .xml	Microsoft Access 2000-2003 .mdb	Text .txt, .asc, .log, .dat
Flat ASCII .flat	Microsoft Excel .xlsx	Zip .zip
GIS .grc	Microsoft Excel 1997-2003 .xls	

Figure 3-2. File types that Alteryx can connect to

The ability to connect to a wide variety of files makes the scope of potential use cases wider as well. It will become easier for you to answer questions like "Well, do you think Alteryx will support [insert file type here]?" or "Do you think we can connect to data [insert data source here]?" There are actually very few sources you cannot connect to directly. In this section, you will learn how to connect to three of the most commonly used file types. With this knowledge, you can connect to any of the other sources in the same way. The configurations can be different from file to file but the principles are still the same. As I will continue to reference throughout this book, the Alteryx help documentation is really great if you need support on a specific topic.

Connecting to Comma-Separated Values Files

To connect to comma-separated values (CSV) files, drag and drop the Input Data tool onto the canvas. Then, open your configuration window pane (double-click the tool) and look at what is configured (see Figure 3-3).

Next, choose the CSV file you want to connect to by entering it in the "Connect a File or Database" field. In this example, you will connect to the *Emergency_vehicle_response_times_by_state.csv* file that is located in the following Samples directory: *C:\Program Files\Alteryx\Samples\data\StartHereData*.

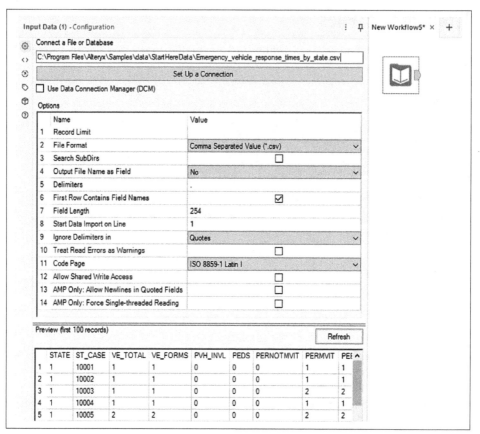

Figure 3-3. Input Data configuration

You can also connect to files by dropping the file onto the canvas or copying and pasting the file location.

To connect to the CSV example file, first click "Set Up a Connection." In the Data connections dialog window that pops up, select Files on the left side and click Select File (see Figure 3-4).

In the "Open a data file" dialog box, navigate to the file you want and click Open (see Figure 3-5).

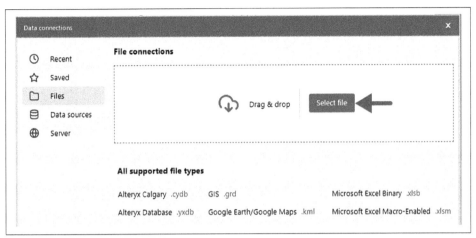

Figure 3-4. Select file

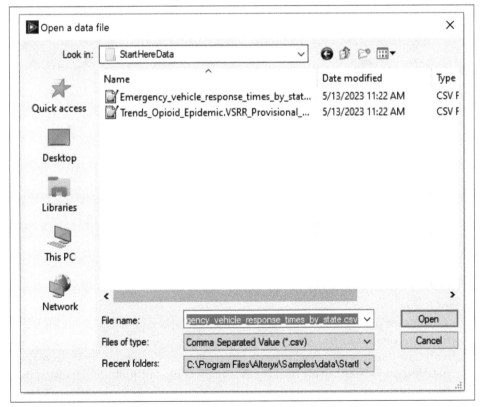

Figure 3-5. Open data file

Over time you will find that Alteryx Designer does things to make your life easier and more efficient. For example, in our scenario you've successfully picked the CSV file you want to use, and Alteryx Designer has made its best guess as to which configuration options are most suitable, so you don't have to set anything if it is working (see Figure 3-6). You are free to modify every configuration option, if you need to.

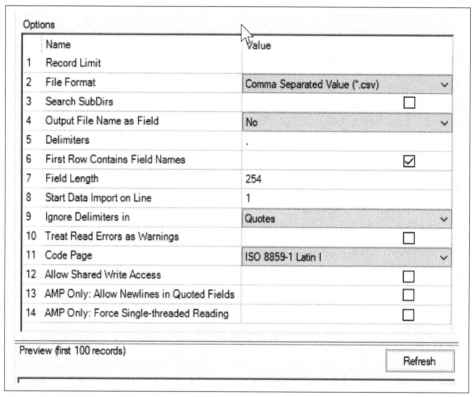

Figure 3-6. CSV input file configurations

Let's look at the options you will see when you connect to a CSV file:

Record Limit

This allows you to limit how many records (rows) are pulled in from the file. I highly recommend using this when working with large data sets to speed up your workflow development. It's also easy to forget that you set this limit, so make a note for yourself either on the canvas using a comment tool or by putting it in the annotations.

File Format

This option allows you to select the file type, informing how the following options are set.

Search SubDirs

Use this option when you'd like to read in multiple inputs and search beyond the folder of the files you have selected. Note that the inputs must contain the same structure, field names, length, and data types.

Output File Name as Field

This option allows you to create a field (column) that contains the filename as a value. This is really helpful when you are pulling in many files at the same time. We will talk about how to do this later in the chapter.

Delimiters

This option allows you to specify any delimiters that are in your data. This is really useful when working with text data, as you won't always have comma-delimited data but maybe data that is separated by tabs (\t), spaces (\s), pipes (|), or even no delimiters (\0). (Note that with this last option, you force the Input Data tool to output all data in a single column.)

First Row Contains Field Names

This option tells Alteryx Designer whether or not you have headers on your data. If you don't, you want to make sure you select this; otherwise, the first row of data will be designated as your header.

Field Length

This option allows you to set the maximum length of your fields. You only need to change this if you see you have extra-long data values. Most of the time, you won't need to modify this.

Start Data Import on Line

This is a great feature that allows you to select which record (row) to start with at import. Say, for example, you have a CSV file that is system generated and puts a bunch of useless information in the top 10 rows of your file. You can tell the Input Data tool to start at row 11, where your data actually starts.

Ignore Delimiters in

This option allows you to ignore delimiters that might be part of the actual data. For example, if you have the delimiter set to a comma, then in a field you happen to have a value of quoted text like "Hello Joshua, I see what you did there!" you don't want that comma to cause a separation of your data. So, if you were to choose "Quotes," that comma after "Joshua" would be ignored.

Treat Read Errors as Warnings

Normal functionality in Designer is to error if you try to bring in multiple files that don't share the same data structure. This feature allows you to bypass this and not let Designer cause an error.

Code Page

A specific code page enables a computer to identify characters and display text correctly. This is not often used, but if you ever have a file that is using a different code page, then you have the option to change that for Designer to read the file correctly.

Allow Shared Write Access

This option allows you to read a file that might be in the process of being updated, like a log file.

AMP Only: Allow Newlines in Quoted Fields

Records by default wouldn't be read sequentially downward one line. For example, line 10 could be read before line 9. Sometimes you will need this option to ensure the file is read the classic way.

AMP Only: Force Single-threaded Reading

If you find that there are issues in how your data is being read using AMP, you can use this option to read data single-threaded.

The last feature that is available on most Input Data tools is a small sample of data (100 rows) that is brought in as a preview (see Figure 3-7). This is very helpful to know, as it helps answer two questions: 1) can Designer see your data? and 2) is the formatting correct? You will often find issues with your data here in the preview first. This allows you to configure the options we just reviewed and then click Refresh to get a new preview.

Preview (first 100 records)   Refresh

	STATE	ST_CASE	VE_TOTAL	VE_FORMS	PVH_INVL	PEDS	PERNOTMVIT	PERMVIT	PERSONS	COUNTY	CITY	DAY	MON
1	1	10001	1	1	0	0	0	1	1	127	0	1	1
2	1	10002	1	1	0	0	0	1	1	83	0	1	1
3	1	10003	1	1	0	0	0	2	2	11	0	1	1
4	1	10004	1	1	0	0	0	1	1	45	0	4	1
5	1	10005	2	2	0	0	0	2	2	45	2050	7	1
6	1	10006	1	1	0	0	0	2	2	111	0	8	1
7	1	10007	1	1	0	0	0	2	2	89	1730	8	1
8	1	10008	1	1	0	1	1	1	1	73	350	3	1
9	1	10009	1	1	0	0	0	1	1	117	47	13	1
10	1	10010	2	2	0	0	0	2	2	33	0	5	1
11	1	10011	2	2	0	0	0	2	2	83	0	7	1
12	1	10012	3	3	0	0	0	6	6	95	1500	9	1
13	1	10013	1	1	0	0	0	1	1	87	0	10	1
14	1	10014	1	1	0	0	0	1	1	11	0	11	1
15	1	10015	1	1	0	0	0	1	1	127	0	11	1

Figure 3-7. Data preview

If you are using network-based files or many files from a folder(s), then you won't be able to utilize the preview.

Now, recall my four-step process for building a workflow from Chapter 2: after you drag and drop a tool from the tool palette (step 1) and onto the canvas (step 2), you then configure it (step 3) and run the workflow (step 4).

You've done steps 1–3. Now, do the last step to see your CSV data come into Designer and view it in the Results window (see Figure 3-8).

Record	STATE	ST_CASE	VE_TOTAL	VE_FORMS	PVH_INVL	PEDS	PERNOTMVIT	PERMVIT	PERSONS	COUNTY	CITY	DAY	MONTH
1 1		10001	1	1	0	0	0	1	1	127	0	1	1
2 1		10002	1	1	0	0	0	1	1	83	0	1	1
3 1		10003	1	1	0	0	0	2	2	11	0	1	1
4 1		10004	1	1	0	0	0	1	1	45	0	4	1
5 1		10005	2	2	0	0	0	2	2	45	2050	7	1
6 1		10006	1	1	0	0	0	2	2	111	0	8	1
7 1		10007	1	1	0	0	0	2	2	89	1730	8	1
8 1		10008	1	1	0	1	1	1	1	73	350	3	1
9 1		10009	1	1	0	0	0	1	1	117	47	13	1
10 1		10010	2	2	0	0	0	2	2	33	0	5	1
11 1		10011	2	2	0	0	0	2	2	83	0	7	1
12 1		10012	5	5	0	0	0	6	6	95	1500	9	1
13 1		10013	1	1	0	0	0	1	1	87	0	10	1
14 1		10014	1	1	0	0	0	1	1	11	0	11	1
15 1		10015	1	1	0	0	0	1	1	127	0	11	1
16 1		10016	2	2	0	0	0	2	2	81	2340	13	1
17 1		10017	1	1	0	0	0	1	1	97	0	14	1
18 1		10018	1	1	0	0	0	2	2	1	0	16	1
19 1		10019	1	1	0	0	0	1	1	121	0	19	1
20 1		10020	2	2	0	0	0	3	3	121	2910	15	1

Figure 3-8. Results window

Great work! You've successfully brought in CSV data. Let's not stop here—let's bring in even more data.

Wait, I Got an Error!

If you received an error message after trying to run the workflow (see Figure 3-9), take a look at what the message is telling you. I find that so many users don't read the actual text of the error message. Most times (not always), the error message will tell you exactly what you need to fix.

Figure 3-9. Workflow error

You can also quickly get to the messages you want by clicking on the message type—Errors or Warnings, for example—which helps in long workflows that have many messages. If you are still stuck, this is where the Alteryx community can come in handy. You can simply post a message in the discussion threads to get your questions answered.

Connecting to Excel Files

Connecting to an Excel file starts off the same exact way as connecting to a CSV file. Drag and drop the Input Data tool onto the canvas and choose the file you want to bring in (see Figure 3-10).

Our example uses this sample data set: *C:\Program Files\Alteryx\Samples\data\Start HereData\Excel.CustomerResponderData.xlsx*.

Once you choose the Excel file, notice that an Excel file doesn't have the same configuration options as the CSV file. In connecting to Excel, you have one option that is different (option 3 shown in Figure 3-10): "Table or Query." This option allows you to choose which sheet inside of the Excel workbook you want to connect to.

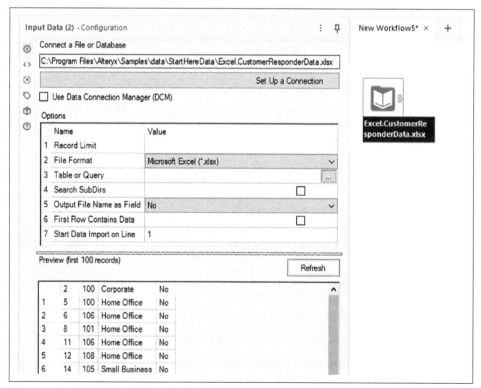

Figure 3-10. XLSX file input

If you click the ellipsis button to the right of that option, you will get the window shown in Figure 3-11.

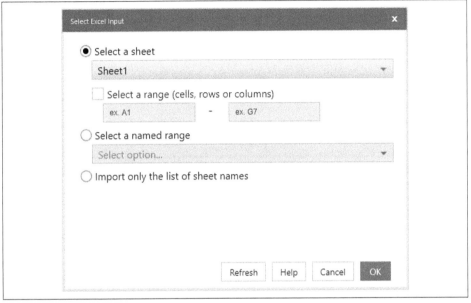

Figure 3-11. Select Excel Input

The three options you now have available are important to know and understand:

Select a sheet
> This option allows you to choose the individual sheet in the Excel workbook you want to connect to. You can even choose a specific range of cells within that specific sheet to read.

Select a named range
> There is a feature inside Excel that allows you to name a range of cells. This option allows you to see and select that named range.

Import only the list of sheet names
> Instead of reading data from the sheet, this feature provides a list of all the sheets that are in that file, allowing you to read from multiple sheets at the same time.

For this example, select Sheet1 from the first option and click OK. You will notice that Sheet1 is now selected in this option (see Figure 3-12).

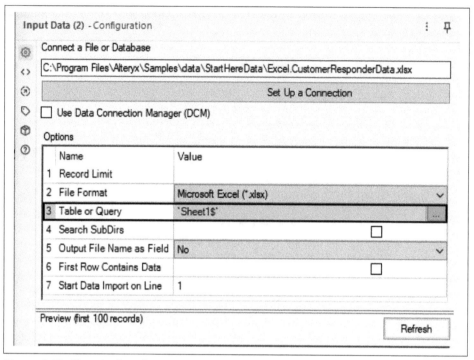

Figure 3-12. Sheet1 selected

You have dragged and dropped a tool from the tool palette (step 1) onto the canvas (step 2) and configured it (step 3). Now you need to run the workflow (step 4).

Congratulations! You are on your way to taking over the world by storm. OK, maybe just *your* world, but still. Let's continue to learn more about connecting to files in different ways.

Connecting to Text Files

Connecting to text files will be very similar to connecting to a CSV file or an Excel file. In this example, you will connect to an XML file (see Figure 3-13).

First, drag and drop a new Input Data tool onto the canvas and select this file: *C:\Program Files\Alteryx\Samples\data\StartHereData\XML_Parse.Sample_ XML.xml.*

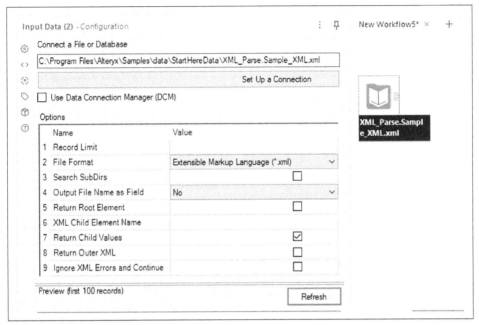

Figure 3-13. Connecting to an XML file

You will notice that Designer has a handful of options available to you specifically geared for XML files:

Return Root Element
This option allows you to output in the data set the root element of the XML file.

XML Child Element Name
Allows you to choose more specifically which element within the XML that you want to read in from the XML file.

Return Child Values
When selected, it will return the values of the root element.

Return Outer XML
When selected, Designer will return the actual XML tag that surrounds the value.

Ignore XML Errors and Continue
This is a useful option when your XML file is not perfect and has some errors because of an XML tag not being closed. By selecting this option, you can ignore those errors. A word of caution, though—you need to be clear as to why you are ignoring them instead of correcting them.

In this example, you are using the base configuration that was selected. Now, let's run the workflow and see what results we get (see Figure 3-14).

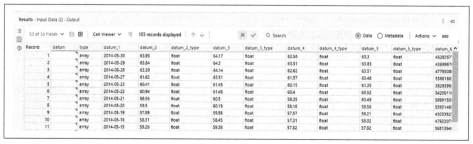

Figure 3-14. XML results

You have now learned how to connect to CSVs as well as Excel files and text files. This can get you started but we don't want to slow down now, right? Let's learn how you can connect to not just a single file but to multiple files at the same time.

Connecting to Multiple Files at One Time

I can still remember when I first started learning Alteryx and mastered pulling in files of all different types—I had workflows with 5–10 inputs for a specific type. I was so proud of myself and built more and more workflows that started like this (see Figure 3-15).

Connecting to multiple files at once is incredibly time consuming. But, as you probably guessed, there are many ways to easily work with many files (even thousands of files) all at once. You can bring in multiple files at once in a few ways, including with Input Data tool wildcards, the Directory tool, and the Dynamic Input tool.

Let's take a look at what wildcards are and how to use them in our Input Data tool to allow us to bring in multiple files at once.

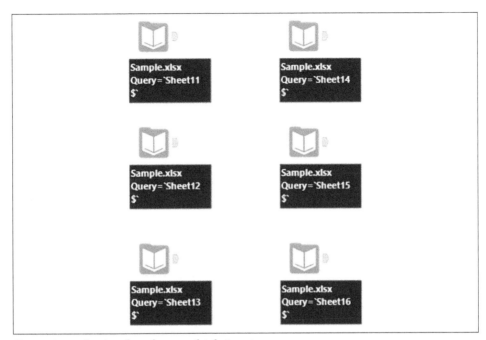

Figure 3-15. Getting data from multiple inputs

Using the * wildcard

When you are configuring an Input Data tool, you can use what are called wildcards. These include * (with the asterisk meaning "all") or ? (for a single character). Let's say you have a folder of 50 CSV files that contain information on each US state. They all have the same number of fields, and the data types for each field are the same. You can add an asterisk wildcard to bring in all of these files at one time (see Figure 3-16).

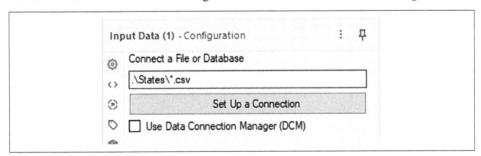

*Figure 3-16. * wildcard input*

When you do this, each file gets read into Designer and the data gets unioned (joined together vertically) into one data set that looks like Figure 3-17.

Results - Input Data (2) - Output

5 of 5 Fields ∨ ☑ ▣ | Cell Viewer ∨ ¶ 49 records displayed ↑ ↓ |

Record	Attrb Code	State	Abbrev.	Population	SpatialObj
1	1	Alabama	AL	4874747	Polygon - View Browse Tool Map Tab
2	4	Arizona	AZ	7016270	Polygon - View Browse Tool Map Tab
3	5	Arkansas	AR	3004279	Polygon - View Browse Tool Map Tab
4	6	California	CA	39536653	Polygon - View Browse Tool Map Tab
5	8	Colorado	CO	5607154	Polygon - View Browse Tool Map Tab
6	9	Connecticut	CT	3588184	Polygon - View Browse Tool Map Tab
7	10	Delaware	DE	961939	Polygon - View Browse Tool Map Tab
8	12	Florida	FL	20984400	Polygon - View Browse Tool Map Tab
9	13	Georgia	GA	10429379	Polygon - View Browse Tool Map Tab
10	15	Hawaii	HI	1427538	Polygon - View Browse Tool Map Tab
11	16	Idaho	ID	1716943	Polygon - View Browse Tool Map Tab
12	17	Illinois	IL	12802023	Polygon - View Browse Tool Map Tab
13	18	Indiana	IN	6666818	Polygon - View Browse Tool Map Tab
14	19	Iowa	IA	3145711	Polygon - View Browse Tool Map Tab
15	20	Kansas	KS	2913123	Polygon - View Browse Tool Map Tab

Figure 3-17. Unioned data set

Using the * wildcard is a really powerful way to add dynamics to your workflows. You can use the * multiple times as well. What if you want to only replace one character? That's where the ? wildcard comes into play.

Using the ? wildcard

Now, imagine having each state broken out for each of the five-year periods we are looking at. We want to bring in only the files that are for the 2010s and nothing from the 2020s. We do this by using the ? wildcard (see Figure 3-18).

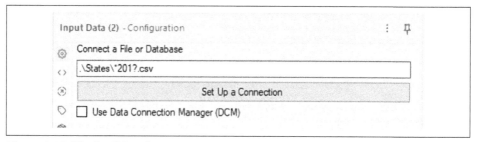

Input Data (2) - Configuration

Connect a File or Database

.\States*201?.csv

Set Up a Connection

☐ Use Data Connection Manager (DCM)

Figure 3-18. The ? wildcard

Figure 3-19 shows the results of bringing only the files that have "201" in the filename and not "202" or beyond.

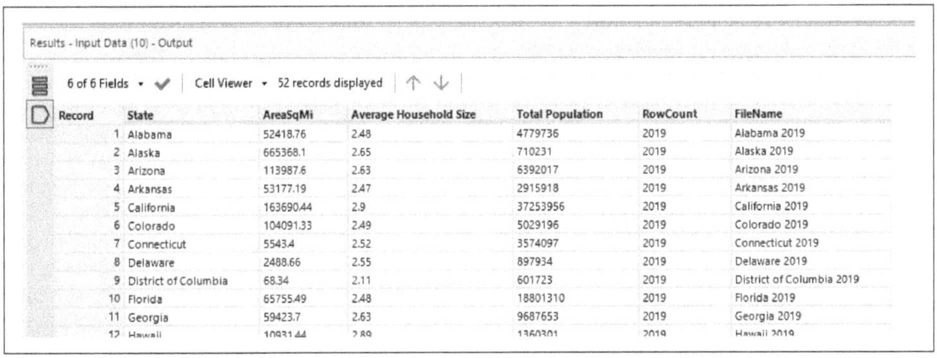

6 of 6 Fields ▾ ✔ | Cell Viewer ▾ 52 records displayed ↑ ↓

Record	State	AreaSqMi	Average Household Size	Total Population	RowCount	FileName
1	Alabama	52418.76	2.48	4779736	2019	Alabama 2019
2	Alaska	665368.1	2.65	710231	2019	Alaska 2019
3	Arizona	113987.6	2.63	6392017	2019	Arizona 2019
4	Arkansas	53177.19	2.47	2915918	2019	Arkansas 2019
5	California	163690.44	2.9	37253956	2019	California 2019
6	Colorado	104091.33	2.49	5029196	2019	Colorado 2019
7	Connecticut	5543.4	2.52	3574097	2019	Connecticut 2019
8	Delaware	2488.66	2.55	897934	2019	Delaware 2019
9	District of Columbia	68.34	2.11	601723	2019	District of Columbia 2019
10	Florida	65755.49	2.48	18801310	2019	Florida 2019
11	Georgia	59423.7	2.63	9687653	2019	Georgia 2019
12	Hawaii	10931.44	2.89	1360301	2019	Hawaii 2019

Figure 3-19. Wildcard results

Two items are important to note here. The first item is that Designer will decide the structure (fields and file types) of the data based on the first file that is read. The second item is that if after that first file there is a file that doesn't match that same structure, that file will be skipped and you will see a warning in your results window after you run the workflow. Designer is expecting all the files in that folder to be the same structure.

One area of interest that I don't cover in this book is connectors. Alteryx Designer has many other connectors to data sources such as Google Sheets, SharePoint, and more in the Connectors tool palette. I highly encourage you to take a look at them and explore if any may be of value to you.

Working with any other file format is very similar to the examples I have provided—you simply need to pay attention to any specific configuration options that are unique to the file type you are bringing in. You will see me repeat this multiple times in this book: you have to know your data. This means knowing what fields you have, what file type it is, what format it is (is it using comma delimiters or tab delimiters?), etc.

Now that we have talked about file types, it's important to realize that files are just one way to connect to data. You can also connect to many different databases, and Designer natively supports many of the most commonly used databases in the world today. We'll explore this topic in the next section.

Connecting with Databases

Working with files is a satisfying experience when everything is working together and you realize you are beginning to automate much of your manual work. However, there is something about connecting to databases that hold potentially millions, if not hundreds of millions or even billions, of records. It's probably like sitting in a Ferrari or a Lamborghini and turning the engine on. It's a lot of power at your fingertips. I still get excited when I start exploring new data sets and start to imagine all the possibilities. There are so many possibilities for connecting to various databases—a few sources are shown in Figure 3-20.

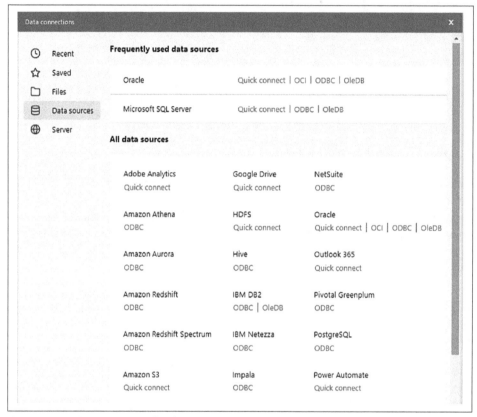

Figure 3-20. Connecting to databases

In this section, you will connect to a database. A word of advice: you'll need to be a bit more persistent than normal here. For the most part, databases can be finicky because there are many moving parts to get working, such as the SQL you write, the driver version, and connectivity. I challenge you to stick with it—it does get easier! If Designer supports it, then you know it will work. It might take some effort and tinkering, based on how it's implemented or the rules at your organization, but it will work. In order to connect to data easily and securely, you will need to understand the Data Connection Manager (DCM).

Data Connection Manager

DCM, as we introduced in Chapter 2, serves as a single access point for your credentials. It allows you to enter and update data source credentials and then reuse those credentials across many tools and workflows. No longer do you have to constantly reenter your credentials and deal with the security issues that come with this. Using DCM will improve your efficiency when connecting to databases by reducing the number of times you have to enter credentials as well as simplifying the process of updating passwords, since you will only have one credential to update.

We will make regular use of DCM throughout this chapter. To ensure that you have DCM enabled for use, go to Options > User Settings > Edit User Settings in the menu bar and click the DCM tab. You will see a screen like Figure 3-21.

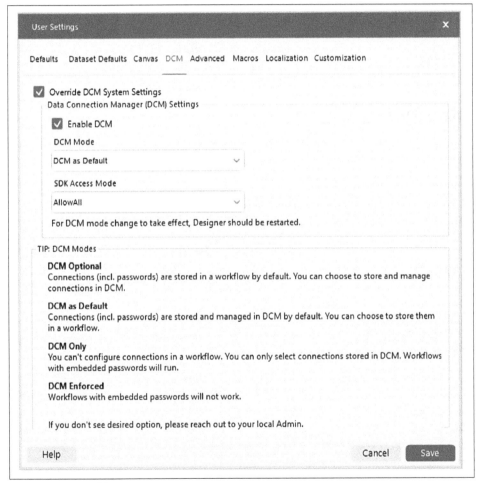

Figure 3-21. Enabling DCM

Notice that the checkbox next to Enable DCM is checked. You also have the option to select a specific DCM Mode. I recommend starting with "DCM as Default" unless you have a compelling reason not to.

Making a Connection to a Database

Designer can connect to databases in two ways. The first way is via Open Database Connectivity (ODBC). The second way is via Object Linking and Embedding Database (OLEDB). The simplest way to know which one to use is to remember that ODBC is geared for relational databases only and depends on using SQL exclusively to "talk" to the database. OLEDB, on the other hand, is more robust and can not only connect to relational databases but also to many other forms such as hierarchical databases, graphical databases, and more.

If you are only connecting to a SQL database, then ODBC is just fine. You'll learn how to connect to databases using both options; then you can choose which option you prefer. It's not likely you will see huge performance gaps with one option over the other, unless you are pulling hundreds of millions of records or more of data.

Drivers and DSNs

If your organization is managing data sources via DCM, then some parts of this section might not be relevant to you. However, I still think it's useful to cover so you understand how it works.

In order to connect to ODBC, you need to knock out a few other steps first. You'll need to ensure you have the right ODBC database driver, and then you will need to create a DSN (Data Source Name) that Designer will use to connect to. To determine if you have the right ODBC driver, you need to first check what the requirement is by going to the Alteryx documentation on data sources (*https://oreil.ly/AjAZK*). Find the data source you want to connect to and see what version you need. For example, if I want to connect to a database using Microsoft SQL Server 2016, I will go to the page on Microsoft SQL Server 2012, 2014, 2016 and see that Designer has been validated on ODBC Driver 11, 13, 13.1 and SQL Server Native Client 10, 11. So, I have five different versions of drivers that should work.

Let's check our machine to see if we have any of those drivers already installed. Click the Windows icon in the bottom left corner and type **ODBC**. You should see an item for ODBC Data Sources (64-bit). When that application opens, go to the Drivers tab (see Figure 3-22). There, you can see the drivers installed for data sources. You can see if any of the drivers you need are there. If they aren't, you will need to install them.

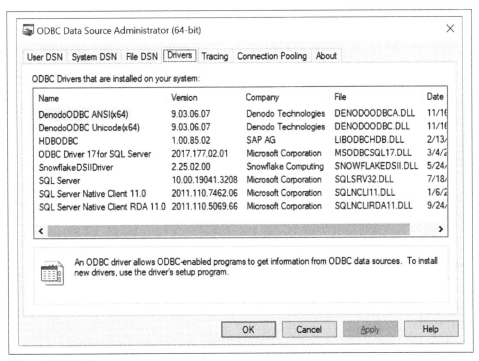

Name	Version	Company	File	Date
DenodoODBC ANSI(x64)	9.03.06.07	Denodo Technologies	DENODOODBCA.DLL	11/16
DenodoODBC Unicode(x64)	9.03.06.07	Denodo Technologies	DENODOODBC.DLL	11/16
HDBODBC	1.00.85.02	SAP AG	LIBODBCHDB.DLL	2/13/
ODBC Driver 17 for SQL Server	2017.177.02.01	Microsoft Corporation	MSODBCSQL17.DLL	3/4/2
SnowflakeDSIIDriver	2.25.02.00	Snowflake Computing	SNOWFLAKEDSII.DLL	5/24/
SQL Server	10.00.19041.3208	Microsoft Corporation	SQLSRV32.DLL	7/18/
SQL Server Native Client 11.0	2011.110.7462.06	Microsoft Corporation	SQLNCLI11.DLL	1/6/2
SQL Server Native Client RDA 11.0	2011.110.5069.66	Microsoft Corporation	SQLNCLIRDA11.DLL	9/24/

An ODBC driver allows ODBC-enabled programs to get information from ODBC data sources. To install new drivers, use the driver's setup program.

Figure 3-22. Drivers

I am going to assume that you have the right driver installed, or you were able to install it. Once you have that part complete, you now need to create a DSN using that same ODBC Data Source Administrator (64-bit) application.

Many who are new to working with databases, and especially setting up connectivity, get stuck on the DSN creation step. They know they need to create a DSN but aren't sure which one to create—a user DSN or a system DSN. The difference between a user DSN and a system DSN is access. A user DSN is only accessible by the user who created it, while the system DSN is available to all users who might use that machine. Later on, we will discuss running workflows as a service account. If you do that, you will need to have a system DSN. For now, you can create a user DSN. Let's walk through the steps to create one.

If you don't have a DSN set up or want to set up a new one, I would recommend using Microsoft Support (*https://oreil.ly/__20h*) to help.

Follow these steps to create a user DSN:

1. In the ODBC Data Source Administrator window, on the User DSN tab, click Add.

2. Select the driver you want to use, then click Finish.

3. The specific instructions for that driver/connection will be presented. Go through the items and configure the driver for the database you want to connect to. Once that's done, click Finish.

4. You will now see a Test Data Source button. It is always good to ensure that you set up the connection correctly; you can confirm by testing the connection.

Now that you have successfully created the user DSN, you are ready to connect to a database from Alteryx. Are you excited yet? You should be!

Connecting to Data Using ODBC and DCM

You will connect to data using ODBC quite often, so it's very important for you to understand the steps early on and become proficient in building a connection that works.

You'll first need to set up a connection that can be used by this workflow or any other workflow you build going forward. Let's walk through the steps you need to do for this:

1. In Designer, drag and drop an Input Data tool onto the canvas.

2. Ensure the "Use Data Connection Manager (DCM)" checkbox is selected and click "Set Up a Connection" in the configuration window (see Figure 3-23).

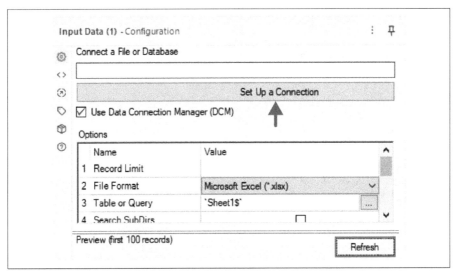

Figure 3-23. Setting up a connection to data using ODBC

3. Click "Data sources" on the left and then ODBC under the data source you want to connect to. For this example, use Microsoft SQL Server (see Figure 3-24).

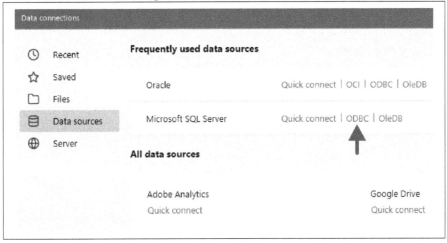

Figure 3-24. Connecting to data via Microsoft ODBC

4. In the Connection Manager, select the "+ New" blue button in the top right corner (see Figure 3-25).

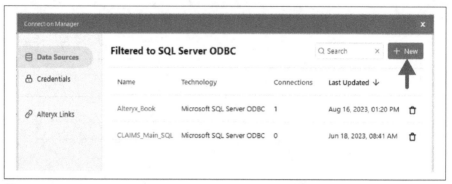

Figure 3-25. New connection

Once you have a connection created, simply click the connection you want in the window. For example, in Figure 3-25, I could click the CLAIMS_Main_SQL connection. We'll get there, but let's first ensure you have a connection fully set up.

5. In the New Data Source window, fill in the name of the connection you are creating in Data Source Name. Make this name very specific so it is clear what this data source is for. Then, pick your ODBC DSN by clicking on the wheel next to the text box (see Figure 3-26).

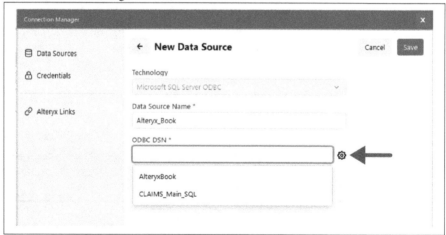

Figure 3-26. Adding a New Data Source

6. When the ODBC Data Source Administrator window pops up, select the ODBC connection (on the User DSN or the System DSN tabs) you'd like to use and click OK (see Figure 3-27).

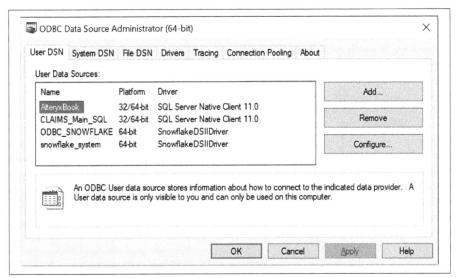

Figure 3-27. Selecting the ODBC DSN

7. Once the ODBC Administrator window closes, make sure the DSN you selected is in the ODBC DSN field. Click Save (see Figure 3-28).

Figure 3-28. Confirming and saving the new ODBC DSN

8. Before we can connect a credential to our data source, we need to create a credential by clicking Credentials on the far left. Click "+ New" and enter the information you have for authenticating to your data source. Click Save (see Figure 3-29).

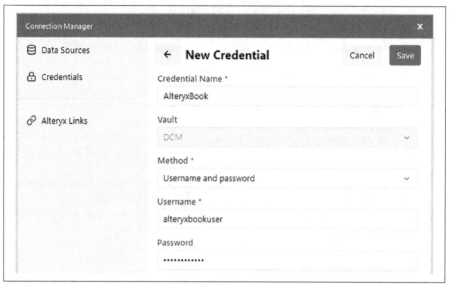

Figure 3-29. *Creating a New Credential*

9. Now that you have the credential created, you can click Data Sources on the far left and select the connection we just created in steps 5–7. On the next screen, you will see that we have the data connection but now also need to link the credential we want to use. To do this, click Connect Credential on the right side (see Figure 3-30).

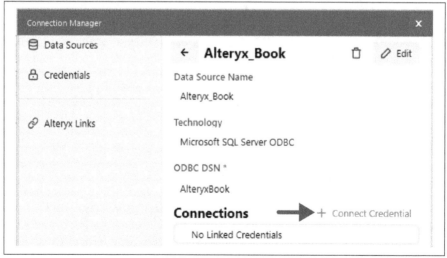

Figure 3-30. *Connect ODBC and credential*

10. Select your authentication method and the credential you just created. Before clicking the blue Link button, I highly recommend clicking Test Connection to ensure you see a "Connection test succeeded" message (see Figure 3-31).

Figure 3-31. Test connection and link credentials

11. Click Connect (see Figure 3-32).

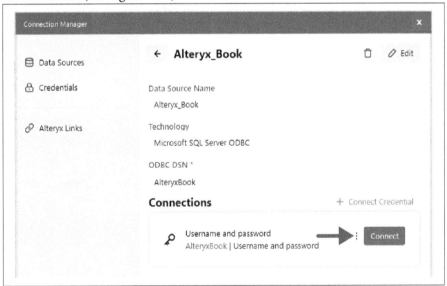

Figure 3-32. Connect to data source

12. A pop-up dialog box will open (see Figure 3-33) and you will have four options to choose from:

Tables
   Select a specific table of data that is in your database.

Visual Query Builder
> Select multiple tables and join them.

Stored Procedures
> Select a previously created and stored procedure.

SQL Editor
> Copy and paste your SQL Editor or modify a previously written query.

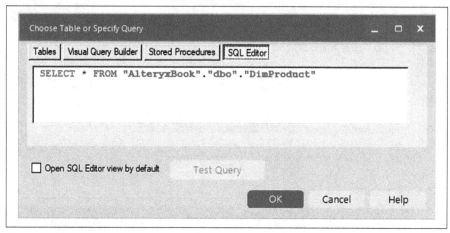

Figure 3-33. Connect to data source by choosing a table or specify query

13. Once you have built your query, click OK and the screen will close.

14. Run your workflow (via either Ctrl+N or clicking the Run button on the right). If your query was successful (fingers crossed), you will see data that is pulled from your database (see Figure 3-34).

 SQL queries that select a large number of rows could take a long time to run. It might be worth adding a limit statement, initially, for testing.

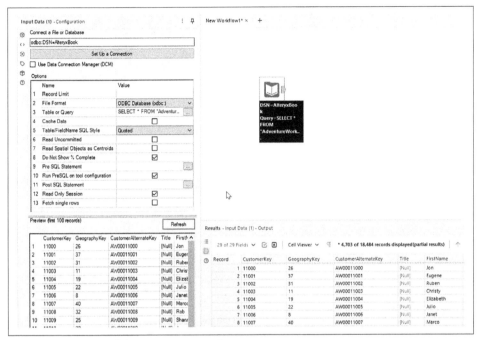

Figure 3-34. Successful connection to a data source

You are now able to set up a successful connection to your database using ODBC. Let's take a look at a very similar example using OLEDB connections.

Connecting to Data using OLEDB

If you want to connect to a data source via OLEDB, there are some minor differences from setting up an ODBC connection. With an OLEDB connection, you don't use the DSN. Instead, follow these steps:

1. Go to the Data sources section of the Data connections window, just as with ODBC, but this time click OleDB (see Figure 3-35).

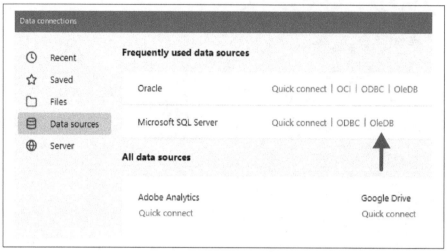

Figure 3-35. Connect using OleDB

2. The Data Link Properties window will pop up. Choose the driver you want to use and click Next (see Figure 3-36).

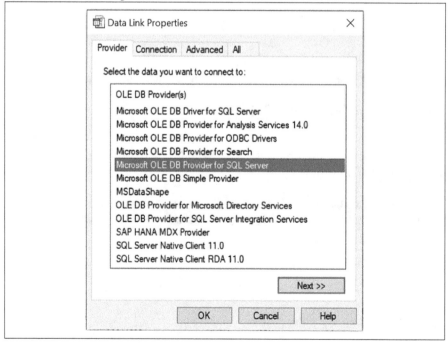

Figure 3-36. Data Link Properties

3. Configure the connection tab. Then, click Test Connection to confirm you get a successful connection.

4. Once the window closes, run the workflow and see your data!

We've covered a lot on the Input Data tool and working with files and databases. Let's take a quick look at the other tools in the In/Out tool palette.

More Tools in the In/Out Tool Palette

As you go through the book, it's important that you learn about as many tools as you can. In each chapter, I will introduce you to more and more tools so that at the end of this book you have a firm grasp on all the tools. You don't need to know every little configuration or detail right now, but make sure you have a general understanding of what the individual tools are used for. If you come across a tool that you think you might want to use, you can do a deep dive into its configuration.

Many tools have example workflows. Also, if you hover over the tool inside the palette, you'll see a description of what that specific tool does.

The In/Out tool palette encompasses all those tools focused on the input or output of data with Alteryx (see Figure 3-37). Since this chapter is about getting data *into* Designer, I want to briefly cover those specific tools. I will skip the Output Data tool, as the next chapter covers outputting data.

Figure 3-37. In/Out tool palette

Browse Tool

The Browse tool, as we saw in Chapter 2, is a powerful and useful tool that you will come to depend on in nearly every workflow you build:

You can use the Browse tool to view data coming from the tool it's connected to. You can see data profile information for multiple columns at once in a single, holistic view, or you can select a single column of data. You can view information on data type, number of records, data quality, and a variety of statistics. This is an excellent tool to better understand your data. Many people I know use the Browse tool as their first step after connecting to their data, in order to explore and better understand what their data is telling them.

 When clicking on a tool anchor, the Results preview might show you partial results, but the Browse tool will always show all records.

Date Time Now Tool

The Date Time Now tool is simple, but very useful:

It provides the date and time for your data at the moment it's run, and based on a format you choose. This is great for logging times of workflow runs as well as using the current date and time in your workflows.

Directory Tool

I referred to the Directory tool earlier in this chapter, and now I want you to understand generally what it's used for:

It allows you to list all the files in a specific directory. You can specify any search parameters, including using wildcards (* and ?). For example, you can list only CSV file types in a directory. You can also configure it to look in all the subdirectories. You will be able to see how powerful this is when you enter a shared drive that holds tens of thousands of files and you want to list only specific files in specific subfolders.

Map Input Tool

The Map Input tool is used to draw or select a map object to use as an input in a workflow:

This is a very useful tool if you'd like to present a map as an input, where the user could click or select an area on the map. You can draw or select a point, line, or polygon from a map and then convert that into a spatial data type. We will talk extensively about spatial tools and spatial data throughout this book, but specifically in Chapter 15.

Text Input Tool

The Text Input tool simply allows you to manually create data:

When you are building workflows off of sample or test data, you can quickly use this tool to create a hardcoded list, some dummy data, or even a placeholder for Analytic Apps. It also allows you to have some static data, if needed, like the address of your company or a list of names that doesn't change. There are many useful hacks that can be used in the building of workflows. One popular hack is that you can copy data from the Browse tool and then right-click on the canvas and paste it. You can also do this from many other applications, especially Excel where you can select a group of rows and columns, copy it, and then paste it directly onto the canvas. A Text Input tool will be automatically created with that copied data. Another hack you can use is in building Analytic Apps, where the Text Input tool becomes a placeholder for a value that the user will provide. We will talk all about that use case in Chapter 14, when we cover Analytic Apps.

Conclusion

By now you should be familiar with the tools and steps you need to perform to connect to individual files, multiple files at one time (using wildcards), and even databases (in two different ways)! You've also been introduced to the In/Out tool palette. I am aware that's a lot of information to absorb. If you find that you don't feel 100% solid on a particular area, I recommend going back and rereading the section on it and working through the steps again. It will behoove you to become very comfortable with bringing in data to Alteryx. There is nothing better than just plain old practice. The users who go on to love Alteryx are those who are persistent and curious. Start with one of the input tools and dig into each part of it, understand what happens when you change the delimiter or see what the Map Input tool provides you. If you are so inclined, I challenge you to go back to Chapter 2 and take that initial workflow you built off of Excel and build a new one using a database connection. In the next chapter, we'll cover the rest of the In/Out tool palette by talking about how to get data out of Designer—specifically, how to save data to a machine or server.

CHAPTER 4

Getting Data out of Alteryx Designer

Just as there are so many different formats that you can use to get data into Designer, there are also just as many formats and methods to get data out of Designer. You could output your data to simple sources, like a CSV file or an Excel file, but you can also output directly to databases, web sources, and major data visualization tools like PowerBI and Tableau. Most users output data either to files, like Excel and CSV, or to databases, like Microsoft SQL Server. In this chapter, you'll learn how to do both.

Like I've said in earlier chapters, Designer is extremely flexible and powerful, and can build well-designed reports and outputs in various formats that allow you to automate both reporting and analysis. This chapter will focus on the Output Data tool, but I will introduce many more tools for outputting data, which we will cover in detail in Chapters 9 and 10.

Files Versus Databases

Many of us in the analytics industry never took a formal class or received training on using databases. In fact, most of us probably received more training on using Excel for our projects than anything else. As we discuss outputting data, I want to use this opportunity to challenge you to consider if using databases might actually be better for you. There are two reasons I am posing this challenge.

First, Designer makes it so easy to interact with databases—both getting data in and getting data out. Second, there are so many features that databases provide. You may think that working with files is easier and quicker, but I would like you to challenge that assumption. With a little work, you can work more effectively and efficiently using databases.

More specifically, I see three key benefits of using databases over files:

Central location
Anyone who has used files to store data can attest to the mess that occurs over time in one's file storage. Folders and folders of data are just spread out and, many times, are hard to get to unless you happen to be extremely organized at all times. Having a database in which to store data makes more sense in that it's all in one central location. Databases don't care if the data is one row or one billion rows; they can handle any size.

Scale and flexibility
You can't beat the power of a database. Users who have tried to put 500,000 rows of data into an Excel sheet know that most file types were not built to scale well. That flexibility of being able to go from one record to one billion records is powerful. The flexibility of a database is also demonstrated in its ability to store all different data types in one place. Having a database that can store JSON formats, spatial formats, and standard table formats means users do not have to manage multiple file types based on the data.

Access and control
Having files that contain valuable data spread out all over a machine is a risk for companies and the user. If a user leaves their laptop logged in, by chance, and someone takes the opportunity to rummage through files, there is no way to stop them from grabbing a file sitting on the desktop and emailing it to themselves or someone else. It's there, open and exposed. With a database, however, you can secure your data—it's stored on servers that are within the walls of a company and can be properly looked after.

For as long as I can remember, databases have represented "real" analytics, at scale. I assure you that files are just as important for analytics, and we'll discuss next.

Output to Files

The main way to output data to a file is by using the Output Data tool, which is the main topic of this chapter. This tool has many features that go above and beyond simply outputting data. Let's start off by taking a look at how we would output to a single CSV file. Then, we will look at outputting to Excel as well as Alteryx's proprietary database format YXDB.

Alteryx has a few file types that are proprietary and only used with Alteryx Designer and Server. One of them is a database file format called YXDB. This file format is the most efficient file type for reading and writing in Designer because it has no size limit, is compressed for maximum speed, and includes additional metadata that references the source of the data and how the data was created. There is no row limit—no other file format, other than text, supports as many rows.

Output to a CSV File

To output to a CSV file using the Output Data tool, first drag and drop an Output Data tool to the canvas and ensure it's connected to the tool that you want to output data from (see Figure 4-1).

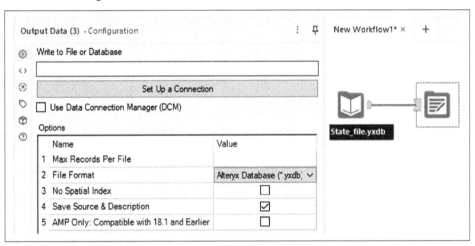

Figure 4-1. Output to CSV file

To configure the Output Data tool, you will need to tell Designer where you want to save the output file. You can do this just like you would for the Input Data tool, by clicking on the down arrow on the right side of the Configuration window, which will open up the Data connections window (see Figure 4-2).

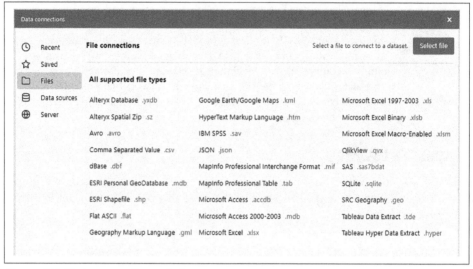

Figure 4-2. Data connections window

In the Data connections window, select the CSV option. Then, in the next window, choose a name for the file (see Figure 4-3).

Figure 4-3. Save a data file in CSV format

Click Save. You have completed the configuration for outputting the data to a CSV file on your machine! Remember, you can also change the configuration, if needed (see Figure 4-4).

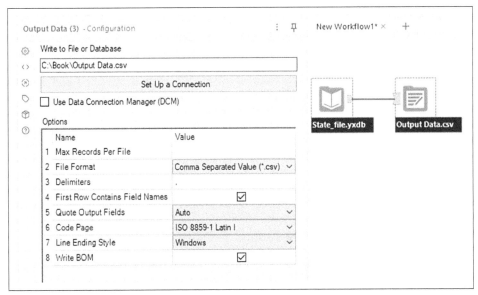

Figure 4-4. CSV configuration options

Let's dig into some of the configuration options for CSV files.

Configuration options

In general, it's important to understand the configuration options you have available to you for the Output Data tool, as there are many options that can determine whether you are able to properly read the file. There are also nice little tricks that will take 2–3 steps out of your workflow just by getting the right options set. Let's take a look at those options:

Max Records Per File

This option allows you to specify how many records get written out. If you are in development mode and just testing, you could set this to, say, 10 records so that it's fast until you need to run it fully.

File Format

This is the option that you use to choose your file type.

Delimiters

This is very important to pay attention to, as it is the actual character that separates your data into columns. If you try to output to a file and all the data is ending up in one column, then it's likely your delimiter is incorrect.

First Row Contains Field Names
> This option allows you to specify whether your data contains headers or not.

Quote Output Fields
> This option is similar to the Input Data tool option, which ensures that values don't get haphazardly cut off by quotes.

Code Page
> This is the option that allows you to specify the code page. Most of the time, you'll never need to modify this.

Line Ending Style
> If you are working with files from different systems (Unix, Mac, or Windows), then you might need to configure this option in order to properly write the files.

Write BOM
> This option allows you to include or exclude the byte order mark (BOM) in the output.

Once you have run your workflow with the configured Output Data tool, it's very easy to open the file from Alteryx. Let's talk about how to view the output file.

Viewing the output file

In the Results window, you will notice that any input or output that is listed is also set as a hyperlink that you can click on to open that file. You can also filter your logs quickly by clicking on the headers of your Results pane to see only the Warnings or Messages, for example (see Figure 4-5).

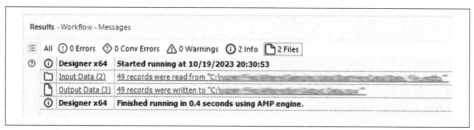

Figure 4-5. Results window

Output to an Excel File

Outputting to an Excel file is very similar to outputting to a CSV file, with just a couple of different options. You will still need to choose the file you want to write to, but instead of clicking the down arrow and selecting a file, you can just type (or copy and paste) the filename and location into the text box. If typed correctly, with the file extension *.xlsx*, then it will automatically recognize and set the default configuration. It's important to note that if you go through the process of clicking on the down arrow and using the interface to select the file, some of the options (like Max Records Per File and File Format), as well as the sheet name selection, will be automatically set. If you type the file path and name, you will need to configure manually as well as use the "|||" (pipe delimiters) at the end with the sheet name to specify what exact sheet you want to use (see Figure 4-6).

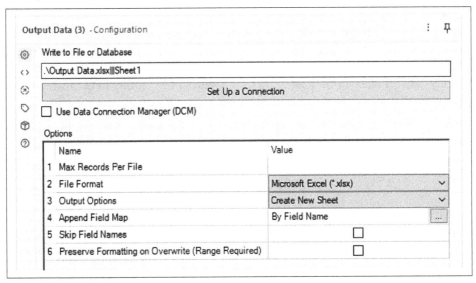

Figure 4-6. File path

An important item to keep in mind is that the sheets of an Excel file are best thought of as tables of a database. They operate in much the same way. Let's talk more about how we can configure the output.

Configuration options

The most important option for outputting to Excel is the third option in Figure 4-6 (Output Options), which allows you to choose the criteria for output of the file. You need to ensure that you have set this correctly, or it could cause errors the second time you run the workflow. When outputting to Excel, you have four configuration options to choose from:

Append to Existing Sheet
> Use this option if you have a file/sheet already created that you want to add to.

Overwrite Sheet or Range
> Use this option if you want to replace a sheet or range.

Overwrite File (Remove)
> Use this option if you want to replace an entire workbook.

Create New Sheet

Use this option if each time you run, you want a new sheet created. Caution: if that sheet is already created, Designer will throw an error telling you it can't be written to because it already exists.

Output to a YXDB File

Outputting to YXDB is probably the easiest way to output. For many use cases, for example where a file is required and the data set is also quite large or where owners of a data set don't want that data modified, it's a really good option if you want to quickly put the data in an easy format and don't have requirements to report or present the data.

To output your data into the YXDB format, simply follow the steps just like you did for CSV and Excel, and choose the location where you want the data to be stored. Remember, Designer is going to do as much as it can to help you by automatically setting configurations when you choose the file type (see Figure 4-7).

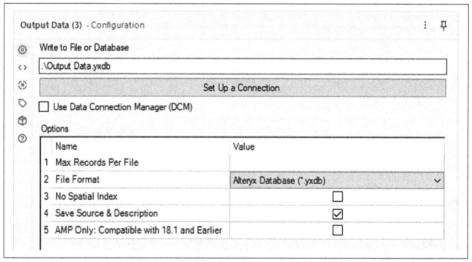

Figure 4-7. Configurations for the YXDB file type

Spend some time getting comfortable using YXDB file types. It will definitely help you on your Alteryx journey. Now, as important as it is to be able to output to files such as YXDB, I would argue that outputting to databases is even more important. Let's make sure you get a solid understanding of how Alteryx Designer allows you to output to databases.

Output to Databases

As stated in the last chapter, Alteryx Designer supports nearly all of the most widely used data sources in the world—Microsoft SQL Server, Amazon S3, MongoDB, MySQL, and even newer sources like Snowflake and Databricks. It's fun to think of all the combinations of data sources one could read from and write to! This is one of the reasons why Alteryx is so flexible. If you need to move data from Excel to Amazon S3, you can. If you need to move data from Microsoft SQL Server to Snowflake, you can. To make this happen, you will need to understand how to use the Output Data tool for your respective data source. I will not cover every data source in this book, but I will give a couple of examples that should be helpful, as they operate in a similar manner.

In the last chapter, you learned how to connect to databases as well as how to use the Input Data tool. Here, you are going to connect to ODBC or OLEDB in the same way with the Output Data tool as you did with the Input Data tool. If you need a reminder of how to set up a connection or a credential, and connect them, then I recommend reviewing that part in the last chapter. There are a couple of nuances with the Output Data tool, however, that I will cover in the following examples.

Output to Microsoft SQL Server

First, you will bring in an Output Data tool from the In/Out tool palette and configure it. To configure the tool, select "Set Up a Connection" (see Figure 4-8).

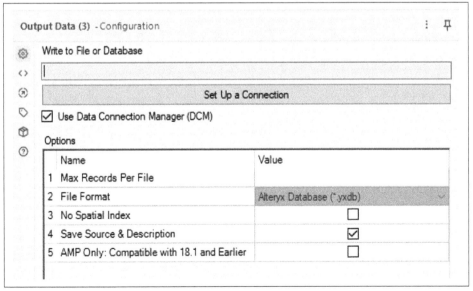

Figure 4-8. Configuring the Output Data tool

Once the Data connections window is open, select the database with which you want to connect. In this example, choose ODBC for Microsoft SQL Server (see Figure 4-9).

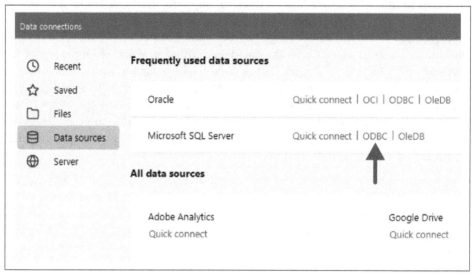

Figure 4-9. Microsoft SQL Server ODBC

Upon selecting the connection you want, you will see a window that will be different depending on the type of connection you make. Because you are connecting to ODBC, you will see the Connection Manager (see Figure 4-10).

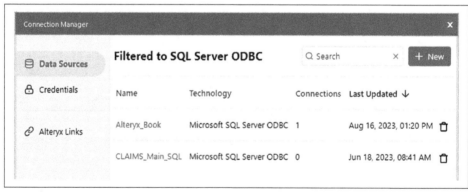

Figure 4-10. Connection Manager

As I've said, when you're new to working with Designer, it's important to play around a little. Give yourself time to explore and test different options so that: 1) you become more familiar with the different options, but more importantly 2) you learn which options give you what you want (ease of use, performance, or even a functioning connection).

In the SQL Server ODBC Connection window, choose your DSN and assign the appropriate credentials. There is one configuration step that is unique to the Output Data tool and that's the Output Table selection. You will need to tell Designer what table you want to write out. Once you have entered a table name, click OK (see Figure 4-11).

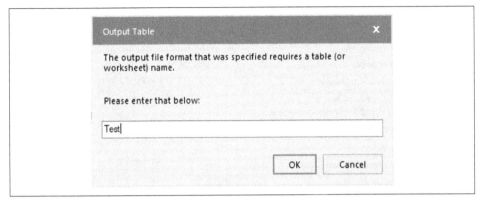

Figure 4-11. Output Table

You will now see the Configuration window populated with the base settings. Let's go through the options so you know what you can change or update.

Configuration options

While we discussed Max Records Per File and File Format earlier in this chapter, Connection ID and Table were set as part of the connection, and for the Output Data tool there are quite a few important options that are different. These options will differ slightly depending on whether you connect using ODBC or OLEDB:

Output Options
> You have many options for how you want to write the data. You can do every-thing from Append, to Delete Data & Append, to completely dropping the table or deleting data before writing. You also have the option to conduct Updates. All of these options allow you to be very precise in your workflows, to update as much or as little as you need (see Figure 4-12).

  To use the Update statements within the Output Options, you will need to ensure you have Primary Keys on your table.

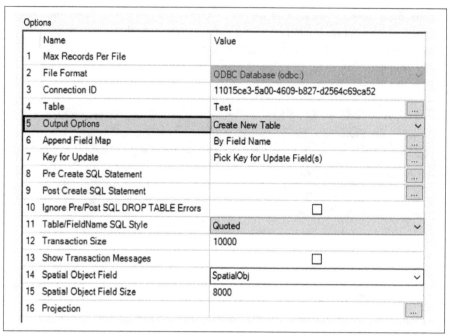

Figure 4-12. Output option to create new table

Append Field Map
This option allows you to map different fields of your output to the table/sheets fields that exist in the output source.

Key for Update
If you are conducting a database update action, then you could use this in order to provide a key to the database.

Pre Create SQL Statement
This option allows you to run a SQL statement prior to your main update/output. This is very useful if you need to create a temporary table, delete specific data, update a table, or even run a stored procedure prior to writing the data to the table specified in the Output Data tool configuration.

 You will likely need to use the OLEDB format in order to use stored procedures.

Post Create SQL Statement

This is the same option as the Pre Create SQL Statement that allows you to run a SQL statement, but in this case it is after writing the data to the table specified in the Output Data tool configuration.

Ignore Pre/Post SQL DROP TABLE Errors

If errors are passed back from the database, then they are ignored. This keeps the workflow from erroring out.

Table/Field Name SQL Style

Depending on the type of database you are connecting to, you might need to modify this if the SQL style of your table and/or field names need to include quotes or not.

Transaction Size

This is the number of rows that are written to the database at a time. If you are working with large database queries, you'll want to determine an optimal size for your database, which depends on factors such as available memory.

Show Transaction Messages

This option allows you to display a message for each transaction in the results log of the workflow. Each message contains the sum of records written up to that transaction.

Spatial Object Field

This option allows you to set the spatial object to include in the output. Spatial files can only contain one spatial object per record.

Spatial Object Field Size

This option allows you to set the size of the spatial object.

Projection

The method used to portray a part of the spherical Earth on a flat surface is called a map projection. If you are working with spatial data, this option allows you to select the projection type to output. By default, Projection is blank and outputs to WGS 84. For in-depth information on Projection Support, visit the Alteryx help documentation (*https://oreil.ly/Cleq4*).

Once you set the configuration options to your preferences, then simply run the workflow. If you got it right, you will see data in your database. Work through this cautiously and connect with someone if you need a little extra help. Once you get it, you'll be empowered to make some amazing workflows!

Output to Multiple Sources

A helpful feature within Designer is its ability to write out to many different sources at one time. You can write out to both files and database tables, and split the data based on a field's values. For example, let's say you have a table that shows Sales Territory information (see Figure 4-13).

SalesTerritoryRegion	SalesTerritoryCountry	SalesTerritoryGroup
Northwest	United States	North America
Northeast	United States	North America
Central	United States	North America
Southwest	United States	North America
Southeast	United States	North America
Canada	Canada	North America
France	France	Europe
Germany	Germany	Europe
Australia	Australia	Pacific
United Kingdom	United Kingdom	Europe
NA	NA	NA

Figure 4-13. Sales Territory information

If you need to split each Sales Territory Group into its own sheet or table, you can output this data to four different tables—one for each group (North America, Europe, Pacific, and NA). To be clear, the number of tables, files, or sheets created depends on the number of distinct values in the column you choose.

To configure this option, check the box at the bottom of the Output Data tool Configuration window that says, "Take File/Table Name From Field" (see Figure 4-14).

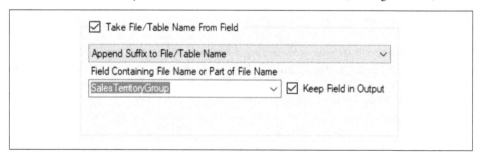

Figure 4-14. Take File/Table Name From Field

You will then decide which option you want to use for the output option (see Figure 4-15).

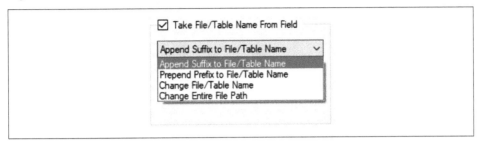

Figure 4-15. Output option

Let's walk through some examples for each of these output options.

Append Suffix to File/Table Name

This option allows you to output to the tables or files for each value of the field that you've selected. Let's say you chose "Test" as the data source name. What you would see, if we use our SalesTerritoryGroup example, are the tables shown in Figure 4-16. Notice how, for each region, the region (aka the SalesTerritoryGroup) is appended to the Test table.

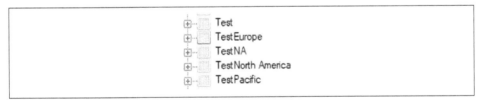

Figure 4-16. Table suffix

Prepend Prefix to File/Table Name

This option behaves the same as the Suffix option, except the names of the fields will be prepended to the beginning of the file/table names. For example, if we wrote out to Excel sheets, we would see something like Figure 4-17, where the region is prepended to the beginning of each table name (sheet name).

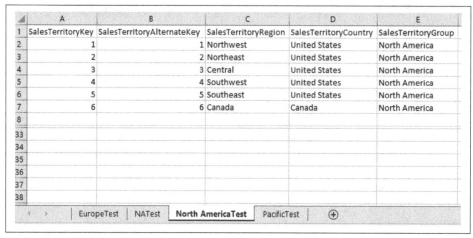

	A	B	C	D	E
1	SalesTerritoryKey	SalesTerritoryAlternateKey	SalesTerritoryRegion	SalesTerritoryCountry	SalesTerritoryGroup
2	1	1	Northwest	United States	North America
3	2	2	Northeast	United States	North America
4	3	3	Central	United States	North America
5	4	4	Southwest	United States	North America
6	5	5	Southeast	United States	North America
7	6	6	Canada	Canada	North America
8					
33					
34					
35					
36					
37					
38					

EuropeTest | NATest | **North AmericaTest** | PacificTest | ⊕

Figure 4-17. Table prefix

Change File/Table Name

With the previous two options, the output is adding to the names either by appending or prepending. This option changes the entire file/table name. Instead of seeing the "Test" name, if we use the Change File/Table Name option, we can make the output a bit cleaner (see Figure 4-18).

Europe | NA | North America | Pacific | ⊕

Figure 4-18. Change File/Table Name

Change Entire File Path

There are numerous creative ways to use this option. One that is very useful is when you are working with CSV or TXT files and you want to write out to multiple files that happen to be in different directories. If you choose this option, to write out to the CSV format, you can also get very specific and dynamically build the file paths. Let's say that for each Territory Group we have a corresponding folder, and in each folder we want to output the corresponding files by Territory Region. The formula could look something like Figure 4-19. (More on building formulas in Chapter 5)

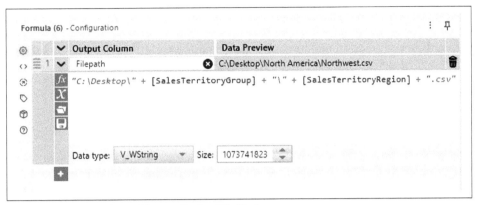

Figure 4-19. Formula to Change Entire File Path

If we look at what one of the Sales Territory Groups would look like, we would see something like Figure 4-20. Each Sales Territory Region became its own CSV file within its North America Sales Territory Group.

Name	Date modified	Type	Size
Canada.csv	4/9/2021 7:40 AM	CSV File	1 KB
Central.csv	4/9/2021 7:40 AM	CSV File	1 KB
Northeast.csv	4/9/2021 7:40 AM	CSV File	1 KB
Northwest.csv	4/9/2021 7:40 AM	CSV File	1 KB
Southeast.csv	4/9/2021 7:40 AM	CSV File	1 KB
Southwest.csv	4/9/2021 7:40 AM	CSV File	1 KB

Desktop › North America

Figure 4-20. Sales Territory file outputs

You have complete freedom to determine dynamically where files are placed and how they are named. As another example, you could push all the Europe Sales Territory Group files to a "European" folder on a completely different server or shared drive, if you wish. The important idea here is that Designer is flexible enough to allow you to build that logic into your workflow, so you do not have to do it manually.

Conclusion

Outputting your data from Alteryx is a powerful feature that allows you to get data into the format you need but also do it dynamically and with precision. It's important to know there are many more tools that allow you to output data in a specific format. These tools include:

- Write Data In DB
- Render Tool
- Amazon S3 Upload
- Google Sheets Output
- MongoDB Output
- Publish to PowerBI
- Publish to Tableau Server

- Salesforce Output Meta
- SharePoint List Output
- API Output
- Blob Output
- Python Tool
- R Tool
- Run Command

You are now able to update the data you want as well as output data in batches across multiple files or tables. In this chapter, you learned how to write out to both files and databases. Again, I challenge you to break any assumptions you may have around always writing out to files. Maybe a database can be more advantageous for you. You have some specific options, like pre and post SQL statements, that can help you manage your output to databases. These options are important to understand, but I recommend spending time learning the options I covered in this chapter to help you make the most of the output tools.

So far, we have covered getting your data into and out of Alteryx Designer. I now want to show you how to get started using Alteryx Designer to clean your data. This is an important and critical step in your journey to becoming proficient, as well as understanding more complex topics in Alteryx Designer!

CHAPTER 5

Cleaning Your Data

Who made this mess? Let's clean it up! Cleaning your data should not be as hard as cleaning the room of a 5-year-old who loves paint and LEGO bricks (trust me, it's not as easy as you think). For those of us who have spent enough time working with data, we know it can get messy, dirty, and downright unusable. Data is like a lot of things in life—it's fragile and requires a lot of care and attention. I believe it shouldn't be a hard task to provide that care and attention, and that's primarily because Designer makes it so simple and straightforward.

Before we get started, please remember that each chapter in this book is additive. You will build on your knowledge of tools and techniques as you go through the book. You will learn things in this chapter that will help you in nearly every other chapter going forward. If you get to a new chapter and feel a bit overwhelmed, feel free to roll back and reread, think, and practice more. The goal, as I've stated, is to turn you into an absolute, bona fide Alteryx rock star. Let's do this.

When we talk about having "clean data," what do we mean, exactly? We are talking about cleaning up all the nuances in our data that *don't* help us tell the story we are trying to tell. Usually, when I refer to "clean data," I am referring to five specific factors:

- We don't have null values.
- We don't have missing values.
- We don't have duplicative data.
- We don't have incorrect or "bad" values (bad is subjective, of course).
- We do have all the data we need (refers to adding data).

In this chapter, you will become very comfortable with the tools in the Preparation tool palette. This collection of tools is primarily focused on filtering, cleaning, creating formulas, and creating data. The Preparation tool palette (see Figure 5-1) is one of the most important and useful set of tools, and you will use it over and over again.

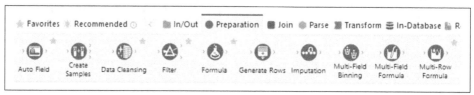

Figure 5-1. Preparation tool palette

You can always recognize the Preparation tools by their blue color and circle shape:

We will cover the different scenarios and use cases when you need to clean data. Combined with what you learned in Chapters 3 and 4, the information in this chapter will enable you to create clean and highly valuable data sets going forward, as well as rearrange rows and columns as needed.

Knowing When You Have Dirty Data

Before you learn how to clean your data, let's look at a great way you can tell you have data that needs to be cleaned. Designer helps you do or see things easily, and one of those things is the quality of your data. There are many ways to check the quality of your data in Designer, but I'll discuss two of the easiest and most common: the Results window and the Browse tool.

The Results Window

We discussed the Results window in Chapter 2 and made the case for how important it is. But in the context of cleaning data, it is even more important. The Results window has a nice feature built into it that analyzes each column of data and gives you high-level statistics. You can see this via the colored bar across each column of data (see Figure 5-2). If you hover over it, you will get the values.

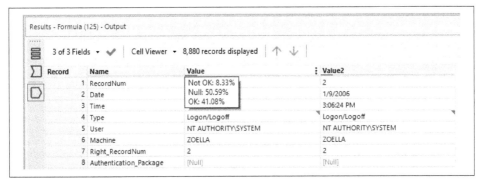

Figure 5-2. The Results window

In Figure 5-2, notice the bar atop the Name column is all green, indicating that it is good. However, the bar atop the Value column shows red, yellow, and green. The values you see if you hover over the column header correspond to these colors. So, what does "Not OK" really mean? It means that there are quality concerns in your data that need to be addressed. If you look at the value of Record 4, you will notice a red triangle in the upper right corner, indicating that this is one of those data quality issues to look at. If you hover over the Value in Record 4, you will see that the value has trailing spaces (see Figure 5-3).

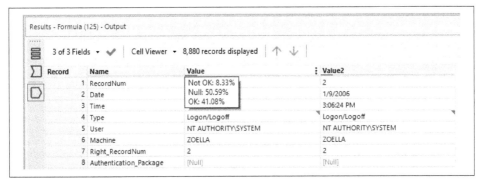

Figure 5-3. Red triangles indicating data quality concerns

You will need to fix that. That may be the only issue you have throughout your data, or you may need to address further issues. The Results window will give you hints about any other data issues you may need to address.

The Browse Tool

The Browse tool has taken monumental leaps in its usefulness from when it was originally created:

I still remember when it just returned data only. It was a utility tool that ensured you could always see the full data set you were working with, but now it's much more powerful. It is no longer a tool only used for viewing data; it now has the capability of data profiling, which gives you an easy way to assess the quality of your data.

By running a workflow that has a Browse tool attached to your input data, you will see something like Figure 5-4.

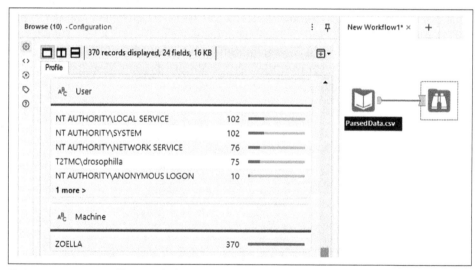

Figure 5-4. Data profiling with the Browse tool

Fun fact: the Browse tool shows the entirety of the data set, while the Results window only displays up to 1 MB of data from each tool, by default. However, with the Browse tool you can see all your data. That doesn't mean you really need to see all your data all the time, but it's a useful function, especially when you want to see the profiled data.

This is OK, but you are not getting the full picture. There is a useful feature that allows you to pop out this Configuration window. Click the square icon drop-down in the top right corner of the Configuration window and click "New Window (All Records)" (see Figure 5-5).

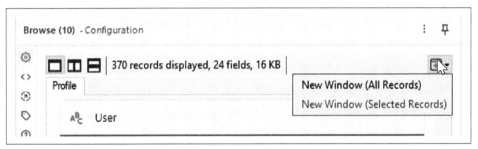

Figure 5-5. New Window (All Records)

You will then have a window pop up that will allow you to maneuver around your Configuration window. You will see two tabs: Table and Profile. The Table tab is simple but useful. It allows you to view all your data in granular detail.

 You can copy any of this data from the Data tab, right-click on your canvas, and paste it directly into a Text Input tool to use as a test data set.

The Profile tab is where the money is at. You can see your data quality at a high level, and you can click any of the column headers and get more detail and visualizations of the data (see Figure 5-6).

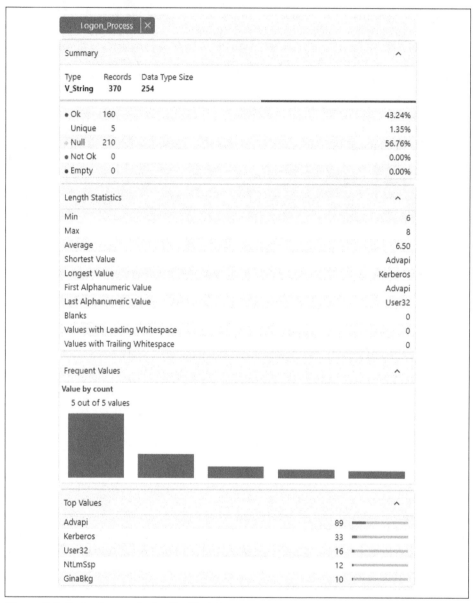

Figure 5-6. Data shown via the Profile tab

You can also look at this same data in the form of bar charts by clicking on the chart icon in the top right corner next to the filter icon (see Figure 5-7).

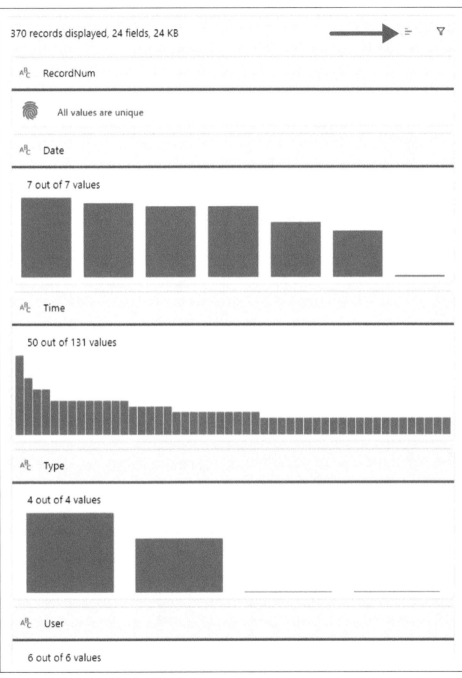

Figure 5-7. Data profile visualization

As you can see, the Browse tool provides so many different ways to look at your data and both find and understand the quality of your data. Now that you can spot your dirty data, let's look at some tools—specifically in the Preparation tool palette—that you can use to clean up any messes you find. First, let's take a look at how you can filter your data.

Filtering Your Data

Removing bad or unimportant data is a critical part of getting to a clean and valuable data set. In this section, you're going to learn how you can remove the data you don't need. It is considered a best practice to remove unnecessary data from your data set as soon as possible in the workflow. The less data that needs to be processed, the more efficient and quickly the workflow can run.

Filter Tool

Filtering rows of data using the Filter tool is both easy and also surprisingly powerful:

You can use the simple Basic Filter to select a single criterion, or you can use the more powerful Custom Filter option that lets you build complex conditions or conditions using more than one column. I highly recommend you don't try and create super complex filters but rather find ways to keep it simple, like chaining multiple, easily configured Filter tools together—this will help you later on when your workflows get bigger and more complex.

One of the greatest parts of this Filter tool, and something that Excel users love, is that it separates your data into two parts. One part is the data that evaluates to true for the filter command, and the other part is the data that evaluates to false. You don't lose visibility of data. In Excel, if you filter on a column, you lose visibility into that data. Let's dig into some of the Filter options.

Basic Filter

The Basic Filter is exactly what it sounds like. It allows you to create basic filters (such as "CustomerID > 30" or "Year = 2020") for your data that test for a single condition (see Figure 5-8).

Figure 5-8. Basic Filter

To use this filter, connect a Filter tool to your data set (see Figure 5-9).

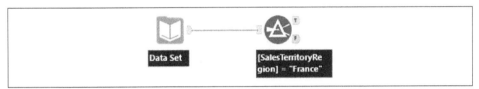

Figure 5-9. Connect a Filter tool to your data set

Once you have the tool connected, you will set the Basic Filter settings (see Figure 5-10).

Designer builds expressions in the "Custom filter" field. It's useful to understand what is actually happening with the formula you are building, and how it's formatted. Having this understanding makes it easier to build on the formulas and/or modify them after using the Basic Filter.

In the Basic Filter, the first drop-down is the field you want to filter your data by. In this example, choose the field "SalesTerritoryRegion." The second drop-down is the operator. The operators that appear in the list depend on the data type of the column you selected to filter by. The third column is the value you want to filter to. The most important part here is to remember that you are building an expression that evaluates to true or false. In Figure 5-10, I am saying, "Show me all the records where SalesTerritoryRegion is equal to France." I am also saying, "Any records where SalesTerritoryRegion do not equal France should be marked as False." I find that it helps me tremendously to talk through this logic, to ensure I am writing true and false to the right locations.

Figure 5-10. Configured Basic Filter

When you click the "T" anchor of the output of the Filter tool, you'll see that the true output is all those records related to France (see Figure 5-11).

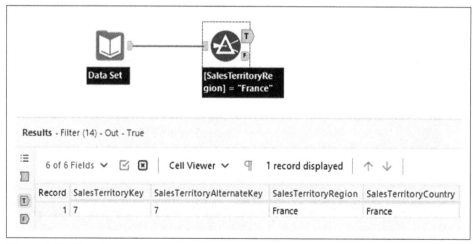

Figure 5-11. T anchor

If you click the "F" anchor, you'll see all the other records that have evaluated to false (see Figure 5-12).

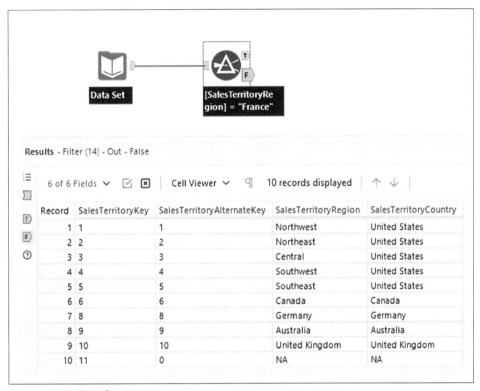

Figure 5-12. F anchor

Custom Filter

The Custom Filter option is very powerful. This filter option allows you to not only check for more complex expressions but also for multiple conditions. For example, a Custom Filter could check if color = blue and number = 4. To use it, simply click the radio button to choose this option. Doing this actually enables a feature in Alteryx Designer that you will use in many other tools: the Expression window.

The Custom Filter allows you to handle quite extensive logic using the Expression window. This is actually quite simple to understand but nearly infinite in its application. Using only the operators AND and OR, you can create combinations of logic-based statements that have some very different outcomes.

Be diligent when you are using the Custom Filter. The whole idea of using Alteryx Designer is to make your life easier and simpler. If you create a formula or filter in the Expression window that's two miles long, then whom does that help? It's sometimes challenging to keep things simple and easy, but I challenge you to not go down the road of building complexity into your workflows. Use multiple tools or simplify what you are trying to do in some way that doesn't add to the complexity of the task. Remember, each workflow should be easy to read and understand.

The Expression Window

The Expression window (see Figure 5-13) is one of the features you will use very often, as it's incorporated into many tools, not just the Filter tool. It's in the Formula tool, the Multi-Row Formula tool, the Multi-Field Formula tool, the Error Message tool, and many more. The Expression window has four main functionalities you should be aware of: functions, columns and constants, recent and saved expressions, and save expressions.

Figure 5-13. Expression window

Functions

The "*fx*" button is what enables you to search and find a function to bring into the Expression window. The functions are broken down into categories (see Figure 5-14).

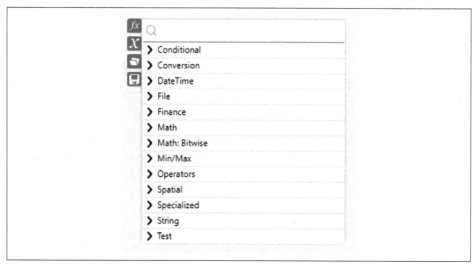

Figure 5-14. Functions categories

Columns and Constants

The variable X button gives you access to the columns and constants in order to bring them into your Expression, if needed (see Figure 5-15).

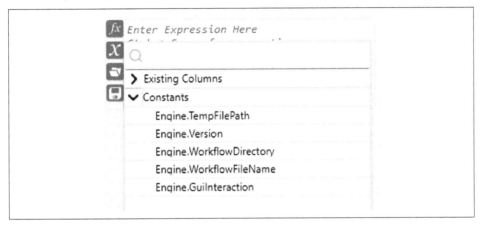

Figure 5-15. Constants

Recent and Saved Expressions

This is where you can find any recent expressions you have used as well as any expressions that you have saved. If you are writing out long or intricate formulas and you want to reuse them, this is the place to go (see Figure 5-16).

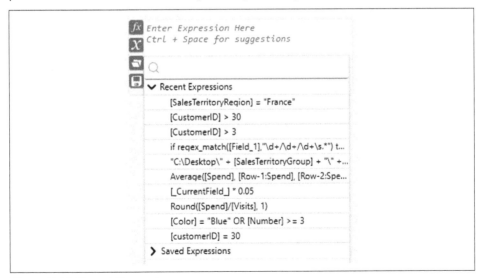

Figure 5-16. Recent Expressions

Save Expression

If you would like to save expressions that you can use over and over again, then this is where you can do that. Anything saved here will then show up in the Recent and Saved Expressions section (see Figure 5-17).

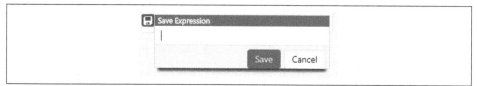

Figure 5-17. Save Expression

Filtering examples

Let's look at a couple of filtering examples to ensure that you understand how to write filter statements that will work.

Finding missing data. Say you have a data set that has some missing values you want to find so you can properly fix or remove them (see Figure 5-18).

PERMVIT	PERSONS	COUNTY	CITY	DAY	MONTH	YEAR	DAY_WEEK
1	1	127	0	1	1	[Null]	5
1	1	83	0	1	1	[Null]	5
2	2	11	0	1	1	2015	5
1	1	45	0	4	1	2015	1
2	2	45	2050	7	1	2015	4
2	2	111	0	8	1	[Null]	5
2	2	89	1730	8	1	2015	5
1	1	73	350	3	1	2015	7
1	1	117	47	13	1	2015	3
2	2	33	0	5	1	2015	2
2	2	83	0	7	1	[Null]	4
6	6	95	1500	9	1	2015	6
1	1	87	0	10	1	[Null]	7
1	1	11	0	11	1	2015	1
1	1	127	0	11	1	[Null]	1
2	2	81	2340	13	1	2015	3
1	1	97	0	14	1	[Null]	4

Figure 5-18. Missing data

As you will start to find out, there will be many different ways to approach each problem. Figure 5-19 shows one way you might create a filter to find records with missing YEAR values, using the IsEmpty operator.

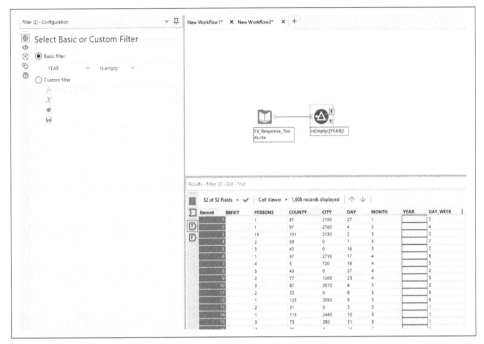

Figure 5-19. IsEmpty operator

Finding specific values. Say, for example, you are looking for any records where the vehicle took an Interstate Highway (I), State Route (SR), or County Route (CR). In the example shown in Figure 5-20, you can see that those specific entries all have one thing in common: they all contain a dash (-) in their name. So, we are going to use that to filter only those vehicles using the Contains operator.

Filtering your data is one of the most important things you can do in your workflows. It's also important to remember that it's a best practice to filter your data immediately after bringing it into your workflow. If you bring in 100,000 rows of data, but you only need 5,000, then you don't want to process 100,000 records and wait each time you run. Filter the data right away and it'll have a positive impact on the speed of your workflow.

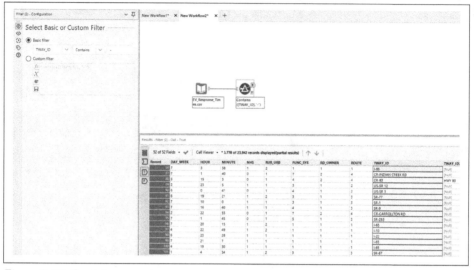

Figure 5-20. Contains operator

The Filter tool is one of the most widely used tools in Designer, so spend the time to get good at using it. Let's now talk about another widely used tool that you will definitely use on a daily basis: the Select tool.

Select Tool

The Select tool is one of the most commonly used and more important tools you need to know:

Although the Select tool doesn't exactly filter data, it has some important functionality in terms of removing data from your workflow. It allows you to not only remove fields, but also rename fields, change data types, and change the size of the data type.

To use this tool, drag it onto your canvas, connect it to the tool you want, and configure it (see Figure 5-21).

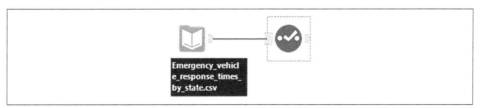

Figure 5-21. Connect a Select tool to your Input Data tool

Let's dig into the Select tool a bit deeper.

Configuring the Select tool

When configuring the Select tool, there are four areas you'll want to pay close attention to: the checkbox, and the Type, Size, and Rename columns (see Figure 5-22).

Field	Type		Size	Rename	Description
☑ CustomerID	Int16	▾	2		
☑ Store Number	Byte	▾	1		
☑ Customer Segment	String	▾	14		
☑ Responder	String	▾	3		
☑ First Name	String	▾	10		
☑ Last Name	V_String	▾	18		
☑ Address	V_String	▾	28		
☑ City	V_String	▾	13		
☑ State	String	▾	2		
☑ Zip	Int32	▾	4		
☑ Lat	Double	▾	8		
☑ Lon	Double	▾	8		
☑ *Unknown	Unknown	▾	0		Dynamic or Unknown Fields

Select (2) - Configuration · Options ▾ · Search

Figure 5-22. Select tool configuration

Alongside each field name is a checkbox, and the checkbox determines whether the field gets to stay in the workflow or is removed from the data going forward. The Type column determines what data type that field will be. This has quite important implications, so we'll cover that here.

> It's important to note that this same Select tool functionality is present in many other tools, like the Append Fields tool, Find Nearest tool, Join tool, Join Multiple tool, Select In-DB tool, and Spatial Match tool, all of which we will cover in this book.

Data types

In Designer, there are six main data types that you will use in many tools, not just in the Select tool. These are important to understand because they have implications for your building successful workflows. For example, if you are trying to add a string value and a numerical value, you will get an error. In Joins, Formulas, and many other tools, the data types matter. The six data types you'll work with in Designer tools are:

- Strings (String, WString, V_String, V_WString, V_String: Forced)
- Numbers (Byte, Int16, Int32, Int64, FixedDecimal, Float, Double)
- Dates and Time (Date, Time, DateTime)
- Boolean (0 or 1; true or false)
- Spatial objects
- Reporting objects

There are some important items to note for a few of the data types:

- The W in WString and V_WString stands for Wide and accepts any Unicode character, so this data type is often used when you need special characters like both Japanese and Chinese characters.
- The V in VString and V_WString stands for Variable, and the length of the field adjusts to fit the entire string within the field.
- The numeric data types really come down to whether there is a decimal and the size of the number you are using. The different sizes are:
  — Byte: 8 binary digits (bits) long. A byte field is a positive whole number that falls within the range 0 to 255, or 2^8.
  — Int16: a numeric value without a decimal equal to 2 bytes, or $-(2^{15})$ to $(2^{15})-1$.
  — Int32: a numeric value without a decimal equal to 4 bytes, or $-(2^{31})$ to $(2^{31})-1$.
  — Int64: a numeric value without a decimal equal to 8 bytes, or $-(2^{63})$ to $(2^{63})-1$.
  — FixedDecimal: a numeric value with a decimal. A FixedDecimal is the only numeric data type with an adjustable length.
  — Float: a standard single-precision floating-point value. It uses 4 bytes and can represent values from +/– 3.4×10^{-38} to 3.4×10^{38} with 7 digits of precision.
  — Double: a standard double-precision floating-point value. It uses 8 bytes and can represent values from +/– 1.7×10^{-308} to 1.7×10^{308} with 15 digits of precision.

- The DateTime data type is specific in Designer and follows the 18-character yyyy-mm-dd hh:mm:ss string format, with Date being the first part (10 characters) and Time being the second part (8 characters).

- The spatial object can consist of a point, line, polyline, or polygon.

Aside from selecting which fields you want to keep and which data type and size you want for each field, you can also rename columns. Many times, our data is not in the clean and nicely named format we would like when it comes to us. We have the option to set the name of the field so that, going forward, it will be named appropriately.

Select tool options

In the top left corner of the Configuration window, you will see the Options dropdown. It contains many options for you to choose from (see Figure 5-23).

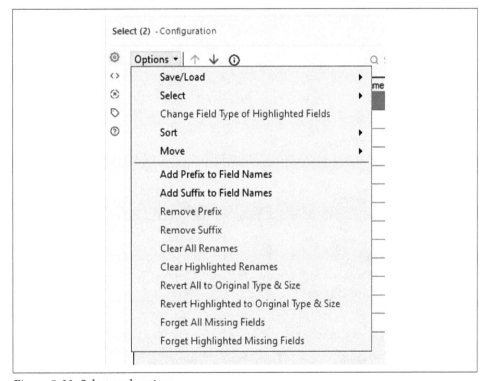

Figure 5-23. Select tool options

These options include:

Save/Load

   This option allows you to save the Field Configuration as a YXFT file. The Alteryx Field Type File (YXFT) is a special type of text file that can be used in other workflows to not only save time in configuring the tool but also to ensure you don't accidentally miss a configuration step.

Select

   This option allows you to select or deselect all or highlight columns. Options include Select All and Deselect All.

Change Field Type of Highlighted Fields

   This option allows you to change the data type of all highlighted columns at once.

Sort

   This option allows you to sort the column order in ascending or descending order. Options include Sort on Original Field Name, Sort on New Field Name, Sort on Field Type, or Revert to Incoming Field Order.

Move

   This option allows you to move highlighted columns to the top or bottom of the list.

Add Prefix to Field Names

   This option allows you to add a prefix to the selected or highlighted column name.

Add Suffix to Field Names

   This option allows you to add a suffix to the selected or highlighted column name.

Remove Prefix or Suffix

   This option allows you to remove the prefix or suffix from the selected or highlighted column name.

Clear All Renames

   This option allows you to remove the new name for all columns.

Clear Highlighted Renames

   This option allows you to remove the new name for all highlighted columns.

Revert All to Original Type & Size

   This option allows you to undo all changes to type and size in all columns and use the original values.

Revert Highlighted to Original Type & Size
This option allows you to undo changes to type and size in the selected or highlighted columns and use the original values.

Forget All Missing Fields
This option allows you to remove all columns that are no longer included in the data.

Forget Highlighted Missing Fields
This option allows you to remove all highlighted columns that are no longer included in the data.

As with the Filter tool, it is a best practice to eliminate any fields of data that you are not going to use from the beginning. Keep only what you need to actually process your data set. The Select tool is a great way to do this but it's not the only one. There are many other tools that you have available, like the Select Records tool. Let's take a look at that next.

Select Records Tool

The Select Records tool allows you to be very precise in the request for records:

You can specify exactly which rows you want. With Select Records, you have four basic options that you can specify:

- A single row
- A range of rows
- All rows before or after a specified row(s)
- Multiple rows

In Figure 5-24, the –100 value says you want all records up to 100. The 10–90 value says you want a range of data, specifically rows 10–90. The 250 value is pulling a specific row of data, and 1000+ says you want all records from 1,000 to the end. You can use one of these options or all four at the same time.

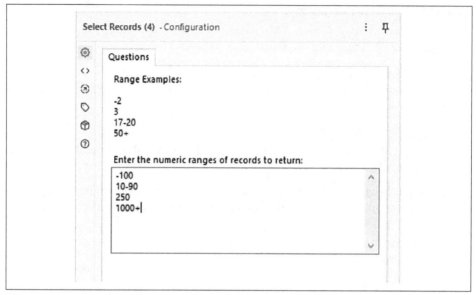

Figure 5-24. Select Records tool configuration

The Select Records tool is powerful, so try and remember to use it when you need it. It's an option when you would like to filter the data set down for testing or development purposes. Let's now take a look at the Unique tool.

Unique Tool

The Unique tool is a powerful data-cleansing tool that allows you to separate unique and duplicate data based on the fields you select:

For a simple example, imagine we want to find the unique records of Letters and Numbers (see Figure 5-25).

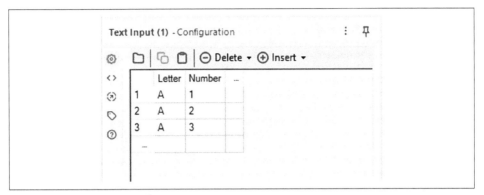

Figure 5-25. Unique records

If we run this through the Unique tool with the Letter column selected, you will see that Row 1 will be marked as Unique and will therefore come out of the U anchor. The other 2 rows will come out of the D anchor (see Figure 5-26).

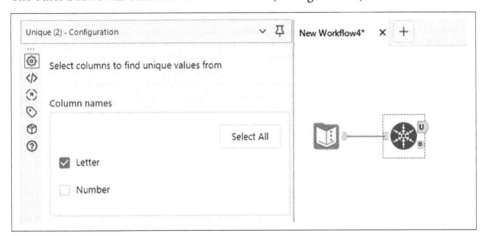

Figure 5-26. Unique tool configuration

If you want all columns to be compared and unique, you can select the "Select All" button. It's important to note that the data is sorted based on the unique columns you've selected. If a specific sort order is desired, use the Sort tool right before the Unique tool to assign the specific sort order of the file (see Figure 5-27).

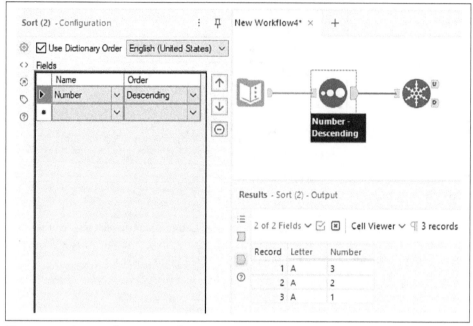

Figure 5-27. Sort and Unique tools

Now, since you sorted by number, the last row has become sorted to the top and the result out of the U anchor is Number 3. The Unique tool is used when you want to ensure that any duplicates in your data are either filtered out or addressed.

Sample Tool

The Sample tool is another helpful tool to have in your arsenal:

It allows you to filter down to a specified number, percentage, or random set of the rows. For example, I can filter the first row of each group of items. The Sample tool also allows you to apply the option you selected to a group of records.

The Sample tool, like many other tools we'll cover in this book, is a powerhouse tool that allows you to do many things in one tool that would be painful or complex if you had to write SQL or code in order to mimic the functionality (see Figure 5-28).

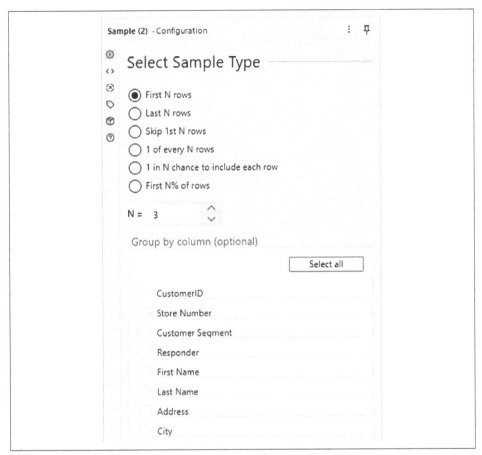

Figure 5-28. Sample tool configuration

For example, here is a list of items the Sample tool could help you with:

- Provide the first 1, 5, 10, or any number of records in your data (first N rows)
- Provide the last 1, 5, 10 or any number of records in your data (last N rows)
- Skip the first 1, 5, 10, or any number of records in your data (skip 1st N rows)
- Pick out 1 of every number of rows (1 of every N rows)
- Pick out 1 in N chance rows (1 in N chance to include each row)
- Pick out the first 1%, 5%, 10%, or any percentage of records (first N% of rows)
- Complete any of the above by a grouping of records

It's important to understand that the "Group by column" function simply means that if you want to do any of those items in the list above, you could. So, for example, instead of getting the first 1, 5, or 10 items of the entire data set, if you grouped by City you could get the first 1, 5, or 10 items for every unique City in the data set. It's a useful way to get the top records by a specific column—top earner by region, bottom performer by state, and so on.

Simply by including a Sort tool before the Sample tool, you can add even more options. For example, you would be able to reverse the order, and getting the "first N rows" would actually be the equivalent of getting the "skip last N rows." Another cool way to use the Sample tool and speed up the process of building workflows is to put a Sample tool at the very beginning of your workflow to only take the first 100, 1,000, or 5,000 records. Most of the time, you do not need the entire data set to build your workflow. Since you are going to be running it many times, it behooves you to keep it small until you complete the workflow and can test it against the larger data set.

Cleaning Your Data

I am going to go out on a limb here for just a moment (with the potential of being banned from certain social circles) and say something very important: cleaning data can be a lot of fun!

There, I said it. I know it's a crazy idea for some, but I particularly love the challenge of taking dirty, nonvalued, disparate data sets and turning them into something that provides insights. There is something satisfying about being able to make that happen. In this section, you will learn to love this, too. There is a nice handful of tools in Designer that you can use to clean your data. I won't go into theory too much, if at all, but know that there is actually much more on the topic of data cleaning that falls into the field of data engineering—way more than I can cover in this book.

When you think about "cleaning" your data, you should ask yourself a few questions that will drive a lot of your actions:

- Are the metadata/data types correct for each field?
- Do I have any blank or null values?
- Do I have any data in an incorrect format (i.e., a specific data format)?
- Do I have unwanted characters in my data (i.e., punctuation that shouldn't be there)?
- Is my data standardized (i.e., different names for the same thing)?

If you consistently ask these questions each time you bring in data to Designer, then you will avoid having to go back to fix issues that show up in your reports or analysis. In this section, I'll cover some of the tools you'll use to answer the questions about the cleanliness of your data.

Auto Field Tool

The Auto Field tool is a powerful utility tool but also one to use with a little caution:

Connected to your workflow, this tool will scan through all the records in the data and find not only the correct data type but also the smallest size necessary for each selected field. Doing this could not only make the size of the data you're working with smaller, and therefore faster, but it can also shrink the size of any file outputs.

If a column being scanned has a single value in it that is a string but all other values are numerical, then it will default to string as that is the only data type that can fulfill all data values. You want to use caution because this can create performance problems, especially if you are working with very large data sets. Each time you run it, the Auto Field tool will scan every single value in the columns you selected—that can slow you down very fast. My advice is to use it as a one-time discovery tool, then use the Select tool to implement what the Auto Field tool has discovered for you. It's important to remember that, in most cases, you would not use this tool against a database input—the database would already have data types set to what they should be as Designer brings those in. That's assuming the database administrators are managing data quality!

Unlike the Select tool, you cannot force the data type with the Auto Field tool. However, you can combine the two to create a more powerful outcome. I will show you how to do that shortly, but first you need to understand how to use the Auto Field tool. The tool configuration is quite simple (see Figure 5-29). You just need to select the fields you want to be scanned and have the data types adjusted.

If you have the Auto Field tool make changes to your data, then the question becomes, "How do you see that the changes definitively happened to your satisfaction before moving on?" Well, you need the metadata tab for that! Let's dive into it now.

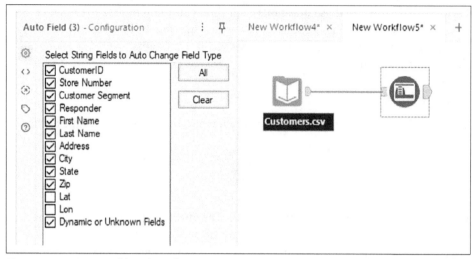

Figure 5-29. Auto Field tool configuration

The Metadata tab

Designer allows you to view the data types for each of the columns. To see those values, click Metadata in your Result window (see Figure 5-30).

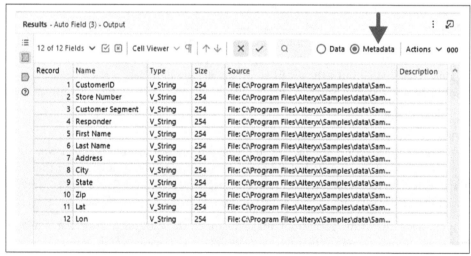

Figure 5-30. Metadata tab

This Metadata section gives you the underlying information for your data set, including the size, type, and name of your fields. You can see the data type and the size of every column. Notice in Figure 5-30, before the Auto Field tool runs, all the data records are of type V_String and size 255. However, if you look at the metadata after the Auto Field tool is applied (see Figure 5-31), you'll see the records have been corrected.

Results - Auto Field (3) - Output

12 of 12 Fields ✓ ☑ ☒ | Cell Viewer ✓ ¶ ↑ ↓ | ✕ ✓ Q ○ Data ◉ Metadata | Actions ✓ 000

Record	Name	Type	Size	Source	Description
1	CustomerID	Int16	2	File: C:\Program Files\Alteryx\Samples\data\Sam...	
2	Store Number	Byte	1	File: C:\Program Files\Alteryx\Samples\data\Sam...	
3	Customer Segment	String	14	File: C:\Program Files\Alteryx\Samples\data\Sam...	
4	Responder	String	3	File: C:\Program Files\Alteryx\Samples\data\Sam...	
5	First Name	String	10	File: C:\Program Files\Alteryx\Samples\data\Sam...	
6	Last Name	V_String	18	File: C:\Program Files\Alteryx\Samples\data\Sam...	
7	Address	V_String	28	File: C:\Program Files\Alteryx\Samples\data\Sam...	
8	City	V_String	13	File: C:\Program Files\Alteryx\Samples\data\Sam...	
9	State	String	2	File: C:\Program Files\Alteryx\Samples\data\Sam...	
10	Zip	Int32	4	File: C:\Program Files\Alteryx\Samples\data\Sam...	
11	Lat	V_String	254	File: C:\Program Files\Alteryx\Samples\data\Sam...	
12	Lon	V_String	254	File: C:\Program Files\Alteryx\Samples\data\Sam...	

Figure 5-31. Metadata after Auto Field tool is applied

Ensuring you are assigning the appropriate types to your data will save you tons of time and stress. When you create calculations later in your workflow, you will need the data types to be correct. For example, a number and a string cannot be added together.

Auto Field tool + Select tool combo

Throughout the book, you will see me return to the concept of single tools having a lot of capabilities by themselves but having exponentially more power in combination. It's one of the most important concepts to grasp. If you follow me at all on social media, you know I talk about design patterns in Alteryx A LOT, and this is why. If you can learn to use powerful combinations of tools, then you have nearly unlimited possibilities. Let's take a look at just one combination here.

The Auto Field tool enables you to scan a data set and choose what the metadata should be. The Select tool can't do that scanning, but it can set it and force it. For example, if a value comes into the Select tool and it's a four-digit number but should be a four-digit string, the Select tool can force it to be a string. Now, if you think about how we would use both of those tools, what you can do then is use the Auto Field tool to do the discovery and tell you what the metadata should be. That can be fed into the Select tool, and those field settings can be saved by going to Options and Save Field Configuration (see Figure 5-32). (Note: it will save to a YXFT file.)

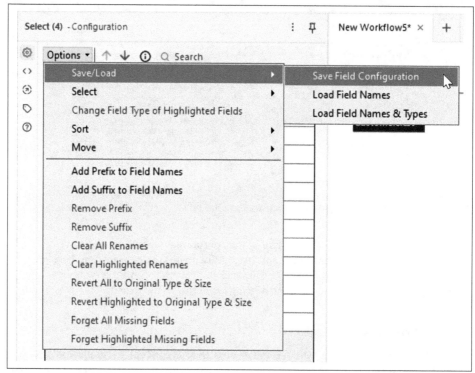

Figure 5-32. Save Field Configuration

Once you save it, you have essentially captured the insights that the Auto Field tool has provided and can now delete the Auto Field tool so that you aren't running it each time. Then, in your Select tool, go to Load configuration to set what you just saved (see Figure 5-33).

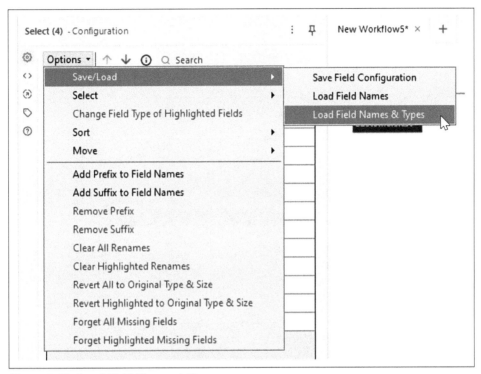

Figure 5-33. Load Field Names & Types

Viola! You now have a Select tool doing the work of the Auto Field tool by setting those data types.

Data Cleansing Tool

The Data Cleansing tool is like the Swiss Army knife of Designer tools:

It has a lot of different configuration options to use, which you can see in Figure 5-34.

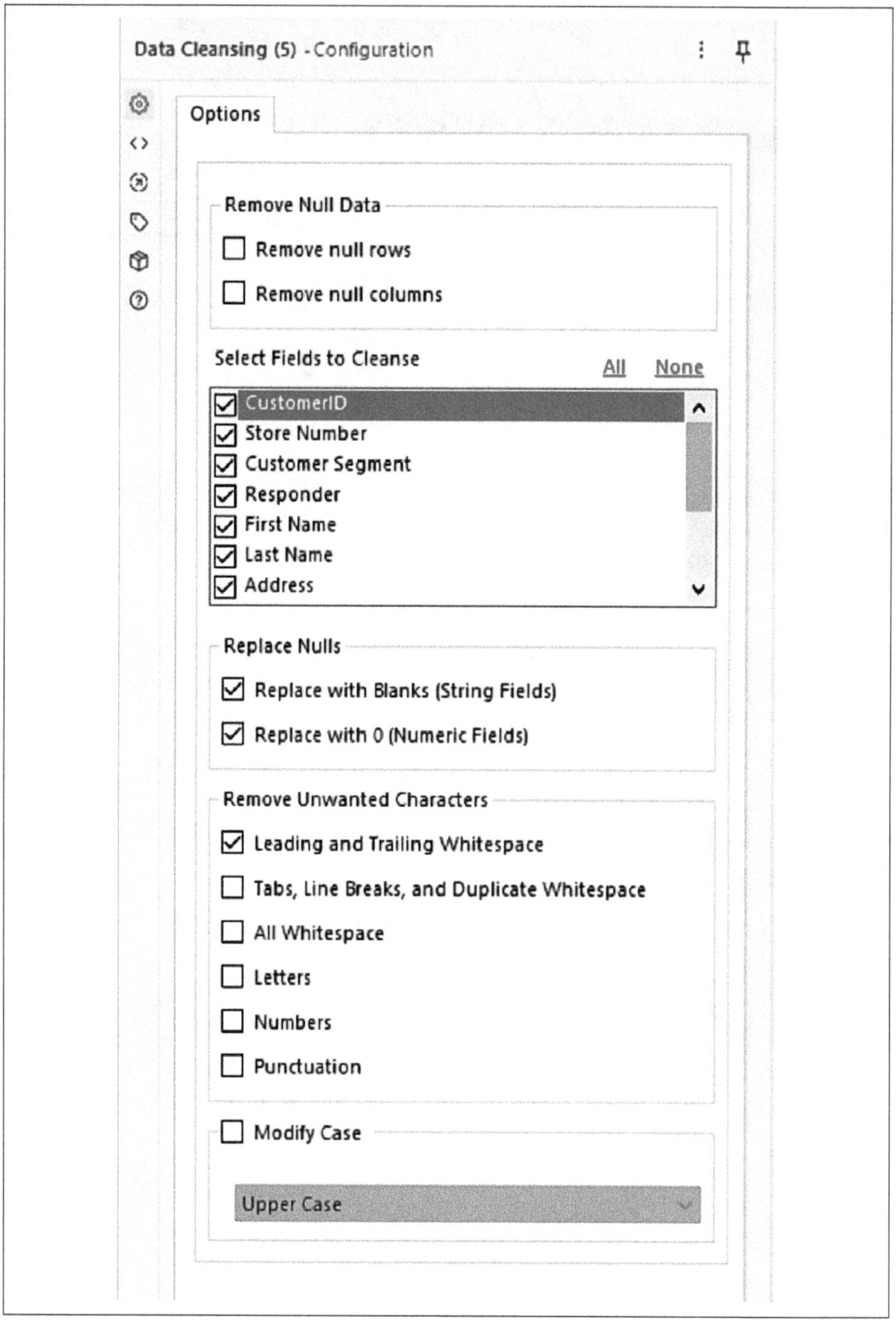

Figure 5-34. Data Cleansing tool configuration

In general, you have three main options, with many suboptions: Remove Null Data, Replace Nulls, and Remove Unwanted Characters. The first two options deal with how you want to address null values in your data—you can remove them entirely or you can replace those values. There are scenarios when you wouldn't want null values, such as if you are preparing data for a predictive model. Or, if you are trying to communicate data issues, you might want null values replaced with a standard value. Either way, that is a decision you need to make. Removing unwanted characters means you can remove leading and trailing whitespace; remove any tabs, line breaks, and duplicate whitespace; remove all whitespace; remove all the letters in a field; remove all the numbers in a field; and remove any punctuation. Lastly, the Data Cleansing tool allows you to modify the case to what you would like. All of these things are quite difficult and tedious in other tools like Excel. Here, it is as simple as a checkbox.

 In this book, we will talk a lot about the idea of building dynamic workflows. You don't want to spend days and weeks building a work of art only to have to rebuild it each time something changes. We need to think ahead and expect the unexpected.

Remember that the Data Cleansing tool is one that is not dynamic and is also what we call "expensive" in that it takes up processing time. If used in a situation where the fields are changing on different runs of the workflow, then the Data Cleansing tool won't pick up those new fields. If you find that you need this option, consider replacing the Data Cleansing tool with the Multi-Field Formula tool, which we cover later in this chapter.

Imputation Tool

The Imputation tool is one that I don't see being used very often, but it's an important tool to know and use:

Like the Data Cleansing tool, the Imputation tool can help you handle null values but it offers even more options. It allows you to replace null values, or a specified value, with the average of that column, the median, the mode, or a specified value. As you build more workflows, you'll find yourself wanting more flexibility. You want to be fast and not have to think through every little change and update you need to make to your data. Get in, quickly remove null values, and get out. You can impute one or many columns with the values you want. It might look something like Figure 5-35.

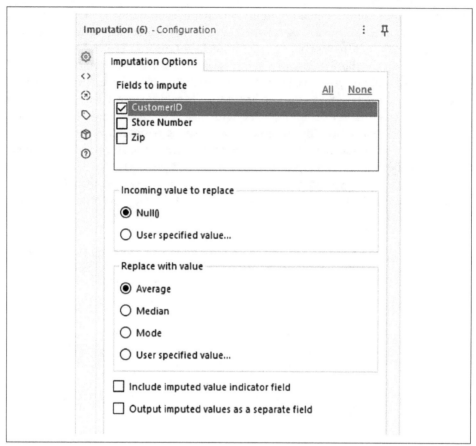

Figure 5-35. Imputation tool configuration

Sort Tool

I am willing to bet the Sort tool will be in your top 10 most used tools within Designer. That is because it is so useful in many regards:

Yes, it sorts, but it also allows you to sort in a more robust way with multiple columns and potentially different directions for each column. On top of that, it supports other tools like the Sample tool, Tile tool, and many more (see Figure 5-36).

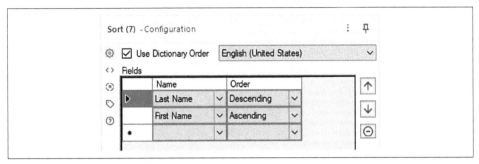

Figure 5-36. Sort tool configuration

Writing Expressions

Understanding how to write expressions using different tools in Designer is important. If you are writing formulas, then you are doing one of two things: creating new fields or modifying existing fields. When we talk about the Multi-Row Formula tool later in this chapter, you will see that you have new types of variables that you can incorporate into your expressions that you don't have available in other tools. Make sure you are aware of the context in which you are writing your expressions.

Compound Expressions

As I mentioned earlier, the Custom Filter allows you to create multiple expressions called compound expressions. There are some nuances to these types of expressions that are important to understand. When we create compound expressions, we use one of two operators: AND or OR. Using the AND operator, you could see something like Figure 5-37.

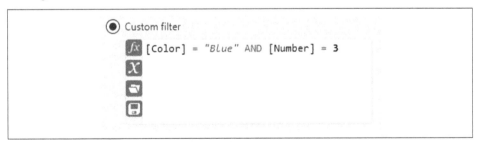

Figure 5-37. Compound expression using the AND operator

The most important thing to remember with the AND operator is that you need *both* statements to be true in order for the overall expression to be true. If you have four or five statements using the AND operator, then all of them need to be true in order to evaluate the entire expression as true. In Figure 5-37, only if the color is blue AND the number is greater than or equal to 3 does the record become true. However, with the OR operator only one of the statements needs to be true. Look again at this example (see Figure 5-38).

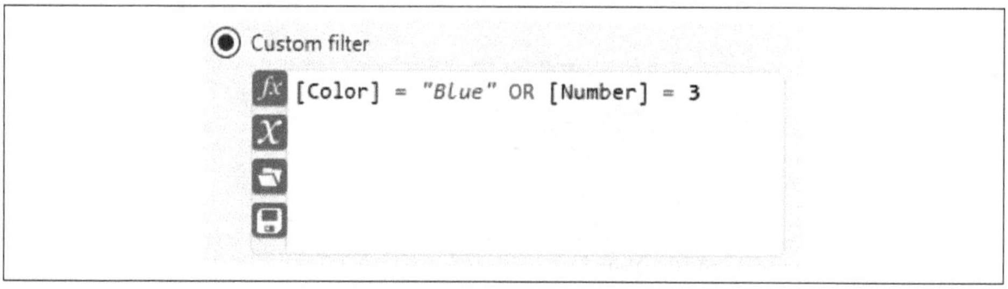

○ Custom filter

fx [Color] = "*Blue*" OR [Number] = 3

Figure 5-38. Compound expression using the OR operator

Now with the OR operator, only one of the statements needs to be true in order for the entire expression to be true. If you want to use both AND and OR operators together, you can use parentheses to separate and evaluate them using the order of operations rule (see Figure 5-39).

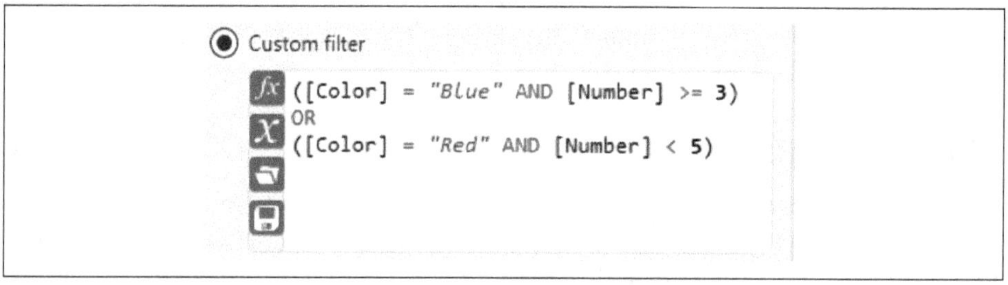

○ Custom filter

fx ([Color] = "*Blue*" AND [Number] >= 3)
OR
([Color] = "*Red*" AND [Number] < 5)

Figure 5-39. Compound expressions using AND and OR operators

Formula Tool

The Formula tool gives you so much power in its ability to create workflows that clean, modify, or add data:

You can use the tool's expression editor to write your formulas. You have two basic options with the formula tool: modify a field or create a new field. If you choose to modify an existing field, you will not be able to change the data type of the field. However, if you create a new field, you can.

There are many ways to use the Formula tool, but here is a brief list of some of the most common applications:

- Apply conditional statements to your data
- Convert numbers and strings
- Format and parse dates
- Extract file paths

- Apply financial algorithms or mathematical calculations
- Analyze spatial data
- Cleanse and modify string data
- Perform validation tests on data

Your time will be well spent learning the many different use cases for the Formula tool. Now, let's look at how you can change the value of an existing field using the Formula tool.

Modifying an existing field

Being able to modify an existing field in place is one of the most liked features among Excel users moving to Alteryx because you no longer have to create tons of columns in order to build calculations—you can literally modify a column in place based on other field values. To modify an existing field, add a Formula tool to the workflow and connect it. From there, open the Configuration pane and select the Output Column drop-down (see Figure 5-40).

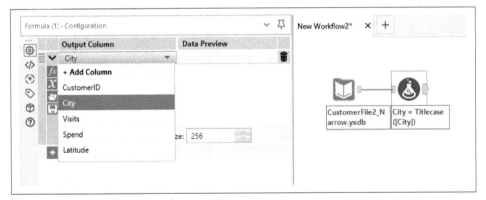

Figure 5-40. Formula tool configuration

Then select the column you want to modify. In Figure 5-40, I am selecting "City" as the column I want to modify. Once you have selected the column, write your expression.

It's important to note that whatever you write here will *replace* the existing value. In this example, you have a data set where the City name has both capitalized values and some with all uppercase letters. You want to standardize that so it's uniform. The expression you would write in this example is shown in Figure 5-41.

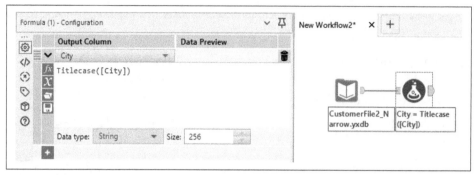

Figure 5-41. Titlecase function

Here, you are taking in the values that were in your data, converting them to title case, and saving them back into that same field. Notice that the data type drop-down is grayed out. That's because, again, you can't modify the data type for an existing field; you can use the Select tool if you need to do that. If you look at the updated data set, you will see that the City is now uniform (see Figure 5-42).

Record	CustomerID	City	Visits	Spend	Latitude
1	1	Denver	1	206.95	39.723993
2	2	Denver	1	228.27	39.666517
3	3	Aurora	1	432.44	39.671027
4	4	Aurora	4	2101.11	39.649212
5	5	Denver	1	1404.09	39.668677
6	6	Denver	2	962.61	39.765623
7	7	Parker	4	552.53	39.557372
8	8	Denver	1	25.37	39.748755
9	9	Aurora	2	7026.44	39.642421
10	10	Denver	2	1838.64	39.695401

Results - Formula (2) - Output — 5 of 5 Fields — Cell Viewer — 90 records displayed

Figure 5-42. Uniform data set

Creating a new field

As I mentioned earlier, you can also create new fields in your data based on values from your data or completely standalone values. For example, you could categorize a single data set before you join it with another.

To create a new field, choose "+ Add Column" (see Figure 5-43).

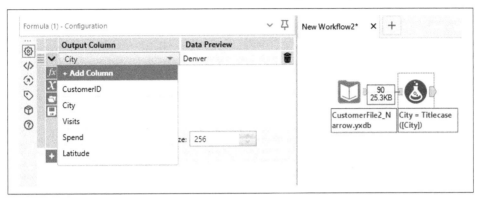

Figure 5-43. + Add Column

Once you select the + Add Column from the drop-down, you must immediately name the column. If you don't, your workflow will error out when it runs.

In Figure 5-44, I am creating a calculation of average spend per visit and I am setting the data type to FixedDecimal with Precision of 19 and Scale of 2.

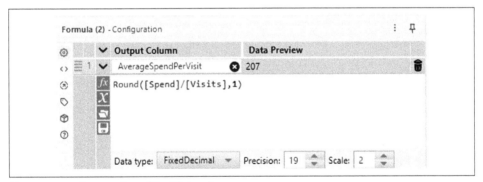

Figure 5-44. AverageSpendPerVisit column

After creating this new column, run the workflow and notice an additional column of data where the average spend per visit, is calculated for each row (see Figure 5-45). This is going to look different when we talk about the Multi-Row Formula tool later on, as we will be able to look up and down rows to create calculations.

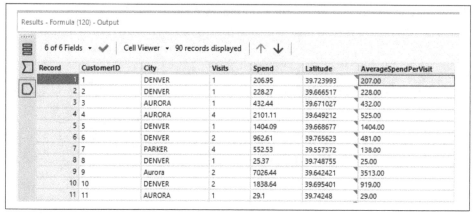

Figure 5-45. Average spend by row

Creating multiple calculations

One of the features that Designer users appreciate is the ability to create multiple expressions in a single tool. Unlike Excel, where each formula that you create is a new column, in Alteryx you don't need to create new columns. You can create multiple calculations that all work off the same field. However, if you want to create a new column, you can do that. You can simply add another column by clicking on the blue square with a white plus sign (see Figure 5-46).

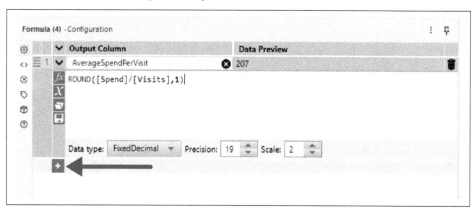

Figure 5-46. Add new column

Creating many expressions is a powerful feature, but think carefully about how you would use it. If you have 10 expressions in one tool, then you are reducing the ability for the workflow to be easy to visualize and understand. Anyone reviewing your workflow or trying to build off of it would have to click each formula. It might make sense in some situations to break out the expressions using a couple of Formula tools if it improves the understanding for other users.

 Before you go creating expressions for every column or many columns at one time, keep reading. The information in the next section on using the Multi-Field Formula tool can save you a lot of time and effort.

Multi-Field Formula Tool

The Multi-Field Formula tool takes all the power of the Formula tool and brings it up a notch. It allows you to write expressions against not just one column at a time, but as many as you want.

The overall idea of the tool is very simple. You select the columns that you want a formula to apply to, choose if you want to modify in place or create new columns, and then write your expression. This is very much like the Formula tool but with some subtle differences (see Figure 5-47).

First, notice in Figure 5-47 that you modify all the columns of a specific data type. For example, if you wanted to add 100 to each of your numeric columns, that would make sense. But you can't add 100 (the number) to all of your string values. If you put quotes around it, which turns it into a string value (i.e., "This is some text" + "100"), then you could but it likely wouldn't make sense to do that.

Second, notice the CurrentField variable. This is used in a couple of the tools and it's a useful feature. It is used to represent a bucket of all the fields you have selected. Let's say you created an expression in order to capitalize all your string fields and you have 10 string fields to be modified. The CurrentField will be the bucket of all those fields, and at runtime it will cycle through each one to apply that expression to your data.

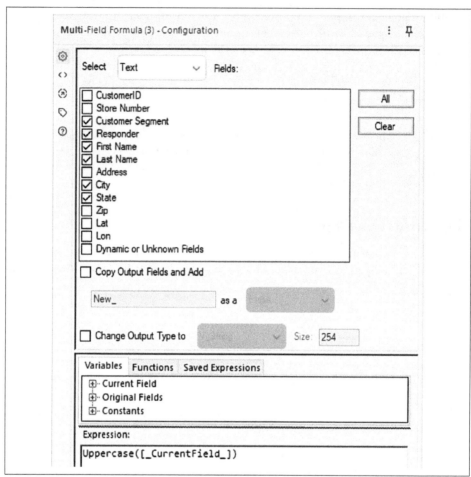

Figure 5-47. Multi-Field Formula tool configuration

If you ran the workflow with the configuration above, you would see that all your text fields would be capitalized (see Figure 5-48).

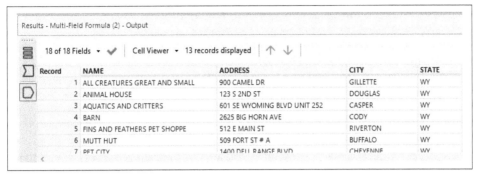

Record	NAME	ADDRESS	CITY	STATE
1	ALL CREATURES GREAT AND SMALL	900 CAMEL DR	GILLETTE	WY
2	ANIMAL HOUSE	123 S 2ND ST	DOUGLAS	WY
3	AQUATICS AND CRITTERS	601 SE WYOMING BLVD UNIT 252	CASPER	WY
4	BARN	2625 BIG HORN AVE	CODY	WY
5	FINS AND FEATHERS PET SHOPPE	512 E MAIN ST	RIVERTON	WY
6	MUTT HUT	509 FORT ST # A	BUFFALO	WY
7	PET CITY	1400 DELL RANGE BLVD	CHEYENNE	WY

Figure 5-48. Multi-Field Formula output

Third, notice that you can output fields to existing columns and you can change the data type. In fact, this is the only tool without the Select tool configuration that can change the data type of an existing field. If you want to standardize all your text fields to the V_String data type with size 8, you can do that. This is yet another way you can do groups of actions all at the same time instead of having to modify the data type individually on each field.

Multi-Row Formula Tool

For many of you coming from Excel, the Multi-Row Formula tool might at first feel like a brain twister!

The Multi-Row Formula tool enables functionality that isn't commonly known in Excel (i.e., Index/Match Lookups) and is unnecessarily complex and complicated (nested if statements looking across and up and down columns). However, the Multi-Row Formula tool simplifies such tasks and frankly goes beyond the capability of Excel.

At its core, this tool flips the script of reading across a row like the Formula tool does and it allows you to read up and down a column. Yes, amazing. Now, the Multi-Row Formula tool can only update one column per tool instance, so if you want to update multiple fields, you need to have an additional tool instance for each one. The tool can both update existing fields in place and create new ones. Again, like the Multi-Field Formula tool, there are some nuances and differences when creating expressions.

The first one is around the Num Rows configuration item. The Num Rows value is what gives you access to the number of rows above or below the value the expression is run on. For example, if I set the Num Rows value to 3, that means when I write an expression, I can calculate using two rows behind or two rows ahead (the actual row is counted as the third). When you change the value of Num Rows, it's immediately affected in the variables section below.

The second difference is regarding the Variables. The variables' values are going to look much different and foreign at first. Everything is in reference to the row, but that's actually what you want. Remember you are not calculating across a row. You are calculating down the column.

Let's say I wanted a running three-month average of the last three months at any given point in time (every row). Figure 5-49 is what that would look like using the Multi-Row Formula tool.

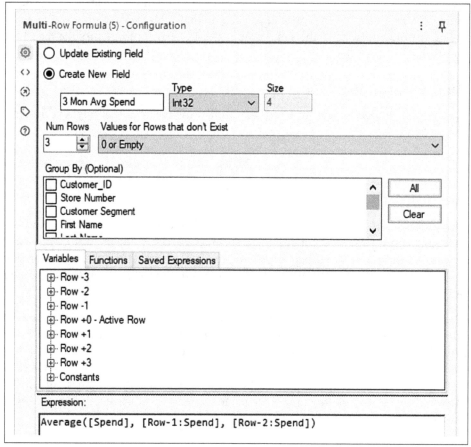

Figure 5-49. Multi-Row Formula tool configuration

In the Multi-Row Formula tool, you have access to the same function library, Variables and Constants, and Saved Expressions you would in the Formula tool.

Now that you can do running averages across a data set, let's turn up the heat by simply adding one thing. Let's run the three-month averages by each and every group of items in the data set. To do this, simply check the Customer Segment box in Group By and rerun the workflow. You'll see that your average three-month value is by group. You could do this easily for three-month, six-month, nine-month, and even yearly aggregations.

Creating Data

Creating data may seem unrelated to the topic of cleaning data, but I would argue that it is. When I refer to "cleaning data," what I mean is that I want to take data in whatever condition it is in and make it valuable and ready to use. Most times, this means cleaning the data, but many times you'll also need to add data to give it more power, more context, and more insight. You can do this by simply "creating" new columns or new rows.

Creating New Columns

I've introduced many tools that can be used for creating new data. The Formula, Multi-Row Formula, and Multi-Field Formula tools can all create new columns. These tools are highly flexible and powerful.

A couple other tools that can help you in creating high-value fields (columns) are the Record ID tool and the Tile tool. Both of these tools give you the ability to create IDs, or markers, alongside the data you already have. Want to mark every fourth row? No problem. Want to mark every new row of a new section? No problem. Let's dive in further!

Record ID tool

The Record ID tool name hints at what it does: adds a record ID to your data:

You would want to do this to not only mark your rows but to keep track of each individual record as you manipulate it. Say, for example, you want to filter your data. By adding a record ID column, you now know when you filter your data which records specifically got filtered. As you do aggregations, pivots, and other operations to the data, you don't lose which records are which.

You can get a bit creative in your use of this tool, as well. If you just want a data set where each row has a sequential number assigned to it, then you can use the standard configuration of setting the starting value to 1 (see Figure 5-50).

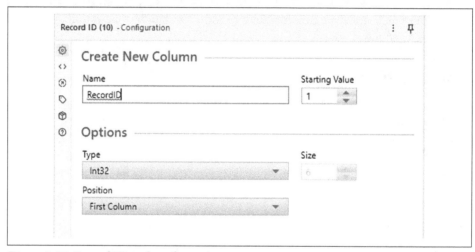

Figure 5-50. Record ID tool configuration

With a little creativity, you can pull off some very useful functions. One idea is to add a Sort tool right before the Record ID tool to sort it by a specific ranking or level. Then, when you add the Record ID column, it could actually take on the role of the "rank" value.

Tile tool

The Tile tool is one of those tools that many users simply don't understand. So, I'm going to spend a little time here walking you through its usefulness, and I encourage you to spend a little time getting familiar with it:

The Tile tool is actually very useful and, when used correctly, can save you time and effort by giving you groups of records to use. The tool simply assigns a value (a tile) based on ranges in the data. When you use the Tile tool, two fields are appended to the data. The first one is the Tile number, which is the assigned tile of the record. The second one is the Tile sequence number, which is the number of the record's position within the Tile. The tool can be configured with one of five methods:

Equal Sum
Assigns records to a tile, where each tile has roughly equal total values.

Equal Records
Each tile is assigned the same number of rows.

Unique Value
For every unique value in a specified field(s), a unique tile is assigned. If multiple fields are specified, a tile is assigned based on that combination of values.

Manual
The user can specify the cutoffs for the tiles by typing a value on a new line for each range.

Smart Tile
Creates tiles based on the standard deviation of the values in the specified field. The tiles assigned indicate whether the record's value falls within the average range (=0), above the average (1), or below the average (–1).

With these options, you can categorize the rows of data into groups based on some very specific criteria. Some use cases for the Tile tool include:

- Create rankings across multiple groups
- Add IDs to your data that allow it to be pivoted (every 10 rows is another set)
- Create sample groups

Creating New Rows

Creating new rows is another way to create data in order to make the data set more valuable or accurate. This is also sometimes used as a step toward getting to a final answer. For example, perhaps you have a list of dates but you know some are missing. You can simply use tools to create those missing values or rows. The formula tools can't create new records, but there are a couple of tools that can, like Generate Rows and Oversample Field. Other tools, like Joins and Parse, can create records based on joining or breaking out previous records.

Generate Rows tool

The Generate Rows tool is another notable tool that can help you create or build a more robust data set:

You can use the tool without any input and just create a column of data that is dynamic, like a list of values. You can duplicate rows and actually build what is called a "scaffold," which we'll cover next. When you have missing data, but you have the records available for the categories, you would use the Imputation tool we discussed earlier. However, if you don't have the records at all in your data, then you would need to create them. That's where the Generate Rows tool comes in to help you create scaffolding, or to build out those values that you are missing.

Scaffolding

Scaffolding is an important concept that not everyone is familiar with. In the physical world, it's a temporary structure (*https://oreil.ly/UwHUJ*) that builders use to support a work crew and materials to aid in the construction, maintenance, and repair of buildings. In the data world, it's the data structure that you can use to build out your data set. If you are missing rows and/or columns of data, scaffolding can help to build them so that all dates or values are accounted for even if the data value is null or zero.

One common use case for scaffolding I've hinted at is dates. If, for example, you have two dates such as a start date and end date but you want to fill in the details in between those two dates, then you need to build the scaffolding to do that. You would use the Generate Rows tool to accomplish this. If you only had a start date and an end date, you could build out something like what is shown in Figure 5-51.

The idea and practice of scaffolding will force you to change how you think about data, foundationally. It isn't just rows and columns. Data has a structure. The scaffolding is the structure of data. If you think a building is just floors and rooms, then you miss the fact that the leaning tower of Pisa is slanted or that the pyramids are well...pyramids. Think about how the structure of the data set contributes to your information, and in turn, the insights you want to pull out.

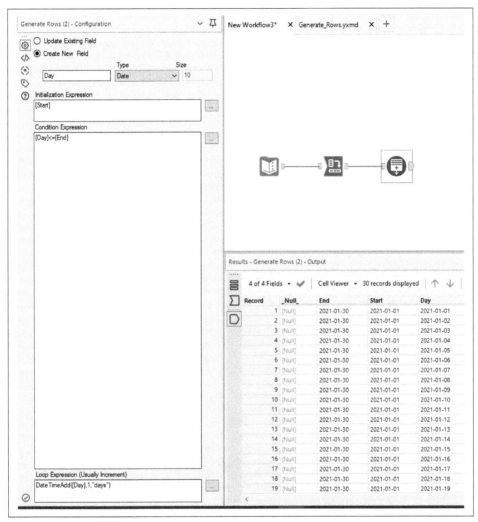

Figure 5-51. Scaffolding

Conclusion

Wow! We covered a lot of tools and techniques in this chapter, but that was to be expected considering cleaning your data is one of the most valuable and important things you can do with Alteryx Designer. You learned how to identify dirty data and, specifically, what to look for. You learned how to filter your data and use the powerful Expression window to write complex and compound expressions. You learned about the different ways to clean your data.

You also learned how to create data via formula tools that construct new columns and rows of insightful information, and the critical concept of scaffolding. We covered so many tools in this chapter that you might not feel like you have a strong grasp on them yet, and that's OK. I encourage you to go back and experiment with them until you feel comfortable. I assure you; you will get there. Like I noted at the start of the chapter, each chapter in this book is additive and you'll reuse many of these tools in future chapters. In the next two chapters, we are going to close out Part I by diving into joining and summarizing your data.

I hope you are starting to appreciate the utility of Alteryx Designer. If you really want to get good at using Designer, nothing beats practice. Do it over and over. You will be amazed at how what you learn now will pay off in the near to immediate future.

CHAPTER 6

Joining Your Data

"A SQL query goes to a bar, walks up to two tables and asks...
...Can I join you?"

Ah, data jokes never get old! Joins are one of the most commonly used tools and for the right measure. They allow a key functionality in Alteryx—joining data sets from multiple data sources easily and efficiently. Some join tools, however, can be challenging to use if you don't learn how they operate and, more specifically, how to think about joining data. It's important to note that relational databases are built on the key principles of set theory; some would argue they're built entirely on these principles. It's also important to understand how set theory works in order to make the most of joins in Alteryx and even troubleshoot why you might be missing data or be unable to join two data sets. Don't worry, I'll make it very easy for you!

After training and talking with so many Designer users over the years, I have uncovered some ideas that help make understanding Designer easier. I try to find simple ideas that set new Designer users on a path to approach learning a concept quickly and easily. For example, when I think about joins in their basic form, I start by asking myself: do I need to join data vertically or horizontally? Vertically means I want two data sets to stack on top of each other. Horizontally means I want to join two data sets by using their common fields. This distinction has helped a lot of people think about which tools they need to use from the start.

At the core of it, there are only three joins: cross joins (Cartesian Joins), inner joins (sometimes just referred to as joins), and outer joins. There are three types of outer joins, as well: left outer join (left join), right outer join (right join), and full outer join (full join). Knowing this basic terminology will simplify most of what you need to know about how to use the join tools. We will talk about all the ways you can make these different joins work with your workflow.

If you don't have experience with SQL or, more specifically, SQL joins, then you might want to take a little bit of time to review the basics. This will help you immensely in your understanding of how Designer thinks about joins. A good reference for SQL basics is *Learning SQL* by Alan Beaulieu (O'Reilly).

The Join tool palette (see Figure 6-1) has a relatively small number of tools, but they are tools that you will use in probably every workflow you build.

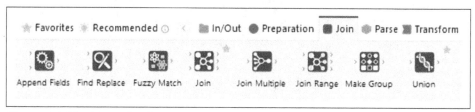

Figure 6-1. The Join tool palette

Join tools are easy to spot, too, with their distinct purple square icon:

Before we get deep into this chapter, it is important to understand that the word "join" is a general term that encompasses all the different types of joins that could happen with your data. You are almost guaranteed to hear someone say, "Just join this table to that table." At first, you may not know exactly what type of join to use, just that you need to somehow join the tables. By knowing the data and what you are trying to accomplish, it will become clear which type of join you need to use. Now, let's jump into the different types so you can start joining data like a rock star!

Vertical Joins

Vertical joins are used when you want to join data vertically, or on top of each other, assuming that there are column names that both data sets share (see Figure 6-2). You would use vertical joins in a case where all the columns in one data set are the same as another data set, but the data values are different. A good example is when you have multiple regions of data. It's the same structure; one is for the northwest and the other is for the southeast. In Designer vernacular (and other data tools), doing a vertical join means "union-ing" the data.

Database administrators (DBAs) and those with a deep knowledge of databases are probably cringing. "Vertical joins? Don't you mean a union?" Yes, smarty-pants. I sure do! Vertical joins are a visual way of describing a union, most of the time. So, let's appease our DBA friends and talk about the wonderful Union tool!

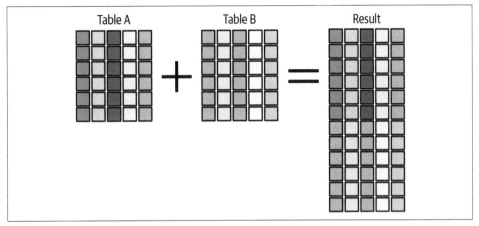

Figure 6-2. Vertical joins

The Union Tool

The Union tool provides a simple way to conduct the vertical join. It is also one of the few tools that can handle multiple inputs, which means it also has a unique anchor that signifies multiple inputs are allowed (see Figure 6-3):

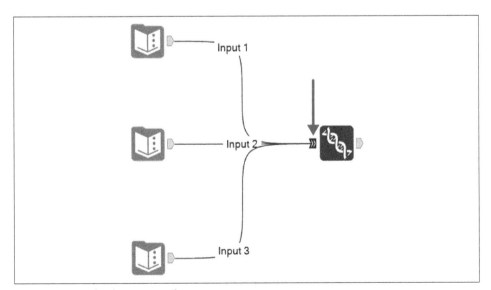

Figure 6-3. Multiple input anchor

The Union tool has three configuration options to choose from (see Figure 6-4), which we'll discuss next.

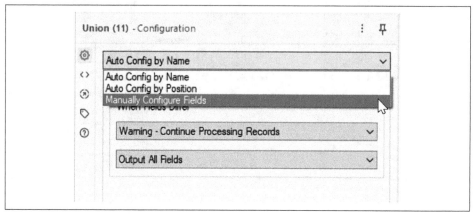

Figure 6-4. Union tool configuration

Auto Config by Name

Auto Config by Name allows you to vertically join two data sets by their names. This expectation that the names of the columns match is important. If the column names don't match, then you will get additional columns in your data. Let's look at an example.

In Figure 6-5, you see that your data records have the same column names.

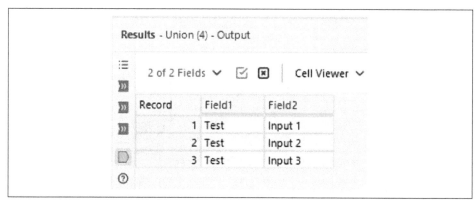

Figure 6-5. Using Auto Config by Name

Each of the three files you are joining has a column named Field1 and a column named Input. Now, what happens if you rename the Input column on each of the three data sets? You would see a mismatch (see Figure 6-6).

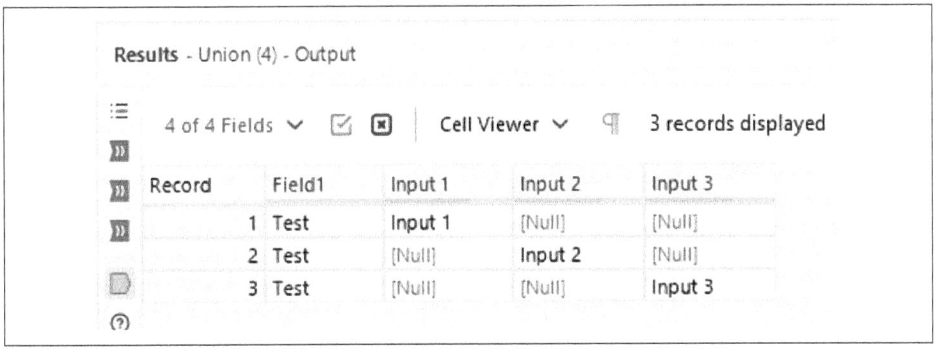

Figure 6-6. Union fields mismatch

Notice how the three columns don't get unified into one single column. This is the downside of using Auto Config by Name. However, if you know the fields are always titled the same, then you could use this option. It's also important to note that the fields don't have to be in the same order.

Auto Config by Position

Auto Config by Position is slightly different in that it assumes that the location of the columns is exactly the same. So, for example, if you have columns A, B, and C in one data set, and A, B, and C in another, then when they are joined the corresponding positions will be joined, meaning column A lines up with column A, Column B with Column B, and so on. The same problem happens with the Auto Config by Name option, though, if your assumption is incorrect. Let's say one data set has Column A, Column C, then Column B, and the second data set has Column A, Column B, and Column C. Any chance you see what is happening? It is OK if you don't! Column A will join fine, but now Column C from the first data set will line up with Column B from the second data set. You need to ensure your assumptions about position are correct if you use this option.

Manually Configure Fields

Manually Configure Fields is the option some use because it allows the greatest flexibility. I like it mostly because I can see that it's going to work the first time. The other reason to prefer this option is that you can even take the situations where the columns aren't lined up the way you want and fix them. Figure 6-7 shows the previous example, where you have different column names in each data set.

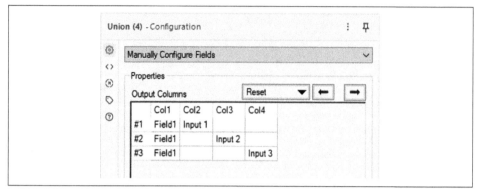

Figure 6-7. Manually Configure Fields

Now, you can click those individual columns and use the arrows next to the Reset drop-down to align them so it looks like Figure 6-8.

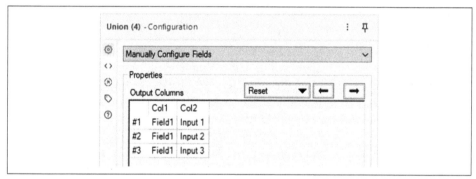

Figure 6-8. Align columns with Manually Configure Fields

One final but important note: the Union tool always uses the first data set you connected to the Union tool and its field names and field order as the field names and field order for the output data set. It matters which data set you connect to the Union and in which order. You can set a specific order for joining your data with the Output Order box at the bottom of the Union configuration window (see Figure 6-9).

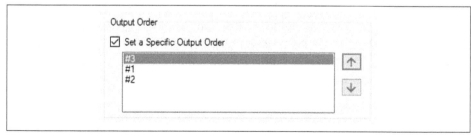

Figure 6-9. Output Order

Remember, with vertical joins, you are stacking the data on top of each other and you need to ensure your columns are lined up with each appropriate field from each of the data sets. Now, if all we had was vertical joins, then life would be easy, wouldn't it? We do not get off so easily. Let's move on to cover the more common and powerful landscape of horizontal joins. They are a bit more complex than vertical joins, but you'll find that once you master joins in general you will be well on your way to becoming an Alteryx Designer pro!

Horizontal Joins

Horizontal joins are much more involved and complex than just stacking data. It's more like stitching together two data sets and ensuring you stitch the right elements of fabric together. Spend some time understanding horizontal joins and building an intuition around how two data sets could be brought together. Horizontal joins are about precisely specifying which data needs to be joined. This will dictate which data you are able to analyze downstream. Let's dig into how you can build horizontal joins using the Join tool.

The Join Tool

The Join tool is likely going to be one of your top five most used tools:

It is the most common tool you will use for bringing data together horizontally, as it can handle both left and right joins as well as inner and outer joins. Right out of the gate, you need to get familiar with the different types of joins you can make happen with this tool, as well as what you can do when you add the Union tool.

The Join tool takes in two data sets. It then allows you to specify whether you want to join by record position or by specific fields (see Figure 6-10).

Joining specific fields has a caveat: you can only join data of the same type. A string field can join with another string field, but a string field cannot join with a numerical data type.

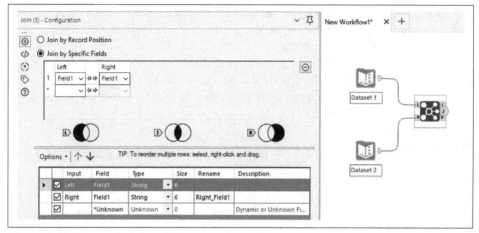

Figure 6-10. Join tool configuration

If you join by record position, then you will see that record 1 of Dataset 1 will be on the same record as record 1 of Dataset 2. If you join by specific fields, you will get a data set where only the records returned are those that match based on a field(s) chosen. You'll also notice you can modify specific items that will be output, like renaming the fields, changing data types, or deselecting fields (exactly like the Select tool!). Also worth noting is that, by default, the Join tool leaves all fields selected with a rename on the right data stream (data coming into the right anchor of the Join tool).

The outputs of the Join tool may seem a bit confusing at first, but let's try to simplify them. There are three outputs: L, J, and R. The L output refers to all the records from Dataset 1 (going into the L input anchor) that *did not* match the field(s) from Dataset 2. The J output refers to all the records from both data sets where the specified field(s) from Dataset 1 *did match* the specific fields from Dataset 2. Lastly, the R output is just the reverse of the L output, where it refers to all the records from Dataset 2 that did not match the field(s) of Dataset 1.

 Get in the habit of counting the records that go into the inputs and comparing that number to what comes out. It can give you a sense of whether your data is getting duplicated based on your join criteria. It's also important to note that if your join criteria are not unique values, you'll end up with more records in the J output than in the L and R outputs. You might actually want this, but more often than not I believe you won't.

As I mentioned earlier in the book, if you combine just two tools, then you can produce an exponentially more powerful effect. Joins are no exception. If you connect the Join tool with the Union tool, you can actually create the outer join sets like you see in Figure 6-11.

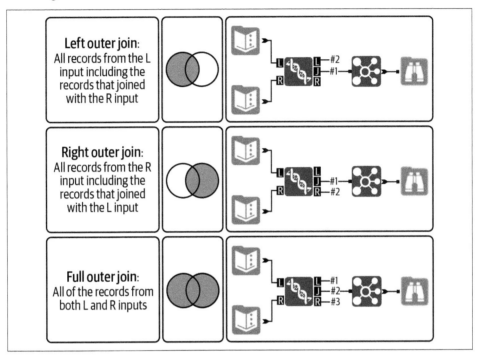

Figure 6-11. Three types of outer joins

One last bit of advice on the Join tool: you might hear me or others explain that joins are "expensive." What that means is that a Join tool can slow down a workflow quite a lot depending on the amount of data and the configuration of the join, as both sets of data must be sorted in order to find matches, and sorting large data sets takes lots of time. Use Join tools sparingly or at least with an important purpose. Don't be afraid to use a join, but if you find yourself with 10 joins in a workflow it's probably time to reassess whether you need all of them or if there might be a better way, especially if the size of your data is considerably large.

The Join Multiple Tool

While the Join tool allows you to join two data sets, the Join Multiple tool lets you connect however many data sets you have at one time:

If you have, say, four or five data sets you can combine on a field or set of fields, it might be easier to use the Join Multiple tool. If you were to use the Join tool, you would end up using three or four of them to stitch together all the data sets.

With the Join Multiple tool, the same setup that we used with the Join tool applies in regard to joining by record position or fields. However, there is an added feature around Cartesian joins, which is basically when you join all the records in one data set to all the records in another data set. This feature is meant to help you avoid making the mistake of joining more data than you intended to by throwing an error on multidimensional joins of more than 16 records (see Figure 6-12).

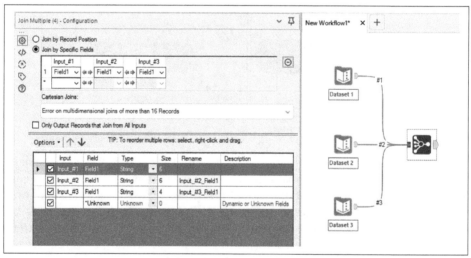

Figure 6-12. Error on multidimensional joins when using the Join Multiple tool

There is also a checkbox available to "Only Output Records that Join from All Inputs." This option represents another way to make sure you are only getting the data you meant to get by specifying the join. Lastly, you'll notice that, just like the Join tool, the Join Multiple tool contains the same features as the Select tool for selecting fields, changing data types, and renaming fields. These features will only apply to the data in the J output (for a normal two-input join). Many people mistakenly assume that whatever changes are made in the Select functionality will also be applied to the L and R outputs.

The Append Fields Tool

The Append Fields tool is a different type of Join tool:

It not only allows you to append data to another data set, but it does so at every row. This is incredibly useful when you need to have a set of values accounted for in a data set. You'll have to proceed with a bit of caution here because you can easily blow up the size of your data set if you aren't paying attention. To give you an example, take a look at Figure 6-13.

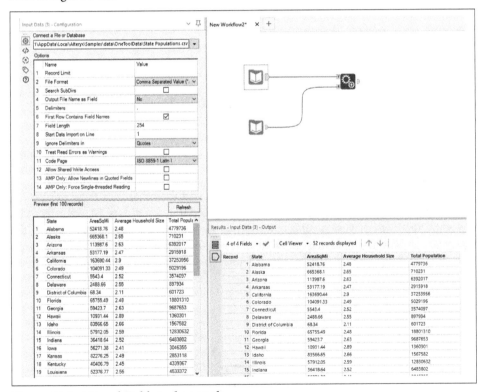

Figure 6-13. Append Fields tool example

You can see that we are starting with a data set that includes US population data by state. Now, let's say you want to append a set of four categorical variables to this data set (see Figure 6-14): Home Office, Consumer, Small Business, and Corporate.

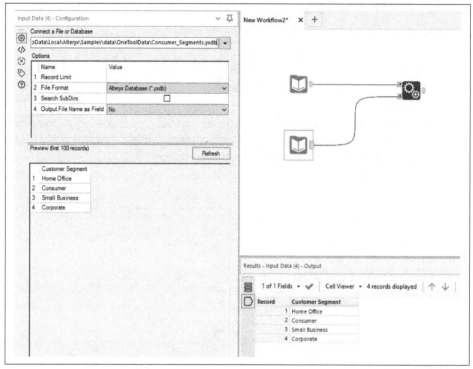

Figure 6-14. Four appended customer segments

When these four values are appended, you will see that your data set went from 52 rows to 208 rows. If you do the math (52 × 4) you see that for, every row in the original data set, four of them exist on the output. So, if you have a data set with 1 million records and you try to append just 50,000 records, you'd end up with 50 billion records!

The Find Replace Tool

The Find Replace tool has multiple use cases that it can solve for:

Together with the Append Fields tool, the Find Replace tool is basically doing a left join with a single key and can be faster than the Join tool, depending on your use case. If you need to make a list of changes to your data, then it's an invaluable tool, as the other ways of doing this (like writing formulas) are a bit more tedious. Find Replace is basically the implementation of a VLOOKUP function that you would use in Excel, but with more flexibility. Just like the VLOOKUP, if there are duplicates in your R input, only the last one will be retained, and since it doesn't sort the data sets like a Join tool, it's much more efficient. You still don't get any L and R outputs, however, which might be just fine.

This tool enables you to find any value in any part of a field and then replace that value with something else, as long as it's a text field. You can also replace multiple occurrences of a value. The other feature that I really like is that you can append fields to a record based on that find. Basically, once I've found a string WOLFMAN in a longer string, I can append a field or a set of fields (see Figure 6-15). That way, I can mark in those records that have what I am looking for and not worry about the records that don't.

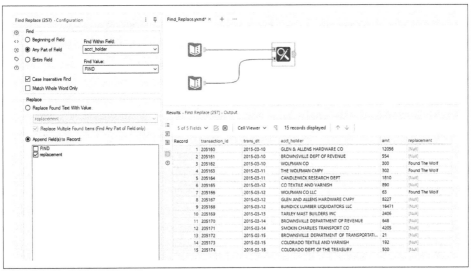

Figure 6-15. Find Replace tool configuration

The Fuzzy Match Tool

The Fuzzy Match tool is one of those tools that a lot of people avoid, and for two reasons. One, as the name implies, it isn't 100% exact. Many users want to make updates to their data based on exact matches but sometimes we really don't have that option. Two, fuzzy matching can be confusing because it relies on an algorithm that we don't fully understand to come up with a match, along with many other configuration parameters that you would need to set. Although this is a relatively advanced topic, I am going to try and make it approachable for you so that you can tap into the power of this tool even if you are just getting started:

First, just because you can't conduct a clean join with your data or an exact lookup doesn't mean you can't still find value in your data or help get your data into a standardized format. We are in the business of cleaning up and creating valuable data sets and the Fuzzy Matching tool can help, even when our data isn't 100% perfect.

Prepping for fuzzy matching

To ensure you can utilize the Fuzzy Match tool successfully, you need to first check off a few items so that your matches are as clean as possible and you can see the results clearly. Let's briefly walk through those checklist items:

Assign record IDs
> You'll want to assign a record ID using the Record ID tool in order to help you see which records matched. Note that if you are using two data sets, make sure that you set the starting value to a different value, as you don't want overlapping IDs.

Clean your data
> You can use a host of different tools to clean your data, like the Data Cleansing tool or the Formula tools (Formula, Multi-Row Formula, Multi-Field Formula). The important thing is that anything you can do to take away inconsistencies in your data, the better the result. For example, if your data isn't standard or some fields have data elements that can be removed, then that will help your fuzzy matching task.

Address accuracy
> In the US, if you have access to the Coding Accuracy Support System (CASS) data set, then you can run addresses through it to standardize them according to the US Postal Service standard. I'll cover the CASS data set in more detail in Chapter 16.

Remove unneeded fields
> This is a best practice for any workflow, but very important with fuzzy matching. You need to get rid of any fields you are not using or that are not important to your efforts.

Now that you are prepped for fuzzy matching, let's look at the process.

The fuzzy matching process

The entire fuzzy matching process in Designer consists of just two steps:

1. Key generation: This step involves creating a key for all records and match fields. Then, you'll record pairs where all the keys match and get moved forward. Many times, this is done for you from within the tool. We'll discuss this more in the next section.

2. Match function field thresholds: For each field in your fuzzy matching, you can set a threshold that is a percentage of how similar the values need to be to pass. In addition to setting a match threshold for each field, you can also set an overall threshold.

Preconfigured match styles

Designer comes packaged with many preconfigured matches where the key generation, match function, and thresholds are already set for you. You can see this listed in Figure 6-16 in the Match Style drop-down.

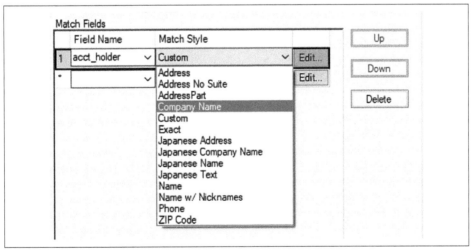

Figure 6-16. Preconfigured match styles

Using preconfigured match styles can save you lots of time and effort, as you can avoid having to configure your own. However, you are able to customize and specify your own configuration, if you like.

Finding matches

The two steps in the fuzzy matching process are simple, but it's easy to miss them when you start to use the tools. Know that when you use the Fuzzy Match tool, it's following those two steps behind the scenes—they're tied into the configuration of the tool. The key generation step happens in the process of finding matches. Those matches are based on the keys generated. When you get into the Fuzzy Match tool, you'll see there are two options available for you to configure the type of fuzzy matching you'll do: Purge Mode and Merge. Let's dig into each of those.

Purge Mode

Purge Mode is used when you want to conduct fuzzy matching within the same data set. This is used to compare all records within the data set to identify duplicates (see Figure 6-17).

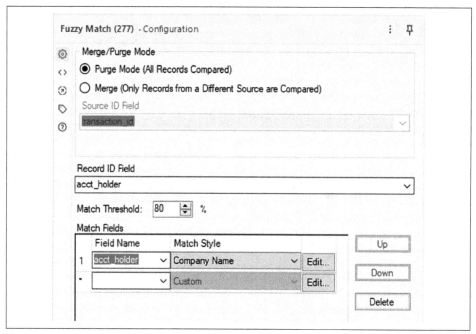

Figure 6-17. Purge Mode

Merge

The Merge option is used when you want to compare data across different sources in order to identify duplicates across different input files (see Figure 6-18).

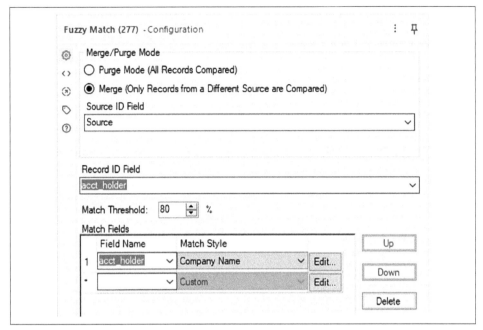

Figure 6-18. Merge

You will need to set each source up with an ID Field.

A few tips and tricks for those new to fuzzy matching:

- Put a unique tool after the Fuzzy Match to ensure you don't bring forward duplicates.
- Start off with a pre-built Match Style drop-down and only when you understand more about fuzzy matching move on to custom styles.
- When merging two data files, use a join to remove any exact matches.
- As fuzzy matching is not exact, it is quite common and in fact necessary to run your module many times with different configurations.

With many tools, and fuzzy matching being the perfect example, you'll need to devote a good amount of time and effort into testing and trying it out. Look at examples and other workflows to get more ideas. There are a lot of configuration options in this tool, and I could write a whole chapter on all the different use cases.

The Make Group Tool

The Make Group tool allows you to create groups of values based on relationships between two columns of data:

It's mostly used with the Fuzzy Matching tool to help group matches, which then lends itself easily to the Find Replace tool. The Make Group tool configuration is simple and just involves specifying two columns (see Figure 6-19).

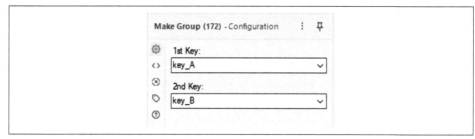

Figure 6-19. Make Group tool configuration

To help you think about how the Make Group tool works, look at Figure 6-20. The input is of a random pair of relationships. From there, they are grouped together based on all the relationships combined. Then, they are output in a Group/Key list.

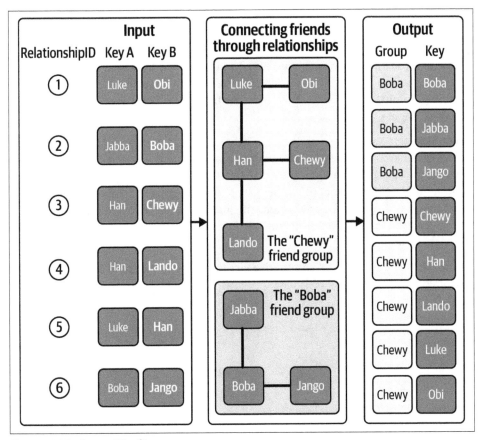

Figure 6-20. Group/Key list

Outputting your matches with keys will make your life easier, as you won't need to manually figure out which groups a particular match belongs to. This is a great tool to combine with other tools to not only find matches that aren't exactly 100% alike, but also to see groups of matches that you wouldn't have been able to find without first doing fuzzy matching.

Conclusion

In this chapter, we covered the Join tool palette in detail and you learned how to join data vertically and horizontally. We also talked about tools that help you to clean up data based on finding and replacing it. We also discussed the technique of fuzzy matching. Joining data is one of the most central and important tasks you will do in Alteryx Designer.

When data sets are connected, they can bring a lot of value to your workflow. Make sure you are aware of the implications of your joins, and ensure that you are doing any data cleanup prior to joining so that your join keys are consistent and you get a good result. Lastly, remember that there are a lot of use cases where combining two or more tools can be helpful. For example, the Join tool and the Union tool make a great team, as do the Fuzzy Match tool and the Unique tool, or the Fuzzy Match tool and the Make Group tool.

In the next chapter, you will summarize your data and learn about tools you can use to aggregate or manipulate your data.

CHAPTER 7

Transforming Your Data

Transforming and aggregating (grouping or summarizing) your data is a critical part of building valuable workflows. Many times, a workflow's entire purpose is to output the counts of something. The number of retailers, the count of employees, the spread of users—all of these are aggregations that give you insight into your focus area. The tools that I will cover in this chapter can take millions or billions of records of raw data and simplify them down to only a few key rows of insightful and understandable data points. We will go deep into the Summarize tool, which I consider to be one of the most valuable tools you have in Designer, period. We'll also cover how to pivot your data to ensure that the data format and readability are what you need. Lastly, we'll cover the rest of the tools in the Transform tool palette to ensure you become a pro at transforming your data.

The Transform tool palette (see Figure 7-1), like the Join tool palette, has a small number of tools in it compared to others we have discussed. However, I will argue that three of these tools are some of the most important tools you will use to build workflows: Summarize, Transpose, and Cross Tab. So, it's important for you to master them. I'll go into detail on why each tool is so important as we work through them in the chapter.

Figure 7-1. The Transform tool palette

You can always identify a Transform tool by its orange color and pentagon-shaped icon:

The more you understand how and why to aggregate and transform your data, the farther you will be on your path toward becoming a pro at working with data in Alteryx Designer. Let's start by exploring the Summarize tool!

The Summarize Tool

The Summarize tool, in my opinion, is the single most powerful tool you have available in Designer based on what it can do natively out of the box:

Some might argue that using R or Python inside of Alteryx (which you can easily do) would be the most powerful tool, because you could essentially build a whole workflow inside of those. But I am not referring to the coding side of things. Straight out of the box, the Summarize tool is the single most capable tool you have at your disposal, and you'll see why by the time we get through this section.

I like the Summarize tool because its capabilities are kind of surprising. Yes, you can group by a value, find the min or max of a group of values, and even find the counts, but there aren't 500 options to configure, like with the Fuzzy Match tool. There are basically two options to configure: the Field and the Action (more on these shortly). The sheer number of combinations is what gives this tool its power. For example, you can aggregate your data by grouping your records by a store and adding together the sales, the quantity, or any other value you have in your data.

At a high level, using this tool simply comes down to choosing the field(s) you want to aggregate and then choosing the action to aggregate them (see Figure 7-2). However, the impact that those two simple options have is enormous.

You can run not only a single action on one field, but you can create multiple actions for each field. Now, that would be impressive if you had just 3 possible actions, which would mean if you had 10 fields and 3 actions, you could potentially create 30 different actions (sum of field 1, average of field 2, sum of field 2, and so on)!

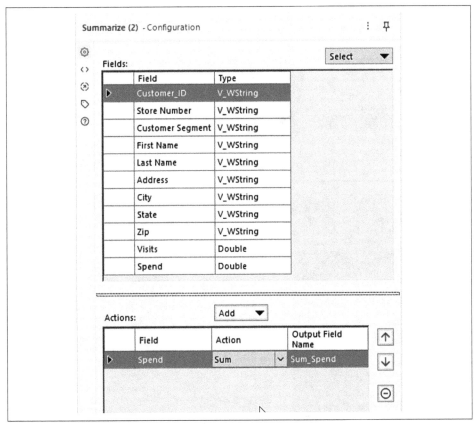

Figure 7-2. Summarize tool configuration

Let's say you select "Spend" as the field you wanted to aggregate. The action selected in Figure 7-2 is "Sum," meaning adding the fields together. However, remember that sum is only one of roughly 40+ actions you have for that one field. You could count the number of values, you could get the max value or the min value in that group of values, and so on.

The magic here is that you don't have just three actions; you have potentially up to 40! Now that you understand what's possible, let's build some aggregations.

Building Aggregations

When you bring a Summarize tool to the canvas and connect it to your data, the data types are extremely important. You need to have your data appropriately cleaned and organized before you summarize because the Summarize tool only enables aggregations for a specific data type. You can see an example of this in Figure 7-3.

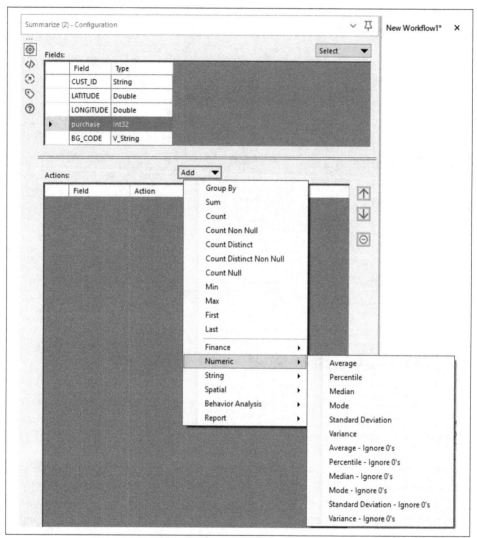

Figure 7-3. Aggregations by data type

Here, you see that the field "purchase" (which is an integer) allows me to use any of the Numeric functions. However, if I select the next field down, "BG_CODE" (which is a V_String), you will notice those Numeric functions are nearly all grayed out (see Figure 7-4).

Again, the data type is important because specific functions are numeric, string, spatial, and even for combining spatial objects, customer profiles, and report snippets.

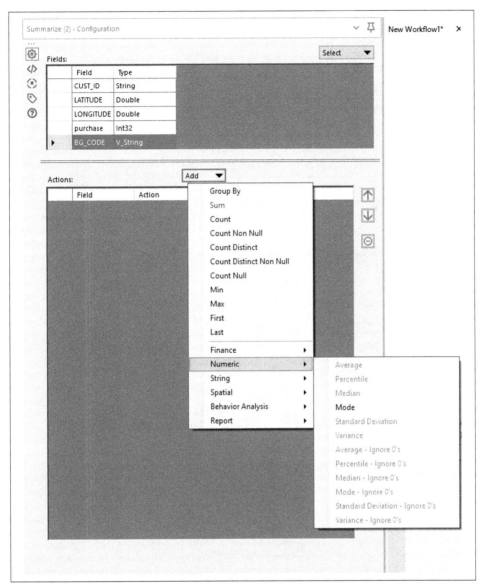

Figure 7-4. Grayed out Numeric options

Let's walk through the process of creating actions. Every situation will be handled exactly the same as in this example, with the only exception being that you might need to specify some parameters (for example, if you are concatenating values). To create an action, simply click the field that you want to aggregate. Then click Add and select the function you would like to use (see in Figure 7-5).

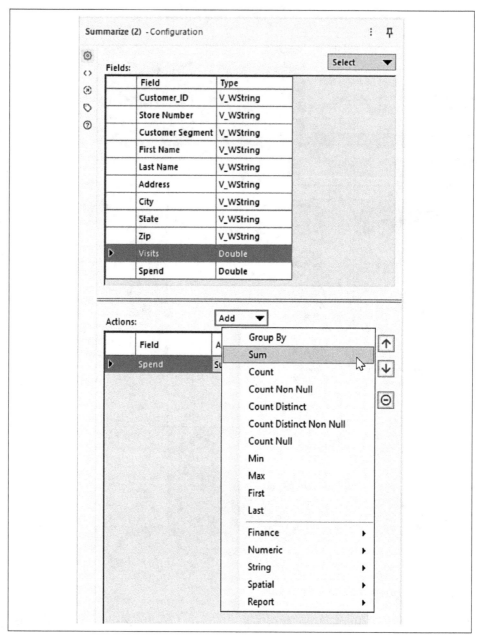

Figure 7-5. Summarize actions

Selecting Sum would result in an action in your field list (see Figure 7-6).

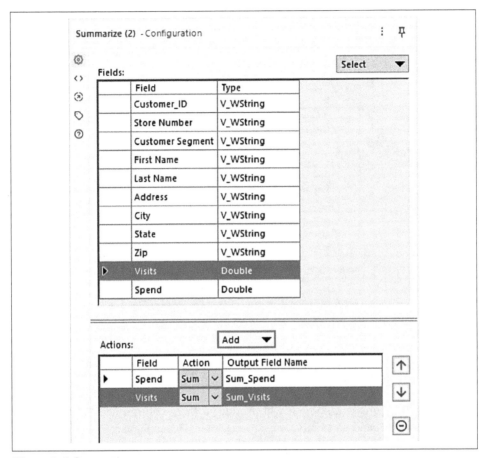

Figure 7-6. Sum action

Now, you can modify the action even after you've selected it, but remember the data type still plays a role. You can also change the Output Field Name to whatever you want by clicking in the Output Field Name and typing what you wish. Designer includes a prefix for numeric actions by default (i.e., "Sum_[field]" or "Avg_[field]"). The most important thing to understand, however, is that the number of fields you have here is the number of columns of data that will be output. If you have two fields here, you will have two columns of data.

To further this example just a bit, let's also add the Group By action to the Customer_ID field and then use the arrows on the right side to position it above the Sum action because the order in the Actions pane dictates the order of these fields in the data set. Let's also rename the fields so they are more user friendly (see Figure 7-7).

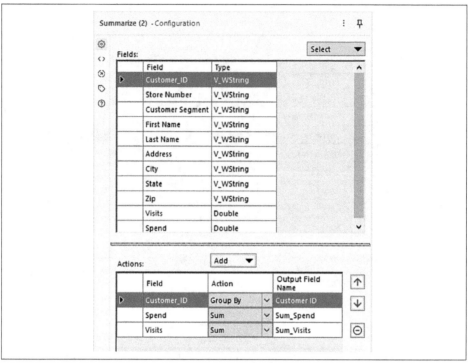

Figure 7-7. Adding Group By action and renaming fields

Now, when this runs you know it will produce a three-column data set, which will show the sum of spend and visits for each customer ID (see Figure 7-8).

If you get a little creative and add just one other tool, you can add many more options. Imagine taking the total for each of these customer IDs and using the Append Fields tool to append the Total Purchase to each one of the customer records. You would then have the base fields to calculate the percentage of the total.

We've talked a lot about the Summarize tool, but there are still more tools that I know you'll find valuable in manipulating your data. Let's take a look at how to pivot your data with the Cross Tab tool.

Results - Summarize (2) - Output

3 of 3 Fields ∨ ☑ ☒ | Cell Viewer ∨ ¶ 2,669 records displayed

Record	Customer ID	Sum_Spend	Sum_Visits
1	457	108.81	1
2	77	64.83	1
3	1328	101.87	1
4	1505	496.85	3
5	281	4.57	1
6	1093	192.69	1
7	1381	1181.49	1
8	2551	639.17	5
9	3330	760.71	2
10	3265	816.71	4
11	676	890.59	2
12	1829	459.47	4

Figure 7-8. Group By output

Cross Tab Tool

The Cross Tab tool and the Transpose tool (which we will cover next) are the two pivot table tools we have in Designer, and they work together quite well:

It's likely that you will get the two tools mixed up. I still do! The easiest way to remember them is that Cross Tab starts with a "C" (columns also start with a "c"), and Cross Tab pivots your data to columns (see Figure 7-9).

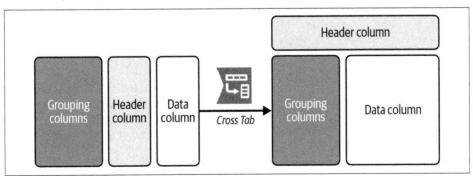

Figure 7-9. Pivot to columns

The Cross Tab tool is used to pivot the orientation of your data from vertical to horizontal. The main reason why you would want to pivot your data is to simply get all the correct values in a single row or column so you can do more calculations on the data, like adding fields together. The Cross Tab tool is fairly easy to configure—you just need to choose which fields you want to stay in place and those become your "grouped" fields. Then, you need to decide which fields you want to be your headers and which fields you want to be your values (see Figure 7-10). Lastly, you need to choose how to aggregate the data. If you have rows of data that are duplicate, then they need to be aggregated, and you can get fairly creative with this feature as well.

Depending on which data type you are using to cross tab, you will be presented with different methods for aggregating. For example, if your data type is a string then the options will be Concatenate, First, and Last (see Figure 7-10).

Figure 7-10. Cross Tab tool configuration

If the Values for New Columns is a numeric data type, you will get a longer list of methods for aggregating, like Sum, Average, Count, Percent, and so on (see Figure 7-11).

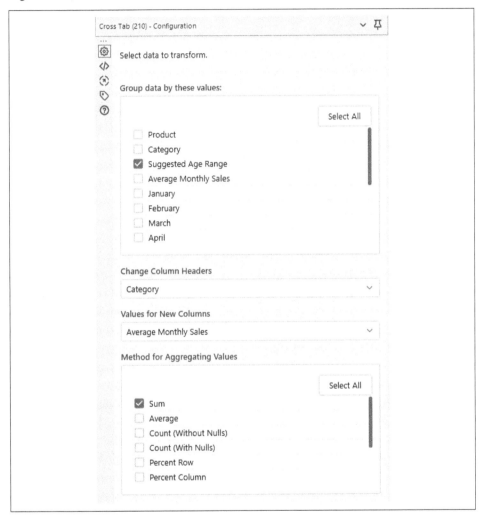

Figure 7-11. Group By Cross Tab

When you pivot your data, you could have a different number of columns because the tool's pivot function depends on the data and how many distinct values you are choosing for your headers. Here's an example that might help you better visualize how the Cross Tab tool works.

Let's start out with a data set that looks like Figure 7-12, then configure the Cross Tab tool, as shown in Figure 7-13.

Record	presidentNo	VicePresidentNo	Pres_or_VP	Name	Dates
1	1	[Null]	President	George Washington	April 30, 1789 - March 4, 1797
2	1	1	Vice President	John Adams	April 30, 1789 - March 4, 1797
3	2	[Null]	President	John Adams	March 4, 1797 - March 4, 1801
4	2	1	Vice President	Thomas Jefferson	March 4, 1797 - March 4, 1801
5	3	[Null]	President	Thomas Jefferson	March 4, 1801 - March 4, 1809
6	3	1	Vice President	Aaron Burr	March 4, 1801 - March 4, 1805
7	3	2	Vice President	George Clinton	March 4, 1805 - April 20, 1812
8	4	[Null]	President	James Madison	March 4, 1809 - March 4, 1817
9	4	1	Vice President	Elbridge Gerry	March 4, 1813 - November 23, 1814
10	5	[Null]	President	James Monroe	March 4, 1817 - March 4, 1825
11	5	1	Vice President	Daniel D. Tompkins	March 4, 1817 - March 4, 1825
12	6	[Null]	President	John Quincy Adams	March 4, 1825 - March 4, 1829
13	6	1	Vice President	John C. Calhoun	March 4, 1825 - December 28, 1832
14	7	[Null]	President	Andrew Jackson	March 4, 1829 - March 4, 1837
15	7	1	Vice President	Martin Van Buren	March 4, 1833 - March 4, 1837
16	8	[Null]	President	Martin Van Buren	March 4, 1837 - March 4, 1841

Figure 7-12. Data prior to using the Cross Tab tool

Figure 7-13. Example Cross Tab configuration

Then you'll see that the presidentNo field will stay in place but the Pres_or_VP unique values of President and Vice_President will be the headers, and the values will be the Name field (see Figure 7-14).

Record	presidentNo	President	Vice_President
1	1	George Washington	John Adams
2	2	John Adams	Thomas Jefferson
3	3	Thomas Jefferson	Aaron Burr, George Clinton
4	4	James Madison	Elbridge Gerry
5	5	James Monroe	Daniel D. Tompkins
6	6	John Quincy Adams	John C. Calhoun
7	7	Andrew Jackson	Martin Van Buren
8	8	Martin Van Buren	Richard Mentor Johnson
9	9	William Henry Harrison	John Tyler
10	10	John Tyler	
11	11	James K. Polk	George M. Dallas
12	12	Zachary Taylor	Millard Fillmore
13	13	Millard Fillmore	

Figure 7-14. Data after using the Cross Tab tool

Now that you understand the Cross Tab tool, let's take a look at the Transpose tool to build our intuition about transforming data in Designer.

Transpose Tool

I believe the Transpose tool is easier to understand and use than the Cross Tab tool, and that's mainly because the output is always the same:

Your output will always be the Key columns and the single data column (see Figure 7-15).

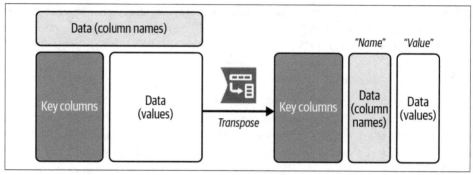

Figure 7-15. Transpose to columns

The Transpose tool is used to pivot the orientation of data from horizontal to vertical, which makes the data useful for further aggregations or common functions such as Group By or Sum. The Transpose tool takes every column that you have not marked as a Key column and reduces it to two columns: Name (which marks the name of the column) and Value (which marks the corresponding value starting with the first row).

Let's look at an example. We'll start with the data set shown in Figure 7-16, where you will notice that the months are columns.

Record	Product	Category	Suggested Age Range	Average Monthly Sales	January	February	March
1	Graphing Calculators	General	13+	84020.17	191817	434	70654
2	Office Supplies	General	All ages	83319.17	156628	82183	125043
3	Encyclopedias	Educational	All ages	79280.75	6299	119153	161717
4	Building Blocks	Fun and Games	3-6	97381.33	8313	184270	186021
5	Books about Dinosaurs	Fun and Games	All ages	106175.58	193667	76441	163244
6	Viggo Mortenson DVDs	Fun and Games	13+	117805.5	181291	178860	144830
7	Clothing	General	All ages	121212.5	6988	71830	69881
8	Frisbee and Frisbee Accessories	Fun and Games	7+	92629.92	4940	105607	53949
9	Legumes	General	All ages	116122.75	73467	154459	92995
10	Microscopes	Educational	7+	602.83	206	324	925

Figure 7-16. Data prior to using the Transpose tool

Now, feed this data set into a Transpose tool and configure it as in Figure 7-17. So, if the original data set contains eight columns and you marked four of them as Key fields, every row will be turned into five rows, each with a Name and Value of the remaining five columns, starting with the first row. There is no aggregation in this tool. You select the Key columns you want to stay put and move forward to your new data set, and then you select the columns of data that you want to be pivoted to a single data column. You can set a parameter to handle your missing columns.

Figure 7-17. Example Transpose tool configuration

You'll end up with a data set that now has the monthly data going down the rows (see Figure 7-18).

Record	Product	Category	Suggested Age Range	Average Monthly Sales	Name	Value
1	Graphing Calculators	General	13+	84020.17	January	191817
2	Graphing Calculators	General	13+	84020.17	February	434
3	Graphing Calculators	General	13+	84020.17	March	70654
4	Graphing Calculators	General	13+	84020.17	April	166571
5	Graphing Calculators	General	13+	84020.17	May	99066
6	Graphing Calculators	General	13+	84020.17	June	64423
7	Graphing Calculators	General	13+	84020.17	July	72846
8	Graphing Calculators	General	13+	84020.17	August	52744
9	Graphing Calculators	General	13+	84020.17	September	16150
10	Graphing Calculators	General	13+	84020.17	October	98130
11	Graphing Calculators	General	13+	84020.17	November	42312
12	Graphing Calculators	General	13+	84020.17	December	133095
13	Office Supplies	General	All ages	83319.17	January	156628
14	Office Supplies	General	All ages	83319.17	February	82183
15	Office Supplies	General	All ages	83319.17	March	125043
16	Office Supplies	General	All ages	83319.17	April	11205
17	Office Supplies	General	All ages	83319.17	May	130896
18	Office Supplies	General	All ages	83319.17	June	31314

Figure 7-18. Data set after using the Transpose tool

The easiest way to think about the Transpose tool is to think of the data going from *wide* to *tall*.

Now, there are several use cases where the Cross Tab and Transpose tools can be used together successfully (see Figure 7-19). Cross Tab and Transpose are basic inverses of each other. You can use Transpose and then reverse it back to Cross Tab. Because the Cross Tab tool aggregates data, it is not always possible to start with Cross Tab.

Figure 7-19. Cross Tab and Transpose tools used together

These two tools are used for what many call "data shaping," which is getting the data set in a shape that is conducive to further analytical calculations. For example, you might have a data set where all your Date values are across the top. This makes it hard to do time series analysis. We want the dates going down the columns, not across. Maybe, in addition to having your dates across the top, you have a second row that is like a nested header and you want that to go across the data but it's tied to the date. You could use the Cross Tab and Transpose tools together to make that use case happen.

Arrange Tool

The Arrange tool allows you to manually transpose and rearrange data columns:

Although the Arrange tool isn't widely used, it has some useful features if you need data to be in an exact format for presentation. With this tool, data is transformed so that each row is turned into multiple rows. Columns can be created by using column description data (see Figure 7-20).

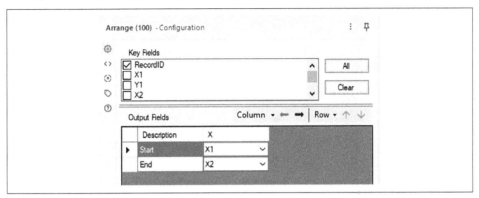

Figure 7-20. Arrange tool configuration

To see what we are doing here, it may help to see an example of the data going into the Arrange tool (see Figure 7-21).

RecordID	X1	Y1	X2	Y2
1	-105.180359	39.979225	-105.059509	39.88445
2	-104.993591	39.736762	-104.979858	39.797986
3	-104.900208	39.888665	-104.933167	39.852829
4	-105.005951	39.81592	-105.018997	39.803261
5	-104.985008	39.868115	-104.974022	39.85731
6	-105.082855	39.742042	-105.054016	39.740458
7	-104.935913	39.803261	-104.910507	39.789017
8	-104.990845	39.952385	-104.990845	39.912896
9	-104.942093	39.727785	-104.937973	39.763686
10	-105.123367	39.82805	-105.109634	39.826995

Figure 7-21. Arrange tool input

Now, with the configuration that you see in Figure 7-20, you would get an output that would look like Figure 7-22.

RecordID	Description	X
1	Start	-105.180359
1	End	-105.059509
2	Start	-104.993591
2	End	-104.979858
3	Start	-104.900208
3	End	-104.933167
4	Start	-105.005951
4	End	-105.018997
5	Start	-104.985008
5	End	-104.974022

Figure 7-22. Arrange tool output

Do you see how we created two Description values, Start and End, and paired them up? Every two rows are now a set. Also notice that because we didn't do anything with Y1 and Y2, those values were just dropped.

Count Records Tool

The Count Records tool is useful but frankly doesn't get much love because you can perform the same function in many other tools:

However, let's not throw it away just yet. It's a good tool to have because you can use it in situations where you need to check and validate that the right number of records came through. For example, the Count Records tool will return zero if no records are present. It simply counts the number of records and gives you that single value, and has no configuration (see Figure 7-23).

Figure 7-23. Count Records results

Running Total Tool

The Running Total tool has some great and useful features, but I would argue it loses its appeal, just like the Count Records tool, because the same tasks can be done in many other, more flexible tools, like the Multi-Row Formula tool. If all you need is the running total, then this is a tool you can use:

The Running Total creates exactly what it says: a running total per row of your data. You might use it if you need to see how a value is increasing as it goes down the rows. Its configuration is simple, too, in that you just select whether you want to Group By anything and then select the column you want to be totaled going down the rows (see Figure 7-24). In this example, we are looking at the quantity of Visits and Spend across customers.

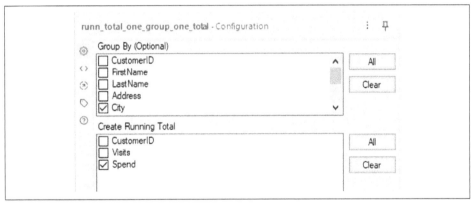

Figure 7-24. Running Total tool configuration

You can see we have selected to group the data by City and then create a running total of Spend. With those two values selected, we would see something like Figure 7-25.

Record	CustomerID	FirstName	LastName	Address	City	State	ZIP	CustomerSegment	Visits	Spend	RunTot_Spend
1	19	DOROTHY	COLE	6561 Welch Ct	ARVADA	CO	80004	Consumer	15	27,192.11	27,192.11
2	24	BELINDA	DEHERRERA	13492 W 67th Dr	ARVADA	CO	80004	Small Business	7	27,828.72	55,020.83
3	30	CYNTHIA	WYAT	9521 W 65th Ave	ARVADA	CO	80004	Small Business	7	2,810.48	57,831.31
4	33	LORENA	GEORGE	7141 Beech St	ARVADA	CO	80004	Home Office	4	3,311.71	61,143.02
5	41	ESTELLA	BICKFORD	6450 Urban St	ARVADA	CO	80004	Home Office	1	62.5	61,205.52
6	49	MARY	WETMORE	7998 W 82nd Pl	ARVADA	CO	80005	Corporate	6	3,413.87	64,619.39
7	57	KATIE	BILLS	6343 Moore Cir	ARVADA	CO	80004	Small Business	1	52.91	64,672.3

Figure 7-25. Running Total output

Notice we have a new column of data called "RunTot_Spend" that is cumulative as you go down the rows.

Weighted Average Tool

The Weighted Average tool is another tool that, like the Count Records and Running Total tools, can sometimes be overlooked since the same tasks can be completed in other tools. But to be honest, it's not as straightforward to accomplish these tasks in those other tools:

If you need to calculate a weighted average for, say, a group of products that exists in categories but the categories are not totally alike, I recommend using the Weighted Average tool. It makes this an easy activity (see Figure 7-26).

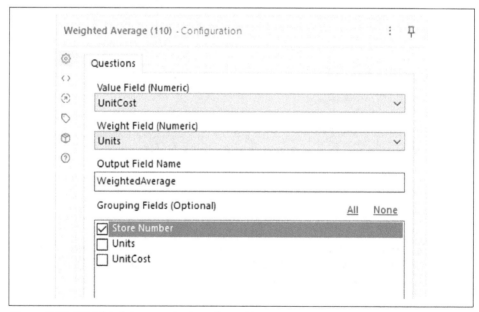

Figure 7-26. Weighted Average tool configuration

In the configuration, you can see that you have a Value Field. That is the field to be averaged. The Weight Field is the field you use to weigh the average. Lastly, you can choose to group by fields, if you like. For example, I will use this tool if I want to weigh the average for each specific store or location.

With this configuration, you can end up with a data set similar to Figure 7-27.

---

2 of 2 Fields ∨   ☑ ⊠   Cell Viewer ∨   ¶   10 records displayed

Record	Store Number	WeightedAverage	
1	100	624.812244	↘
2	101	980.027621	↘
3	102	855.731864	↘
4	103	1208.638587	↘
5	104	875.258855	↘
6	105	779.172378	↘
7	106	906.598712	↘
8	107	803.039937	↘
9	108	898.45375	
10	109	908.422381	↘

Figure 7-27. Weighted Average output

You may notice those red arrows again in Figure 7-27. This time, they're not showing up because we have missing data. When aggregations are done, rounding could occur. These red arrows appear when Alteryx is attempting to make you aware of which level decimal these numbers are being aggregated.

Make Columns Tool

This last tool we'll look at in this chapter is a secret, sneaky, and almost unknown tool. But, because you are reading this book, you are now going to learn about it. It's not even in the Transform tool palette! The Make Columns tool is hiding in the Laboratory tool palette, which we haven't yet discussed. It's a Transform tool, but it's never been put into the main Transform tool palette. It's useful and has helped me on a good number of tricky projects:

At its core, it allows you to move your data into the specified number of columns. It's very useful when you want to transform data that has a pattern, like every third row is the main subject or every tenth row is the beginning of a new record. You can specify if you want to arrange vertically or horizontally, and you can group fields (see Figure 7-28).

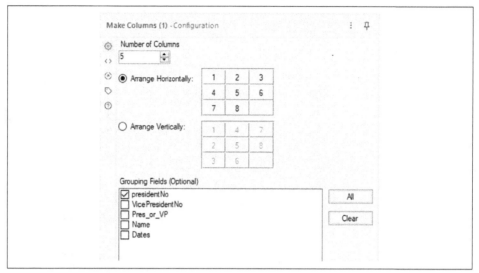

Figure 7-28. Make Columns tool configuration

In our earlier example, you can take a data set of the US Presidents and Vice Presidents and essentially make the President the main focus of each row. So, our data will go from what you see in Figure 7-29, to what you see in Figure 7-30.

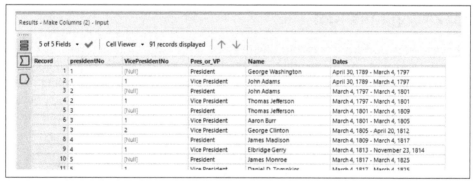

Figure 7-29. Data set before applying the Make Columns tool

Column_1_Pres_or_VP	Column_1_Name	Column_1_Dates
President	George Washington	April 30, 1789 - March 4, 1797
President	John Adams	March 4, 1797 - March 4, 1801
President	Thomas Jefferson	March 4, 1801 - March 4, 1809
President	James Madison	March 4, 1809 - March 4, 1817
President	James Monroe	March 4, 1817 - March 4, 1825
President	John Quincy Adams	March 4, 1825 - March 4, 1829
President	Andrew Jackson	March 4, 1829 - March 4, 1837
President	Martin Van Buren	March 4, 1837 - March 4, 1841
President	William Henry Harrison	March 4, 1841 - April 4, 1841
President	John Tyler	April 4, 1841 - March 4, 1845
President	James K. Polk	March 4, 1845 - March 4, 1849
President	Zachary Taylor	March 4, 1849 - July 9, 1850
President	Millard Fillmore	July 9, 1850 - March 4, 1853
President	Franklin Pierce	March 4, 1853 - March 4, 1857
President	James Buchanan	March 4, 1857 - March 4, 1861
President	Abraham Lincoln	March 4, 1861 - April 15, 1865
President	Andrew Johnson	April 15, 1865 - March 4, 1869

Figure 7-30. Data set after applying Make Columns tool

Now here's a trivia question for you! Who's the only president to have had three vice presidents? Who were they? Arranging the data this way will help you answer that question easily.

The Make Columns tool is such a great tool when you're faced with using Regex and other tools to parse out the data you need. Sometimes all you really need is the Make Columns tool.

Conclusion

Transforming your data is one of the most important, key skills you need to have when working with Designer, so if you find that you don't feel comfortable with any of the main tools we've covered in this chapter (Summarize, Cross Tab, and Transpose) then go back and practice using them. Make sure you know how they are used. Make sure to find ways to incorporate them into your workflows.

This chapter marks the end of Part II, where we've covered the basics of Designer. Congratulations on making it this far in your journey! We are now going to go beyond the basics. You will learn how to use more and more advanced items, from parsing tools to Reporting, In-Database tools, and even Connectors! The next part is probably the heaviest section in the book, but it will definitely take you to an advanced user level and allow you to do things in Designer you didn't even know were possible! Let's get to it.

Beyond the Basics

CHAPTER 8

Parsing Your Data

This chapter is the first in Part III of the book, which takes you beyond the basics. This part includes an action-packed eight chapters that are going to take you from a beginner just getting your feet wet to a full-fledged advanced user swimming in the deep end. You are going to learn how to parse even the most complex data to create attractive reports that are automated. We'll also cover in-database tools and how to document, test, debug, and optimize your workflows—topics that are important to understand to become an advanced Alteryx Design user.

While you may have heard of some of these topics, many are going to be completely new to you. Please stick with me. I assure you that if you can practice and put forth the effort, you will see positive results. These tools are advanced not because they are hard to learn but because they provide superior results, so if they seem challenging just remember: you've got this!

Call me silly, but parsing data is one of the areas of data engineering I love the most. I know a lot of advanced Alteryx users who love it, too. There is just something about turning a nasty, uncleaned, seemingly useless data set into something that can tell you the difference between a million-dollar opportunity and a dud. I suppose it's like the process of diamond cutting, since diamonds are found as rough, dirty rocks. Only until an expert diamond cutter analyzes, cleans, and cuts it does that diamond really show its true value.

Before we learn about the parsing tools in Designer, I first want you to understand what parsing is and what it means to parse your data.

What Is Parsing?

Alteryx Designer is considered to be one of the most flexible tools for working with data and it's in large part due to its capability to parse out data. Parsing data is simply the breaking a data value into parts that can be put into sensical data objects such as street, city, state, and zip code. That definition doesn't give justice to the frustration, challenges, and headaches that specific parsing projects can give.

What if you had to parse out the following?

> 12Avery 495.988525 23SANFORD Liquid Accent™ Tank-Style Highlighters13.0188522 33Xerox 196849.9288523 43Acme® Preferred Stainless Steel Scissors41.6488523 53V701446.6788523 63Xerox 1942011.6788524 73Canon S750 Color Inkjet Printer1451.3788526 85Global Troy™ Executive Leather Low-Back Tilter6362.8590193 95Xerox 1930113.2590197 106Kensington 6 Outlet MasterPiece® HOMEOFFICE Power Control Center1515.1790194

If you didn't have Designer, you would need to be a fairly advanced programmer because parsing this data wouldn't be easy. With Designer, however, it's simple. Once you're familiar with the tools at your disposal, you'll be able to use Designer to chew through problems like this left and right with very little issue. You might even come to like it as much as I do! Let's jump in and start learning the Parse tool palette.

The Parse tool palette (see Figure 8-1) may seem small but each of these tools can handle a pretty heavy list of chores!

Figure 8-1. The Parse tool palette

The Parse tools are built to help you break apart your data so that you can turn it into something valuable. Let's explore the individual tools you need to know to make parsing data a breeze!

Text To Columns Tool

The Text To Columns tool is a great utility tool that allows you to parse out data in many different situations:

Do you have an address all in one field? No problem. Do you have a big, long line of text separated by pipe delimiters? Again, no problem. The Text To Columns tool allows you to split your data based on what it contains—think commas, periods, pipe delimiters, even tabs and spaces (see Figure 8-2).

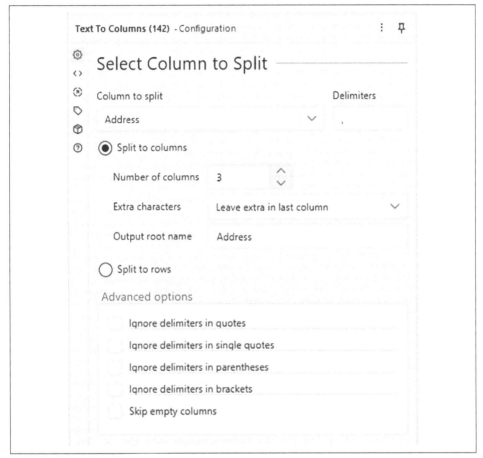

Figure 8-2. Text to Columns tool configuration

 Adding a space as the delimiter will work, but it's invisible and therefore not good for readability. Use the character "\s" instead.

In the tool's configuration, select the Column to split and the delimiter. The delimiter is crucial here because it allows you to be very precise but also flexible. You can put any character you want to split here (it must be a character, not a word), but you can also put any of the white space characters if you need to break apart your data based on spaces or tabs (see Table 8-1).

Table 8-1. White space characters

White space	White space character
Tab	\t
New line	\n
Space	\s
Space or tab	\s\t

Once you have the delimiter, you need to figure out whether you are going to split by columns or by rows. If you know that your data is three columns, then choose "Split to columns." If you have, for example, transactional data in a single row and it's 10 or 100 items (or maybe each row is a different amount), then absolutely use "Split to rows" because you don't know how many rows and want it to be dynamic. Imagine if you had to parse data but you didn't know how many columns were in your data set? You would likely have to keep trying and guessing how many columns you had, over and over again. The "Split to rows" option makes this easy.

If you add a Record ID tool to your canvas before you do the split, you can keep the rows in the same grouping. That way, when they split, you know which original row they came from and you can easily use the Summarize tool to aggregate them back to one row per ID again.

Remember, you also have some advanced options that allow you to ignore or skip certain elements. Sometimes these can come in handy if you have data that is just a bit messy and has extra characters. If you have a data set where you find that your data is parsing on the quotes in, say, a block of conversational text, then you can choose to ignore them. You can ignore quotes, single quotes, parentheses, and brackets as well as skip empty columns.

As I've said throughout the book, learning these tools and building your intuition about when you would need to use them takes time. Be patient and know you'll pick it all up with practice.

DateTime Tool

The DateTime tool is really nice because it handles dates, which are a key data type:

When you work with data long enough, you'll find that dates can be a real pain, and Alteryx is not flexible when it comes to interpreting dates and times. This data needs to be in a specific format, and this tool can convert it from multiple formats, as long as you can specify the pattern. For example, if you have dates coming from database in one format, but you need it in another, the DateTime tool allows you to parse it out into its individual pieces and put it back together. This tool is fairly easy to configure (see Figure 8-3).

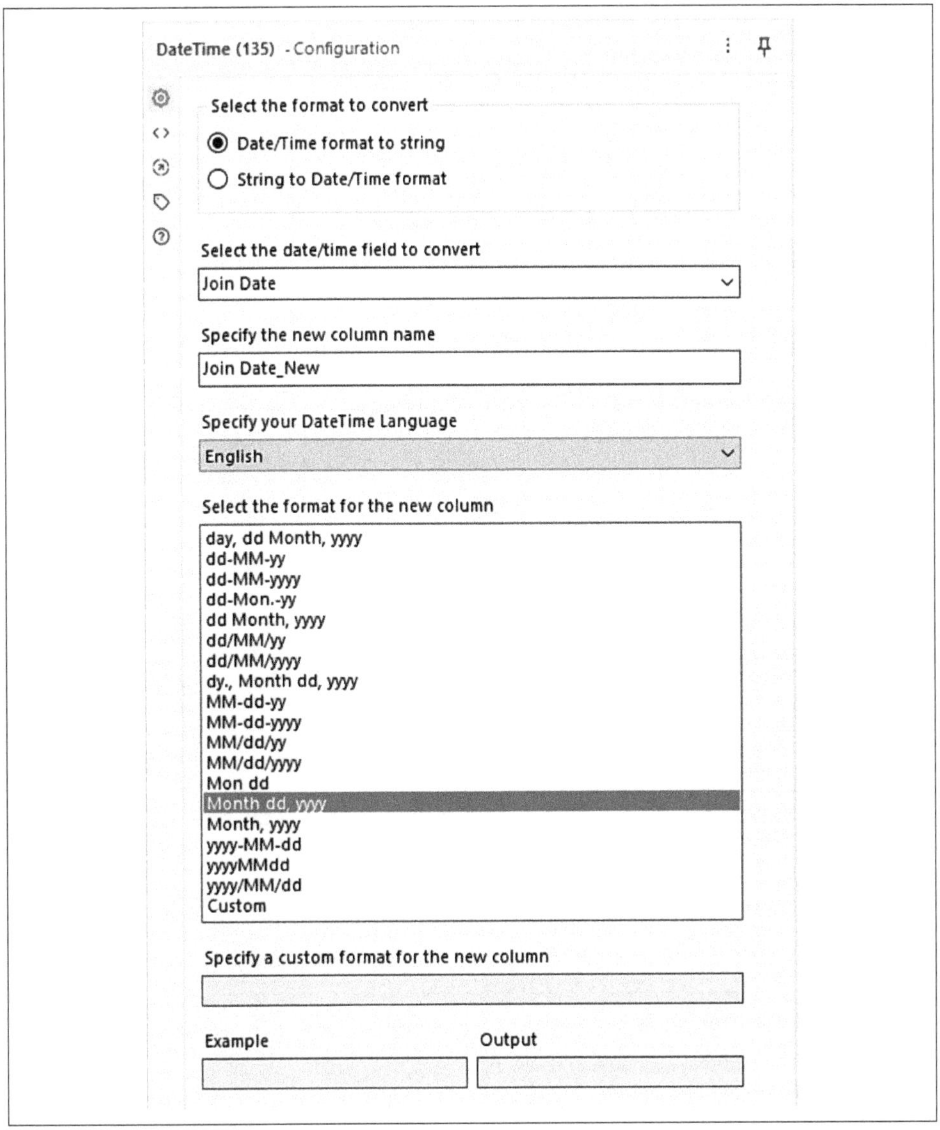

Figure 8-3. DateTime tool configuration

First, select the format you want to convert, then select the date/time field to convert. Specify what the new field name is going to be, and the DateTime language. If you select to convert Date/Time format to string, then you need to select the format you want the data *to be in*, not what *it is in*. If you are converting from string to date/time format, then you need to select the format of the string. You also have the option to customize your format if one of the formats doesn't fully match up.

As we touched on in Chapter 5, when we covered data types, it's important to remember that the DateTime data type is very specific in Alteryx. To work with dates, or do what is called *date math,* you need to ensure that the date fields are in the Alteryx format: YYYY-MM-DD HH:MM:SS.

> *Date math* refers to all the calculations you can do on dates, like calculating the difference between May 01, 2021 and Jan 04, 2021. Alteryx can do all kinds of calculations on dates in the Formula tool.

XML Parse Tool

The XML Parse tool allows you to not only parse out XML, but to select only those specific subsets of data you want:

Simply specify the XML field, and then select the XML element to parse and what you want to return (see Figure 8-4).

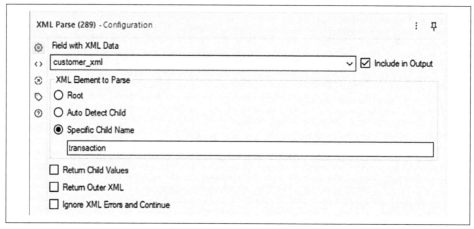

Figure 8-4. XML Parse tool configuration

Let's walk through the various XML elements to parse:

Root
> The base value of the main element, such as the `customer id` in Figure 8-5.

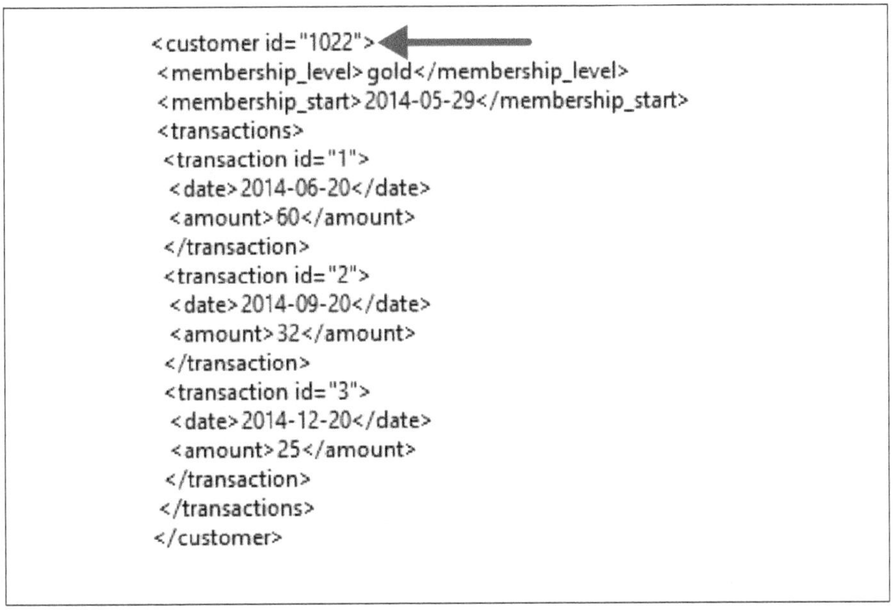

```
<customer id="1022">
  <membership_level>gold</membership_level>
  <membership_start>2014-05-29</membership_start>
  <transactions>
   <transaction id="1">
    <date>2014-06-20</date>
    <amount>60</amount>
   </transaction>
   <transaction id="2">
    <date>2014-09-20</date>
    <amount>32</amount>
   </transaction>
   <transaction id="3">
    <date>2014-12-20</date>
    <amount>25</amount>
   </transaction>
  </transactions>
</customer>
```

Figure 8-5. Root element

Auto Detect Child
> The auto-detected child of the XML block (see Figure 8-6).

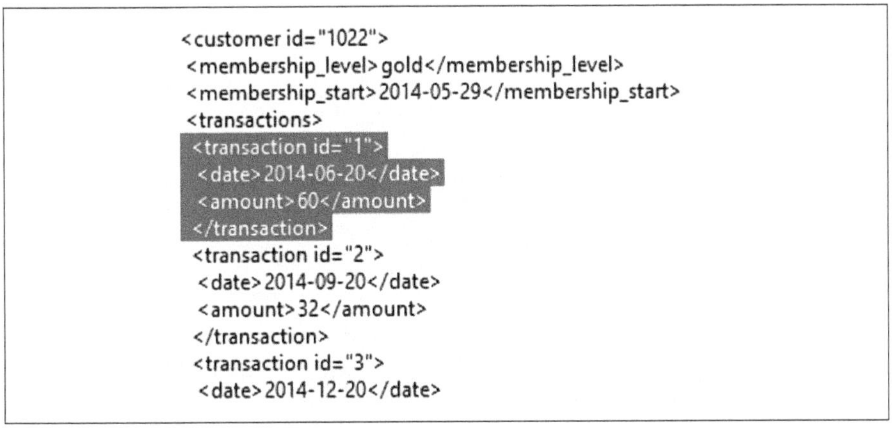

```
<customer id="1022">
  <membership_level>gold</membership_level>
  <membership_start>2014-05-29</membership_start>
  <transactions>
   <transaction id="1">
    <date>2014-06-20</date>
    <amount>60</amount>
   </transaction>
   <transaction id="2">
    <date>2014-09-20</date>
    <amount>32</amount>
   </transaction>
   <transaction id="3">
    <date>2014-12-20</date>
```

Figure 8-6. Auto Detect Child

Specific Child Name

Allows you to specify the exact element you want to parse out, such as "transaction."

Once you have decided which XML element to parse, you can pick what you want to return. You can Return Child Values or Return Outer XML. You also have a parameter to ignore any XML errors. XML Parse is one of those tools that you will likely use somewhat recursively. You may have 3 or 4 of them strung together to fully parse out every piece of data you need (see Figure 8-7).

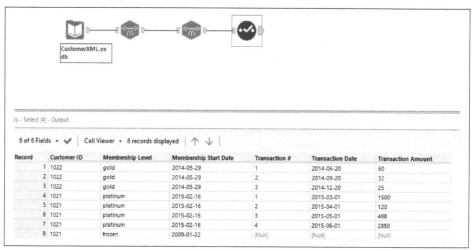

Record	Customer ID	Membership Level	Membership Start Date	Transaction #	Transaction Date	Transaction Amount
1	1022	gold	2014-05-29	1	2014-06-20	60
2	1022	gold	2014-05-29	2	2014-09-20	32
3	1022	gold	2014-05-29	3	2014-12-20	25
4	1021	platinum	2015-02-16	1	2015-03-01	1500
5	1021	platinum	2015-02-16	2	2015-04-01	120
6	1021	platinum	2015-02-16	3	2015-05-01	488
7	1021	platinum	2015-02-16	4	2015-06-01	2850
8	1021	frozen	2009-01-22	[Null]	[Null]	[Null]

Figure 8-7. XML parsing workflow

Now let's take a look at an amazing tool that most people shy away from at first glance: the RegEx tool.

RegEx Tool

The RegEx (regular expressions) tool is one of the most feared tools but is by far one of the most useful based on all the flexibility it provides:

RegEx is essentially used to identify patterns within your data. As it's a scripting language, that means you have nearly infinite ways to use it.

I know some longtime Alteryx users who have never tried to figure out the RegEx tool. I have also seen users run circles around others because they took the time to learn the RegEx tool and understand the power it holds. Do not pass this tool up. Devote an afternoon to understanding how it works and then commit to using it, as you can, in practice. To get started, let's first talk about regular expressions so you understand the main ideas on which this tool is based.

Regular Expressions

A regular expression is a sequence of characters that specifies a search pattern, such as the following:

- `<a .*?>.*?</a>`
- `([^,]*) (?:,|$)`
- `(?:R2D2)`

To the untrained eye, they look like a complete mess of characters, but someone well versed in RegEx would realize they are defined search patterns. Let's take that last sequence in the list and break it down so that you can see it's not a bunch of random characters. First off, in the search pattern `(?:R2D2)` there are two key pieces:

`(?:...)`
> This is the noncapturing group. A noncapturing group allows you to apply quantifiers to part of your RegEx but does not capture or assign an ID, meaning it doesn't allow you to identify it later with an ID.

`R2D2`
> This is the word we want to look for, specifically.

These searches on our data allow us to find a specific, maybe hard-to-find pattern in a string of data. Once we have identified it, we can choose to manipulate the pattern in many versatile ways. As you may know, regular expressions are used almost everywhere—in software systems, networking systems, and many more areas where finding patterns in data is needed, such as searching through computer log files.

As an Alteryx user, making use of RegEx means that you can match any possible pattern in your data, helping you avoid potential roadblocks. Imagine for a second if someone were to send you that same string from earlier:

> 12Avery 495.988525 23SANFORD Liquid Accent™ Tank-Style Highlighters13.0188522 33Xerox 196849.9288523 43Acme® Preferred Stainless Steel Scissors41.6488523 53V701446.6788523 63Xerox 1942011.6788524 73Canon S750 Color Inkjet Printer1451.3788526 85Global Troy™ Executive Leather Low-Back Tilter6362.8590193 95Xerox 1930113.2590197 106Kensington 6 Outlet MasterPiece® HOMEOFFICE Power Control Center1515.1790194

Instead of stressing out and throwing your hands in the air or giving up, you can immediately start looking for the pattern. You know that if you can find a pattern, you can clean it up. You can parse it. That's the power of RegEx and the Parsing tools in Designer. Ninety-nine percent of all data has patterns in it that you can exploit. One of the differences between an expert and an advanced or novice Designer user is how they use the tools at their disposal to find those patterns, including the RegEx tool.

Now, before we get too far ahead of ourselves, I want to give a very simple lesson on building RegEx strings outside of Alteryx so that you have more context as you go through this section.

How to Build RegEx Strings with RegEx101

All the features and functions of the RegEx tool rely on one fundamental thing: the search pattern, or the actual regular expression. We need to be able to write those in order to utilize this tool, so I recommend using the RegEx101 site (*https:// regex101.com*). It will make your life a lot easier in the process of writing and learning RegEx.

I use RegEx101 nearly every time I am working on regular expressions. It is an incredible tool that simplifies a lot of the work in building regular expressions, and it has contributed to my understanding of the topic. This site helps you to write and test a regular expression on a small sample data set. Let me run through an example so you can see how I would use it. Let's use a set of addresses for our example (see Figure 8-8).

Figure 8-8. RegEx101 example

In Alteryx, we'll parse those values, including the address elements, into different fields. I created a search pattern to do this using RegEx101 (see Figure 8-9).

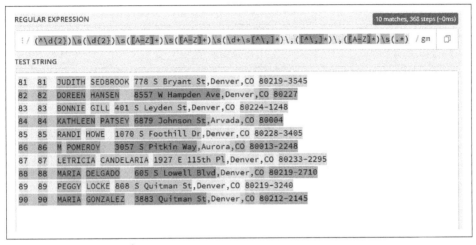

Figure 8-9. RegEx search pattern

Now, this may not be the most efficient way, but I want you to see that the power of RegEx101 is that you start to write these expressions and you can immediately see whether you are finding what you want or not. Now, let's put this into Alteryx. I am going to copy the regular expression and put it into the RegEx tool with the Parse option (see Figure 8-10).

You can see that I went from a single field of data and, based on my RegEx expression, was able to parse out each of the eight fields. Imagine for a moment how difficult this would be in many other tools. You can easily parse out data in 1 tool that others may build out in 10!

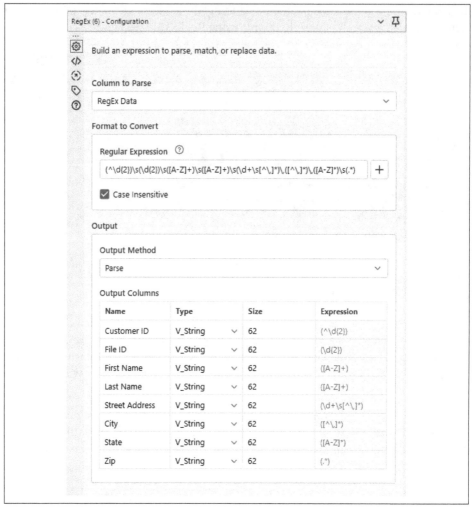

Figure 8-10. Address parse using the RegEx tool

Now that you know what RegEx is, let's deep dive into using the RegEx tool!

Using the RegEx Tool

There aren't many configuration options for the RegEx tool but the ones that you have can produce quite significant results (see Figure 8-11).

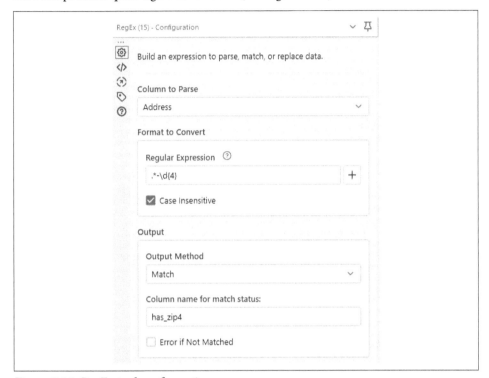

Figure 8-11. RegEx tool configuration

The first item is the "Column to Parse." This is simply the column you are going to apply the regular expression to. The next item is the actual Regular Expression that you came up with. There is a plus sign to the right of the text box, which brings up a drop-down list of many common regular expressions you can use. I will walk you through how to build your own RegEx strings shortly.

Before you have the regular expression written, first decide in which format you need your output. This output component is important. You have four options: Replace, Tokenize, Parse, and Match (see Figure 8-12).

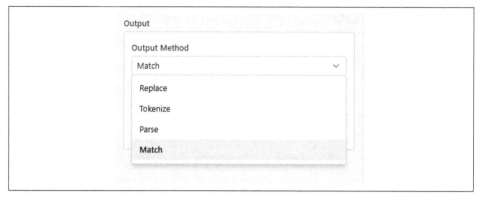

Figure 8-12. RegEx output

Replace

By selecting the Replace output option, you are replacing the regular expression you searched for with a second expression (see Figure 8-13).

Figure 8-13. RegEx Replace

You'll see how powerful this is in the next section, where we will discuss how you can mark specific groups of a pattern within your data and then use those marks as a reference to replace that value.

Tokenize

By using the Tokenize option, you can split data based on the regular expression you create (see Figure 8-14).

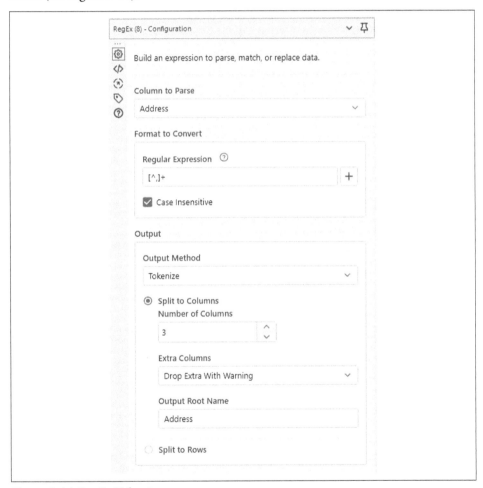

Figure 8-14. RegEx Tokenize

Tokenize captures a repeating pattern and parses it. This is similar to the Text to Columns/Rows tool, except that with Tokenize you focus on the data pattern rather than the separator/delimiter. This is great for things like telephone numbers, addresses, and other items that parse to a well-defined number of columns. However, if you have a pattern in the data and are splitting by that pattern but aren't sure how many columns of data it might be, you can use the "Split to Rows" option.

Parse

The Parse option is extremely useful as it allows you to not only look for multiple patterns but also have each of those patterns output to a different named column with specific data types and sizes. Notice in Figure 8-15 that each output field is defined by a set of parentheses.

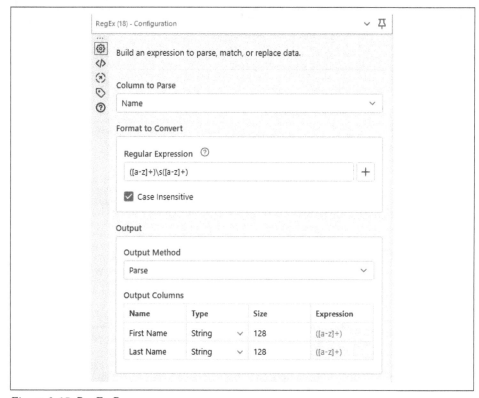

Figure 8-15. RegEx Parse

With one tool and one regular expression, you could potentially parse an entire data set. Wild.

Match

The Match option is a lot like Replace but instead of actually replacing the value, it returns a Boolean value of true or false based on whether it was able to find the value from your regular expression (see Figure 8-16).

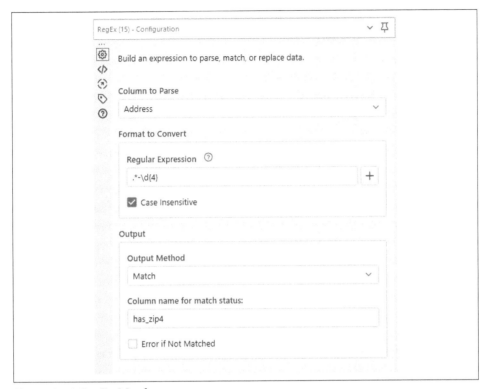

Figure 8-16. RegEx Match

This is great for validation and confirming that something is or is not in your data. You're learning the various aspects of the RegEx Tool, but there may be times when you need help determining what the RegEx should be and look like. For that, we can turn to parsing using the Formula tools.

Parsing Using the Formula Tools

Parsing isn't something that is constrained to the RegEx or Parsing tools. You can use any of the Formula tools to do parsing, as well, and you can even use regular expressions in your formulas! One of the things that I really love is the ability to use regular expressions from the Formula tool. You can build formulas based off of regular expressions, but you can also write more of them in one tool, which in turn makes a complex area of your workflow feel simpler and become easier to understand by other users and leadership.

If you go into the Formula tool and search for "RegEx," you will see the three RegEx formulas (see Figure 8-17).

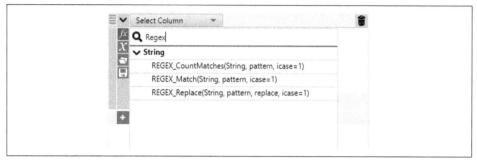

Figure 8-17. Parsing in the Formula tool

You already know that RegEx can handle specific and complicated patterns. You can build a Formula expression that looks something like what is shown in Figure 8-18 for replacing values in your data.

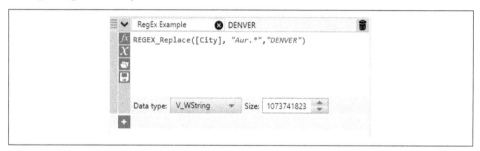

Figure 8-18. REGEX_Replace

The features that the Text to Columns tool provides aren't really portable to the Formula tool. You'd have to create each individual formula expression for each of the fields you want to parse.

However, you can find tons of functions available in the Date and DateTime function groups (see Figure 8-19).

If you want a handy reference to all the functions, and specifically the DateTime functions, check out the documentation (*https:// oreil.ly/By2l8*).

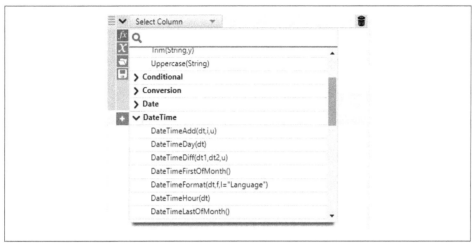

Figure 8-19. DateTime functions

DateTime formulas will tap you on the shoulder many times as you build out workflows. You'll find that they are helpful in taking rather complex or complicated parsing and making it as simple as calling a function. Get used to using them when it makes sense to.

Many advanced users prefer parsing dates using formula functions over the DateTime tool because it allows them to work on fields directly and doesn't create a new field. The DateTime tool creates a new column and then you have to deal with that instead.

Conclusion

Parsing data can be a real challenge, but in Alteryx it's an approachable and straightforward process. Although it does take a little bit of time to learn about regular expressions, they will make all the difference for you. The power you have with the RegEx tool is unmatched by any other tool in Designer. The DateTime tool is critical for helping you parse through dates easily. The XML Parse tool allows you to pull out values quickly from an XML data set. The Text to Columns/Rows tool is essential for breaking your data up into the various fields in the easiest way possible. All of these tools help you to parse your data into formats that are easier to present in reports or that you can more easily work with to process and clean for analysis purposes. Remember, you can also do parsing in Formula tools if it makes sense for your task. This allows you to use the benefits of building formula expressions.

In the next chapter, we are going to switch gears for a moment and learn how to build reports, based on our data, that can be fully automated and delivered to thousands of users.

CHAPTER 9

Reporting

The Reporting tools in Alteryx allow you to build fully automated, pixel-perfect reports and output in formats like PDF, HTML, Excel, Word, and even PowerPoint. You can add charts and maps, as well as tables of data and text, and then order these snippets exactly how you want them. Some examples of the reports and outputs you could build include:

- An HTML page that changes frequently based on data
- A weekly or monthly PowerPoint presentation
- A marketing brochure that is delivered via PDF or Word
- A product catalog with images and text

The number of ways to make different types of reports can be overwhelming. In this chapter, I will walk you through the Reporting tools first so you understand which tool does what. I will cover the element tools that create the snippets you will put into a report, then I will use the various layout tools to organize those snippets. I'll also show you how to output those reports into the various formats. Lastly, I'll walk through an example so that you can see all the pieces working together. Let's get started!

The Reporting tool palette (see Figure 9-1) includes all the Reporting tools that you will need to build everything from simple to highly complex and formatted reports.

Figure 9-1. The Reporting tool palette

I like to think of the Reporting tools as falling into roughly three categories—elements, layout, and output—which all build off of each other. Remember, you can always spot the Reporting tools by their nice orange color and page outline shape:

Let's now deep dive into the report elements, which are the tools that will help you build the pieces of a report.

Report Elements

Report elements are those tools that provide the fundamental building blocks—like a chart, a graphic, or data—to the report. Reports in Alteryx Designer aren't like a dashboard with lots of flashy items for exploratory analysis. They are meant for those users who know what they want, and want it every day, week, or month. Say you want a one-page PDF report on the status of your business emailed to you every morning. That would be a good use case. Let's say you have, like I did, a 100-slide presentation in PowerPoint that takes you weeks to build each time, and you want that automated, monthly, and divided up by five geographies. That would be an even better use case. These Reporting tools have the potential to eliminate thousands of hours of time wasted on building a report manually. Let's say you have a 15-tab Excel report that is highly formatted. You can completely automate it using the Reporting tools in Alteryx.

It's important to understand that when you are building a report, the tools are essentially converting your data into HTML objects behind the scenes. When we get into these tools a bit deeper, you will realize that you can modify these HTML snippets to your liking.

Let's see how these tools work so that we can start to build amazing reports.

Image Tool

The Image tool is fairly straightforward:

It allows you to not only add images to reports but also to bring images into your data set, meaning it doesn't have to be tied to the creation of a report. You can add a corresponding image to each row of your data that shows a product, for example, so that users see a related image when they query the data.

Any image you want to use could be taken from a folder of files at runtime, or a static image could even be stored in the workflow. The tool does not require an input connection and supports PNG, JPEG, and GIF file formats (see Figure 9-2).

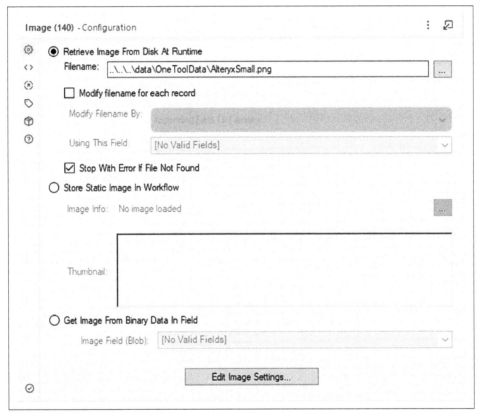

Figure 9-2. Image tool configuration

Configuring the tool isn't difficult. You have three main options:

Retrieve an image from disk at runtime
> With the option to retrieve an image from disk, you have flexibility in that you can pull as many images as you want. Say, for example, you have a list of products and you have a row of data for each of those products. You could pull a unique image for each one of those products.

Store an image in the workflow
> An image can be saved with the workflow so that the workflow can be shared as a single file. The image file size is added to the workflow file size.

Get an image from binary data of a field

   If you need to process image data, you could use Alteryx to turn that binary data into an actual JPEG or PNG, for example.

Users will often use the Image tool to add an image to the header of a report, like a logo or banner (see Figure 9-3).

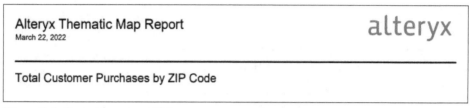

Figure 9-3. Report banner with logo

Like many of the tools that you've learned about already, most of the power in the Image tool will come from your own creativity in how you want to use it. Let's now look at how we could create more interactive and data-driven charts for your reports using the Interactive Chart tool.

Interactive Chart Tool

The Interactive Chart tool helps you create interactive bar charts, line graphs, scatter plots, and pie charts:

These charts allow you to make your reports so much more compelling and data driven.

   We call this tool *interactive* because you can make changes and see the difference in the chart you are creating without having to run the workflow.

These charts and graphs can be used standalone or they can be included as part of a larger report. This tool can be a bit tricky, as it uses a newer form of UI than what we have covered previously—a pop-out window. It also offers tons of options for building charts. Let's go through these options.

Building an interactive bar chart

To begin building an interactive bar chart, you need to perform these three steps:

1. Bring the data you want to use for the bar chart into your workflow.
2. Connect the data to an Interactive Chart tool.
3. Click Configure Chart in the tool Configuration window.

Once you have the chart open, you will see something like Figure 9-4.

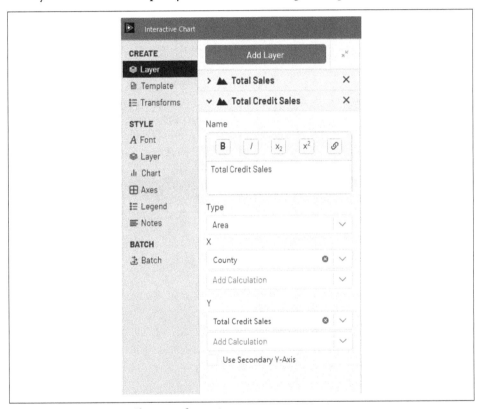

Figure 9-4. Interactive Chart configuration

On the left, you'll see a handful of features and options. Let's go through each one.

Create a layer. Interactive charts are built in layers, which you then format. You can have as many layers as you want. When you add a layer to your chart, there are a few things to specify:

- Name the layer so it's clear what that layer is for.
- Pick the type of chart (such as Area, Bar, Line, or Scatter).
- Depending on the graph type you choose, you might have some other options, like Orientation.
- Pick the X and Y variables that will provide the data for your chart. You can add a calculation to how that X or Y value is displayed. For example, instead of counting the number of instances, you could sum them.

Create a template. If you plan to build relatively complex charts and graphs regularly, it is a good idea to save them as a template so that you can avoid having to do all of the configuration over and over. You can then import those saved templates next time you want to build a chart. It's as simple as going to the Template section, typing the name of the template you want to save, and clicking Save (see Figure 9-5).

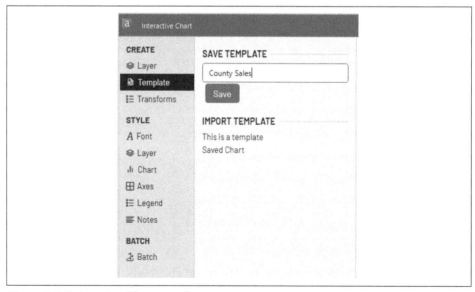

Figure 9-5. Interactive Chart template

Create transforms. Transforms allow you to split out the different data elements in order to format the chart at a more granular level. For example, you could split by Region and you'd see the same data but formatted by each element of the Region (see Figure 9-6). You can format the elements differently in the Style Layer, which we cover next.

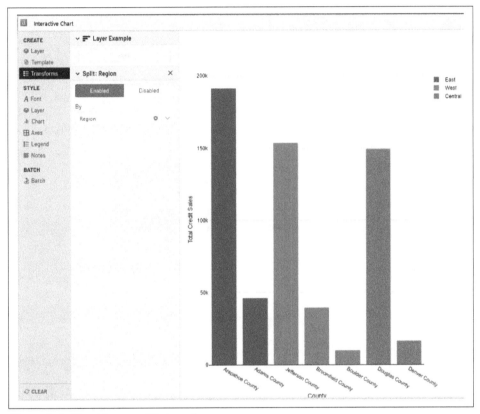

Figure 9-6. Chart layers with transforms

Style fonts.   The Font feature simply allows you to modify the global font style that is used in the chart (see Figure 9-7).

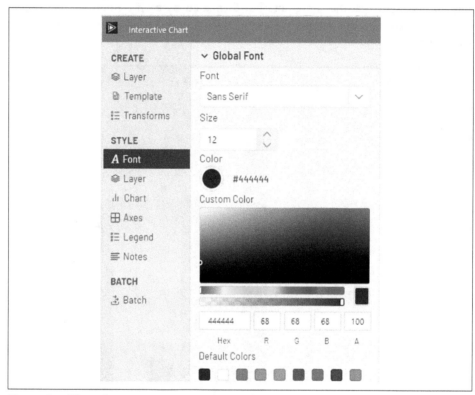

Figure 9-7. Chart font

Style layers. The Layer option in the Style section allows you to format the entire chart more specifically. If you've used the Transforms feature, it allows you to format each individual chart that is available, potentially having very different chart views for different slices of the same data. Notice in Figure 9-8 how you could style the layers of a chart for Total Sales.

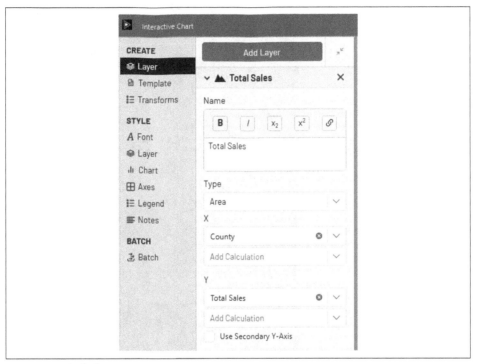

Figure 9-8. Style layers

Style charts. The Chart option allows you to configure the overall chart display. You can set the size units, width, height, background color, margins and padding, as well as hover text and title (see Figure 9-9).

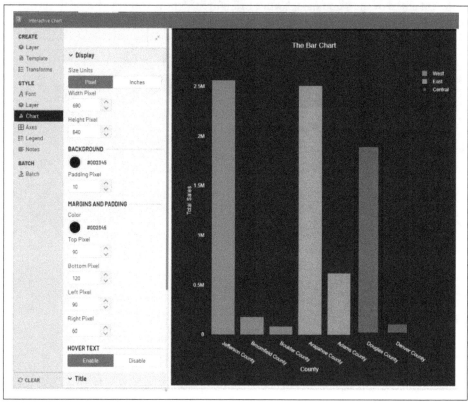

Figure 9-9. Style charts

Style axes. The Axes option allows you to specify how your axes labels and titles are going to be displayed (see Figure 9-10). You can set the title here as well as the display range (you would want to use this if you had too much data to display).

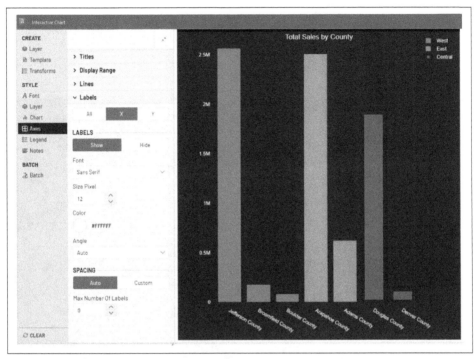

Figure 9-10. Chart axes

Style legends. The Legend option simply lets you configure how you want to display the legend on the chart (see Figure 9-11).

You can move many items on the chart by simply clicking and dragging them, and you can edit the text by clicking on it.

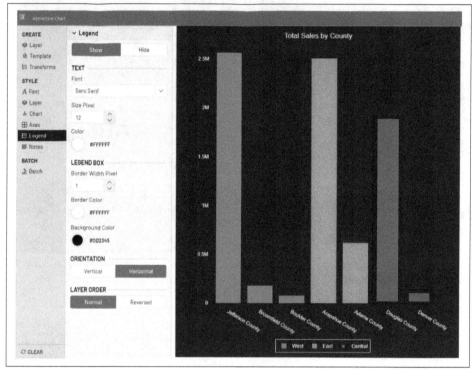

Figure 9-11. Chart legend

Style notes. The Notes option allows you to put customized notes onto the chart (such as pointing out where the data shows a trend in increasing sales, for example). This is a great feature that can help make the chart more compelling and easier to understand (see Figure 9-12).

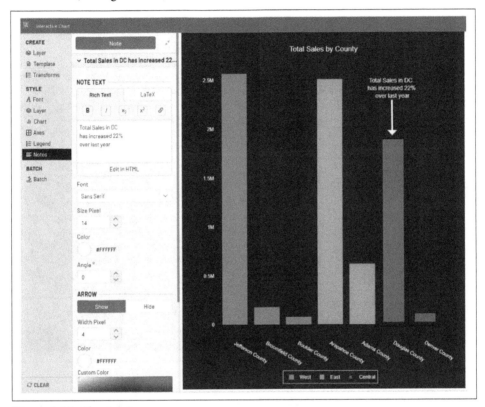

Figure 9-12. Chart notes

Batch. The Batch feature allows you to split the chart by a field value of your choosing. How many batches get created depends on how many categories exist in your data. Each batched report is output as a separate record in your workflow (see Figure 9-13).

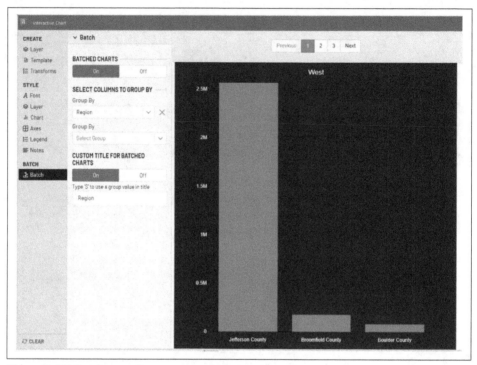

Figure 9-13. Batch reporting

There are a lot of options involved in building an interactive chart, but remember that you can save the chart as a template if you are doing a lot of configurations. Remember to use visual best practices in building your charts—they can become something that is great to look at while also showcasing the story of the data. Let's keep moving and learn about how to put headers and footers on our reports.

Report Footer Tool

The Report Footer tool allows you to set a text footer on each page of your report:

It also allows you to add page numbers (see Figure 9-14).

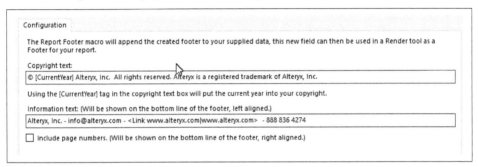

Figure 9-14. Report Footer tool configuration

Now, let's look at the topside and learn how to put a header on our report.

Report Header Tool

Like the Report Footer tool, the Report Header tool allows you to set a header on each page of your report:

You can include the title, date, and an image if you like (see Figure 9-15).

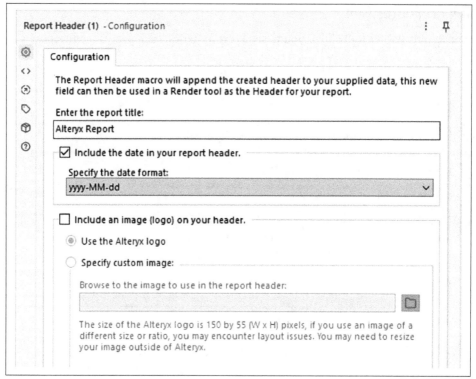

Figure 9-15. Report Header tool configuration

Report Map Tool

The Report Map tool is quite useful, as it creates map visualizations for your reports:

When you use the Report Map tool, you are creating map elements with data that will become part of your report presentation. This enables you to more accurately showcase spatial location data, like states or cities, instead of only using charts and graphs.

It is a highly customizable tool with many features that allow you to display spatial data easily and beautifully. Figure 9-16 shows an example of a thematic map that could be created using the Report Map tool.

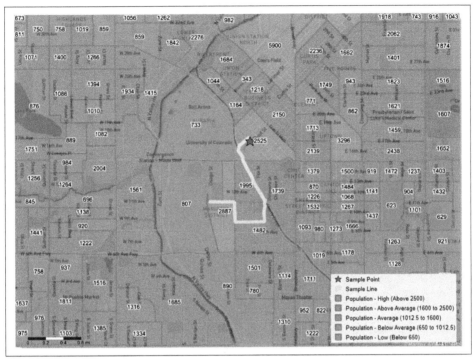

Figure 9-16. Thematic map

There are quite a lot of features that I'd like to cover to ensure you are able to create your own map elements. They fall under four tabs: Settings, Data, Layers, and Legend. Let's look at each of those four tab settings a bit more.

Settings

The Settings configuration tab allows you to set many different aspects of your map. The settings you can adjust are:

Map Size
    Choose how big the map is overall.

Resolution
    Choose which level of resolution can be used.

Scale
    Choose the scale of the map (None, Feet, Meters, Miles, and Kilometers).

Reference Base Map
    Choose which background the data elements lie on top of.

Background Color
    If you are not using a Reference Base Map, you can color the background of the map.

Map Drop Shadow
    Create the entire map with a drop shadow.

Expand Extent
    Expand or contract the zoom level.

Data

The Report Map tool is one of those special tools that can take in multiple data sources. You can identify these tools by noting that the input anchor is different in both shape and color. Notice the two white arrows on the anchor, as well (see Figure 9-17).

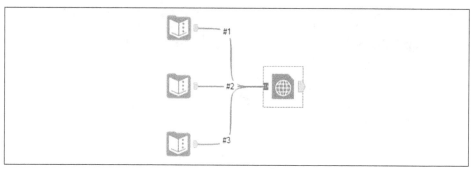

Figure 9-17. Report Map input anchor

This will allow you to create multiple layers of different data sets on your map. Each of your incoming connections from tools will be numbered, and those numbers will correspond to the incoming connections you see in the Data tab.

You can also bring data into the tool directly from a file using the File Connections feature. You can specify the Spatial Field to be used and the field that will act as the label for that spatial object (see Figure 9-18).

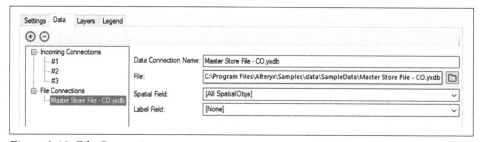

Figure 9-18. File Connections

Layers

The Layers tab allows you to configure multiple layers on your map. If you want to display trade areas (which we explain in more detail in Chapter 14) but also display points within those trade areas, you can use multiple layers (see Figure 9-19).

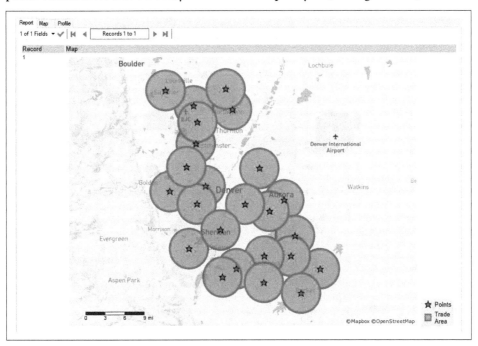

Figure 9-19. Multiple map layers

You can add a layer by clicking on the plus sign and selecting one of the three types of layers: Points, Lines, or Polygons (see Figure 9-20).

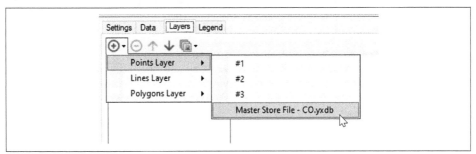

Figure 9-20. Three types of layers

Let's take a moment to cover what the three types of Layers look like. You saw what a Polygons layer looks like in Figure 9-16, where each data element is a polygon of that zip code. You also saw what a Points layer looks like in Figure 9-19, where each red star is a point representing the center of a trade area. Now, Figure 9-21 shows what a Lines layer looks like.

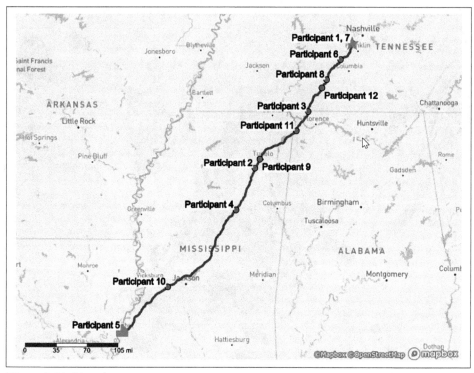

Figure 9-21. Lines layer

Once you click one of the layers, you will see a new item in the list that you can configure further for formatting (see Figure 9-22). Each of your layers will connect to one of the data connections you created in the Data tab.

 The order in which you build layers matters! The top layer in your list corresponds to the topmost layer in your chart. If you find that you have data on that map but you're unable to see it, then look to change the order of the layers by using the up and down arrows.

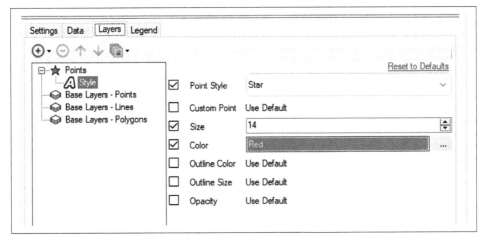

Figure 9-22. Formatting a Points layer

You can have as many layers as you need.

Legend

The Legend tab allows you to fully modify how the legend appears on your map. You can change the position, background color, text color, font, font size, icon width and height, as well as add comma separators (see Figure 9-23).

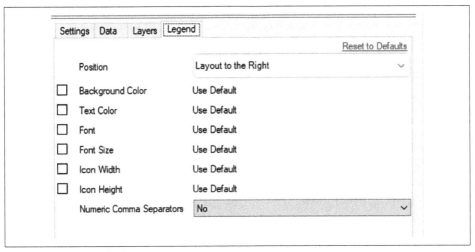

Figure 9-23. Legend tab

There are many things you can do with the Report Map tool and, before I move on, I want to mention just a few ideas that might spur your imagination to create some amazing visualizations. You can create things such as:

- Indexed maps
- Heat maps
- Thematic maps

- Reference maps
- Density maps
- Travel/time maps

Figure 9-24 shows you an example of a map that was built using the Report Map tool, which conveys average rainfall totals in Texas.

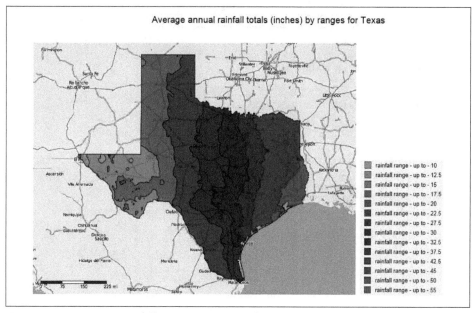

Figure 9-24. Average rainfall in Texas

Let's now look more closely at how we can work with our map legends using the Map Legend Splitter tool and the Map Legend Builder tool.

Map Legend Splitter Tool

The Map Legend Splitter tool is simple and has a single key feature tied to it:

An important point that I touched on briefly in the beginning of this chapter is about what these tools are actually doing. When you pass data through Reporting tools, they are taking that data and wrapping it in HTML code in order to build a presentable object like a data table, map, or chart. What that really means to you is that even if the data you feed into the tool is now in HTML, it's still data. It's still modifiable. The Map Legend Splitter and the Report Map tools are a perfect use case for this idea. The Map Legend Splitter tool allows you to take a legend that was created by the Report Map tool and split it into its value parts. This might not seem like an important thing but splitting the legend allows you to modify it to appear exactly how you want it.

Figure 9-25 shows a simple map built with a legend.

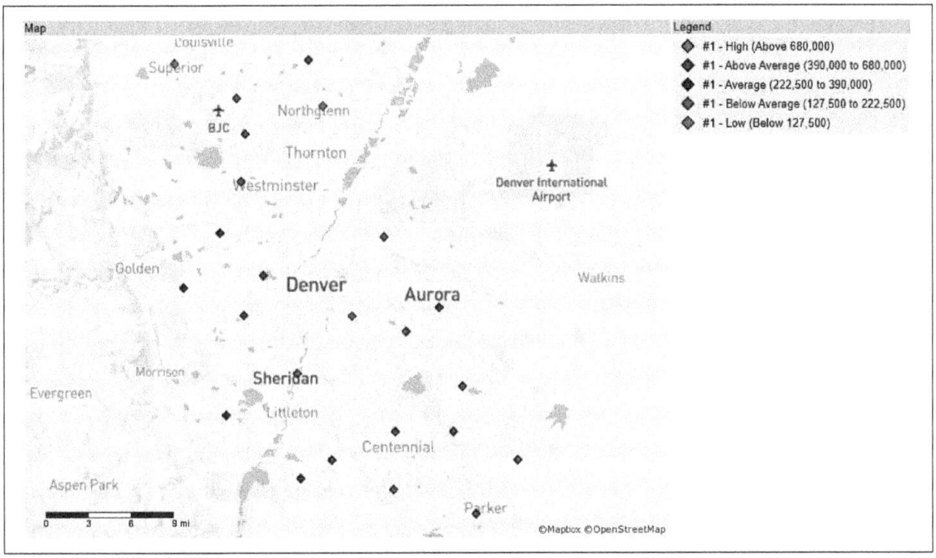

Figure 9-25. Legend example

What if, in this use case, we didn't want the "#1 -" in front of each individual element? Well, we don't have to settle! We can modify it. By building a workflow to first build the map, then using the Map Legend Splitter tool, we can pull out those legend items so that we can modify them (see Figure 9-26).

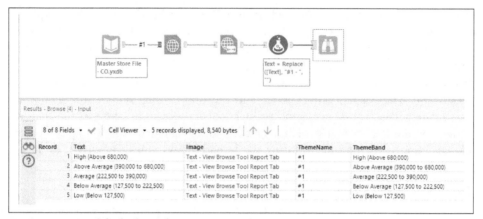

Figure 9-26. Modify the legends

Notice in column 1 ("Text") that the "#1 -" part of each record has been removed using the Formula tool in the Preparation tool palette. There are a handful of other elements that are modifiable as well when you use the Map Legend Splitter tool, but what if we want to lay it on top of the map we originally built? How do we do that? We use the Map Legend Builder tool, of course.

Map Legend Builder Tool

The Map Legend Builder tool allows you to do the opposite of the Map Legend Splitter tool to put together the components of a legend:

The expectation with this tool is that you have built a legend from your data and you are ready to finalize it and lay it on top of the map you've created.

 Make sure you pay attention to how similar these tools' icons look. Always remember the Map Legend Splitter tool has the arrows facing outward, versus the Map Legend Builder tool that has the arrows facing inward.

If we simply build off of what we did in the previous section using the Map Legend Splitter tool, we can just add the Map Legend Builder tool to bring the updates we made to the legend back into the map (see Figure 9-27).

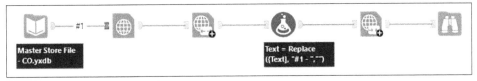

Figure 9-27. Build the legend

When you are building your legends, it's always easier to use the Map Legend Splitter tool first as it will give you the fields (text, image, text style, and image style) you need to build your legends in the configuration (see Figure 9-28).

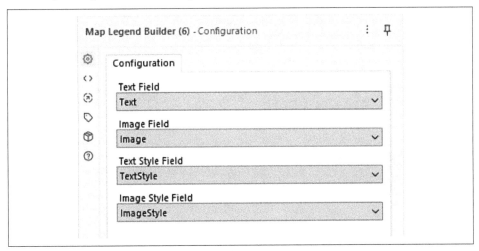

Figure 9-28. Map Legend Builder tool configuration

If you are not modifying a preexisting legend, you can build one from scratch dynamically—just make sure you have these four fields, shown in Figure 9-28, accounted for.

Once you get into building more and more maps, legends will be an important part of your map-building journey, specifically because they help make your maps pop! If you look at any of your map legends and see boring bullet points or just text, know that you can get as creative as you want.

Report Text Tool

The Report Text tool is useful when you need to create highly formatted text elements for your reports or emails:

With this tool, you can create fields from scratch and therefore are not required to have an input into this tool. You can also convert existing fields into report snippets. Lastly, you have the option to use Expert mode, which allows you to specify exactly the layout of text you want. Let's walk through some of these options.

Create a new field

In Figure 9-29, you can see that we have selected "Create new field for this text" in the Text Mode and we have named our Field "Title." Once we have set the Text Mode, we can configure the Text Data section.

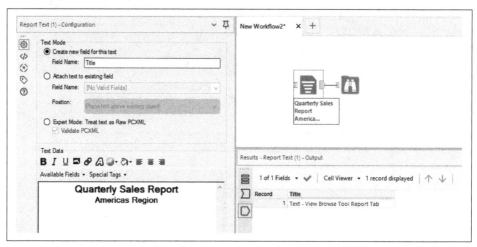

Figure 9-29. Report Text tool configuration

This is where you can configure exactly what the text is going to look like. This doesn't need to be a title or header. It could be a paragraph of data, like maybe a disclaimer or a description of a chart.

The features you have available here are:

- Bold
- Italicize
- Underline
- Add an image
- Add a hyperlink
- Font
- Text color
- Fill color
- Left, center, and right alignment

We'll see in the next example what happens when you have available fields. You also have Special Tags that can be used (see Figure 9-30).

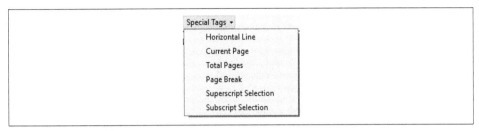

Figure 9-30. Special Tags

Attach text to existing field

With the "Attach text to existing field" option, you can add text or images to a report snippet that is already created (see Figure 9-31).

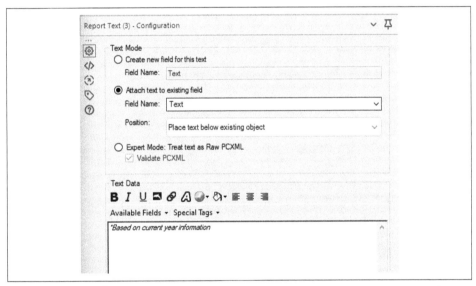

Figure 9-31. Attach text

This allows you to simply append additional text either above, below, left, or right of the original text object, image, chart, or table.

Expert Mode

Expert Mode allows you to put the PCXML (HTML and CSS) directly into the Report Text tool to create a report element (see Figure 9-32).

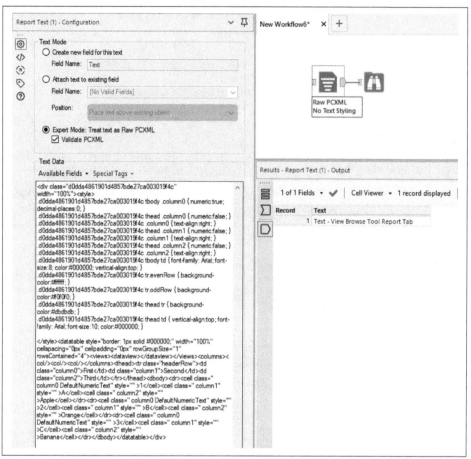

Figure 9-32. Report Text tool using Expert Mode

PCXML

PCXML, as we discussed earlier in the book, is Alteryx's proprietary file output for-mat—the software provides a standard reporting structure across all of its products. The main idea to remember is that these reporting tools are ingesting your data and building it within the PCXML in order for it to be displayed as HTML. You will see PCXML is only in the Reporting Tools within Alteryx Designer. Knowing that this exists and that you have options like Expert Mode will enable you to jump in and build or modify anything to your heart's desire.

Table Tool

The Table tool creates a table element that can be put into a report. It is one of the most commonly used reporting tools and one of the most robust in terms of features:

There are thousands of ways to format tables. I'll cover the main features in this section. With a little creativity, you will see how to use all the options (see Figure 9-33).

Table (9) - Configuration

Table Mode ● Basic ○ Pivot (CrossTab)

Group By
- Store Num
- Address
- City
- State
- ZIP
- Lat
- Lon
- County
- Region
- Total Sales
- Credit Sales
- Total Customers
- Avg Sales per Customer
- Perf Indicator

All

Clear

Table Configuration

Table Width | Percentage | 100 % |

Pivot Style

☐ Bar Graph | Lat | Settings...

☑ Show Column Headings

Per Column Configuration

☑ Store Num
☑ Address
☑ City
☑ State
☑ ZIP
☑ Lat
☑ Lon
☑ County
☑ Region
☑ Total Sales
☑ Credit Sales
☑ Total Customers
☑ Avg Sales per Customer
☑ Perf Indicator
☑ Dynamic or Unknown Fields

Rename Field
Width   Automatic
Alignment (H) Center
Borders   None
Prefix
Suffix
Dec. Places 0
Column Rules Create...

Default Table Settings...   Create Row Rule...

Figure 9-33. Table tool configuration

Table Mode

Table Mode has two main options: Basic and Pivot (Cross Tab). Basic allows you to create standard tables of your data, with the option to create multiple tables broken out by a field using the Group By checkboxes.

Figure 9-34 shows you what a standard table looks like.

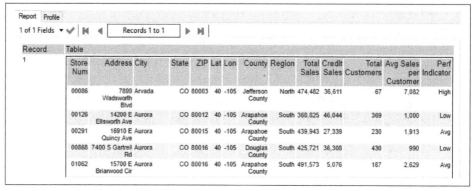

Figure 9-34. Standard table

> The Group By checkboxes don't aggregate; they group values together and create separate tables for each of the unique values.

Using the Group By checkboxes, you get separated tables that look like what you see in Figure 9-35.

The Pivot (Cross Tab) table allows you to create aggregated pivot tables with the help of a Cross Tab tool (see Figure 9-36).

Record Table

1

Store Num	City	Address	State	ZIP	County	Region
00086	Arvada	7899 Wadsworth Blvd	CO	80003	Jefferson County	North
02322	Broomfield	1660 W Midway Blvd	CO	80020	Broomfield County	North
05077	Edgewater	1985 Sheridan Blvd	CO	80214	Jefferson County	North
07244	Lakewood	14500 W Colfax Ave Unit B1	CO	80401	Jefferson County	North
07259	Lakewood	456 S Vance St	CO	80226	Jefferson County	North
07460	Littleton	9390 W Cross Dr	CO	80123	Jefferson County	North
10153	Superior	400 Marshall Rd	CO	80027	Boulder County	North
10470	Thornton	1001 E 120th Ave	CO	80233	Adams County	North
10871	Westminster	10445 Reed St	CO	80021	Jefferson County	North
11623	Westminster	14451 Orchard Pkwy	CO	80023	Adams County	North
11756	Wheat Ridge	5071 Kipling St	CO	80033	Jefferson County	North

2

Store Num	City	Address	State	ZIP	County	Region
00126	Aurora	14200 E Ellsworth Ave	CO	80012	Arapahoe County	South
00291	Aurora	16910 E Quincy Ave	CO	80015	Arapahoe County	South
00868	Aurora	7400 S Gartrell Rd	CO	80016	Douglas County	South
01062	Aurora	15700 E Briarwood Cir	CO	80016	Arapahoe County	South
01150	Aurora	1400 S Havana St	CO	80012	Arapahoe County	South
04576	Denver	7930 Northfield Blvd	CO	80238	Denver County	South
05093	Englewood	6767 S Clinton St	CO	80112	Arapahoe County	South
05697	Glendale	4301 E Virginia Ave	CO	80246	Arapahoe County	South
06425	Highlands Ranch	1950 E County Line Rd	CO	80126	Douglas County	South
06485	Highlands Ranch	1265 Sgt Jon Stiles Dr	CO	80129	Douglas County	South
07819	Lone Tree	10001 Commons St	CO	80124	Douglas County	South
08718	Parker	11150 S Twenty Mile Rd	CO	80134	Douglas County	South
09512	Sheridan	3650 Riverpoint Pkwy	CO	80110	Arapahoe County	South

Figure 9-35. Grouped By table

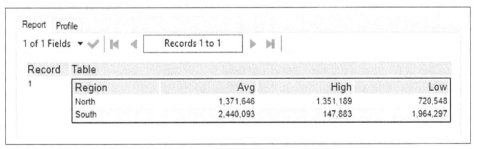

Report   Profile

1 of 1 Fields ▾ ✓ ◄◄ ◄   Records 1 to 1   ► ►►

Record Table

1

Region	Avg	High	Low
North	1,371,646	1,351,189	720,548
South	2,440,093	147,883	1,964,297

Figure 9-36. Pivot table

Table Configuration

You'll want to spend some time playing around with the Table Configuration pane. There are so many different options that you can adjust, down to column-by-column or row-by-row formatting. Let's dig into some of those options.

Table Width. Table Width lets you select the width of the table. There are a few options here:

Automatic
> Sets the minimum width for the data contained within a table

Percentage
> Sets the percentage of the page for the table to be displayed, where 100% is the entire width of the page

Fixed
> Sets the width of the table, in inches

Depending on how you are building your reports, you might want to have the table width scale to whatever space you want it to fill. This is particularly important when the table size might change. However, if you are trying to create balance in a report, you might want to use Percentage to ensure that your elements are taking up only a certain percentage of the page. Now, if you want your reports to be exact and you know that even if the data changes it won't misalign your report, you will want to force the element spacing by using the Fixed option. Just be aware that if your reports are dynamic, you might not have accounted for the different alignment and spacing of different data sets.

Pivot Style. Pivot Style is only available (not grayed out) when you've selected the Pivot (Cross Tab) Table mode. The Pivot Style (see Figure 9-37) is used when you have data coming in from the Cross Tab tool.

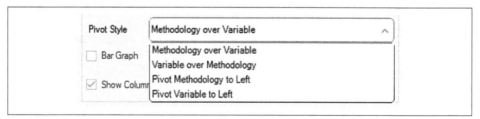

Figure 9-37. Pivot Style

The "Methodology over Variable" style displays each performance indicator (i.e., Avg, High, Low) as a column across the top of the table (see Figure 9-38).

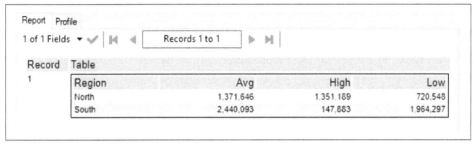

Figure 9-38. Methodology over Variable

"Variable over Methodology" displays each performance indicator as a column across the top of the table, and the Sum (in our example, the sum of the total sales grouped by Region), as shown in Figure 9-39.

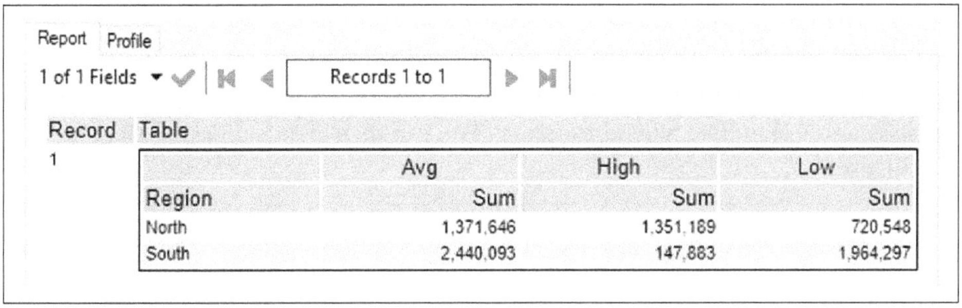

Figure 9-39. Variable over Methodology

"Pivot Methodology to Left" displays each performance indicator as a column across the top of the table, and the Sum of the total sales grouped by Region for each row (see Figure 9-40).

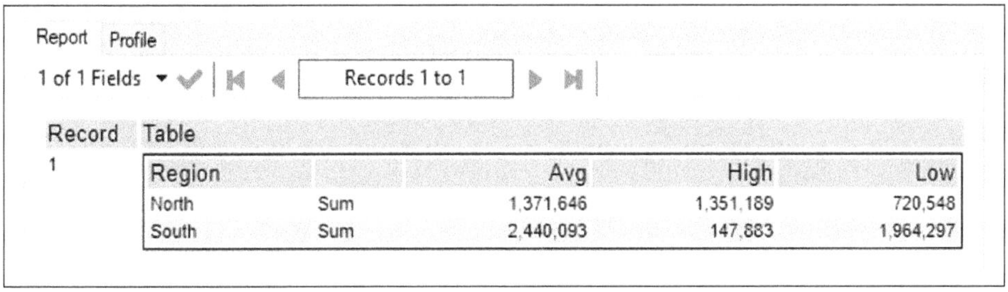

Figure 9-40. Pivot Methodology to Left

Finally, "Pivot Variable to Left" displays each performance indicator on the left side of the table, and the Sum of the total sales grouped by Region for each on the right (see Figure 9-41).

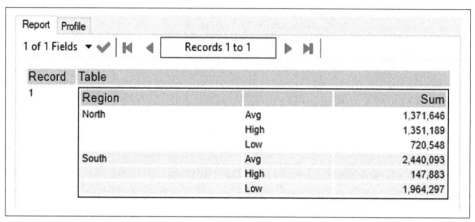

Figure 9-41. Pivot Variable to Left

Bar Graph. The Bar Graph allows you to add a bar graph to the table as well modify the look and feel in the Style Editor panel. You can then create tables of data that look like Figure 9-42.

Store Num	City	Address	State	ZIP	County	Region	Total Sales 3		523
00086	Arvada	7899 Wadsworth Blvd	CO	80003	Jefferson County	North	474,482	67	
00126	Aurora	14200 E Ellsworth Ave	CO	80012	Arapahoe County	South	368,825		369
00291	Aurora	16910 E Quincy Ave	CO	80015	Arapahoe County	South	439,943	230	
00868	Aurora	7400 S Gartrell Rd	CO	80016	Douglas County	South	425,721		430
01062	Aurora	15700 E Briarwood Cir	CO	80016	Arapahoe County	South	491,573	187	
01150	Aurora	1400 S Havana St	CO	80012	Arapahoe County	South	461,845		
02322	Broomfield	1660 W Midway Blvd	CO	80020	Broomfield County	North	176,237	143	
04576	Denver	7930 Northfield Blvd	CO	80238	Denver County	South	129,950		450

Figure 9-42. Bar graph added to table

By going to the Style Editor panel and selecting "Formula" in the Color Mode drop-down field, you can dynamically color the bars based on a formula (see Figure 9-43).

The Show Column Headings option is only shown when you are using the Pivot (Cross Tab) Table mode or when you don't have the Bar Graph selected.

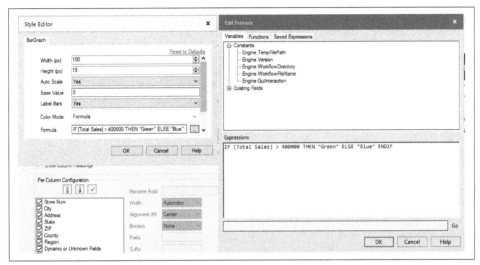

Figure 9-43. Dynamic coloring

Altering the colors of the bars allows you to produce tables like the one shown in Figure 9-44.

Store Num	City	Address	State	ZIP	County	Region	Total Sales	
00086	Arvada	7899 Wadsworth Blvd	CO	80003	Jefferson County	North	474,482	67
00126	Aurora	14200 E Ellsworth Ave	CO	80012	Arapahoe County	South	368,825	369
00291	Aurora	16910 E Quincy Ave	CO	80015	Arapahoe County	South	439,943	230
00868	Aurora	7400 S Gartrell Rd	CO	80016	Douglas County	South	425,721	430
01062	Aurora	15700 E Briarwood Cir	CO	80016	Arapahoe County	South	491,573	187
01150	Aurora	1400 S Havana St	CO	80012	Arapahoe County	South	461,845	
02322	Broomfield	1660 W Midway Blvd	CO	80020	Broomfield County	North	176,237	143
04576	Denver	7930 Northfield Blvd	CO	80238	Denver County	South	129,950	450
05077	Edgewater	1985 Sheridan Blvd	CO	80214	Jefferson County	North	421,493	361

Figure 9-44. Dynamic color bar charts

Per Column Configuration. The Per Column Configuration is a powerful feature for building highly customized tables. You have a ton of options to configure each and every column of data to exactly what you want. You can see the features available to you by clicking on any one of the columns (see Figure 9-45).

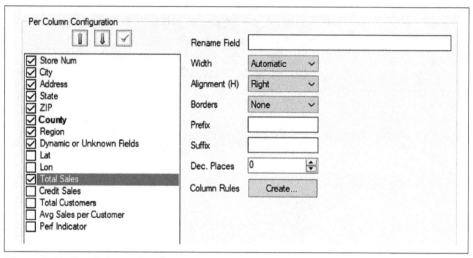

Figure 9-45. Per Column Configuration

The Column Rules feature offers you even more flexibility in formatting. Column Rules allow you to apply a rule to a specific column and have it applied based on the data or formula you wish. Do you want to highlight a column based on a threshold being passed? You can do that (see Figure 9-46).

Figure 9-46. Column Rules

Default Table Settings. At the bottom of the Table Configuration pane, there are two buttons: Default Table Settings and Create Row Rule (see Figure 9-47). Let's discuss each of them.

Figure 9-47. Table Configuration buttons

Default Table Settings holds all the settings you might want to set as default (see Figure 9-48).

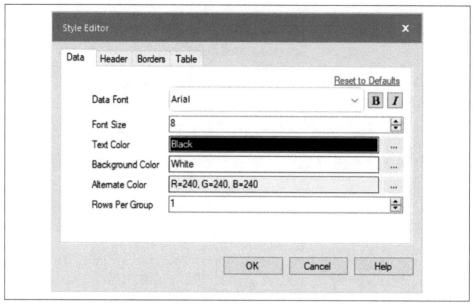

Figure 9-48. Default Table Settings

Here, you can configure just about everything that has to do with your table, from the data to the headers, borders, table, and bar graph. This sets the global view of your table. If you want the entire table to have size 8 Arial font, then you would set that in this window. You can modify specific elements, like text color, in column or row rules; this sets the initial settings.

> You won't see certain tabs (like Header or BarGraph) in the Style Editor if you don't have them selected in the main configuration.

Create Row Rule. Row Styling Rules are exactly the same as the column rules, but they apply rules at a row-by-row basis. (see Figure 9-49). This is a great feature for creating, say, bold total rows in your reports.

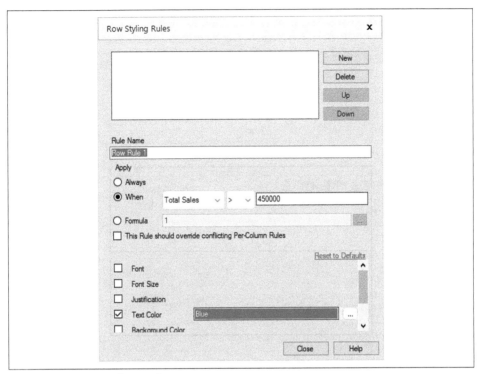

Figure 9-49. Row Styling Rules

The most important thing about Row Styling Rules is to understand the setting in the middle of this window that reads "This Rule should override conflicting Per-Column Rules." If you have two rules that conflict with each other, this allows you to write row rules that will take precedence over the column rules you've created. An example of this would be if you have a row rule that says color a row blue if total sales are greater than 450,000, but the column rule says the column should be colored red if total sales are over 500,000. If this option is not selected, then the column rule will hold a higher priority.

An easy way to know if you have a row rule set up is to notice whether the text on the button is bold (see Figure 9-50).

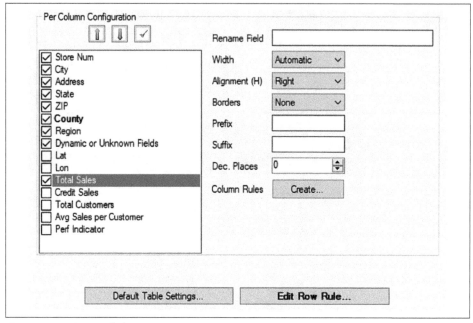

Figure 9-50. Row rule button

You have learned how each of the report elements work. You should have a decent amount of understanding in order to know which tools would be used for which function and how to configure them. We are now going to talk about how to use all these tools together to create dynamic and visually appealing reports that can be fully automated.

Report Layout

So far in this chapter, you have learned about creating snippets, or objects that are only part of a larger report or document. Although there are use cases for just creating a table or a chart, you will often be tasked with creating a report that combines all these snippets into one. That's what the Layout tool and the Visual Layout tool are meant to do. Their job is to help you organize all the snippets into a formatted report that looks exactly the way you want.

You can use two tools to organize these snippets: the Layout tool (which is good for highly structured reports where you want control over every little detail), or the newer Visual Layout tool (not yet in the Reporting tool palette at the time of writing, which helps you put together the report using a visual layout so you can have a better understanding of where things will be laid out in the report). At the end of the day, it's pretty much a matter of preference as they both export the same thing: a report.

Layout Tool

The Layout tool helps you combine the snippets you created using the report elements tools:

A workflow might look something like Figure 9-51.

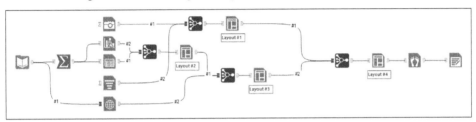

Figure 9-51. Report layout workflow

Notice you have four different instances of the Layout tool in this workflow. That's because the Layout tool combines snippets in only two ways: vertically or horizontally. You can combine as many as you want, but if you are combining multiple snippets vertically you won't be able to align anything horizontally from within that tool instance. You would need to have another instance where you take the report layout that has elements joined vertically and join it with another snippet horizontally.

In Figure 9-51, Layouts #1 and #2 are both joining snippets horizontally. Layout #1 (see Figure 9-52) is combining an image with text from a text tool side by side.

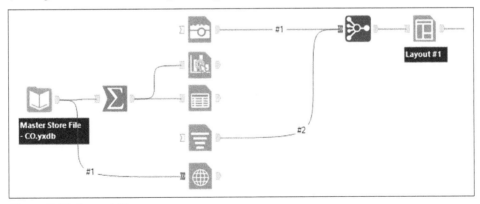

Figure 9-52. Layout #1

Layout #2 (see Figure 9-53) is joining a chart and a table side by side.

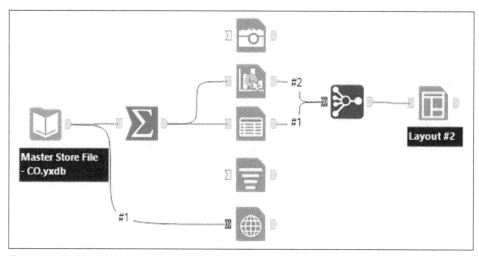

Figure 9-53. Layout #2

Then, Layout #3 (see Figure 9-54) is taking the layout from #2 (which is a chart and a table) and vertically adding a map below.

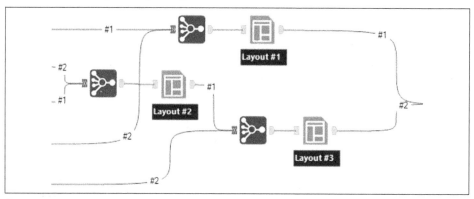

Figure 9-54. Layout #3

Lastly, Layout #1 and Layout #3 are brought together vertically to create the overall report.

 Notice in this example that I am using a Join Many tool, but you can easily use the standard Join tool (Join by Record Position) or the Union tool for building vertical layouts as well.

The report that is made as a result of this workflow looks like Figure 9-55.

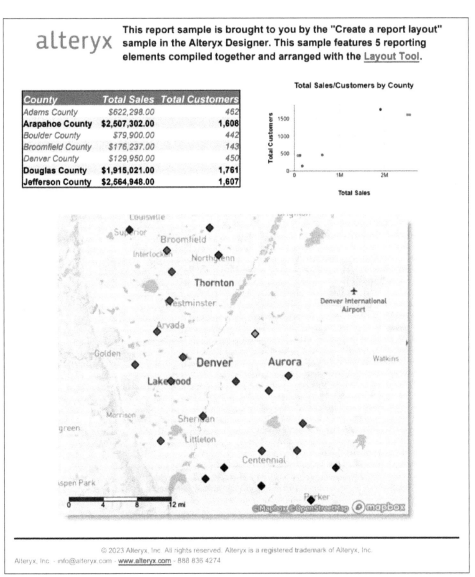

© 2023 Alteryx, Inc. All rights reserved. Alteryx is a registered trademark of Alteryx, Inc.
Alteryx, Inc. - info@alteryx.com - www.alteryx.com - 888 836 4274

Figure 9-55. Resulting report

Now that you understand how the Layout tool works for connecting the snippets and building the report, let's look at the layout configuration to understand how we can configure this tool.

Layout Mode

Layout Mode has three different options for you to choose from in the drop-down. You can select "Each Individual Record" (see Figure 9-56), which allows you to lay out each of the individual snippets.

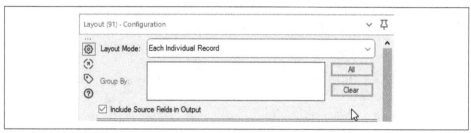

Figure 9-56. Layout Each Individual Record

"Each Group of Records" allows you to create batch reports by selecting a field in the Group By section. Lastly, you have the option to use All Records Combined, which combines all the records from one data field or snippet. Most of the time, if you are creating standard reports, you will use Each Individual Record.

If you want to use the data coming into the report further downstream, then keep the "Include Source Fields in Output" selected. Otherwise, uncheck this option in order to have only the reporting output.

Layout Configuration

The Layout Configuration (see Figure 9-57) is what you will use to determine how the different reporting snippets will be laid out.

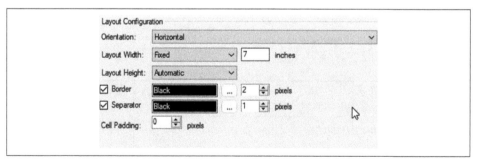

Figure 9-57. Layout Configuration

The first option is the Orientation, which determines if you will stack your snippets horizontally or vertically. You also have two additional options in the list of drop-down values in Orientation to line up your table columns: Vertical with Section Breaks, or Vertical Merge Contents.

With Vertical with Section Breaks, it's important to note that the type of break you end up with will vary depending on file type:

- For XLS and XLSX, a section break is equivalent to a new sheet within a workbook.
- For PDF, DOC, DOCX, and RFT, a section break is equivalent to a new page.
- For HTML and PCXML, a section break is not created; it's all one scrollable web page.

So, if you have two snippets you are bringing together and you create a section break, then those two snippets will be on either different sheets or pages.

The Vertical Merge Contents option simply allows you to line up all the table snippets so that they are aligned.

Below Orientation, Layout Width allows you to select the width of the layout of the elements you are combining. Automatic will set the minimum display width for the data contained within a snippet. Percentage sets the percentage of the page, where 100% is the entire width of the page, and Fixed sets the width of the data, in inches. Layout Height can be set to Automatic or Fixed.

You can add a border around the group of snippets you want, as well as a separator and cell padding to have items spaced apart from each other.

Per Row Configuration

Your choice of orientation (vertical or horizontal), will determine if you see the Per Row Configuration or the Per Column Configuration option (see Figure 9-58).

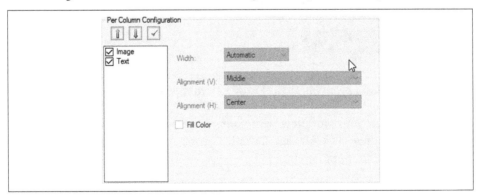

Figure 9-58. Per Column Configuration

With vertical orientation, you will see the Per Row Configuration, while horizontal translates to Per Column. Per Row or Per Column Configuration is where you choose the order of the snippets you want to lay out. You can use the arrows to move one snippet above the other. The Height and Alignment can be set, but know that they are also dependent on the Layout Height option you chose in conjunction with your orientation. Height and Alignment work together to ensure that all your elements are aligned on the page in the most appealing manner.

Visual Layout Tool

The Visual Layout tool is powerful and has actually been around for quite some time:

Like I mentioned earlier, it doesn't sit within the Reporting tool palette. Rather, it sits in the Laboratory tool palette.

The Visual Layout tool doesn't do everything that the standard Layout tool does, but it makes it easier to adjust the layout of snippets. You don't get the specificity of features you get with the Layout tool, but many times you won't need it. You'll notice a difference right away when you go to the configuration of the tool (see Figure 9-59).

Figure 9-59. Manage Layout button in Visual Layout tool configuration

If you plan to run your workflow with your reporting tools connected to the Visual Layout tool, then click Manage Layout. A window will pop up that looks like Figure 9-60.

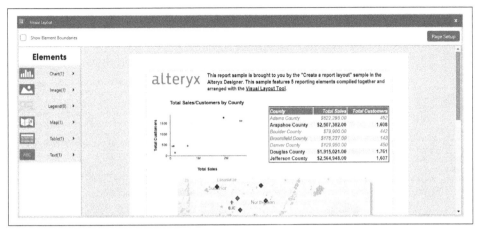

Figure 9-60. Visual Layout tool configuration

You can now work with each element of your report in a GUI that lets you see how it will output before it's actually output. You can set the type of file and size requirements in Page Setup at the top right corner.

To move the elements around to fit your desired layout, simply hover over the individual object (such as a chart) and then click the black bar and drag it to the position you want. You will notice that once you start dragging, borders of the objects will show up to guide you on where to put the objects (see Figure 9-61).

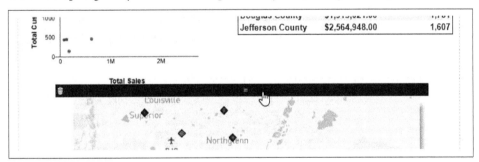

Figure 9-61. Drag by border

This can be just one step in a workflow where you bring many pieces together. From here, you can add other report snippets to build amazing reports that are data driven and aesthetically pleasing.

Overlay Tool

The Overlay tool is useful if you want to overlay one reporting snippet onto another:

The most obvious use case for this tool is overlaying a legend onto a chart. Many users I talk to like using the Interactive Chart tool for creating overlay titles on charts, but if you are building a report using the reporting tools and have something you'd like to overlay in a specific place, then this might be the tool you need.

For example, if you build a map with the default settings for the legend, we might start off with the view shown in Figure 9-62—a map with the legend pushed to the right and wrapped, as each line of text is too long to fit in the space.

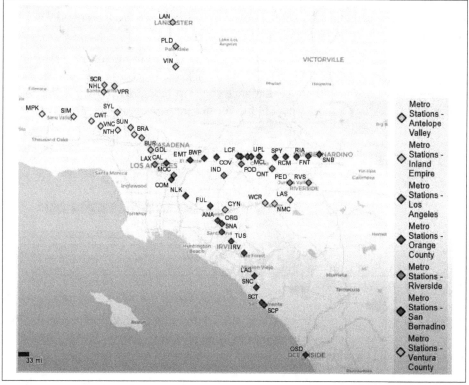

Figure 9-62. Legend overlay on right

Prior to using the Overlay tool, I would use the Map Legend Splitter, Formula, and Map Legend Builder tools to separate and format the legend. Now, by using just the Overlay tool, I am able to build a map with an overlay of a nicely formatted and color-coded legend that looks a lot better (see Figure 9-63).

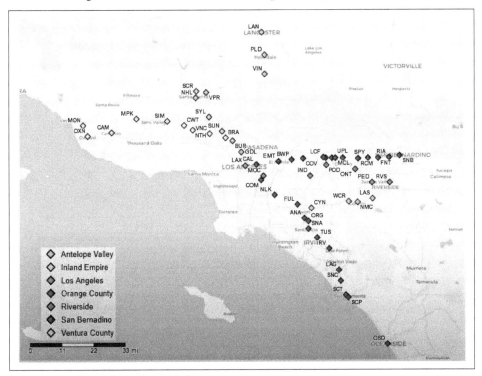

Figure 9-63. Legend overlay on left

Now, configuring the Overlay tool is quite simple as long as you remember one thing: you first need to select your base layer (see Figure 9-64).

Your Base Field is the bottommost layer that you'll work with. The other object, whether it's a text field or image, will be the additional layer that goes on top of the base layer.

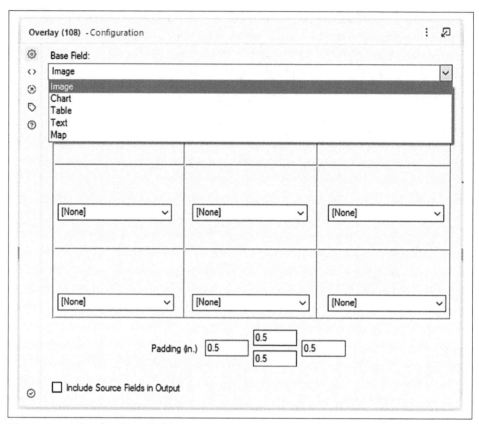

Figure 9-64. Overlay Base Field

For example, you can see in Figure 9-65 that we have decided to put the Text object into the top-left quadrant.

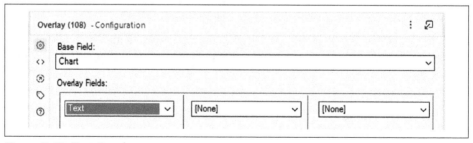

Figure 9-65. Text Overlay

This will take whatever text exists in that text object and lay it on top in the top left of the chart object. With the Overlay tool, you can improve the look and feel of your visualizations.

Now that we have covered the Overlay tool and how we can lay out reports using the Layout tool and the Visual Layout tool, let's shift gears to outputting our reports. This is going to bring it all together so you'll be able to completely build an end-to-end report.

Report Output

We've discussed how to build the elements needed for a report, as well as using Layout tools to get them positioned just right on a page. Now let's get into the tools you have at your disposal to output these reports into various formats.

Email Tool

The Email tool could arguably be the best tool in the Reporting tool palette:

The Email tool enables you to send emails of anything you want from your workflows. Here's a list of ideas:

- A monthly report to the managers on your team
- A weekly status report to your team
- A daily health check report of your systems
- A table of data that will be used in analysis on other projects
- A ping to a chatbot giving someone an update on when a workflow is complete
- A highly formatted HR report to individual employees

The Email tool isn't difficult to use, either (see Figure 9-66).

The Email tool supports a DCM connection in order to provide a secure and authenticated experience for those that require it. It is similar to the setup of DCM connections to data sources. If you don't require DCM then the first thing you'll need to do is get your organization's SMTP information, which you can usually do with a simple call to your service desk or IT group. SMTP, which stands for Simple Mail Transfer Protocol, is an application used by mail servers to send, receive, and relay outgoing email between senders and receivers. Once you get that information, populate the SMTP and port fields. You may or may not need the encryption or SMTP authentication, depending on how your organization has SMTP set up.

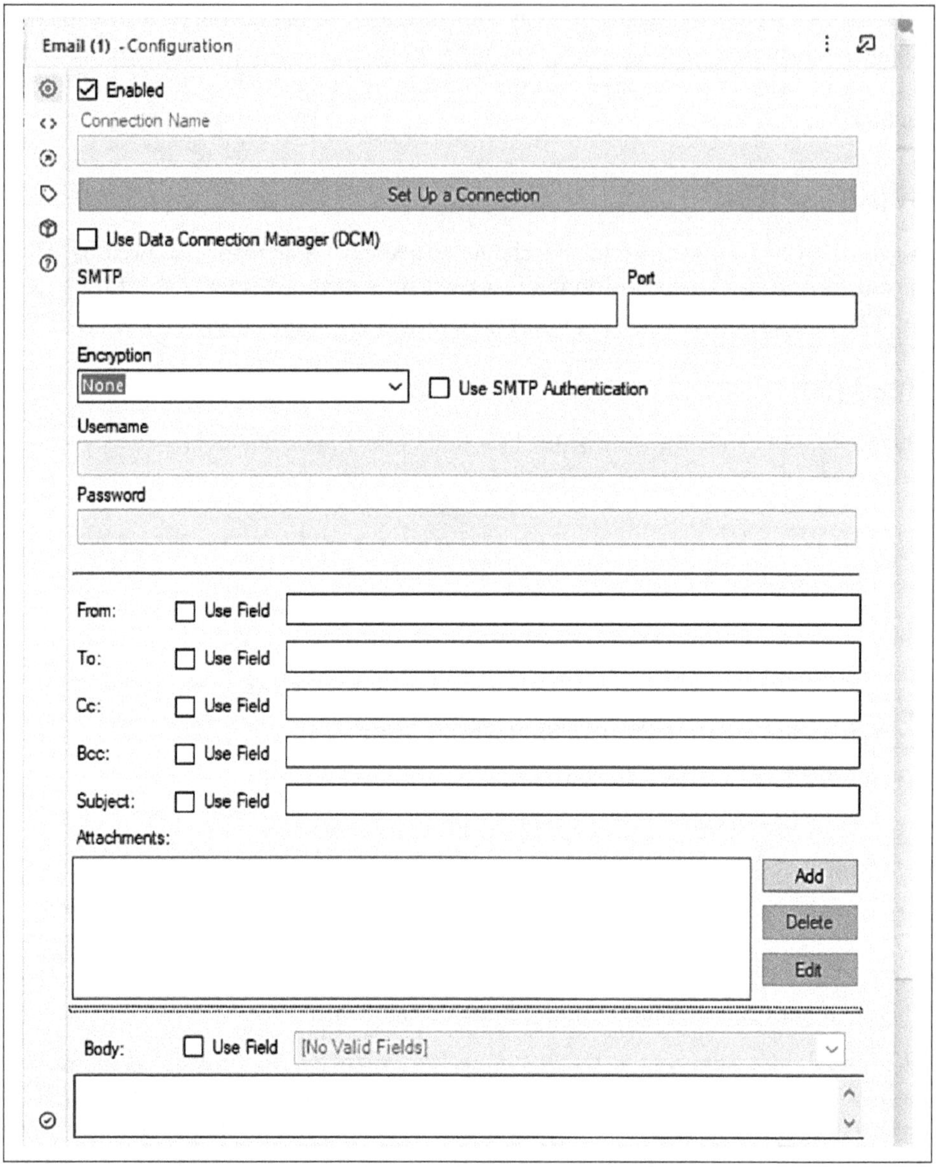

Figure 9-66. Email tool configuration

From there, you will choose what to populate in your email. On all the addressee fields, as well as in the Body field, you can use a field from the data coming into your Email tool by clicking the Use Field checkbox and selecting the field you want to use. You can also manually populate these fields if you want to.

You can also attach files to the email, such as files that the workflow created, or even a full PDF report that is highly formatted. Any of the reporting tools you've learned about can also be used in the body of your email. For example, you could use the Image tool to bring in a banner, the Text tool to bring in formatted text, and even the Map tool to bring in an image of a map based on data in your workflow. You can make your email look as nice as any manually created email you have seen!

Insight Tool

The Insight tool solves for a fairly specific use case, enabling you to create an interactive dashboard with charts and text that is then published to the Alteryx Gallery (or Server) for users to view:

The idea is to create a standard dashboard that can be refreshed at any time.

There are some cool features in the Insight tool, like creating a drill-down on a chart (where you can see multiple levels of information in an interactive report) or add dynamic filters on a chart.

Render Tool

The Render tool allows you to take all of your highly formatted reports and output them to many different formats:

You can output reports to the following file types:

- HTML file (*.html*)
- Composer file (*.pcxml*)
- PDF document (*.pdf*)
- RTF document (*.rtf*)
- Word document (*.docx*)

- Excel document (*.xlsx*)
- MHTML file (*.mht*)
- PowerPoint presentation (*.pptx*)
- PNG image (*.png*)
- ZIP file (*.zip*)

You can also batch your reports so that you send a slice of your report to only a specific group of people. We'll discuss this more in the next section. Now, let's dig into how to configure the Render tool.

The ZIP file contains an HTML file and a folder with all of the HTML file dependencies, such as images.

Configuration

Configuring the Render tool is fairly easy (see Figure 9-67).

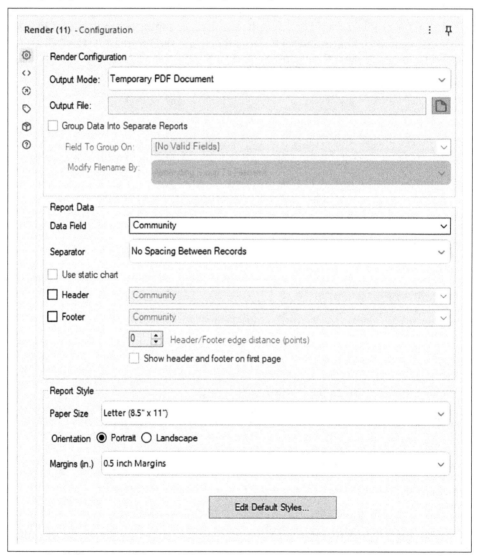

Figure 9-67. Render tool configuration

In the Render Configuration section, you will set the Output Mode. You'll notice that there are many options that say "Temporary." This just means it's going to output from the workflow once it's complete. If you are just prototyping or building the output, this is a great option. Choose the nontemporary option only when you need the report to be saved somewhere. If you want to output to a specific filename and location, select the "Choose a Specific Output File" option at the bottom of the list and then set the details in Output File.

In the Report Data section of the Configuration window, you will first see the Data Field drop-down. Data Field is the incoming field of data that you will be using for your report. If you want a separator in your report, you can enable that next. The "Use static chart" checkbox is only available when using the Temporary HTML File or Temporary Composer File output modes. This checkbox allows you to choose whether you want to use a static chart or keep it interactive. You can provide a field that becomes the Header and/or Footers and set the edge distance, as well as choose whether you want to show the header and footer on the first page or not.

The Report Style section is straightforward. Just choose your paper size, orientation, and margins. However, it's important to note that you can control the Text Style of the report using the Edit Default Styles button. You can see the details that this button pulls up in Figure 9-68.

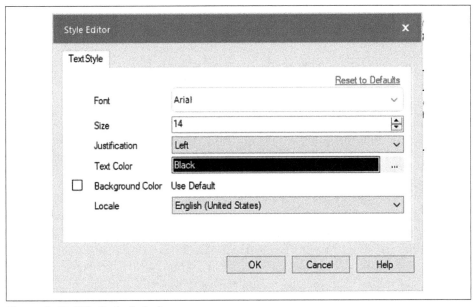

Figure 9-68. Edit Default Styles

Most of the time, you will use the Render tool to output after you've built your layout of reporting snippets. When you are building your layout of reporting snippets, make sure you spend the time to get them laid out the way you like first, as your Render tool isn't going to have much control over the layout and structure of the report.

Advanced Reporting Topics

Once you start getting more familiar with report elements, layouts, and rendering, it's time to take your reporting skills to the next level by learning some advanced ways to approach tools and techniques in Alteryx Designer. In this section, we will look at a couple of advanced topics such as building out reports and batch reporting.

Things to Consider When Building a Report

When you get started with the reporting tools, you will need to practice getting to the point where you have a beautifully crafted final report. You've learned a lot about the tools separately but very little about putting them together to create a report. I want to make sure you have a model to use to know you are capturing all the main components of building a report.

Here are some questions that I think about before I get started:

- What is the output going to be? PDF, Word, PowerPoint? (This will guide you on layout.)
- What data will be used? (This will guide you on what you will need to build in your workflow.)
- Are there going to be maps, charts, or graphics?
- Is this a single report or batch reports?
- How will this report be delivered? Email, file folder, output to window?

A general process for building a report in Alteryx Designer could look like: "gather data > build report snippets > build layouts > add header/footers > render and email."

Batch Reporting

One capability that Alteryx Designer users consistently like is the ability to create processes to clean up data and output batch reports. This is a huge return on investment of time and effort. Imagine being able to eliminate all the manual work to create multiple versions of the exact same report. I can tell you from direct experience there is no greater feeling than the aha moment when you realize this can be done, and quite easily.

Batch reporting means taking a report you've created (i.e., not batched) and converting it into a batched report. These steps are a great guide for building batch reports:

1. Visualize the end result.

2. Create a nonbatched report workflow.

3. Test for accuracy.

4. Convert to batch mode.

5. Test again.

6. Review layout and render options.

Now, let's assume you have a report like the example in Figure 9-69.

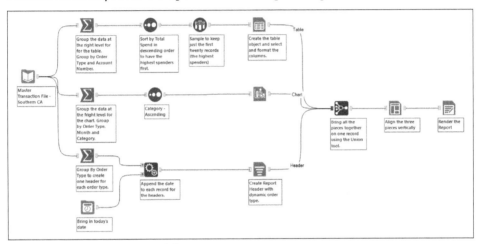

Figure 9-69. Batch report workflow

With this workflow, you can start to visualize the end result of having a single report that fulfills steps 1 and 2. With this report, you can follow on to step 3 of testing for accuracy. Next comes the part that is critical for this section: converting to batch mode.

Convert to batch mode

Converting to batch mode is where the real magic happens. First, you need to understand that there is no single switch for converting a single report to a batched report. Instead, you will follow the process of converting each reporting tool to a grouped/batched form and then bringing them together. Each tool might handle a batch differently but the idea is still the same—you Group By on each tool, then bring them together.

Second, you need to figure out how you want the reports to be batched. Do you want a single PDF with the data separated per page? Or do you want to have completely separate documents? You can do either.

For example, if we want to batch a table of data that's being used with the Table tool, then that means simply creating the Group By. In this example, I am grouping by the Order Type, which will start to create those batches for each order type in my data (see Figure 9-70).

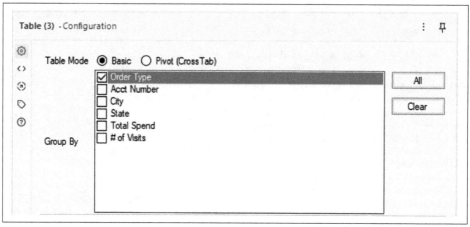

Figure 9-70. Group By Table

The output is important to understand. You now want to see the different rows of data once you've set that Group By and run the workflow (see Figure 9-71).

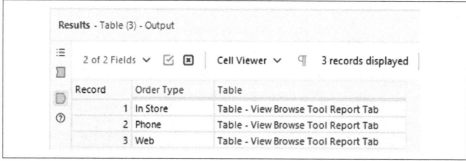

Figure 9-71. Order Type by row

For each reporting tool you are using, you want to achieve the same thing. What's critical here is that you Group By the same fields. If, for example, you choose to Group By an Order Type, then when you configure the charts with the Interactive Chart tool you want to also batch by Order Type. If you are using text, then you want to add the Order Type field into the Report Text tool as well. When you bring all these outputs together, you want to see something like Figure 9-72.

Chart	DateTimeNow	MyHeader	Order Type	Table
Chart - View Browse Tool Report Tab	07/06/2022	Text - View Browse Tool Report Tab	In Store	Table - View Browse Tool Report Tab
Chart - View Browse Tool Report Tab	07/06/2022	Text - View Browse Tool Report Tab	Phone	Table - View Browse Tool Report Tab
Chart - View Browse Tool Report Tab	07/06/2022	Text - View Browse Tool Report Tab	Web	Table - View Browse Tool Report Tab

Figure 9-72. Batch rows

Now you have each row representing the data for a single batch. In Figure 9-72, for example, you have three Order Type batches: In Store, Phone, and Web.

Now that we have those individual batches prepared, we need to prepare the layout like we would do for a single report. That part isn't too different from what we've already covered. However, because we have the data configured on a row-by-row basis, the layout will group the three elements (Chart, Table, and Text) into a single layout for each row. You will still have three records of data, but now only one main column called Layout.

Lastly, you need to set up and configure the Render tool, which will give you the opportunity to either build a single report with three separate sets of charts, tables, and text, or build three documents each with its own set of report objects. It's important to keep in focus that if you want to have three different reports in one document, you can use the "Output Mode of Temporary…" (PDF, DOC, XLS, etc.). However, if you want different documents, you need to specify the filename and type.

If you get everything configured correctly and batched, you'll have a report like the one shown in Figure 9-73 that is focused on the specific category or field value.

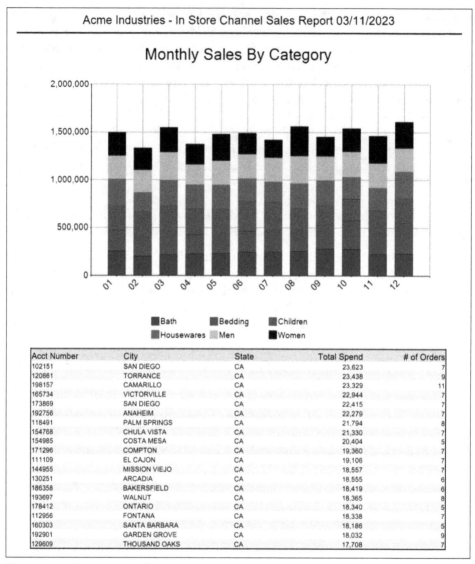

Figure 9-73. Report example

Conclusion

Outside of data preparation, few activities are as manual and time-consuming as reporting. However, it doesn't have to be that way. You can fully automate beautiful reports using the tools I covered in this chapter and free yourself to do bigger and better things. The key steps to reporting in Alteryx Designer are to figure out the desired components, or parts, of your reports (i.e., charts, tables, graphs), build your snippets, set up your layout, and then determine how to render those layouts and to whom they will be delivered. Going from a single automated report to as many report slices as you need is just a simple configuration with batch reporting. I want to ensure you understand that reports can be standardized, pixel perfect, and fully automated. Take the time to learn these tools so that you can create something extraordinary for your next project!

In the next chapter, we are going to explore an interesting part of Alteryx Designer for users who work with databases. You will learn how to improve your workflow speeds by more than 10 times just by using the In-Database tools. Let's get to it!

CHAPTER 10

In-Database Tools

Even if you already have some familiarity with Alteryx Designer, the In-Database (In-DB) tools are likely new to you, so I will take the pleasure of introducing them to you in this chapter. This is a set of tools you absolutely need to have in your back pocket if you work with databases in any way. I am going to help you understand what In-DB tools are, what they do, and why they are so important. You are likely going to learn these tools quickly, as many of them are similar in configuration to the tools you have learned already, with some important nuances; they just execute in a different way. First, let's jump right in and learn what In-DB tools are.

What Problem Do In-DB Tools Solve?

The In-DB tools enable almost all of the same data operations as the standard tools—like the Select tool, Formula tool, and Summarize tool—but with a key distinction: The data does not leave the database. In-DB tools connect to your database. When the workflow runs, it takes the commands you have created within your tools, sends them to the database, and processes the query. The workflow does not send the data back. It keeps everything on the database, instead of bringing the data over the network to your machine. The data will only return once you've told the database that you want all the data to come back to your machine via data output or other tool.

Consider a workflow that uses the standard input tool and connects to a database in order to pull, say, 10 million records. Once you have pulled those 10 million records, you are going to filter down to only the records you want, which may be only 10,000 or 20,000. It's important to understand what's *actually* happening here. You are sending a query from Alteryx to the database, then the database processes that query and completes it. It then sends those 10 million records back to the machine across the network. You are then processing all that data in memory on your machine. Your query will likely take well over five minutes, and that's not even taking into consideration the time needed for the rest of your workflow to further analyze the data. Now imagine if you had to run that workflow five times a day—the impact would be significant.

It likely only took the database 10 seconds or less to complete the query. You're probably wondering why a query would take five minutes to complete if the database executed the actual query part in only 10 seconds. The rest of the time is eaten up almost exclusively by the transfer. The key reason why data can be slow is not the database (assuming it's built and configured correctly); it's always the *movement* of data. Moving data around when it's not necessary is a bad idea. Imagine if you had 10 of those queries in the workflow. Now your workflow takes over an hour to run when it should take less than a minute. This is exactly why In-DB tools are so useful—they can drastically reduce not only the time you spend developing but also the impact to the database, improving the overall efficiency of the workflow. It is common to see workflows reduce from one hour when using standard tools to 1–2 minutes or less when using In-DB tools.

Remember, a database is able to process data much faster than your machine. It's a database, so processing data is its sole purpose, and database vendors ensure that their systems are fine-tuned to be the best data-crunching machines possible. Why pull all of the data to your machine all of the time when a database can do it better and faster? You shouldn't. Now that you understand what problem In-DB tools solve, let's learn how we can tap into their power.

How Does an In-DB Workflow Work?

In-DB tools can easily work with standard tools in Alteryx Designer. Data is streamed into and out of an In-DB workflow using the Data Stream In and Data Stream Out tools (which we cover in more detail later in this chapter), or by connecting directly to a database using the Connect In-DB tool (which we will also cover later). The key here is to look at the anchors going into and coming out of the In-DB tools. They are different. The blue anchors are an indicator that the tool can only connect to other In-DB tools. However, you'll notice in Figure 10-1 that the Data Stream In and Data Stream Out tools have both blue and green anchors, which enables the conversion from standard tools to In-DB tools.

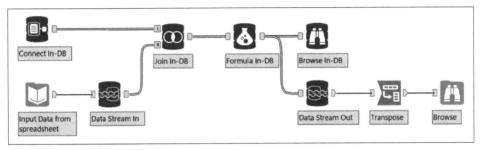

Figure 10-1. In-DB workflow

In this chapter you will learn a lot about how to build In-DB workflows in the context of some best practices. Since some readers may be new to working with databases, it's always helpful to understand best practices before going wild and querying an entire database looking for a single value. Following are some best practices:

Do not pull the entire table of data, also referred to by database folks as the select *
approach.

> You almost never need the entire table of data. Become more surgical and learn to pick out only the fields you need by writing more precise SQL queries. When you are trying to learn what's in the table, get used to using row limits of 100, 1,000, or even 10,000 to filter the data to a snippet of it.

Limit use of In-DB Browse or Data Stream Out tools.

> These are fine when you are learning or when you are building a simple work-flow, but streaming data out and browsing means that the data is coming across your network and slowing down your workflow. If you are pulling data from a database into an Excel spreadsheet, for example, do all the data processing with In-DB tools and stream out only when that data set is ready go straight to the Excel sheet.

Optimize your queries.

> The SQL queries that Alteryx generates from the tools might not always be the most efficient and effective for that particular database. If you have queries that are pulling back a lot of data, it might be a good idea to optimize that query, meaning rewrite the query in a way that the database can handle more quickly and efficiently.

We've talked about why In-DB tools are important, how they generally work, and some best practices. Let's now learn about the individual In-DB tool configurations so you can start building your own In-DB workflows.

The In-DB Tool Palette

The In-Database tool palette contains all the tools you will need to connect and query data from a database (see Figure 10-2).

Figure 10-2. The In-DB tool palette

Connect In-DB Tool

The Connect In-DB tool is critical to understand from the beginning as it's one of the tools that allows you to connect to your database:

When you learn about the Data Stream In tool and the Dynamic Input tool later in the chapter, it will be helpful to already understand the Connect In-DB tool.

In addition to connecting to your database, this tool submits your initial query. You want to make sure that you are being efficient while also not forgetting a field or rows that you need for your analysis. Let's first look at how you can connect to your database.

Connecting to your database

To connect to your database, you first need to do a couple of quick checks to ensure you have everything you need:

1. Ensure you have access to the database you want to connect to.
2. Ensure you have the details of your database. This includes the data source (i.e., Microsoft SQL Server, Oracle, Teradata), server name, database name, and potentially the username and password.

Before we set up a connection to your database, you need to have "line of sight" to the database. This means that your computer must be able to "see" or connect to the database. This is one of the first things you'll troubleshoot if you can't create a connection. Many times, corporate security systems like firewalls or VPNs can block this connection from happening, and a simple request can get it resolved.

Setting up your first in-database connection

To set up your in-database connection, first open a new workflow (canvas), drag and drop the Connect In-DB tool onto the canvas, and double-click on the tool to open the configuration window. You'll notice that the configuration window is very simple, with just two fields: "Connection Name" and "Table or Query" (see Figure 10-3).

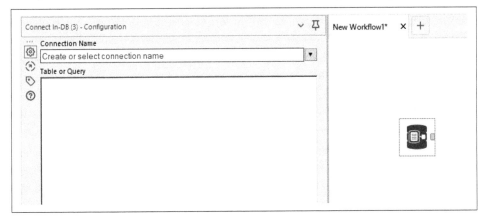

Figure 10-3. Connect In-DB tool configuration

In the Connection Name field, click the drop-down arrow to open the connections menu (see Figure 10-4).

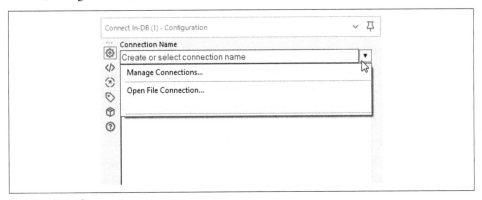

Figure 10-4. Connections menu

Click Manage Connections, which will open the Manage In-DB Connections window. This window allows you to create a new connection or modify a preexisting connection. For this example, you'll create a new connection (see Figure 10-5).

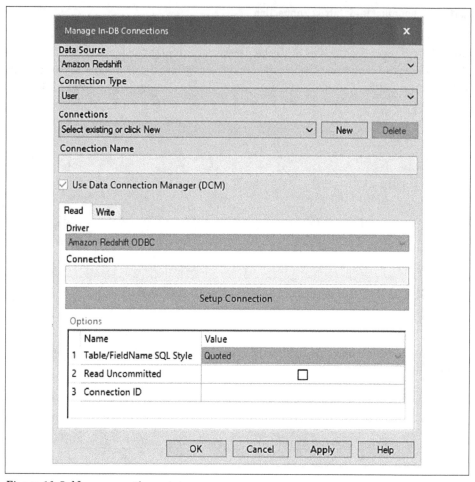

Figure 10-5. New connection setup

To start, pick your Data Source. The list of Data Sources includes everything that is currently supported for Alteryx Designer as of the version you have installed (see Figure 10-6).

> There is an entry in the Data Source list called "Generic ODBC." If your data source isn't listed here, you can try and connect using this generic connection.

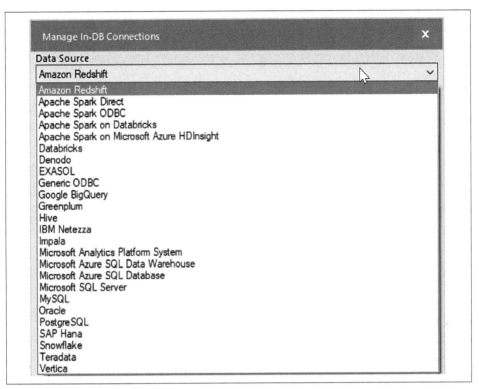

Figure 10-6. Data Source list

I selected Microsoft SQL Server. I am going to focus on SQL Server simply because it is the most popular data source among Alteryx Designer users. You might run into options that I haven't covered here that are specific to your database. A quick look at documentation specific to your database should help you clarify what you need.

 To dig deeper into databases and practice with In-DB tools, download SQL Server Database Developer Edition (*https://oreil.ly/ EgcMD*), SQL Server Management Studio (*https://oreil.ly/xbKIT*), and a sample database for free (*https://oreil.ly/a1PdE*).

The next field you'll see is the Connection Type. There are three connection types: User, System, and File (see Figure 10-7).

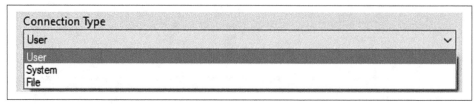

Figure 10-7. Connection types

The User connection type allows you to create a connection that only you can use. The System connection type is only visible if you run Designer as an Administrator, and allows you to create a connection that can be shared. Lastly, the File connection type allows you to create a connection and save the settings as a file (INDBC). This allows you to package the file connection with the workflow. For this example, set up a User connection type.

Next, configure the connection. Just as with the standard input tools, you can also configure the Connect In-DB tool to use a DCM connection. If you have set up other connections for this particular data source before, you'll see them in the drop-down menu. If this is your first connection, click the New button to the right (see Figure 10-8).

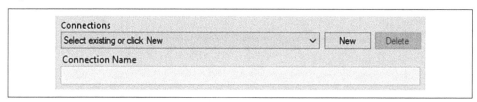

Figure 10-8. New connection

When you click New, all of the field boxes are cleared for you to configure. If you decide not to use DCM, you'll set a Connection Name. If you don't want the default settings, you can set the password encryption as well.

Now configure the Read and Write tabs, which drive the connection to your database (see Figure 10-9).

Depending on the Data Source you've selected, the values in the Driver drop-down will change. Once you've selected the driver, set up your connection string. Click the arrow next to the connection string box and click New Database Connection. If you are using SQL Server, you will see the Data Link Properties window (see Figure 10-10).

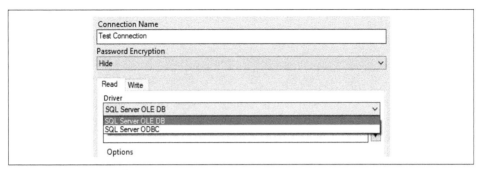

Figure 10-9. Driver selections

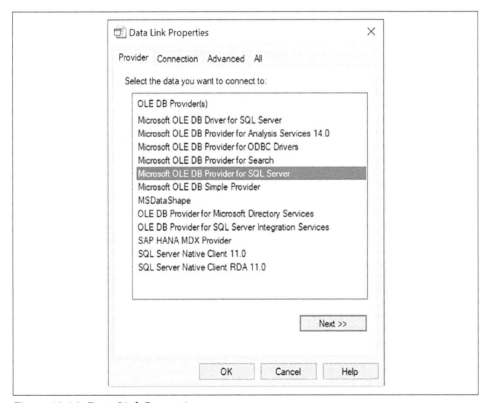

Figure 10-10. Data Link Properties

If you are using other data sources, you will likely see the ODBC window and will need to configure the ODBC connection to your data source.

You may need to install database drivers at this point, if you don't have them.

From the Provider tab, the driver will usually be selected for you. If not, select the appropriate data connection and click Next. On the Connection tab, enter your server name, login information, and select the database you want to use on that server. Once you have all that information set up, click Test Connection. If everything works, you will see a "Test connection succeeded" message (see Figure 10-11).

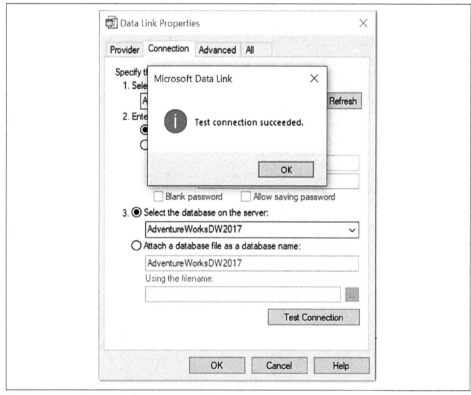

Figure 10-11. Test connection successful

Click OK to close the message and then OK again to close the Data Link Properties window. You will notice that the Connection String field is now populated (see Figure 10-12).

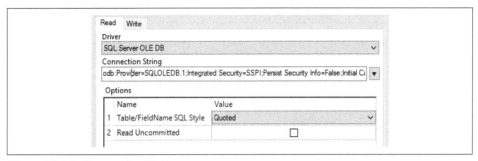

Figure 10-12. Connection String

You are not quite ready, though. You still need to configure the Write tab. Unless you want to use a different driver, it's a lot easier to just set the driver to "Same as Read Driver." That way, you won't have to handle any further configuration (see Figure 10-13).

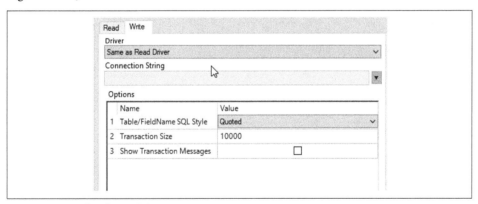

Figure 10-13. Configure Write settings

Once you have both the Read and Write tabs configured, or you've set up your connection using DCM, click OK. The "Choose Table or Specific Query" window will open, which allows you to start building your query against that database connection (Figure 10-14).

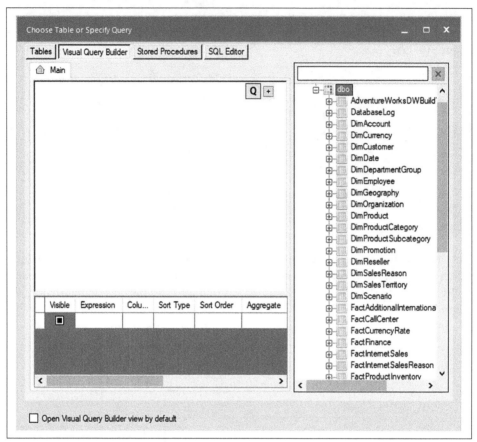

Figure 10-14. Visual Query Builder

Congratulations! You have successfully set up your first connection to use In-DB tools in Designer.

I want to mention one last important piece of information before we move on to other tools. Using In-DB tools might seem a bit awkward at first, as you are so used to "seeing" your data or at least a lot of it. Using In-DB tools is a bit of a paradigm shift. I'll demonstrate what I mean.

First, I am going to configure a simple query in our Visual Query Builder and click OK (see Figure 10-15).

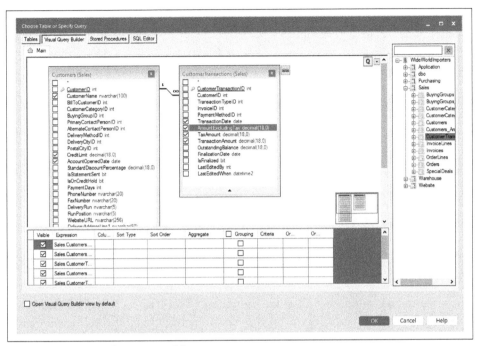

Figure 10-15. Visual Query Builder

Now we have a query in our Configuration window (see Figure 10-16).

Figure 10-16. SQL query in Configuration window

Let's run the workflow and see what records come back. Wait…what the…huh?? There is nothing there! (See Figure 10-17.)

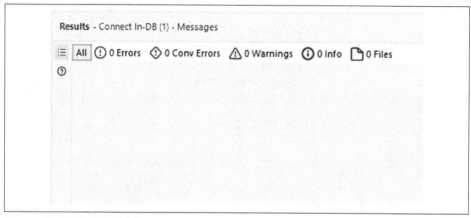

Figure 10-17. In-DB results

You are probably wondering if I broke something or set it up incorrectly. I assure you this is working fine. Do you remember back in the beginning of the chapter when I explained that the reason for using In-DB tools is to help keep the data at the data source and NOT bring everything back? Well, that's what happened here. I didn't tell it to give me anything back locally; I just told it to run a query. It worked perfectly. Now, let's look at the Browse In-DB tool so we can see what happens when you ask for just a little data to come back.

Browse In-DB Tool

The Browse In-DB tool is a bit different than the standard Browse tool:

The standard Browse tool includes features to do data profiling. The Browse In-DB tool does not. It's a very simple tool that allows you to pull back data from your In-DB workflow.

The Browse In-DB tool has two features you can configure: the number of records you can pull back and whether you would like to enable caching or not. Caching is enabled by default (see Figure 10-18).

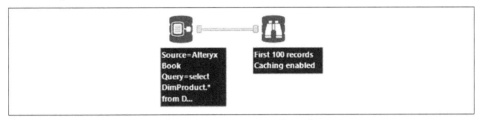

Figure 10-18. Caching enabled in Browse In-DB tool configuration

If the database connection or query (including the number of records to browse) does not change, then the query *will not be rerun*. Instead, the records that display in the window are pulled from the cache.

Once you run the query with the Browse In-DB tool, you will see records output in the Results pane (see Figure 10-19).

Record	CustomerName	AccountOpenedDate	TransactionDate	CreditLimit	TransactionAmount	TaxAmount	AmountExcludingTax
1	Aakriti Byrraju	2013-01-01	2013-01-01	3500.00	2645.00	345.00	2300.00
2	Bala Dixit	2013-01-01	2013-01-01	2000.00	465.75	60.75	405.00
3	Tailspin Toys (Head Office)	2013-01-01	2013-01-01	[Null]	103.50	13.50	90.00
4	Tailspin Toys (Head Office)	2013-01-01	2013-01-01	[Null]	511.98	66.78	445.20
5	Sara Huiting	2013-01-01	2013-01-01	2400.00	809.60	105.60	704.00
6	Alinne Matos	2013-01-01	2013-01-01	3858.75	494.50	64.50	430.00
7	Wingtip Toys (Head Office)	2013-01-01	2013-01-01	[Null]	694.03	90.53	603.50
8	Ingrida Zeltina	2013-01-01	2013-01-01	2600.00	296.70	38.70	258.00
9	Tailspin Toys (Head Office)	2013-01-01	2013-01-01	[Null]	204.70	26.70	178.00
10	Tailspin Toys (Head Office)	2013-01-01	2013-01-01	[Null]	119.60	15.60	104.00
11	Wingtip Toys (Head Office)	2013-01-01	2013-01-01	[Null]	14.95	1.95	13.00
12	Wingtip Toys (Head Office)	2013-01-01	2013-01-01	[Null]	263.35	34.35	229.00
13	Wingtip Toys (Head Office)	2013-01-01	2013-01-01	[Null]	2794.50	364.50	2430.00
14	In-Su Bae	2013-01-01	2013-01-01	3600.00	747.50	97.50	650.00

Figure 10-19. Browse In-DB tool results

Now that you can run a query and get back data, you are well on your way to successfully using In-DB tools. Let's dive deeper into the rest of the tools.

Summarize In-DB Tool

The Summarize In-DB tool is similar to the standard Summarize tool, except that it doesn't have all the actions available that the standard tool does:

Let's say you want to see the total transaction amount per customer. Just like you would with the standard Summarize tool, you would Group By CustomerName and sum on TransactionAmount (see Figure 10-20).

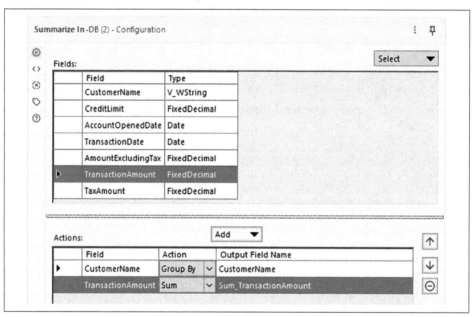

Figure 10-20. Summarize In-DB tool configuration

Then, when you run the workflow, you would see something like Figure 10-21.

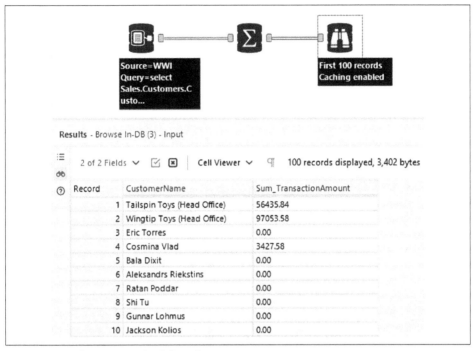

Figure 10-21. Summarize In-DB tool output

The biggest, and really only, difference between the standard Summarize tool and the In-DB version is the number of actions you can take. With the Summarize In-DB tool, the actions shown in Figure 10-22 are available to you.

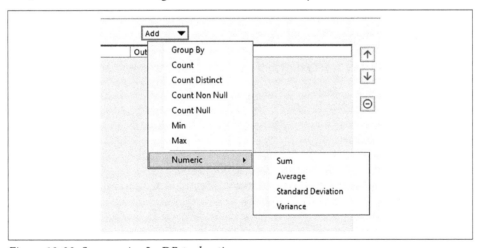

Figure 10-22. Summarize In-DB tool actions

Select In-DB Tool

The Select In-DB tool is also similar to the standard Select tool:

The only difference is that you can't change the data type.

Remember, the Select tool just allows you to select or deselect fields that you don't want in your data set (see Figure 10-23).

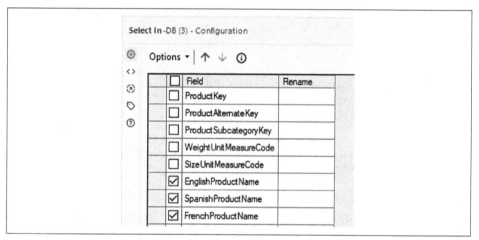

Figure 10-23. Select In-DB tool configuration

Sample In-DB Tool

The Sample In-DB tool is very different from the standard Sample tool:

Although it doesn't offer all the different options, it does offer the important ones: the number and percentage of records. It also enables you to sample records based on the order of the data (see Figure 10-24).

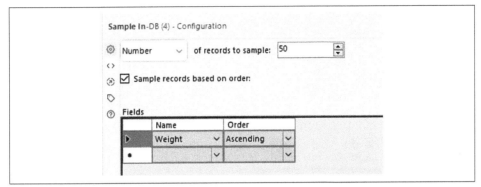

Figure 10-24. Sample In-DB tool configuration

Union In-DB Tool

The Union In-DB tool is nearly identical to the standard Union tool:

You can auto configure by Name or Position.

Also, when the fields are different you have the same options to determine how you will handle them (see Figure 10-25).

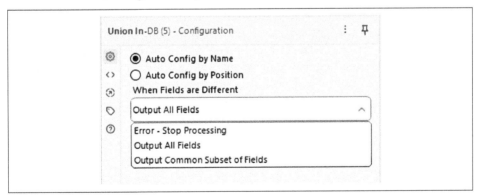

Figure 10-25. Union In-DB tool configuration

The overall use and methods you use with the Union In-DB tool stay the same, as well (see Figure 10-26).

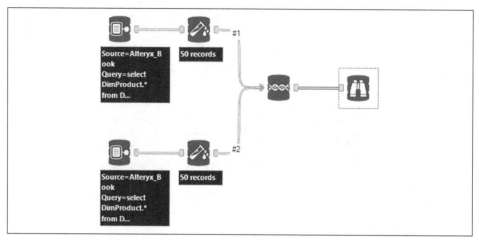

Figure 10-26. Union In-DB workflow

Join In-DB Tool

The configuration of the Join In-DB tool is distinctly different from the standard Join tool in a few ways:

First, you can only join by specific fields, not by records. Second, you don't have the Select Type menu where you can rename fields and change data types. Third, you can only conduct one join type per tool. Obviously, you could have multiple joins in your workflow, but you only have one output per tool (see Figure 10-27). All of the joins you need to do can be done with this tool, but you might need to be a bit more explicit and even use multiple tools to make it happen.

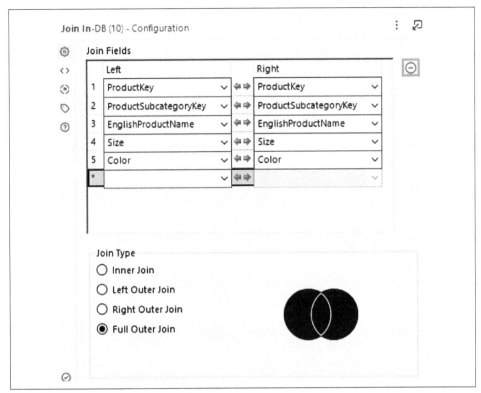

Figure 10-27. Join In-DB tool configuration

Formula In-DB Tool

The Formula In-DB tool is also distinctly different from the standard Formula tool, but it's still incredibly powerful:

It's different mainly because you are no longer able to use the Alteryx syntax for creating formulas; you will need to use SQL.

Alteryx-specific functions will not work for In-DB tools such as Filter In-DB or Formula In-DB. Instead, you will use SQL operators and functions as if you were writing a SQL expression (see Figure 10-28).

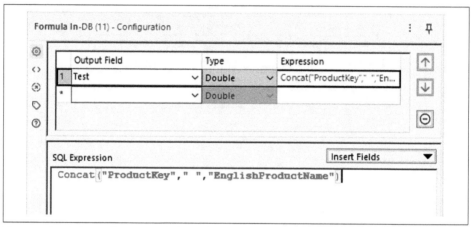

Figure 10-28. Formula In-DB tool configuration

You are still able to put multiple formulas in one tool. However, you aren't able to use the previously created fields in a succeeding formula, as shown in Figure 10-29.

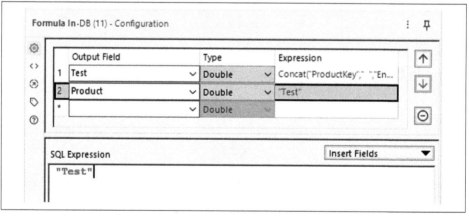

Figure 10-29. Formula on previous field

If you need to use a field you created in another formula, you can simply bring another Formula tool onto your canvas. Let's say, for example, you have a field that is actually a date but it's stored as a string and you want to change the data type. With the Formula In-DB tool, you would use the CAST function (see Figure 10-30).

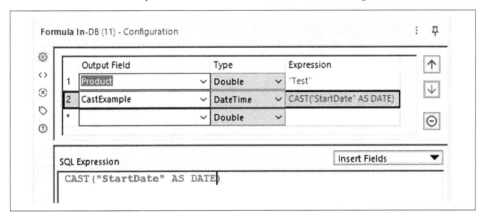

Figure 10-30. CAST function

The Formula In-DB tool, while different, is still powerful and useful. It just takes a little time to get used to it. Now that we understand the shift we have to make for the Formula In-DB tool, let's discuss a similar tool—the Filter In-DB tool.

Filter In-DB Tool

The Filter In-DB tool is similar to the standard Filter tool in that you have both basic filter and custom filter options:

Just remember, this isn't in Alteryx format but common SQL format. It's also important to remember that even if you need to build a custom filter, you should use the basic filter to get started.

Just like with the standard Filter tool, as you write the basic filter, the custom filter expression window will be populated. I've always used that as an in-the-moment reminder of the format I need (see Figure 10-31).

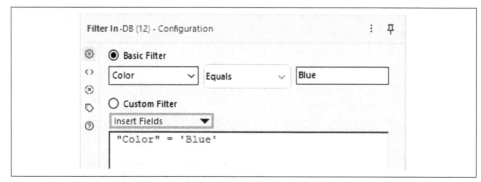

Figure 10-31. Filter In-DB tool configuration

We can also do compound expressions with the Filter In-DB tool, where we filter based on multiple criteria. Don't forget that your expression must always evaluate to a true or false value. If we want to expand our expression in Figure 10-31, we could add another criterion, for example, filtering for any products where the expected delivery date is greater than a specific date (see Figure 10-32).

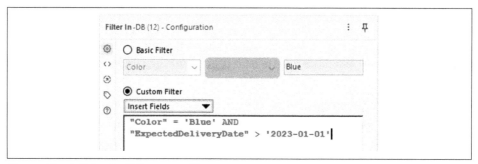

Figure 10-32. Filter In-DB custom filter

Just like all the other tools with expression windows, Alteryx Designer doesn't care how you space out your expressions as long as they are valid. You can have everything in one line or put each expression on a different line to make it easier to read, like I did. You can use extra spaces or tabs as well to make it suit your style.

I could even do something silly like what is shown in Figure 10-33.

You can see that I've used multiple lines by hitting enter and I've put a bunch of spaces in the text. None of that matters, as it doesn't affect the overall query. It's all about the syntax; if that's correct, then you are good to go!

Figure 10-33. Custom expression

Remember, keep it simple and usable. It's easy to build simple expressions, but once you start to build more complex expressions, pay attention to ensuring it remains simple to read, understand, and use. If you are building a filter that has 15 different compound expressions that no one but you can understand, then you've gone too far and need to rethink how to make it easier. Sometimes that means using multiple filter tools, or maybe using better documentation inside the expression. Maybe you don't use that particular tool, but rather a collection of other tools. Remember: *keep it easy.*

Dynamic Output In-DB Tool

The Dynamic Output In-DB tool is a tool that does just one thing, but it's very useful if you need it:

This tool allows you to output not only the connection details, but also the query information from anywhere in your workflow.

This is huge when you build complex workflows and you need to understand what query is being sent back to your database. You could even use it to build a base query to which you can dynamically generate many versions of the query and resubmit to the database. Let's look at an example.

In Figure 10-34, I am outputting the query and connection name directly from the initial query. The query is exactly what was sent to the database. Notice I have clicked on the green Browse tool.

Figure 10-34. Query and Connection Name

You can see the exact query going to the database—this is exciting! You could put a Formula tool after the Dynamic Output In-DB tool and come up with variations of that query. Now, what happens if we add a Filter tool? How does the query change? What does a filter look like now in that query? Well, let's take a look (see Figure 10-35).

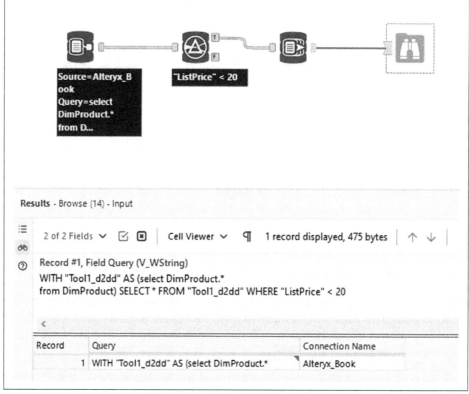

Figure 10-35. Query with filter

Whoa! Now that's cool. We can see that by adding a filter where "ListPrice" < 20, the original query was put into a subquery and the filter was applied to that subquery. Now you could dynamically update that value of "ListPrice" to any other price and send those to the database. That's powerful.

I've only shown you the output values of Query and Connection Name, but there are many other output fields that you can pull out as well (see Figure 10-36).

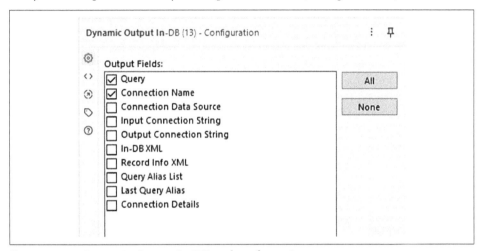

Figure 10-36. Dynamic Output In-DB tool configuration

With these output fields, you can do some pretty cool work in terms of dynamically changing which database, table, or query is run based on a given situation.

Dynamic Input In-DB Tool

Now that you understand how the Dynamic Output In-DB tool works, let's take a look at how the Dynamic Input In-DB tool works:

The Dynamic Input In-DB tool is a bit simpler and feeds off of the Dynamic Output In-DB tool. At its simplest, it takes a Connection Name and a Query, or Query Alias List, and uses that connection to run the query (see Figure 10-37).

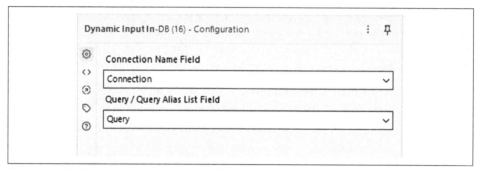

Figure 10-37. Dynamic Input In-DB tool configuration

You probably noticed that I used "Query" or "Query Alias." As you saw in the Dynamic Output In-DB tool, a WITH statement was added after the filter. The Dynamic Input In-DB tool cannot use that query with a WITH statement (you'll get an error) so we give it the Query Alias List instead (see Figure 10-38).

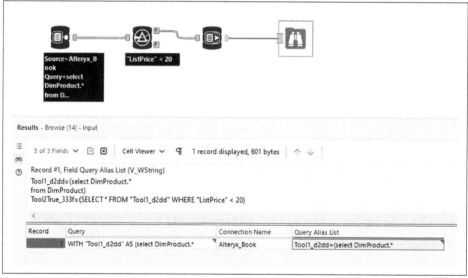

Figure 10-38. Query Alias List

If we give the Dynamic Input In-DB tool a Connection Name and Query Alias List, then we see it just runs that query and provides the results (see Figure 10-39).

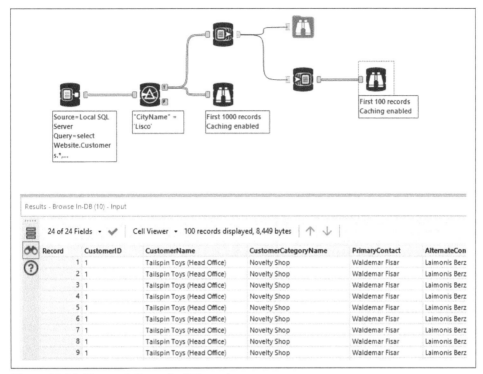

Figure 10-39. Dynamic Input In-DB results

Now that you have the connection information and the query in text form, you could do all kinds of creative query generation and execution based on input from users or results. Imagine you have a workflow that runs once a day and checks a table for any new records. If any new records are returned and based on a value or set of values in that data, you could run any number or combination of queries to process or investigate that data.

You now know how to get data into the workflow and can connect to pull data dynamically, but you also need to know how to write data. Just like all the other operations you would need to do in a database, you want to make sure that you are doing this one "In-DB" as well.

Write Data In-DB Tool

The Write Data In-DB tool mimics the standard Output Data tool in a few aspects, but it obviously focuses on working with databases:

Four main output modes are available to you in the Write Data In-DB tool:

Create New Table

If you want to create a brand new table from your workflow, this is the option to select. This option is used mostly at the beginning of a project, to create the tables you will need to update or modify later on. It's not usually something that you will use over and over, but there are indeed use cases for it. To configure this option, provide only a Table Name (see Figure 10-40).

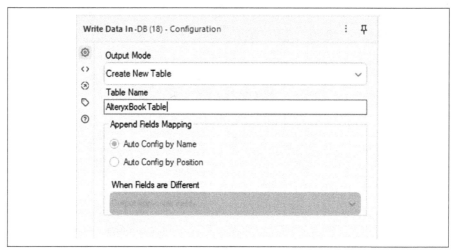

Figure 10-40. Create New Table output mode

Delete Data & Append

This output mode option assumes that you already have a table and are now going to delete data (rows) and append new ones. You use this option if you need to update a table with new data or update values that already exist in the table. To configure this option, provide a Table Name and determine whether you want to auto config by name or position (see Figure 10-41). When you select the "Auto Config by Name" option, Designer will look to match the header (the Name) of the fields in the table to what you are providing. "Auto Config by Position" refers to the column in the table where the field exists.

For example, consider a table with three columns. The first column is position 1, the second column is position 2, and so on. So, position 1 of the existing table would be expected to match position 1 of the data you are providing. The last option, "When Fields are Different," gives you some options in case the fields are different. You could either tell it to stop processing and throw an error so you are notified, or you could tell it to proceed by outputting the applicable (or matching) fields.

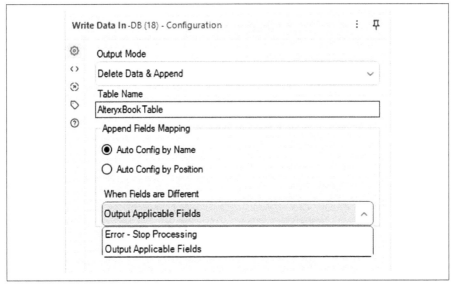

Figure 10-41. Delete Data & Append output mode

Overwrite Table (Drop)

Overwrite Table is really just a more forceful option than Delete Data & Append. Where Delete Data & Append keeps the table intact and just updates the necessary data, Overwrite Table blows away the whole table and re-creates it with the data you provided. This is useful if you just want to have a place to throw data and don't care if the previous data in the table is deleted (see Figure 10-42). To configure this option, provide the Table Name. The Append Fields Mapping selection criteria are grayed out since they are not needed.

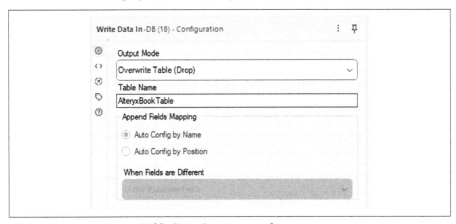

Figure 10-42. Overwrite Table (Drop) output mode

Create Temporary Table

This option allows you to output data into a table that only exists for the current session. This option is useful when building workflows and macros where you need to hold the metadata or subqueries of data in place temporarily in order to process your data (see Figure 10-43).

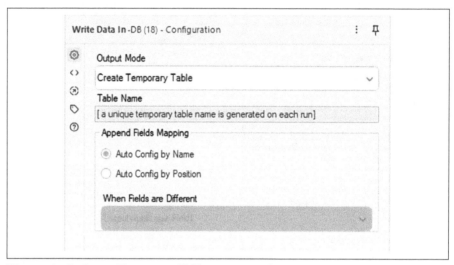

Figure 10-43. Create Temporary Table output mode

The key thing to keep in mind is that you are still operating "In-DB," which means that the data you are querying isn't leaving the database. The data you queried is going to be put into a table that is temporarily available. Once you are done with that query and close the connection, that table will be erased. Temporary tables are a useful tool when you are moving different sets of data around with the goal of creating a data set you will use for analysis.

Data Stream In Tool

I have purposefully saved the two Data Stream tools for last, as I think they are the most important. These tools allow you to move from In-DB to standard tools, or the reverse. More often than not, you will find that it's difficult to build workflows that use 100% In-DB tools. In most cases, there will be Excel files or other data that exists outside of the database that needs to be brought in.

The Data Stream In tool is what brings your data from standard tools to In-DB tools and allows you to go from using the standard tools to using In-DB tools:

Configuring the Data Stream In tool should be quite easy now that you have the hang of things—you just need to set the Connection Name and the Creation Mode. The Creation Mode is how you will write the data in the database (see Figure 10-44).

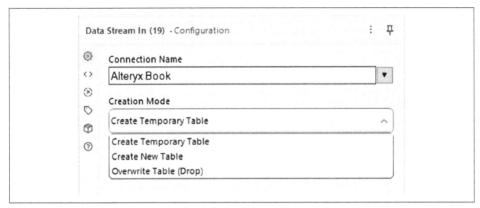

Figure 10-44. Data Stream In tool configuration

Just as with the Write Data In-DB tool, you have the option to create a temporary table, create a new table, or overwrite one that's already created (see Figure 10-45). In database terms, we think of this as "landing" your data. If you are doing this frequently, you might want to think about whether you need this data to persist (i.e., not get deleted) or if you can just use a temporary table (i.e., you are going to process this data and create a report or an output).

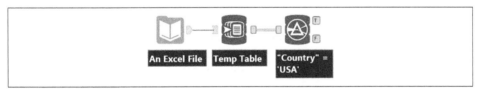

Figure 10-45. Temporary table

Notice that, in Figure 10-45, the input anchor is green. This means that it can only connect to standard tools. The output anchor of the tool is blue, which means that only In-DB tools can connect to it.

Data Stream Out Tool

The Data Stream Out tool is the opposite of the Data Stream In tool. It allows you to go from In-DB tools and take the data out to standard tools:

You will need this if, for example, you want to take data from a table and output to a file or use tools that only exist in standard tools.

If you wanted to connect to a database, filter to a specific set of records, and then output to an Excel file, you would use the Data Stream Out tool (see Figure 10-46).

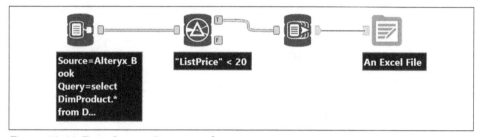

Figure 10-46. Data Stream Out example

 Please do not try to query a million-record table and try to output to Excel (or any file) so you can analyze it using standard tools unless you absolutely need to. If you have the data in a database, try to learn and use the In-DB tools. Your processes will be astronomically faster and more efficient. As with all things in life, there is no permanent line in the sand on this idea. Take it as a best practice that can save you massive headaches. Your goal with using In-DB tools is to gain performance and efficiency, and you lose that the moment you stream out the whole data set. Ideally, you analyze "In-DB" and output the very last data set that is going to be shared.

You will not see databases or queries the same after learning how to use In-DB tools. If you are like me, you might even get a bit frustrated when you see queries that take more than 20 minutes, now that you can query data in seconds. Help me save the sanity of our fellow analysts and teammates and ensure they are using In-DB tools whenever possible.

Transparency in Using In-DB Tools and Designer

Although I am an Alteryx evangelist, I believe that transparency about how things actually work is extremely important and only makes us better. As quick as I am to support Alteryx and 95% of what they build and do, they don't always get everything perfect. There are areas that, frankly, are hard to build for or that just need more attention.

I would put the In-DB tools in that category. They are good and useful and have only gotten better and better with nearly each release. However, databases in general are complex and complicated pieces of software.

To be clear, Alteryx hasn't designed for every single feature and functionality that each database vendor has built into its own products, and it's not reasonable to expect that. However, there are areas that should be designed for, and it's reasonable to expect that Alteryx Designer taps into the core functionality of a specific database's features, whether it's speed, efficiency, or other operations.

An example where this has been done well is the bulk loader feature that many databases like Oracle, SQL Server, and Teradata have. Alteryx can tap into those features and provide you, the user, with an easy path to use those features. An area that can be criticized, though, is ensuring that the SQL that is being built and sent to a database is the most efficient that exists. Database vendors spend millions of dollars just to ensure that data is being retrieved or updated in the absolute fastest and efficient way possible. Alteryx Designer should tap into that, but historically that hasn't always been the case.

The takeaway here is to not be blinded by the idea that any software company is flawless. Even the greatest developers aren't, and there are going to be areas that can always be improved. Get good at using the tools and understanding why things work the way they do, and where they work well and don't. That little insight has made me a much better Alteryx developer and architect overall. It's fun to push the limits to see how well something works. How many records can Alteryx Designer process? How long does it take to query a bazillion records and in which scenario? How fast can data move with certain machine configurations? Fun. Fun. Fun.

Additional Tips and Tidbits

There are endless tips and tidbits on In-DB tools, but I've limited the list below to those that I think will be most useful for you:

- In-DB processing requires 64-bit Alteryx with 64-bit database drivers.
- You cannot query from multiple databases with In-DB tools, as there will be an architecture mismatch.
- There are six predictive tools that have In-DB support. When a predictive tool with In-DB support is placed on the canvas with another In-DB tool, the predictive tool automatically changes to the In-DB version. To change the version of the tool, right-click the tool, point to Choose Tool Version, and click a different version of the tool.
- To run workflows on Alteryx Server, the ODBC driver must be configured as a System DSN. For In-DB processing, the Connection Type must be "System."

I may have missed the one bit of information you really need, and for that I apologize profusely. I hope we can still be friends.

Conclusion

In-DB tools are an amazing creation from the developers of Alteryx Designer. Their capabilities allow you to go from a one-hour workflow process to potentially just a couple of minutes. You can easily connect to a database and run all your queries on the database without having to bring any of that data in memory to your machine, thus slowing down the process. You can tap into the power of the database's speed, efficiency, and execution.

You are now able to connect to your database, pull data out, put data in, and update data. You can analyze the data in-database and, if needed, you can convert from or to standard tools. Get familiar with the In-DB tools so that, if the opportunity presents itself, you can tap into a database without much trouble. Lastly, get to know how your databases work and what you can reasonably expect for performance. Now, we'll discuss a toolset that the majority of Alteryx Designer users don't know of (but you will soon!). This toolset—the Calgary tools—can greatly enhance your development skills, especially when working with big data sets.

CHAPTER 11

Calgary Tools

In this chapter, you will learn about a collection of tools that allow you to tap into data sets up to billions of rows with runtimes in seconds. Yes, billions. Yes, in seconds. You are going to learn what the Calgary tools are and, more importantly, how to use them and why they are so powerful if you are ever working with large data sets.

Calgary is a special type of proprietary data engine from Alteryx that allows you to store and conduct analysis on Calgary databases, which can contain billions of records. In more practical terms, this means that you can load a huge amount of data into a Calgary database—a proprietary file database format that can be stored like any other files on your machine and with indexes—and the time it takes to retrieve that data is orders of magnitude faster than if you were to pull from a standard database.

If you have spent a decent amount of time working with large data sets, you know that nothing is more frustrating than building queries to count items (number of products, customers, locations) from millions (or even billions) of rows of data. It's painfully slow without the right software. Calgary tools allow you to not only break that barrier but do so with a level of flexibility that allows you to write the specific queries you need (e.g., the number of products with at least $10M in sales and 500 customers).

Alteryx designed the Calgary tools with their users in mind. The UI and configuration of these tools is quite easy. There are only five tools in the Calgary tool palette (see Figure 11-1) but they allow you to solve the big challenge of handling a large number of records.

Let's jump into the tools and talk through some examples.

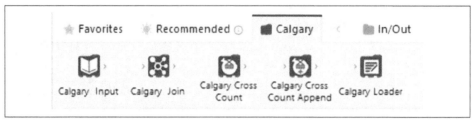

Figure 11-1. The Calgary tool palette

Calgary Loader Tool

Your first step when using the Calgary tools will be loading data into a Calgary database, which is what the Calgary Loader tool is for:

You will use the Calgary Loader tool to create a Calgary database (CYDB file). You load anything you want into a Calgary database, and each field contained in the input file can be indexed to maximize the Calgary database performance. There is an approximate 2-billion-record limit on a single Calgary database (2^{31}, to be more precise), so it is best used for data sets in the 100- to 33-million-record range. If you need more than 2 billion records, you can simply use multiple database files.

When configuring the Calgary Loader tool, you don't need to set much. You will set the name of the database you want, the indexing type, and choose the fields you would like indexed (see Figure 11-2).

In the configuration window of the Calgary Loader, you will select the "Load base Calgary Table and/or 1 or more standard indexes" option. You will then see a list of fields from that CYDB. Along with those field names, you will see the columns Data, Index, and Index Type. The Data checkbox is like the Select tool, and if unchecked, it does not go through to your subsequent tools. The Index checkbox tells the Calgary tool whether to create an index on that specific column. Lastly, the Index Type column gives you the option to use Auto or set manually to High/Low selectivity (see Figure 11-3).

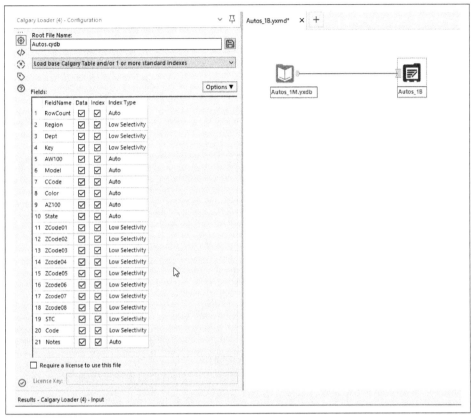

Figure 11-2. Calgary Loader configuration

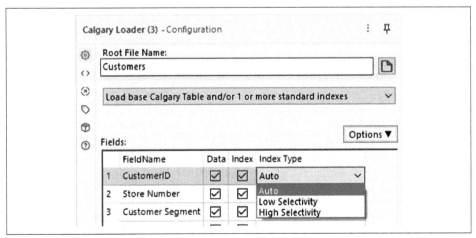

Figure 11-3. Selectivity

I will talk more about the Index Types in the next section. You can also set a single advanced index, which can be a bit easier than having to see potentially hundreds of indexes individually. When you set a single advanced index, you get a new set of configurations that will look like Figure 11-4.

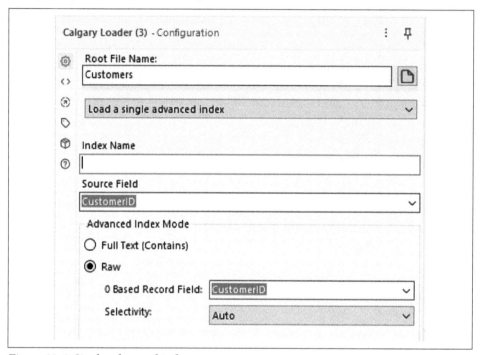

Figure 11-4. Single advanced index

You create the index name, then select the source field and advanced index mode you want. The options in Advanced Index Mode are:

Full Text (Contains)
Full Text will search the field for a specific value, which can be in any part of the value of the field.

Raw
Raw is a special mode used with standard indexes, used to create and index multiple fields. For Raw Indexes, you need to specify both the 0 Based Record Field, which is the record ID, and the Selectivity: High, Low, or Auto.

Now you know how to configure the Calgary Loader, but I want to touch a little bit more on indexes for those who aren't familiar with them. They can be a bit confusing, but they are really important, not just for the Calgary tools but also for working with databases in general.

Calgary Indexes

A database index is a data structure that improves the performance and speed of data retrieval. It is a method that allows the database to avoid having to go through every record each time to search for data based on your query. Now indexes aren't necessarily a requirement per se, but they are a great asset for you to use, especially if you are querying databases over and over. It is the reason why when users ask me about working with large amounts of data, I advise them to put it into a database, as the tools you have available (like indexing) will make your life much easier when you are working with the data.

I won't assume that everyone reading this is interested in the mechanics behind how data gets pulled from a database; however, for any of you who find or need performance for your queries, I urge you to spend a little time digging into this topic. Whether you are querying a billion records and want that to go faster or maybe you just have a specific query that you want to run faster, knowing more about database indexes will help you. I just want to cover a small subset on the topic of indexes to get you started, including why Calgary indexes are different.

How do I know which fields to index?

Knowing which columns to index can be a bit challenging, but now that you know a bit more about indexing and what the purpose of an index is, you'll have a clearer perspective on what columns you might need. The great thing is that you don't have to get this perfect the first time. You can put a few indexes in and then query the data to ensure you are getting the results you want. If not, add another index or more.

When we discuss normal databases (rather than Calgary), there are considerations you need to make around which indexes to create. This is because every time you do an insert or update to the database, it will impact the time the overall query takes, because that data needs to update the indexes. It may not be a drastic increase, but even small changes can add up fast.

Now with Calgary it's a different situation. You cannot update the data once it's loaded, so you don't really need to consider the performance impact on updates or inserts. You can index everything up front and the impact (of slower time to load) will only occur one time when you do the initial load. You can put a few indexes in and then query the data to ensure you are getting the results you want. If not, add another index or more.

As you saw earlier, there are two different modes for creating nonspatial indexes:

High Selectivity Index
A high selectivity index is used for fields that contain very unique records, like addresses or names.

Low Selectivity Index

A low selectivity index is used for fields that contain repetitive data, like gender or state abbreviation.

If you want Alteryx to automatically apply the index mode with high or low selectivity based on the data, select an auto mode.

Where are my indexes stored?

When you complete the load via the Calgary Loader tool, you will have chosen to save your *.cydb* file to a specific location on your computer. The indexes go in that same directory, but they'll have a different file extension of *.cyidx* (for Calgary index). Figure 11-5 shows what you should see once a Calgary load is complete with indexes.

Name	Status	Date modified	Type	Size
> Book > Calgary				
Customers.cydb	⊘	10/24/2023 10:59 AM	Calgary Database	222 KB
Customers_Indexes.xml	⊘	10/24/2023 10:59 AM	XML Document	3 KB
Customers_Address.cyidx	⊘	10/24/2023 10:59 AM	CYIDX File	46 KB
Customers_City.cyidx	⊘	10/24/2023 10:59 AM	CYIDX File	11 KB
Customers_Customer Segment.cyidx	⊘	10/24/2023 10:59 AM	CYIDX File	10 KB
Customers_CustomerID.cyidx	⊘	10/24/2023 10:59 AM	CYIDX File	25 KB
Customers_First Name.cyidx	⊘	10/24/2023 10:59 AM	CYIDX File	22 KB
Customers_Last Name.cyidx	⊘	10/24/2023 10:59 AM	CYIDX File	30 KB
Customers_Lat.cyidx	⊘	10/24/2023 10:59 AM	CYIDX File	48 KB
Customers_Lon.cyidx	⊘	10/24/2023 10:59 AM	CYIDX File	47 KB
Customers_Responder.cyidx	⊘	10/24/2023 10:59 AM	CYIDX File	10 KB
Customers_State.cyidx	⊘	10/24/2023 10:59 AM	CYIDX File	9 KB
Customers_Store Number.cyidx	⊘	10/24/2023 10:59 AM	CYIDX File	11 KB
Customers_Zip.cyidx	⊘	10/24/2023 10:59 AM	CYIDX File	13 KB

Figure 11-5. Completed Calgary load

Now that you have a solid understanding of the Calgary Loader tool and indexing, you have the power to get data into a database format that can help you not only scale to larger and larger data sets, but also ensure that those big queries are also performant. Let's now shift gears a bit and get into reading data so you can build workflows using your new Calgary database.

Calgary Input Tool

Now that you've created your CYDB file, you can retrieve data from it with the Calgary Input tool:

If you were hoping that the Calgary Input tool would be the same as the standard Input tool, I am sorry to inform you that it isn't. But once you understand how it works, you'll be querying data in no time. When you drag a Calgary Input tool onto the canvas, you'll see the configuration window shown in Figure 11-6.

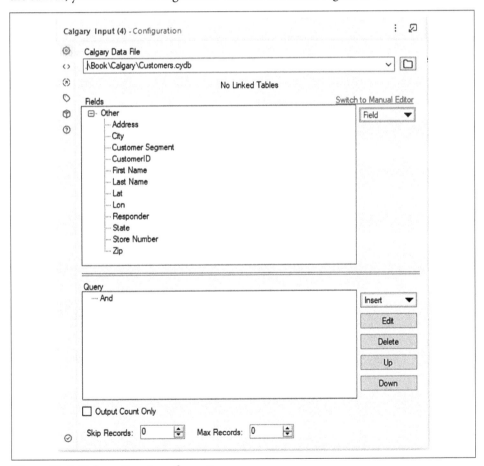

Figure 11-6. Calgary Input configuration

Everything you do to select fields is eliminative, meaning that each query is essentially a filter meant to bring back only what you are looking for. If you don't provide a query, it will return all records in that database.

To show you what a query looks like without any additional filters, follow these steps:

1. Drag the Calgary Input tool onto the canvas.

2. Select a Calgary data file. (If you didn't create one using the Loader in the previous section, you can always use one of the samples in *C:\Program Files\Alteryx\Samples\data\SampleData\CalgaryData*.)

3. Set Max Records (on the bottom of the configuration window) to 1,000 to ensure your query is quick.

4. Click Run to run the workflow.

If this is indexed it shouldn't take more than half a second to run. Now, that's the baseline (see Figure 11-7).

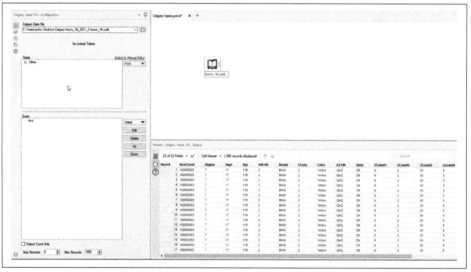

Figure 11-7. Calgary Input query

Let's take a look at what happens when we set some parameters that filter the data. To set a query, you first need to expand the "Other" list in the Fields window (see Figure 11-8).

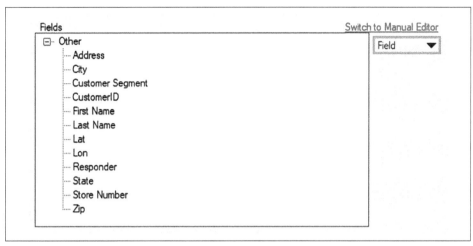

Figure 11-8. Field list

From here, you have two options to build the query. For Option 1 (this is the custom option), you can double-click on the field you want to filter (in this case, I double-clicked City), and you would then see Figure 11-9.

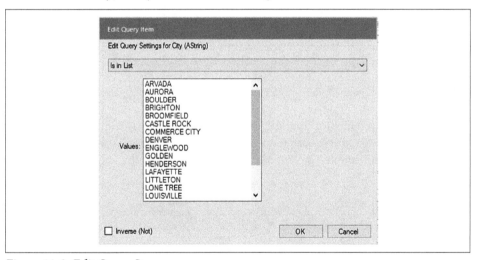

Figure 11-9. Edit Query Item

For Option 2, you can single-click on the field and then use the Field drop-down to the right, like in Figure 11-10.

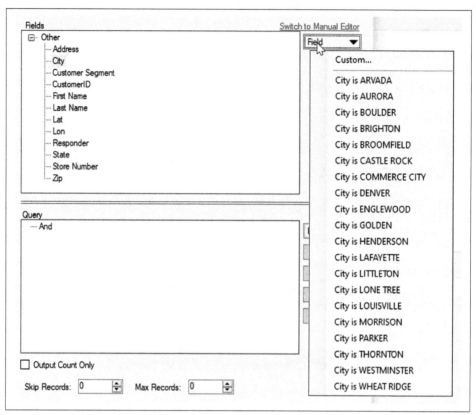

Figure 11-10. Field drop-down

Option 2 is more efficient if you just want to quickly select a field value to filter on. However, if you want your query to be a bit more robust, you will want to use Option 1. The custom (or double-click) option provides a more substantial list of options (see Figure 11-11).

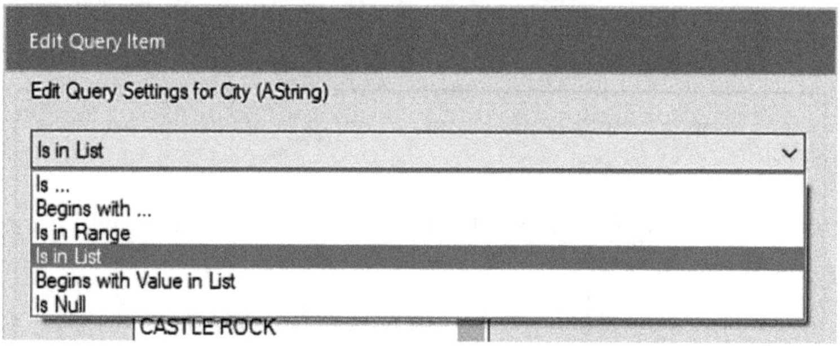

Edit Query Item

Edit Query Settings for City (AString)

Is in List

Is ...
Begins with ...
Is in Range
Is in List
Begins with Value in List
Is Null

CASTLE ROCK

Figure 11-11. List of query options

Say, for example, we chose the value Denver as our value to filter. Figure 11-12 shows what it will look like.

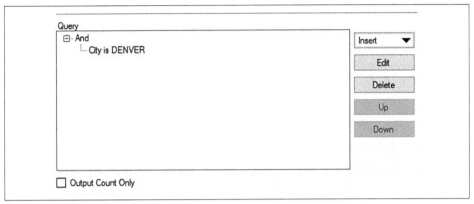

Query
⊟·· And
 ┊···· City is DENVER

Insert ▼
Edit
Delete
Up
Down

☐ Output Count Only

Figure 11-12. Query option

You can actually combine queries by using the Insert drop-down and choosing operators. Now when we run with this "City is Denver" query, notice we only get those corresponding values returned (see Figure 11-13).

Results - Calgary Input (4) - Output

12 of 12 Fields ∨ ☑ ☒ | Cell Viewer ∨ | 1,166 records displayed | ↑ ↓

Record	CustomerID	Store Number	Customer Segment	Responder	First Name	Last Name	Address	City	State	Zip
1	2	100	Corporate	No	JEAN	SMITH	376 S JASMINE ST	DENVER	CO	80224
2	3	100	Corporate	No	JULIA	CARRERA	846 S UMATILLA WAY	DENVER	CO	80223
3	5	100	Home Office	No	LINDA	TREVINO	5360 ZUNI ST	DENVER	CO	80221
4	6	106	Home Office	No	H	MACK	1599 WILLIAMS ST	DENVER	CO	80218
5	9	105	Home Office	No	VIVIAN	GAULDEN	4497 CORNISH WAY	DENVER	CO	80239
6	10	100	Home Office	No	PAMELA	WRIGHT	2316 E 5TH AVE	DENVER	CO	80206
7	11	106	Home Office	No	MARIA	GONZALEZ	3883 QUITMAN ST	DENVER	CO	80212
8	12	108	Home Office	No	WANDA	MAYBERRY	1965 YUKON ST	DENVER	CO	80214
9	21	100	Small Business	Yes	AVIVA	HEIFETS	3490 S BELLAIRE ST	DENVER	CO	80222
10	23	107	Corporate	Yes	LUCINDA	MAIA	4896 HARLAN ST	DENVER	CO	80212
11	24	105	Corporate	No	ROBIN	WALLIN	2855 ADAMS ST	DENVER	CO	80205
12	35	103	Small Business	Yes	VALERIE	GINSBURG	2100 16TH ST	DENVER	CO	80202
13	36	105	Small Business	No	LEIGH	WALLNER	200 RAMPART WAY	DENVER	CO	80230
14	37	106	Small Business	No	STACY	GILSON	4464 W GILL PL	DENVER	CO	80219
15	42	106	Consumer	No	TERESA	WIDENER	1330 YUKON ST	DENVER	CO	80214
16	46	101	Home Office	No	DIANE	ARONSON	6780 E CEDAR AVE	DENVER	CO	80224
17	49	101	Corporate	No	CAROLYN	EDWARDS	4480 S TENNYSON ST	DENVER	CO	80236
18	53	100	Corporate	No	DANA	COLLINS	4762 E ARKANSAS AVE	DENVER	CO	80222
19	57	100	Consumer	No	LYDIA	MAZANTI	10 S SHERMAN ST	DENVER	CO	80209

Figure 11-13. City Denver query

Three other features on the bottom of the configuration window are:

Output Count Only
    Get high-level counts.

Skip Records
    Skip a specified number of records.

Max Records
    Select a max number of records to return.

Let's take a look at field categories within the Calgary Input tool.

Field Categories

While the list of fields has just "Other" as the header, you can change this so it looks more user-friendly like I've done in Figure 11-14.

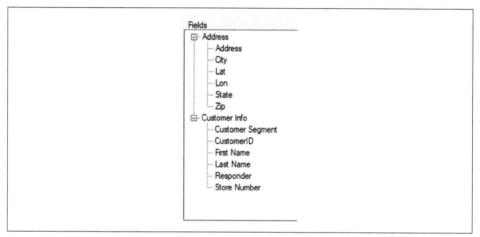

Figure 11-14. Friendly group headers

You simply right-click on the field header and select "Edit Index MetaInfo" (see Figure 11-15).

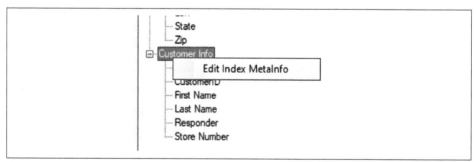

Figure 11-15. Edit Index MetaInfo

Then, in the new window, you can either Rename or Add New Category. Once you add a new category, you can drag and drop the fields you want in that category (see Figure 11-16).

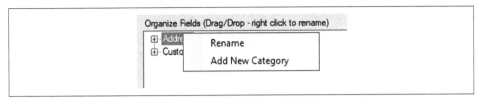

Figure 11-16. Meta Info Editor

You can also change the index properties like Index Name, Default Query Type Range, and Values (see Figure 11-17).

Index Properties
General   Range   Values

Index Name: CustomerID
Default Query Type: Is ...
Short Field Name: CustomerID
Long Field Name: CustomerID

Figure 11-17. Index Properties

Linked Tables

You may have noticed the No Linked Tables message on the top of the configuration pane. I won't go into depth on this feature here but if you need to use linked tables, which would allow you to link two Calgary databases, there is an Analytics App available to you under Options > Run Analytic Apps called "Calgary: Create Link Between 2 Tables" to help with this process, as well as additional documentation (*http://help.alteryx.com*) (see Figure 11-18).

Now you are able to pull data and filter it in the database before running. Let's look into the Calgary Join tool next.

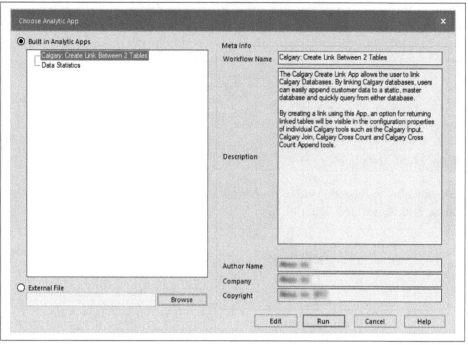

Figure 11-18. Create Link Between 2 Tables

Calgary Join Tool

The Calgary Join tool contains some nicely hidden features:

It operates quite a bit differently than a traditional Join tool. Think of it more as a Filter tool that adds (or joins) data based on the data you provide. For example, if you have a data set of a specific car you are interested in, then a good use case is to have all historical data on that car, its parts, its prices, and sales or manufacturing data over time in a Calgary database where you can query for just the information you need about that specific car. You don't want to be querying the entire historical database and pulling through a workflow each time. To start, you'll connect the Calgary Join tool to a workflow (see Figure 11-19). Let's jump right in!

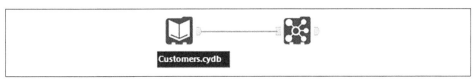

Figure 11-19. Calgary Join workflow

In the configuration pane, you first select the Calgary data you want to join records from (see Figure 11-20).

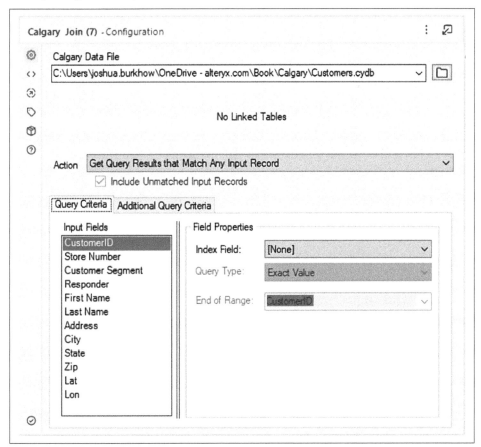

Figure 11-20. Calgary Join configuration

To make the join valid, you want to have fields/values in your data that can be matched, or joined, with the Calgary data. In the Action list, we have a handful of different ways we can match our data to the Calgary data (see Figure 11-21).

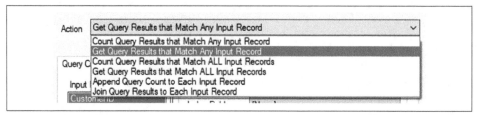

Figure 11-21. Action options

Rather than go through each one individually, I want you to see that there are basically two options here: Count or Get. Count is simple; it gives you the number of those records with the values you specify from your query. Get gives you the entire set of data that matches the query you created. You also have the last two options where you can append or join those counts or records to each of your input records. Maybe you want to know how many items are available or you need to output that data to stakeholders. Those options become very useful then.

In the following example, you can see that we chose Region and Color of cars as our Input Fields, and are using the *Autos.cydb* data set to append the query count to each input record (see Figure 11-22).

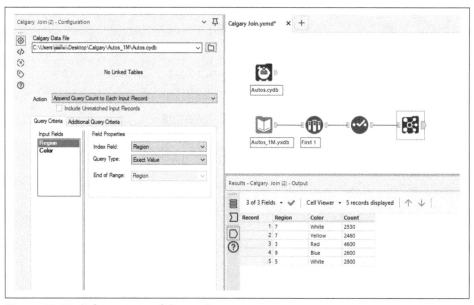

Figure 11-22. Calgary Append Query Count

Notice that you have three columns with the region, color, and count. Now, we'll go through that same example but with "Join Query Results to Each Input Record."

Instead of getting the counts of those records, you get the full record of detailed data (see Figure 11-23).

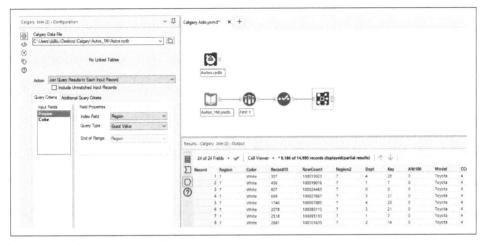

Figure 11-23. Join query results

The Calgary Join tool gives you the power to quickly pull from large data sets. When you work with large data sets, you need to be good at filtering the data *before* you pull it. What's so great about the Calgary tools in general, and this Join tool in particular, is that you can easily filter your data. On top of pulling the data that joins your input, you can also filter that data by using the Additional Query Criteria on the second tab. This tab (see Figure 11-24) looks exactly like the configuration for the Calgary Input tool.

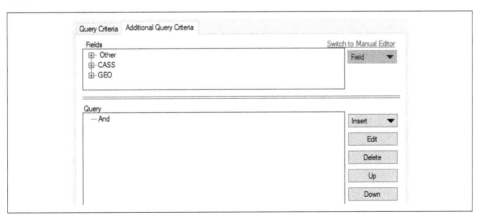

Figure 11-24. Additional query criteria

Now you have the information you need to query large data sets smartly! Let's now jump into a couple more tools that will bring you to the next level.

Calgary Cross Count Tool

To query large data sets intelligently, you don't usually query all fields for the entire record—that wouldn't make sense as you wouldn't be able to read or even see all of the results. Most of the time, you will want to get counts of something. When using our earlier Customer data set, you may want to know: how many customers responded? This is where tools like the Calgary Join can be useful, but the Calgary Cross Count tool takes it even further by helping you find the counts of rows that match a query in a Calgary database:

Instead of having to pull a set of data and summarize the counts you need, you could pull the counts on the first step.

Once you get into its configuration, you'll see the Calgary Cross Count tool is basically the same as the Calgary Input tool; the difference is that the query criteria are now on another tab. The Calgary Cross Count tool will let you create a straight line count of rows for a field or set of fields (Figure 11-25).

With this configuration you will have a list of the counts of who responded and didn't (see Figure 11-26).

Again, you can add as many fields as you want to count but it's going to give you a count of the rows with that combination of values.

If you are dealing with huge amounts of data, you might want to consider filtering the data with the Calgary Input and Calgary Join tools. Remember, in this tool you have the Additional Query Criteria tab available to filter your data set down to what you are looking for.

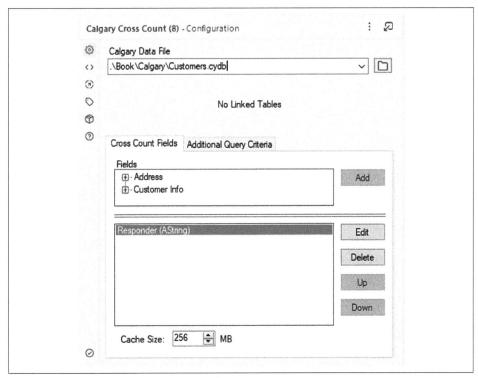

Figure 11-25. Calgary Cross Count configuration

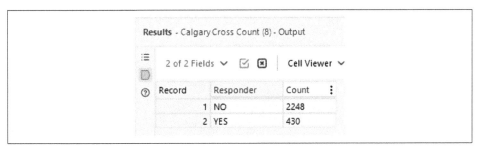

Figure 11-26. Calgary Cross Count output

Calgary Cross Count Append Tool

The Calgary Cross Count Append tool, as you can imagine, is very similar to the standard Calgary Cross Count tool. However, it has the added features of the Calgary Join tool, too:

The Calgary Cross Count Append tool takes an input file and appends counts at a row level that exist in the Calgary database. Where this becomes really amazing is when you, for example, have a location (or a spatial object in Alteryx vernacular) and you want to get counts of things like the number of stores, buildings, or houses based on that location. You can do exactly that using this tool by joining on a spatial object and then returning either the row counts of a specific set of values that are connected to that location or appending the results for more granular detail.

You would configure this first tab just like the Calgary Join tool (see Figure 11-27).

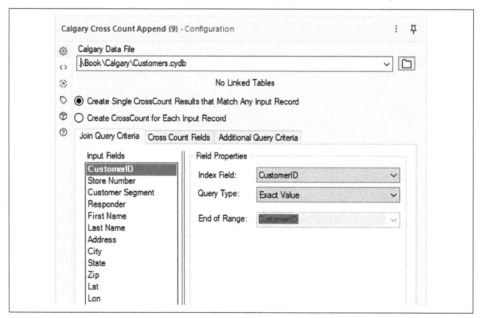

Figure 11-27. Calgary Cross Count Append configuration

Notice there are just two options here. Option 1 obtains the counts of rows that "join" to the fields you are providing via the Calgary Input tool. This results in a clean list of the values of the fields from the Cross Count Fields tab as well as each of their counts (see Figure 11-28).

Results - Calgary Cross Count Append (9) - Output

2 of 2 Fields ∨   ☑ ☒ | Cell Viewer ∨

Record	CustomerID	Count
1	10	1
2	100	1
3	1000	0
4	1002	0
5	1003	1
6	1005	1
7	1006	0
8	1008	1
9	1009	0
10	101	1

Figure 11-28. Calgary Cross Count Append results

Option 2 allows you to not only create the counts but to do it at the input row level so that all the detail is brought along. This is the "append" part of the tool (see Figure 11-29).

Results - Calgary Cross Count Append (121) - Output

7 of 7 Fields ✔   Cell Viewer ▾ 123 records displayed   ↑ ↓   Search

Record	Lat	Long	Name	Centroid	SpatialObject_TradeArea	CASS_CarrierRoute	Count
27	41.956069	-70.662367	Plymouth Rock Landmark	Point - View Browse Tool Map Tab	Polygon - View Browse Tool Map Tab	C012	1
28	41.956069	-70.662367	Plymouth Rock Landmark	Point - View Browse Tool Map Tab	Polygon - View Browse Tool Map Tab	C013	2
29	41.956069	-70.662367	Plymouth Rock Landmark	Point - View Browse Tool Map Tab	Polygon - View Browse Tool Map Tab	C014	2
30	41.956069	-70.662367	Plymouth Rock Landmark	Point - View Browse Tool Map Tab	Polygon - View Browse Tool Map Tab	C015	0
31	41.956069	-70.662367	Plymouth Rock Landmark	Point - View Browse Tool Map Tab	Polygon - View Browse Tool Map Tab	C016	0
32	41.956069	-70.662367	Plymouth Rock Landmark	Point - View Browse Tool Map Tab	Polygon - View Browse Tool Map Tab	C017	0
33	41.956069	-70.662367	Plymouth Rock Landmark	Point - View Browse Tool Map Tab	Polygon - View Browse Tool Map Tab	C018	0
34	41.956069	-70.662367	Plymouth Rock Landmark	Point - View Browse Tool Map Tab	Polygon - View Browse Tool Map Tab	C019	0
35	41.956069	-70.662367	Plymouth Rock Landmark	Point - View Browse Tool Map Tab	Polygon - View Browse Tool Map Tab	C020	0
36	41.956069	-70.662367	Plymouth Rock Landmark	Point - View Browse Tool Map Tab	Polygon - View Browse Tool Map Tab	C021	0
37	41.956069	-70.662367	Plymouth Rock Landmark	Point - View Browse Tool Map Tab	Polygon - View Browse Tool Map Tab	C022	0
38	41.956069	-70.662367	Plymouth Rock Landmark	Point - View Browse Tool Map Tab	Polygon - View Browse Tool Map Tab	C023	0
39	41.956069	-70.662367	Plymouth Rock Landmark	Point - View Browse Tool Map Tab	Polygon - View Browse Tool Map Tab	C024	0
40	41.956069	-70.662367	Plymouth Rock Landmark	Point - View Browse Tool Map Tab	Polygon - View Browse Tool Map Tab	C025	0
41	41.956069	-70.662367	Plymouth Rock Landmark	Point - View Browse Tool Map Tab	Polygon - View Browse Tool Map Tab	C026	0

Figure 11-29. Calgary Cross Count Append output

Remember, just like most of the other Calgary tools, you can provide additional query criteria in order to cut down the amount of data you are looking at.

Conclusion

In this chapter, you learned about the powerful and practical Calgary tools. These tools will help those who work with large amounts of data and want to extend their data power by tapping into billions of rows of valuable information. There are only five tools but they can open doors for you to read from billion-row data sets, join to your data sets, give you aggregated counts, and also filter down to only what you want to see or use. You can use Calgary tools with all your other tools, as well.

In the next chapter we get to jump into one of my favorite topics around Alteryx: macros! You will definitely go next-level once you understand how to use Alteryx Designer to create and share macros.

PART IV

Macros and Apps

CHAPTER 12

Interface Tools

If all you had to do each day was read an Excel file, clean it up, and output it to a database, Alteryx would be a useful application for you. However, Alteryx also has so many features and functions that make it a particularly useful tool when it comes to analytics. Once you start using Alteryx more and more, you will find yourself building the same workflows again and again or building the same patterns within a workflow over and over.

Welcome to the world of Alteryx macros and apps! Macros and their sister feature, apps (which we discuss in the next chapters), are game changers in Alteryx Designer.

To build macros and apps, your foundation is the Interface tool palette. You'll use the Interface tools with both. They allow you to build UIs that not only make your workflows more dynamic, but also allow you to build workflows that change parameter settings at runtime based on what the user inputs. In this chapter you will learn about the Interface tools so that you can apply them to build macros and apps.

The Interface Tool Palette

The Interface tools (see Figure 12-1) allow you as a developer to provide an input interface to the user. This will become a critical function that you will use over and over. I am going to walk through each of the Interface tools so that you have a solid understanding of how they work. As you read this chapter, think about how you might build a macro using these Interface tools.

Figure 12-1. The Interface tool palette

Both Alteryx macros and apps use the same Interface tools. Because we'll be covering the macros chapter first, all my examples and explanations are from the point of view of building a macro. However, everything you learn in this chapter will come in handy when we talk about how to build apps using these same tools in Chapter 14.

Macro Input Tool

I'm going to start off with the Macro Input and Output tools, as these two tools are fundamental to every macro you will build. The Macro Input tool allows a user to provide a template for data that will serve as the input to the macro:

The Macro Input tool is responsible for providing the green anchor to the user. If you were to build a simple Macro Input example, it might look something like Figure 12-2.

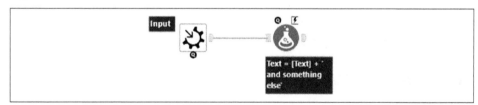

Figure 12-2. Macro Input example

However, if you were able to save this as a macro and provide it to someone else, this is what they would see:

The Macro Input tool configuration options are shown in Figure 12-3.

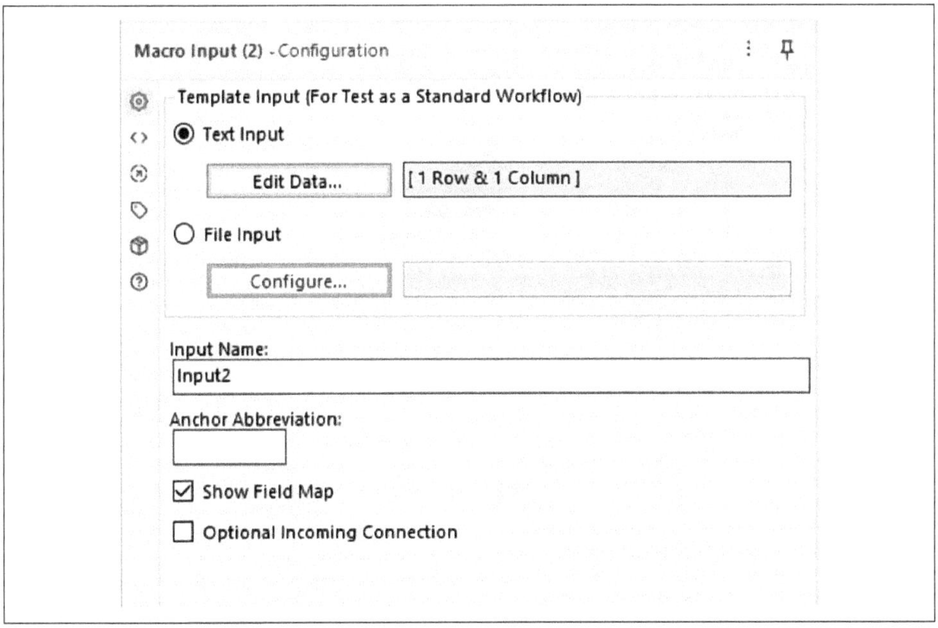

Figure 12-3. Macro Input configuration

The first option is the Template Input. The Macro Input tool needs to know what data you're going to bring into the macro. You have two options here: Text Input or File Input. These are similar to your standard data input tools. Just to be clear, this doesn't have to be the actual data you'll be using, but it needs to be the same structure. The Macro Input tool needs to understand the structure of the data coming in.

You also have the option to name the specific tools so they're easier to find later on. If you have multiple anchors (either inputs or outputs), it might be beneficial to use the anchor abbreviation to delineate which one is which. As a reminder, the Anchor Abbreviation is the letter that is shown on the input or output anchors of a tool. Show Field Map allows you to present the full list of fields to the user to ensure that each field maps up correctly to what your macro is expecting. This becomes extremely useful when incoming fields are not named exactly as the macros are expecting.

Lastly, the Optional Incoming Connection setting allows you to make the use of this input optional. This is a useful feature when you have multiple inputs but only need one of them and you don't want to require a data set. You might want to provide additional analysis based on whether a data set is provided, but skip it if it's not provided.

Macro Output Tool

The Macro Output tool provides an output anchor in your macro. It's similar to the Macro Input tool, but without all the configurations.

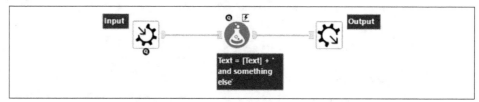

Figure 12-4. Macro Output example

Notice when you add a Macro Output tool, as shown in Figure 12-4, you get an output anchor (see Figure 12-5), just like you did for the Macro Input tool.

Figure 12-5. Macro Output anchor

The only configurable options for the Macro Output tool are the Output Name and Anchor Abbreviation, shown in Figure 12-6.

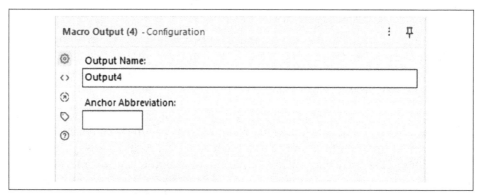

Figure 12-6. Macro Output configuration

With either of these two tools, you can start building a standard macro. If you go to the Workflow Configuration window, you'll see that simply by inserting one of these two tools, the type of file has changed to YXMC (see Figure 12-7).

If you save the workflow to your machine, you will notice that the "Save as type" is now an Alteryx macro with the *.yxmc* extension. Any of the four types of macros will use this extension (see Figure 12-8).

Figure 12-7. Workflow type configuration

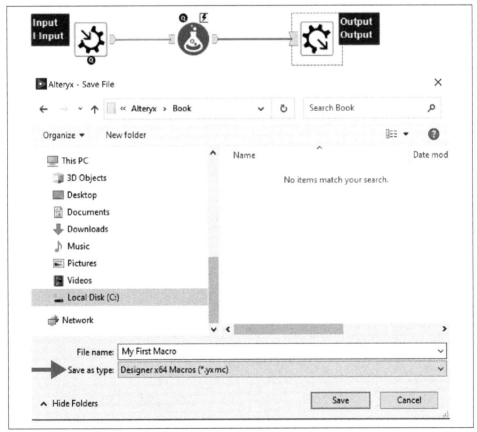

Figure 12-8. Workflow "Save as type"

Once you have the macro saved to your machine, you'll want to bring it into a workflow so you can use it. There are a couple of ways that you can make the macro available to your workflow. One way is shown in Figure 12-9.

Figure 12-9. Insert Macros

Let's walk through the steps:

1. Open a new workflow.
2. Right-click on the canvas.
3. Select Insert.
4. Scroll down to Macros.
5. Choose the new macro you've created.

Once the macro is on your canvas, make sure that the appropriate inputs or outputs are connected. If you were able to do this successfully, then you've built your first macro. Congratulations! Now, let's dive deeper so you can make even more.

Text Box Tool

The Text Box tool simply allows you to take in text from the user:

For example, you may want to capture a name, phone number, or any other bit of textual information that will in turn be used in the workflow.

Now, what's interesting is what it looks like from the Alteryx developer's point of view (see Figure 12-10).

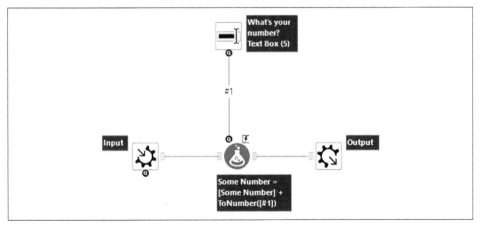

Figure 12-10. Text Box example

There's a bit to unpack with this initial example, and I want to make sure that you get a full understanding of the moving parts here. You can see the Input and Output tools that we added in the previous section, but now you also see the Text Box tool. Notice in Figure 12-10 that the Text Input tool is going into the Formula tool. Since the Text Box tool allows a user to enter text that can be brought into the macro, at runtime, when that text is entered it will go into the Formula tool and be calculated as part of the formula value.

As far as configurations go, the Text Box tool is quite simple (see Figure 12-11).

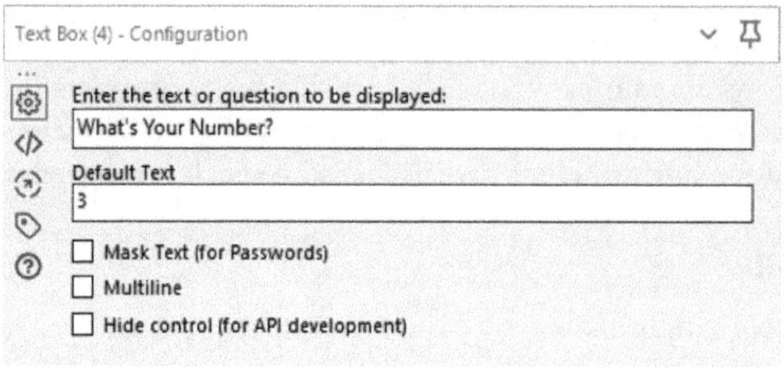

Figure 12-11. Text Box configuration

The first two configuration items ("Enter the text or question to be displayed" and "Default Text") determine what the user will see when they use that macro. They'll type their answer in the text box (I've entered "3" here, for the example we'll walk through shortly). Whatever you enter in the "Enter the text or question to be displayed" will be the question on top of the text input for the user. Ideally this is a question or clear instructions to the user (such as "Enter your name," as you see in Figure 12-12). The "Default Text" box will be whatever value you want the user to start with. That value can always be changed or kept as is.

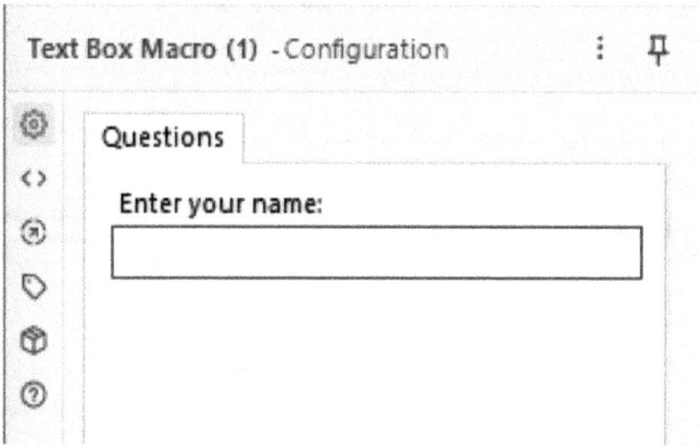

Figure 12-12. Text Box question

The third option in the Configuration window, "Mask Text (for Passwords)," allows you to use the text box as a password field, but not display a password in plain text. You've probably seen this when you sign in to online banking or other secure apps, when your password appears as asterisks as you type it. The fourth option, Multiline, allows a user to enter multiple lines of text in an input. The last configuration item, "Hide control (for API development)," is used when we tap into the SDK and API functionality that Alteryx offers.

Part of the challenge for you here is to learn what to expect, because it's not going to be immediately transparent what's happening when it runs.

First you need to run the macro, which you'll do by entering a value in the text box as I've shown in Figure 12-11. For this example, we'll stick with the number 3 that I entered. Number 3 will now be stored as a question variable (in this case, it's [#1]), which you can see as the connection from the Text Box tool to the Formula tool in Figure 12-13.

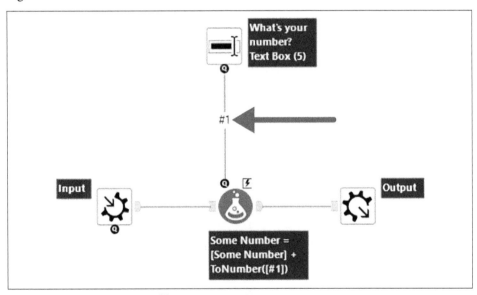

Figure 12-13. Text Box variable

If you were to change the name of that connection, then the name of your variable would change. If we take a look at the formula inside the Formula tool, you will notice that it's using that [#1] variable in its equation (see Figure 12-14).

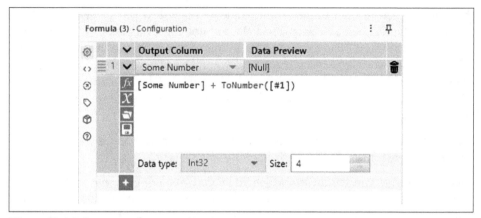

Figure 12-14. Some number equation

Think about this for a second. You entered the number 3, which then gets saved to the [#1] variable, where it gets used in the formula in Figure 12-14. Note that I have set the [Some Number] variable that I just created to 4, so if you calculate this value, it would be 4 * 3 = 12. The important piece here is that the Text Box tool is providing a value *at runtime* into this formula, and the formula is in turn calculating a value based on what that [#1] value is.

We are creating a formula that has variables that can be changed right at the moment a user runs the macro. If you are having trouble visualizing or building the macro, stick with it and keep going through these tools. I assure you it will "click" soon and make perfect sense for you. Everyone has the same struggle.

Let's keep going and add some new tools to your repertoire!

Action Tool

The Action tool is incredibly important for building macros and apps:

It is the glue that binds all the Interface tools and the tools you have in your macro or app. The Action tool is responsible for the modification of a tool based on the Interface tool, meaning that an Interface tool's values cannot be changed without the Action tool making it happen. Let's look at an example to drive this home. Recall from Figure 12-13 that the Text Input tool is connected to the Formula tool. Without that Action tool, the value of the [#1] variable can change, but what if I wanted to change the [Some Number] variable? I will need the Action tool to help me do that (see Figure 12-15).

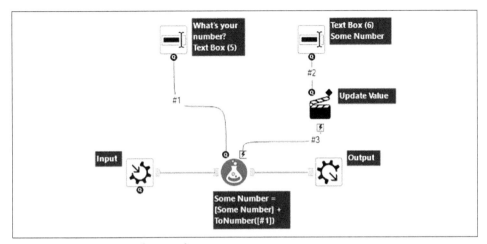

Figure 12-15. Action tool example

As you can see in the upper right, the text input "Some Number" is taking is a number value that is then passed to the Action tool via the [#2] variable. The Action tool gets a bit dynamic at this point because the configuration options change based on what tools are connected to it. It always depends on what is coming in and what tool the Action tool is going to modify. The first piece to understand in the Action tool configuration window is the "Selection an action type" drop-down and the three action types available (see Figure 12-16).

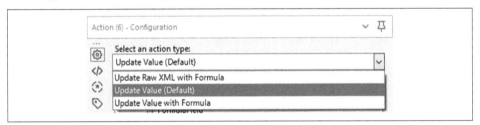

Figure 12-16. Available action types

I want to start with the Update Value (Default) action type, as this will be the most common use case. When you select Update Value, you are telling the workflow to take whatever value(s) are coming in from the user and put them in place of whatever value you selected. This is a critical point. You must tell the workflow where you want that value to update (see Figure 12-17).

Notice in Figure 12-17 that I've selected the expression of the formula as the value I want to update. I've also configured it to replace a specific part of that formula by checking the box "Replace a specific string" and typing exactly which part of that formula I want changed. Through these action types, you can change a value, change the entire formula, or even change the entire XML of a tool! There is literally nothing you can't change for each interaction, which in turn means you have an immense amount of power to do what you need.

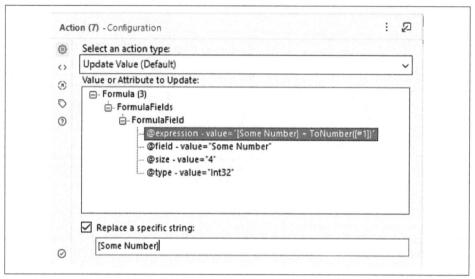

Figure 12-17. Selecting Value or Attribute to Update

One of the more challenging aspects of learning the Action tool is familiarizing yourself with all the possible combinations that you could use by connecting the Action tool to other Interface tools and tools within your workflow. This is something that you will have to experience and practice as you build workflows. I will highlight some other use cases for the Action tool as I cover the rest of the Interface tools.

Numeric Up Down Tool

The Numeric Up Down tool simply allows you to provide a number input to the user:

This tool is simple and has a basic configuration. You can set the minimum, maximum, increment, default, and number of decimal places for the value being set (see Figure 12-18).

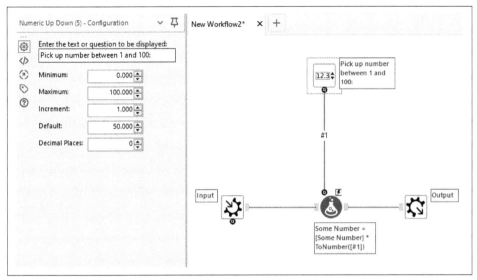

Figure 12-18. Numeric Up Down configuration

Remember, if you want to test that you configured your Interface tool correctly and that values are passing as you expect, you should build a test workflow. Save your macro and then bring it into your test workflow (see Figure 12-19).

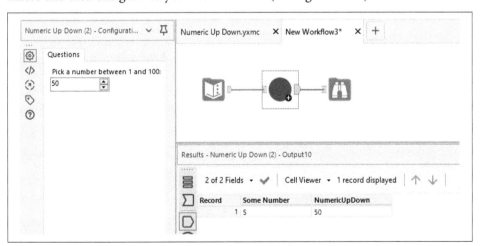

Figure 12-19. Test workflow with Numeric Up Down macro

 You can open multiple instances of Alteryx Designer. If you happen to have multiple screens, it's useful to have multiple instances open so you don't have to switch back and forth. You can have your macro open on one screen and your test workflow on the other.

Radio Button Tool

The Radio Button tool is a bit different from the other Interface tools; it can best be thought of as an enabler to other tools rather than an actual input that takes a value:

With a single radio button, a user can make all kinds of different logic choices that have downstream effects, like whether to include a part of a report, whether to output to different sources and types, or even whether to include specific information. There are two main use cases for this type of tool. The first is to offer a group of radio buttons to the user that would look like Figure 12-20.

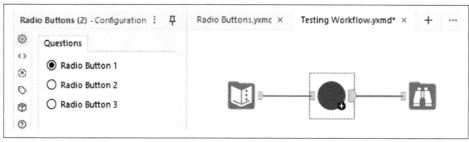

Figure 12-20. Group of radio buttons

You can use your creativity to decide what text will be displayed by the buttons. The key piece to know here is that when you feed that input from the Radio Button tool into something like the Formula tool, the value that gets passed in is either a True (if it's selected) or False (if it's not selected) (see Figure 12-21).

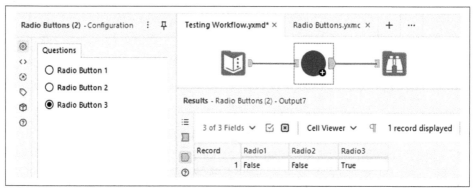

Figure 12-21. Radio Button tool results

While this first use case is helpful, the second use case is my favorite. Since you can build your workflow to provide certain features (or not) based on your user's selection, you can use the radio buttons to open or collapse a whole other group of Interface tools. If you just start out with one radio button, then you have the option of collecting your Interface tools in one group (see Figure 12-22).

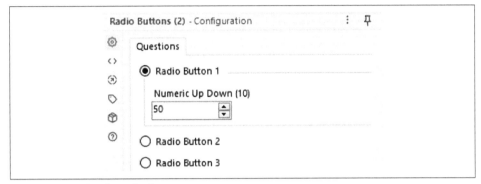

Figure 12-22. Single radio button group

Once you add two or more radio buttons, then you'll have more options, like opening or collapsing those groups (see Figure 12-23).

Figure 12-23. Collapsed group

For this example, you need to use the interface designer to properly lay out the individual groups, which we will cover later in this chapter. That configuration looks like Figure 12-24.

As we get farther along in this chapter, you will find plenty of examples where it makes a lot of sense to use radio buttons to better organize the Interface tools. Always try to keep in mind that the point of having these features in your macros is to benefit and simplify the user experience. Try not to add anything that isn't absolutely essential or that won't improve the user experience.

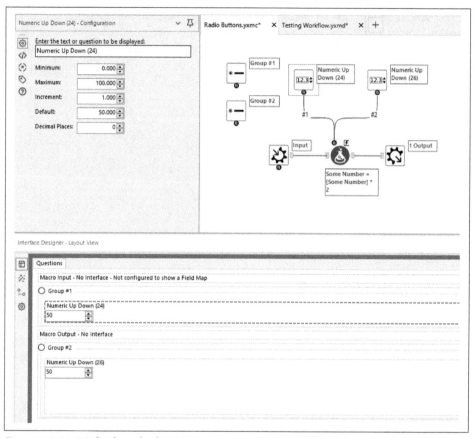

Figure 12-24. Multiple radio buttons

Drop Down Tool

The Drop Down tool gives the user the option to choose from a list of values:

The Drop Down tool is fairly easy to configure as well (see Figure 12-25).

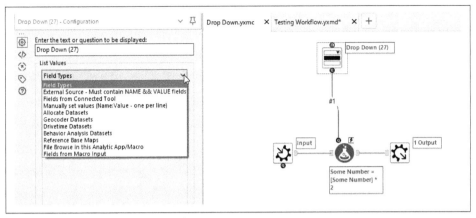

Figure 12-25. Drop Down List Values

If you look at the list of values in the configuration, you will see there are 11 different ways to use this tool. This drop-down list will depend on which of these options is picked and how it is configured. Don't let this overwhelm you—there are a few options that you will use more often than others and you'll quickly become familiar with them:

Field Types
  Used to provide a list of supported field types.

External Source
  Allows you to provide a list from a file.

Fields from Connected Tool
  Allows you to provide a list from an output of a tool.

Manually set values
  Allows you to create a list of name:values.

Data sets (Allocate, Geocoder, Drivetime, Behavior Analysis, Reference Base Maps)
  Allows you to display a data set to populate a list.

File Browse in this Analytic App/Macro
  Similar to the "Fields from Connected Tool" option, it allows you to provide a list to the user from a file.

Fields from Macro Input
  Allows you to create a list from the fields of a macro input. For this, the Q anchor of the Macro Input tool needs to be connected to the Drop Down tool.

The options that you'll likely run into the most are Manually Set Values, Fields from Connected Tool, and External Source. I'd recommend getting used to these options first but certainly be open to exploring and experimenting with the others.

To understand how you can use the Drop Down tool, let's walk through a very simple example. Figure 12-26 shows a simple macro built with a single drop-down that is going to allow a user to select one of three possible options.

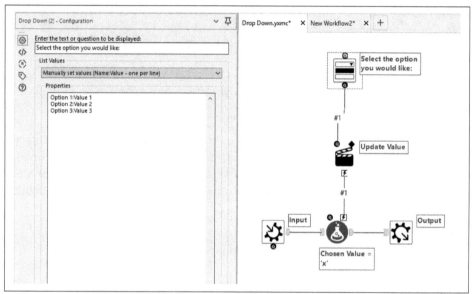

Figure 12-26. Drop Down example

 There is typically an expectation that the drop-down will be dynamic (i.e., it will change) during runtime. In fact, Alteryx determines and populates the drop-downs before the app is run. For it to update dynamically, you must go to chained apps, which we cover in Chapter 14.

The Action tool (see Figure 12-27) is just going to take in the option that was selected and replace the "x" in the formula with the value of that option selected.

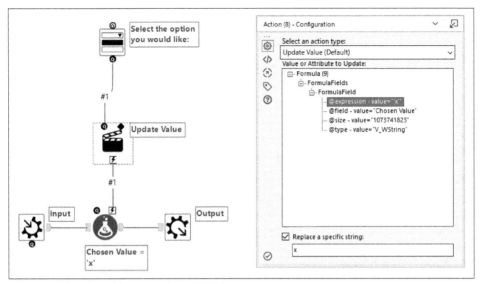

Figure 12-27. Drop Down with the Action tool

Now when a user chooses, let's say, Option 3 (see Figure 12-28), that corresponding value (Value 3) replaces the "x" in the formula value.

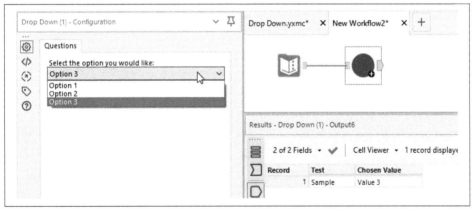

Figure 12-28. Option 3 selected

Check Box Tool

The Check Box tool allows you to display a checkbox to a user, which can turn on or off anything that you'd like:

This allows for quite a few extremely useful use cases.

The Check Box tool is useful when you want to provide an option to include something. For example, let's say you have a standard report and you want to provide an option to include a detailed summary. The user can check the box to include the summary if they want it. You can also provide a list of checkboxes as options that a user may want to include in an analysis or report (which is called a List Box and will be covered in the next section).

When configuring this tool (see Figure 12-29) you only have three simple items to set. First is the text you want to be displayed for the user. Second is the default value (checked or not checked), and third is whether to collapse the group when deselected, which allows you to expand options in the UI.

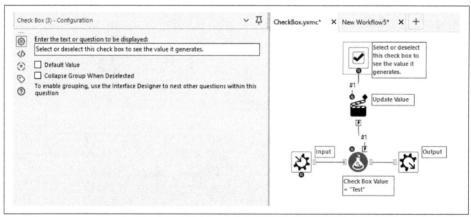

Figure 12-29. Check Box configuration

The important thing to remember is that these Interface tools mainly give you a value to work from. If the user checks the box, then you get the value True. If they don't, then the value will be False (see Figure 12-30).

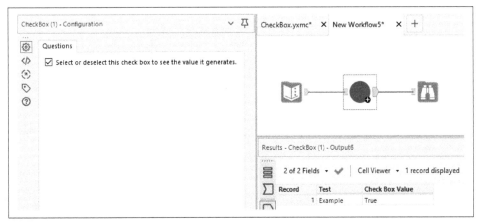

Figure 12-30. Check Box selected

Once you have that value in place, you can build your workflow to operate from that signal. It's all up to you and your creativity as to how it's applied.

List Box Tool

The List Box tool allows a user to make multiple selections from a list:

You might use this when you have four options that you want the user to select from, which will filter the data down to the focus area the user selected.

The List Box tool has a lot of the same configurations as the Drop Down tool, with some additional options (see Figure 12-31). As with most Interface tools, you will set the text that will be displayed to the user. You can also set the default to All Checked if you want all the boxes to appear checked for the user up front. You can take your inputs and generate a delimited list, or you can use any one of the List Values to determine what is going to be in the list (notice they are listed as Name:Value pairs).

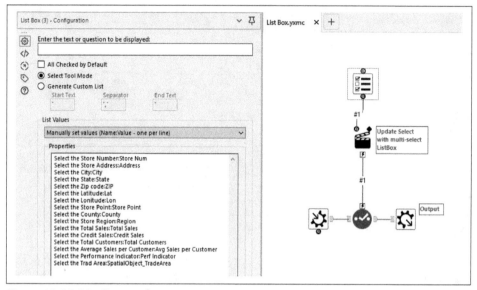

Figure 12-31. List Box configuration

The important thing to remember here is that you need to understand how your values are coming in and what they map to. In the example in Figure 12-31, you can see that we are taking a list of values, and the Action tool is selecting or deselecting fields based on what you chose. The macro view would look like Figure 12-32.

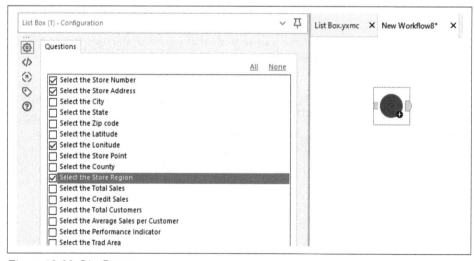

Figure 12-32. List Box macro

Folder Browse Tool

The Folder Browse tool and the File Browse tool, covered in the next section, both open the doors to a lot of functionality. The Folder Browse tool displays a folder browse control, which allows a user to select files or folders from their own machine:

The directory path specified by the end user is passed to downstream tools that the Folder Browse tool is connected to.

The configuration is super simple. You just need to specify the text the user will see when using this object. You'll also see a warning about not being able to use this in apps published to the web (see Figure 12-33). Please ignore this for now—I'll cover it more in Chapter 17 when we discuss the Alteryx Server (or Gallery).

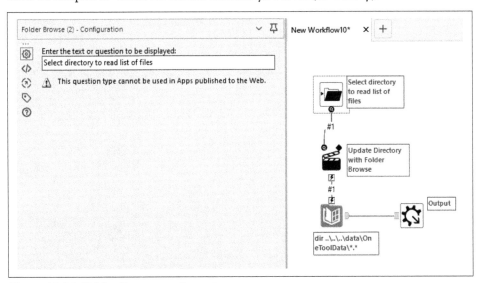

Figure 12-33. Folder Browse configuration

The use of the Folder Browse tool is unique because instead of having to specify the folder ahead of time, the directory tool allows you to have the user specify the folder of files at runtime. Instead of having to select an individual file each and every time, you could select 100 or even 10,000 files at one time to be processed.

File Browse Tool

The File Browse tool is similar to the Folder Browse tool:

The File Browse tool allows a user to choose a single file at runtime to use in a workflow. The configuration, much like with the Folder Browse tool, is fairly simple. You enter the text or question to be displayed to the user, present a Save As dialog to the user, and choose the formatting of the file you want the user to select. If you're going to use the arbitrary file specification, say for a specific file type like TXT, it's important to note the formatting that is available by default (see Figure 12-34). You might have to do much more work for a text file specification versus using the native tools.

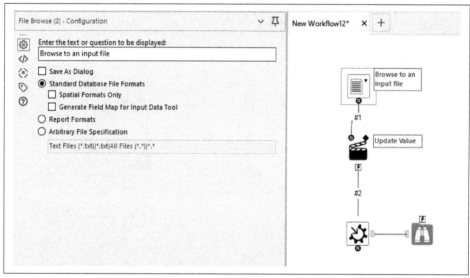

Figure 12-34. File Browse configuration

Once you configure your File Browse tool, save it as a macro, and bring it onto your canvas, you will see a File Browse input in your workflow (see Figure 12-35).

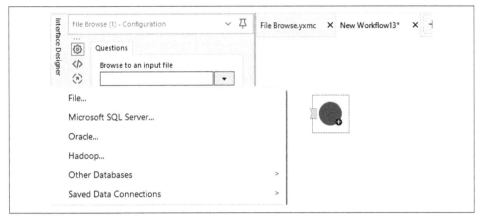

Figure 12-35. File Browse macro

The important things to remember here are:

- You can use the File Browse tool both for inputs and outputs (e.g., if you want the user to specify which exact file to save to).

- You can have as many File Browse tools as needed to cover your inputs or outputs.

- If you happen to select an Excel file, Alteryx Designer will automatically ask which tab you want to use within that spreadsheet.

Date Tool

The Date tool is a simple but important Interface tool:

The Date tool simply allows the user to pick a date that can update any part of your workflow that requires it. It is most commonly used to help filter data based on a date or set of dates. There's really no configuration other than providing the text that a user is going to see (see Figure 12-36). Say, for example, you have a report of sales. By providing a Date tool, a user can choose a specific set of dates for which to present the sales numbers.

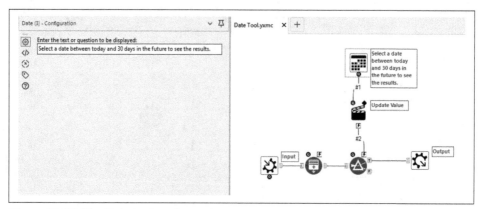

Figure 12-36. The Date tool configuration

The important thing to note on the Date tool is that the format of the date follows the Alteryx standard format: YYYY-MM-DD.

Tree Tool

The Tree tool is a slightly more complex Interface tool, but it's useful enough to be worth the effort:

The Tree tool displays an organized, hierarchical data structure in an app or macro that allows the user to make one or more selections. The selections made by the end user are then passed as values that are separated by a newline character (\n).

There are a few important configurations you need to get right to use this tool properly (see Figure 12-37).

Notice that this is the first time where the Action tool is connected to a Macro Input tool. It's important to build an intuition of what is happening. Here, when a user selects a value from the Tree tool, that value(s) is pushed via the Action tool to the Macro Input.

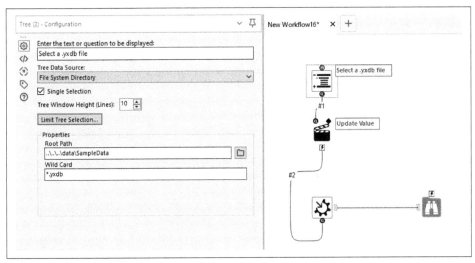

Figure 12-37. The Tree tool configuration

As with most of the Interface tools, you'll have to enter the text or question that you want to be displayed. The next important step is to set your Tree Data Source, which is the location from which the hierarchy is pulled. Here, you have five options (see Figure 12-38).

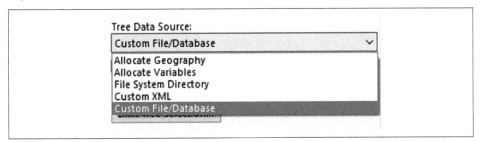

Figure 12-38. Tree Data Source options

The Allocate Geography and Allocate Variables options refer to third-party data sources. The File System Directory option allows you to point at a Windows directory on your machine and use the hierarchy of the folders. Custom XML and Custom File/Database are both file-based sources where you will select a file that has a specified hierarchy.

Using the configuration in Figure 12-37, the UI would look like Figure 12-39.

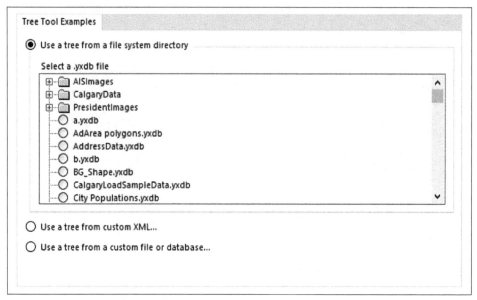

Figure 12-39. Tree tool example

Map Tool

The Map tool is a powerful tool if you're using maps and doing spatial data analysis:

The Map tool is responsible for helping a user interact with a map and turning map interactions (e.g., selecting a location) into spatial data.

The Map tool has quite a few features and configurable options (see Figure 12-40).

As always, enter the text or question to be displayed to the user first. The next configuration will be the Base Map, the background map that is displayed to the user and which everything else lies on top of. I recommend looking at the list of the base maps to find a map that works best for your situation. The next configurable option is the Select/Draw option. This simply allows the user to draw one or more spatial objects on the map—sometimes you only want the user selecting one item at a time (like a city or a state). You also have a Zoom To configuration that allows you to configure the boundaries of the map that will be displayed initially.

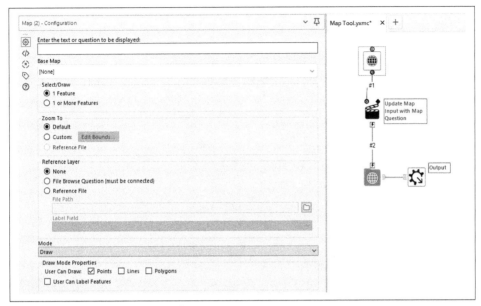

Figure 12-40. The Map tool configuration

The Reference Layer option will add a layer that allows you to use the File Browse Question to connect to a file that would provide information to the user. For example, instead of clicking on 10 different cities you could instead upload a list of those 10 cities. Next, there are two modes that you can choose from: Draw and Select From Reference Layer. With Draw mode, you have a few simple properties where you can allow the user to draw points, lines, polygons, and also label those features. If you happen to have a reference layer, like the points of the stores in your area, then you can switch over to the Select From Reference Layer option.

Now that you've gotten your Map tool configured and saved, you can see how you can present a map on which a user can select a point. That information, which in this use case is a spatial object, is passed to the Map Input tool. Imagine you wanted to create a map where you list all your stores within 100 miles of the user's location that they select (see Figure 12-41).

In this example, a user would click a location (say Oak Hill Park) and then run the workflow to see which stores are closest to that location.

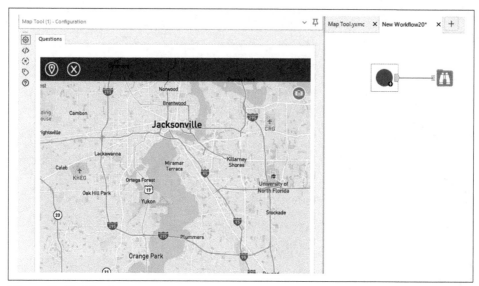

Figure 12-41. Map input

Condition Tool

The Condition tool can build out more complex logic within your applications:

The Condition tool performs similarly to the Filter tool. You can create an expression that evaluates to either True or False. Based on the output of that expression, you can decide to direct your workflow process in different directions (see Figure 12-42). Say, for example, you have a drop-down with two color choices: Red or Blue. Now, if a user chooses Blue, then you can use the Condition tool to process the input and follow a flow that is based on the selection of Blue (e.g., a sales report for the Blue team). A common use case is when you want a user to decide whether to include something, like quarter-on-quarter change, in a report. They can select "yes" and the report will be built with that included.

It's important to build an intuition for what data is being passed through here. When you connect an Interface tool to an Action tool, the Action tool is just responsible for making that real-time update to the tool it's connected to, based on the information coming through. Remember that the Condition tool has all the features and functions of a Filter tool, so you could write fairly complex formulas, but at the end of the day the expression still needs to evaluate to True or False.

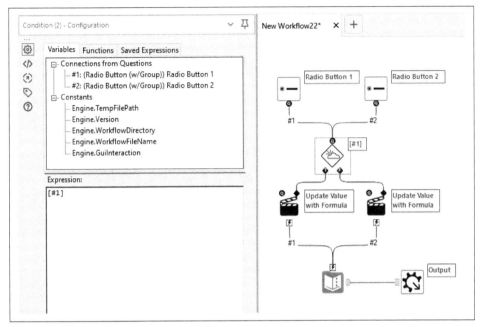

Figure 12-42. The Condition tool configuration

Error Message Tool

As you build more and more macros and apps, you will find that the Error Message tool will become your guiding light for ensuring that users are using the inputs correctly:

It will help to improve the overall quality of your workflows by ensuring that if a user doesn't enter the right value, the workflow doesn't get run and the user is prompted to update the value so it's within the correct parameters.

The Error Message tool serves a similar purpose as the Condition tool, but functions differently. With the Condition tool, the expression will evaluate to True or False and pass that information into the workflow. However, with the Error Message tool, if the expression is True then the system presents an error message to the user and prompts them to modify their input. With macros, this will present an error message to the results window. With apps, it will create a pop-up for the user that appears before they can submit the results.

Let's look at an example in Figure 12-43.

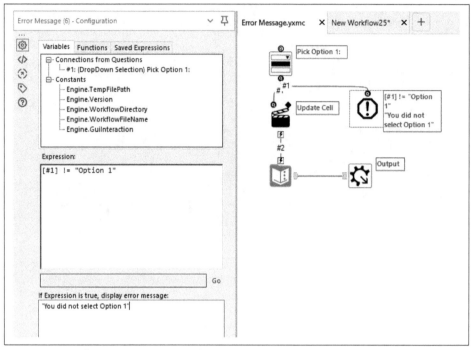

Figure 12-43. The Error Message configuration

In the expression window, you see that I'm looking to make sure the user is selecting Option 1. If they don't, then that expression evaluates to True and will display the error message "You did not select option 1." If we save this macro and try to run it with Option 2 selected, then you will see the error message successfully (see Figure 12-44).

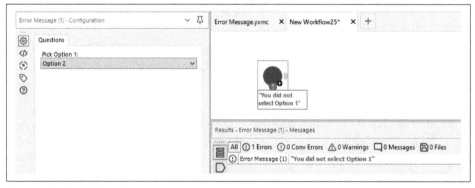

Figure 12-44. Option 2 error message

If there is ever a chance that the user could enter the wrong information (e.g., entering a phone number instead of an email address), then you should use the Error Message tool.

Control Parameter Tool

The Control Parameter tool is solely focused on enabling batch macros:

The Control Parameter tool provides the input values the macro uses for each batch it processes. In general, if you provide three values to the Control Parameter tool, then your macro will run three batches. The quintessential use case is for applying tax rates. Say, for example, we have five states in the US that all have different corporate tax rates. You can use the Control Parameter tool to help ensure that a specific row of data (say, data from the state of Florida) is applied to the right tax situation.

If you find yourself building a workflow and have sets of tools repeating over and over, then it is very likely you have a good beginning use case for a batch macro. A simple example of a batch macro could look something like Figure 12-45.

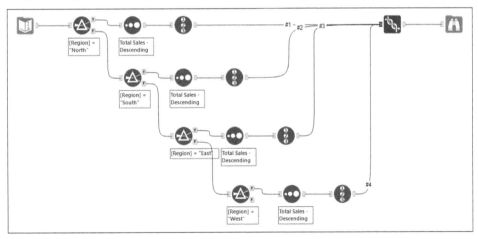

Figure 12-45. Batch macro use case

Here, you can notice that there are four instances of essentially the same workflow process but filtered to each of the four directional values. This cascading set of filters is usually a key indicator that you need a batch macro. However, the batch macro will not cascade like this; it will run the entire data set for each entry presented to the Control Parameter. The correct representation is that the Text Input tool will connect directly to the input of each Filter tool.

The solution to this is shown in Figure 12-46, where there's a single process flow and the Control Parameter tool is responsible for providing the four directional values. This is a very small use case where we could go from 12 tools down to 3, essentially cutting down the size of our workflow by almost 75%. Now, imagine if you had a workflow that had 1,000 tools in it!

A couple of different things happen when you drop a Control Parameter tool onto your canvas. First, the file type automatically changes to a batch macro. Second, when you bring your new macro onto a canvas, you'll see a new type of input with a ¿ (upside-down question mark) (*https://oreil.ly/_VUUq*). There isn't really anything to configure except entering a label for the Control Parameter input (see Figure 12-46).

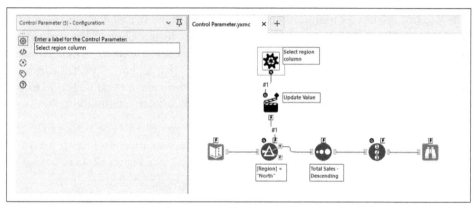

Figure 12-46. Control Parameter configuration

When you bring a batch macro onto the canvas you will also notice a drop-down to choose the field you want to feed into the batch macro (see Figure 12-47).

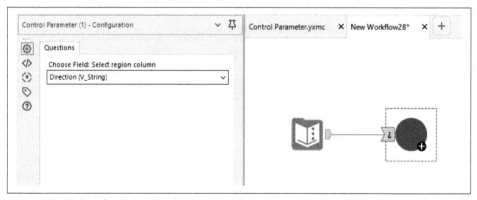

Figure 12-47. Batch macro input

The full power of batch macros is frankly beyond the scope of this book, as the number of use cases easily extends into the thousands (if not more). Batch macros can be extremely powerful, both by adding functionality and by reducing the size and complexity of your workflows.

Conclusion

In the beginning of this chapter, I talked about how macros and apps are a game changer in Alteryx, but to fully use their power, you needed some baseline knowledge about the Interface tools. Throughout this chapter, I discussed all the Interface tools that you will need to know to build robust and highly valuable macros and apps. In the next chapter, you're going to learn how to build your own macros. We'll then jump to apps in Chapter 14.

CHAPTER 13

Macros

A macro is simply a workflow that allows a single tool to be inserted into another workflow. Building a macro allows you to benefit from a standard process that is created once and used as many times as you need. You no longer need to build the same 5-, 10-, or 100-tool workflow. When you can build a macro, a single tool can be used as many times as you need. A macro also has its own file type, the *.yxmc* file extension. Interestingly, most users already use macros without knowing it. Many Alteryx tools are actually macros! Let's talk about one specific example.

With an Alteryx macro, you can create something quite involved (see Figure 13-1).

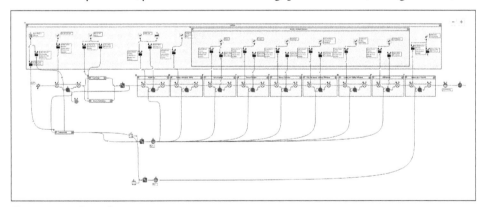

Figure 13-1. Sample macro

Or you can create something that's nicely packaged, like this Data Cleansing Macro:

Note the black circle with white plus sign on the macro in this icon. That indicates that it is a macro, not a standard tool. You can enable that plus sign by going to Options > User Settings > Edit User Settings, going to the Canvas tab, and clicking the box "Display macro indicators on tools" (Figure 13-2).

Figure 13-2. Macro indicator setting

You can get into any of these macros and see the underlying macro by simply right-clicking on the tool and selecting Open Macro: (Figure 13-3).

Figure 13-3. Open Macro

Imagine if every time you needed to build a workflow for a task, you had to build something like 30 tools. Instead, you can build that process into a macro and have a single tool handle it every time.

The impact of macros cannot be understated. I would not consider an Alteryx developer to be "advanced" until they know how to build macros. As a matter of fact, to pass the Alteryx Designer Advanced Certification exam, you must know macros. They are really a big deal. Get it? Got it? Good. Let's make sure you know macros.

Types of Macros

In Alteryx Designer there are technically four types of macros that you can build: standard, batch, iterative, and location optimizer (see Figure 13-4). However, most of us will say there are three main macros, because location optimizer is only used for unique use cases, and frankly it's an iterative macro at its core.

Figure 13-4. Macro types in Workflow tab

You can find the list of macro types in the drop-down in the workflow Configuration pane on the Workflow tab:

Standard macro

The standard macro, as I mentioned in the introduction, is simply a workflow. It is a packaged workflow that can be used as many times as needed. It allows you to do away with the complexity of copying tens or hundreds of tools that define a process and instead allows you to use one single tool that drags onto the canvas just like every other tool. Think of it as enabling you to do many tasks with a single tool.

Batch macro

The batch macro is very powerful and allows you to handle use cases where you need the forEach capability in your workflow. For example, I could use a batch macro if I want to analyze a tax return forEach state or produce a report forEach line of business. The macro runs once for each record or selected group of records in data. This macro requires a Control Parameter tool as an input, which we will discuss further in this chapter.

Iterative macro
> The iterative macro runs a configured number of times or continuously until a condition is met. An iterative macro essentially allows you to handle a while loop inside of your workflow.

Location optimizer macro
> The location optimizer macro is a special type of macro that is usually used in network analyses of locations. I won't cover this much here since it's such a specific use case.

As you can see, each of these macro types has specific uses and benefits. Over time, you will build up a sense of when you need each macro. Many of us who have been building workflows for a good number of years can take one look at a workflow and tell you intuitively if you have a use case or two for a batch macro or an iterative macro. Later in this chapter, we'll look at some of the patterns to be looking for.

Next, let's learn how to manage your macros as you start using or building them.

Managing Macros

Over time, as you build more and more macros, you'll find that you need some sort of organizational method or process to keep all your files together. Fortunately, Alteryx Designer provides an easy way to do this. Go to Options > User Settings > Edit User Settings and click the "Macros" tab (see Figure 13-5).

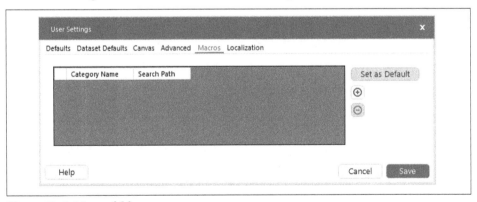

Figure 13-5. Macro folder

By adding a search path for macros (see Figure 13-6), you can then store all your macros in a single folder.

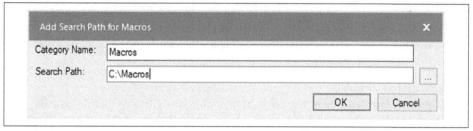

Figure 13-6. Adding a search path for macros

Alteryx Designer will be able to see the macros and present them via a Macros tool palette (see Figure 13-7).

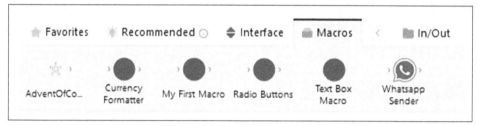

Figure 13-7. Macros tool palette

Let's build a standard macro so you can start to take your Alteryx game to the next level.

Building a Standard Macro

Now that you're familiar with all the tools available to you, let's run through a simple example of building a standard macro so that you can see all the pieces put together.

Step 1: Build a Workflow

Every macro starts off as a workflow. In this example, you'll build a simple macro that allows a user to choose how many records they want to output. You can do that using the Sample tool. Pick any sample file that has a decent number of rows, add a Sample tool set to 100 rows, and then the Browse tool. It should look like Figure 13-8.

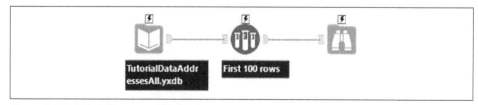

Figure 13-8. Workflow to a standard macro

Step 2: Add Interface Tools

Next, you'll add a Numeric Up Down tool, connect it to the Sample tool, and configure the Action tool. Also, right-click on the Browse tool and convert to a Macro Output interface tool. It should look like Figure 13-9.

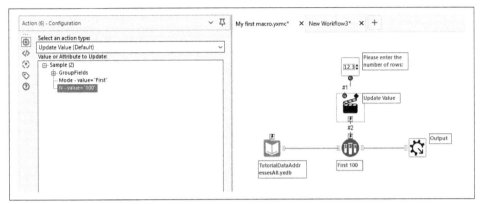

Figure 13-9. Add Interface tools

> You could convert the Input tool to a Macro Input tool to make it more dynamic by simply right-clicking and selecting "convert to Macro Input."

Step 3: Set to Standard Macro and Save

Go into the workflow configuration and set the type to Standard Macro then save it somewhere on your desktop (see Figure 13-10).

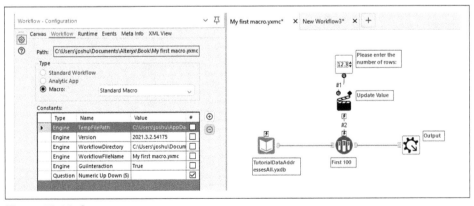

Figure 13-10. Set macro type

Step 4: Insert Macro and Test

Open a new workflow, then right-click and insert the macro into the workflow (see Figure 13-11).

Figure 13-11. Insert macro into a workflow

Then, you'll want to test the macro and ensure the number of records output matches what you chose. If not, you'll need to troubleshoot where it is not working (see Figure 13-12). This comes down to getting good at seeing what value comes in and ensuring that the value and the math involved are correct all the way through.

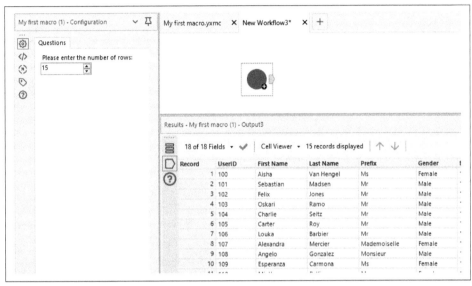

Figure 13-12. Macro test

Congratulations! You've built your first standard macro. Now let's raise it up a notch and run through the steps to build a Batch Macro!

Building a Batch Macro

Batch macros are very similar to standard macros with a single key difference: the Control Parameter. You can sound like a real Alteryx rock star when you see a workflow that has the Control Parameter and say, "Ah, I see you built a batch macro!" That's because a Control Parameter is the single tool that turns a standard macro into a batch macro. As a matter of fact, as I'll show you in a little bit, when you drop the Control Parameter tool onto *any* workflow, it automatically changes the workflow type to a batch macro. The Control Parameter gives it the "batching" functionality. Let's look at a simple example (see Figure 13-13).

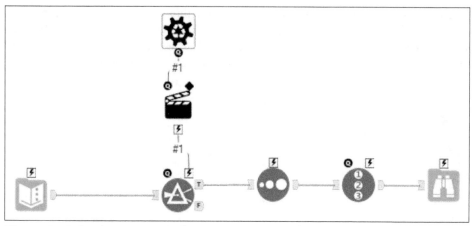

Figure 13-13. Batch macro example

Notice that the Control Parameter connects to the standard tools just like any other interface tool. It's using the same Action tool that you would use in an app or macro to drive the change to the workflow at runtime. Now here's where it gets different in a couple of different ways. First, by adding a Control Parameter you are in turn adding another input anchor to the workflow. When we save this and bring it into another workflow, you'll notice that now not only is there another anchor but it's got that upside-down question mark. Only a Control Parameter has this type of input (see Figure 13-14).

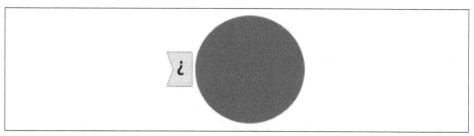

Figure 13-14. Batch macro anchor

All of this shows you what a batch macro is and how it looks, but we haven't discussed the reason *why* we would want to use a batch macro. We will do that now. The reason why we would use a batch macro is because it has the power to exponentially reduce our workflow size and even improve performance in many cases. The easiest way to show you what I mean by "exponentially reduce" is to give you an example of what it looks like in a situation where you don't use a batch macro. Take a look at Figure 13-15 and you'll see a workflow (not a macro) where we have a very simple and easy situation that is quickly getting out of hand. We have 18 similar but different inputs (it could just as well be 1,000 inputs too), we need to pull the same specific columns of data from "each" data set and then apply the same formula to "each" data set before we bring it all together in a Union tool.

I put quotes around "each" on purpose. That is what the batch macro is really all about. It allows you to build a macro that effectively says "for each instance, I want you to apply this process." In our example we are saying, "for each (of the 18 different) inputs, I want to remove the same two fields and add them together before unioning them into a single data set."

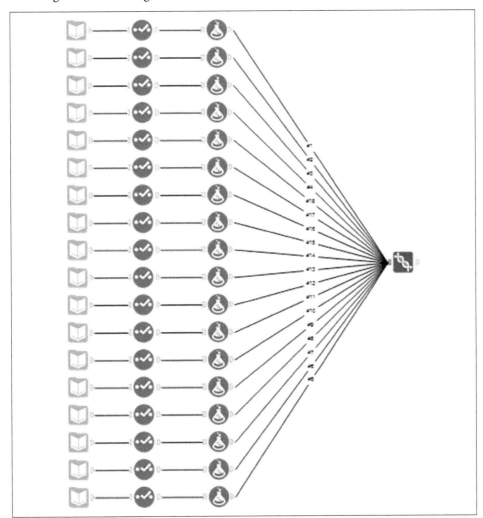

Figure 13-15. Nonbatch macro example

Hopefully, you are getting an itch to know what this process would look like as a simple batch macro. Well, it would look something like Figure 13-16.

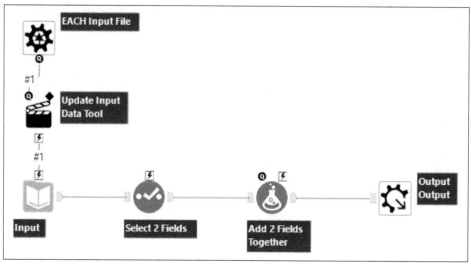

Figure 13-16. Simplified batch macro

Now, you should be looking at this thinking, "OK cool! This just went from 55 tools down to 6!" Meh…that's OK, but I wouldn't say that's mind-blowing. What is mind-blowing is knowing that even if you had to bring in 10,000 inputs and handle them all the same, meaning 30,001 tools total, how many tools would a batch macro then be? Yep, you guessed it: still 6! That is mind-blowing. Do you now understand what I mean by exponential reduction?

The best part is that it isn't even the most mind-blowing part (at least to me). What's even more cool is that when saved and placed into a workflow, it's how many tools now? Yep, 2. It is now 2 that can essentially handle what 30,000 tools or more could do. (See Figure 13-17.)

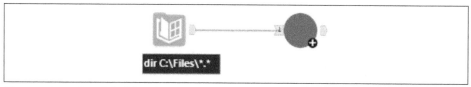

Figure 13-17. Simplified batch macro in a workflow

Even though it's only two tools, I want to describe what's actually happening. As you learned about in Chapter 3 we are using the Directory tool. We are using the Directory tool in our example because it produces a single list of files and their corresponding locations. Now the batch macro is taking that entire list of files and saying, "For each file (aka each record), I'm going to select the two fields I need and I'm going to add their values."

Now there should be two more questions to answer. How does the batch macro know its "for each file" and not something else like "for each letter 'A'"? What happens once the batch macro has gone through the entire list and done it's work? What happens next and how does the data get outputted?

The first question is really critical to understand; you won't be able to use batch macros, let alone understand how they work, otherwise. How the batch macro knows what it's going to use "for each" instance is simple. You set it. Do you remember when I said that dropping the Control Parameter onto a workflow automatically does a bunch of things, like forcing it to be a batch macro, but also adds the upside-down question mark as an anchor? Well it also does one more thing. It adds a question (just like other interface tools do) to the configuration window that allows you to pick what will be fed into the Control Parameter and in turn be the "for each" (see Figure 13-18).

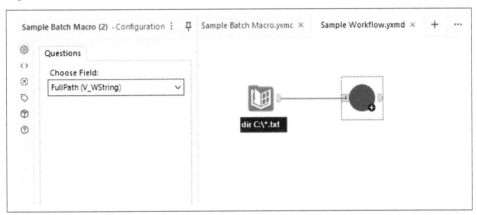

Figure 13-18. Batch macro question

This field you set in the question will dictate what the batches are.

The second question is important as well. When a batch macro completes, it's gone through the 18 files, selected the 2 fields, and added them together. The data is all unioned automatically and exported out the Macro Output tool.

When dealing with batch macros, remember that just because you identify a single record as a "batch" doesn't mean that your output will necessarily be a single record. There could be many rows. Imagine you are reading files and each file has 1,000 rows of data that is read in. Those would all likely be part of one batch. Again, you can have as many batches as you want and need.

It's also important to make it a practice to figure out how many batches you are expecting when you first build your batch macro. Not rows, again, but *batches*. If, for example, I use the information in Figure 13-18 and I see 50 different rows of "fullpath" values come in, then I expect 50 batches.

I've done you a bit of a disservice by keeping this section somewhat short. I usually take two days to teach macros and apps. I want you to understand the parts and mechanics, but you need to expect that it will take practice and effort to really master all types of macros. The topic of macros can easily fit into a decent-size book all by themselves.

Let's not give up now though. Let's dive into an even more exciting topic around macros. Iterative macros!

Building an Iterative Macro

As we jump into iterative macros, you'll need to shift how you've thought about workflows just a bit. I am not going to sugarcoat the fact that iterative macros can be a decent challenge, not because they are actually difficult. I think they are quite easy to understand and build. They can be perceived as difficult because they don't operate with the same paradigm as a standard workflow. However, just like batch macros, they can have a near exponential impact in performance but also allow you to address use cases that you couldn't have up to this point.

With that, let's first talk about what an iterative macro is exactly, and then we'll dig into why they are useful to know and use.

Iterative macros are one of the types of macros, but they are a very unique type. Some of the things they don't have in common with the batch macros are that there is no control parameter type tool that turns it into an iterative macro. To convert a workflow into an iterative macro you will have to go into the workflow settings of the workflow and set it as such (see Figure 13-19).

Another way they differ from batch macros is that, while the batch macro was used to go through a process "for each" instance of that list of items, the Iterative macro is meant to mimic the Do While loop often used in programming languages. The Do While loop in general terms is to Do a process While a statement of some sort is still true, with the understanding that Alteryx Designer will keep doing this process over and over until that statement is no longer true. Let's look at an example (see Figure 13-20).

Looking at this extremely simple example, you can see quite a few important things. First, what is this macro doing? Well, it's taking a single number in via the input. Then it's taking that [Num] value and simply adding 1 to it. Then the Filter tool is doing a check, asking if this number you gave it is less than 10. If it's true, it's going out the T anchor and into the "I" or Iterator output. If it's not, then it's going out the F anchor and into the "C" or Complete Output Tool.

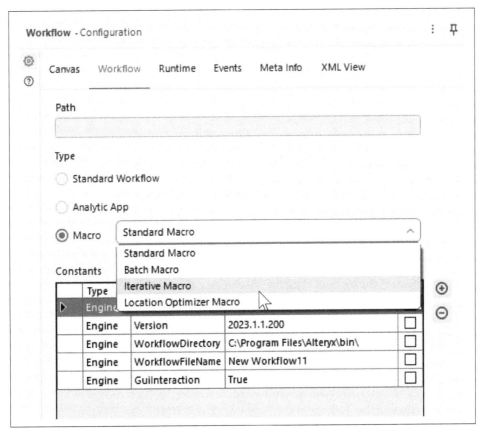

Figure 13-19. Iterative Macro setting

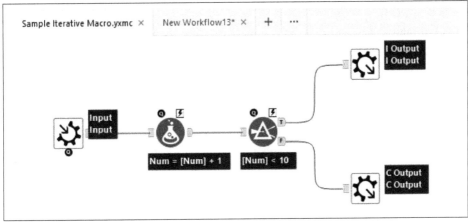

Figure 13-20. Iterative Macro example

Now think about this in the context of iteration. When that number comes out of the "T" anchor, it is less than the value of 10; let's say for this example it's the number 2. It was 1, but then another 1 was added to it before the filter and now it's 2. That 2 is going to go out the "I" output and back into the input at the beginning of this macro.

Let's take a moment here to transparently recognize one of the first difficulties in iterative macros. You can't see that iteration happen. You can do some tricks like adding an output tool right after the input macro tool to get close to seeing if that number that went out of the "I" output came back to the input again, but it's a trick, not the actual thing. As you build more and more iterative macros it will be a bit of a second nature feeling as you'll have a clear understanding not only how iterative macros work but also paired with what you want to have happen.

Let's take a look at another crucial aspect that is not only key to building iterative macros (meaning they can't operate otherwise) but is also different from building a batch macro: the Interface Designer (see Figure 13-21) Remember you can always get to the Interface Designer by clicking on the menu bar at the bottom is you see it, or go to the menu at the top and click the View menu, then Interface Designer.

Notice I am on the settings pane on the far left. The bottom half of this pane is only available once the workflow type has properly been set to Iterative Macro. The first part to pay attention to specifically for configuring an iterative macro to work is to set what the iteration input is. This Iteration Input is the input of the macro that it will circle back to on each subsequent iteration. The Iteration Output is the data that *has not* yet met the criteria for the macro to end. In Figure 13-20, it means that the Filter tool has evaluated the number and it is not yet less than 10. The "Maximum Number of Iterations" setting is pretty clear, meaning it's the maximum amount no matter what it will end on. Even if your logic is wrong (which happens a lot) it will make sure to not go on forever. When the "Maximum Number of Iterations" is hit then these are the options (Error, Warn, Output) that you can dictate to happen. Lastly the Output Mode dictates how the output will happen. It is important that you specifically set the Iteration Input and Output or the macro will not work.

Now, what does the iterative macro look like once it's put into a workflow? Well let's take a look (see Figure 13-22).

You might be thinking, "Wait, how is it just two tools?" You have taken a relatively involved process and you've simplified it to just a macro. Here we are using the text input to offer the number. That number is fed into the iterative macro, and it will loop "while" it is less than 10. Each time it loops through (which is usually quite fast), it is adding 1 to that number. So on the first iteration it might be the number 5, the second iteration 6, the third 7, 8, 9, 10, and finally it stops because when it evaluates to see if it's less than 10, it finds that now it's actually not true. It's false, so it goes out the "C" output and completes the workflow.

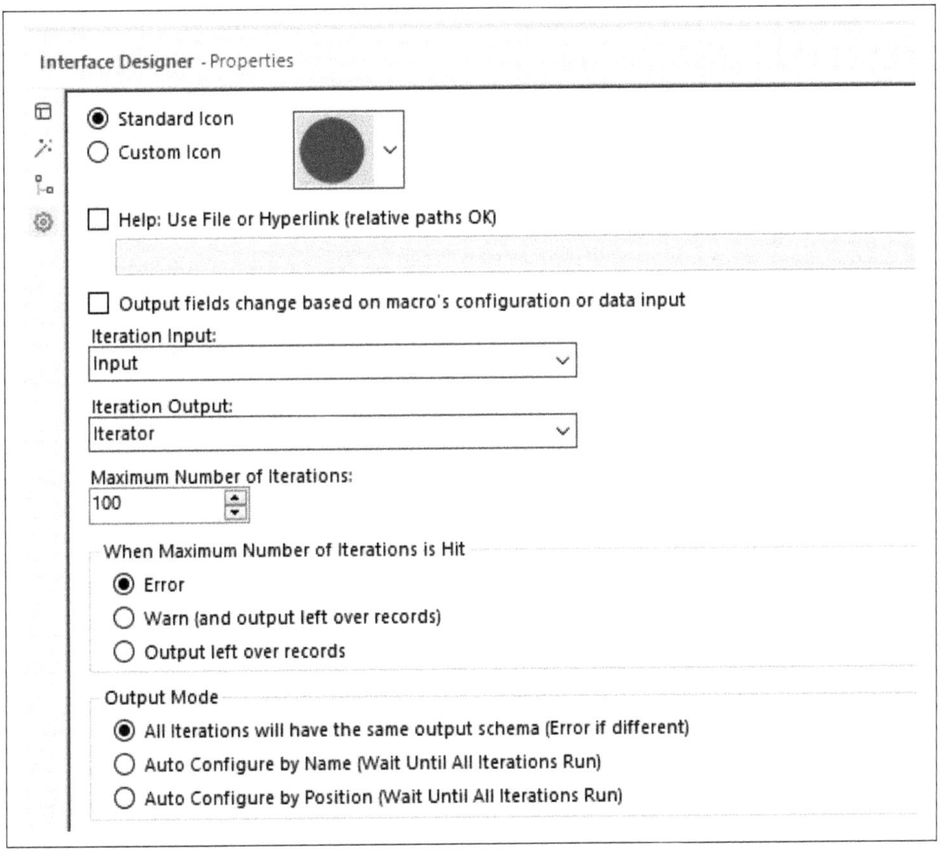

Interface Designer - Properties

- ⦿ Standard Icon
- ○ Custom Icon

- ☐ Help: Use File or Hyperlink (relative paths OK)

- ☐ Output fields change based on macro's configuration or data input

Iteration Input:

Input ⌄

Iteration Output:

Iterator ⌄

Maximum Number of Iterations:

100 ⬍

When Maximum Number of Iterations is Hit
- ⦿ Error
- ○ Warn (and output left over records)
- ○ Output left over records

Output Mode
- ⦿ All Iterations will have the same output schema (Error if different)
- ○ Auto Configure by Name (Wait Until All Iterations Run)
- ○ Auto Configure by Position (Wait Until All Iterations Run)

Figure 13-21. The Interface Designer

Figure 13-22. Iterative Macro in a workflow

As you can tell, there are a few good moving parts to building iterative macros. Please don't let that discourage you. Your ability to advance in using Alteryx requires you to understand these macro types and get fluent with them. I assure you, based on thousands of others who have gone before you, it can be done. It's challenging for sure but very worth learning.

You are now well on your way to doing even much more amazing things. Spend time in this space learning and building macros. They will, over time, become a cornerstone of your workflow development. The more fluent you become in building and testing macros, the more you will find incredible use cases for them. Think of it as building bigger and better tools that have even more utility usefulness than the original tools that you started with.

Conclusion

In the last chapter, I mentioned that macros are a game changer in Alteryx. I'm hoping after learning the Interface tools in Chapter 12, and now starting to build your own macros, you understand that statement with greater clarity. I can assure you that once you've spent some time practicing and building macros, you'll be well rewarded.

Macros might be the single most impactful tool in your Alteryx Designer arsenal. Imagine if you built a workflow that takes something that took 10 hours of manual work, but in an Alteryx workflow it takes 30 seconds. Most people would be astonished at just that, but it gets better than that. Imagine that instead of doing those 10 hours of manual work, say once a week, you can now use just the macro. In one month, you are saving 39 hours and 58 minutes of your time. That's a whole week of time to devote to bigger and better things. Imagine you go on about your year and use your macro but now it's fully automated so you no longer need even 30 seconds. You are saving a week per month. That's three months you've saved in a year!

Now, what would happen if you took that macro that is now saving 25% of your time (assuming you work a standard 40-hour week) and you start sharing it with your colleagues. Every single person who uses that macro is now saving that amount of manual work. Say just 10 people use that macro. You are now not only saving 25% of your time, but also 25% of each of the 10 individuals. That's over two and a half years of work saved each year! You might be skeptical about this but do me a favor and ask around. I've been doing this for more than 10 years and I hear this story at least once a week.

Now, let's take the excitement of macros and apply it to learning Analytic Apps, which can have as much (or even more) impact on your work.

CHAPTER 14

Apps

In this chapter, I cover the important topic of Analytic Apps. An Analytic App, at its core, is a workflow. The key value in building an app is that, when an app is run, it gives the user a chance to choose values right before it runs. The user's choices could change which information is used in the workflow, as well as how it's used, hence making it supremely dynamic. Analytic Apps are one of Alteryx Designer's most valuable features.

For many, apps are less of a technical topic to learn but more an adventure in rethinking how you present data to fellow coworkers and leaders. Apps shift the focus of the workflow from you as a developer to the end user of your data. You literally need to think in terms of different outcomes. Apps are meant for users to interact with the data that you are providing to get more accurate and relevant information.

As you learn the technical aspects of how Analytic Apps work and how to build them yourself, I challenge you to start thinking about how the user(s) will interact with your app. Don't just put three Interface tools on top of your workflow and think that you are building an app. Spend time with the users and ask hundreds of questions about what would be great for them. Get their feedback and build it into the app. Your goal isn't to just build something and walk away. Your goal is always to impact the users in a positive way. Focus on building apps that make their day and, in turn, their lives easier.

Why Use Analytic Apps?

The power of Analytic Apps lies in two key features:

- When you build an Analytic App and publish it to an Alteryx Gallery, any user who has the right access can run the app without needing a license. Imagine an executive who is knocking on your door every week to get a report. You build the report into an app with the features that the executive wants and let them run it whenever they want to.

- By turning your workflows into Analytic Apps, you can build much more dynamic processes that don't require you to constantly update workflows each time you have a slightly different variable.

An analogy that I like to use to explain Analytic Apps is building a submarine sandwich. Imagine if you went into your favorite deli, asked for a submarine sandwich, and they just made you a sandwich without any additional input from you. That is analogous to a workflow—no options and no Interface tools. Now, imagine if you went into that same deli and asked for a submarine sandwich, but this time they asked you, "What type of bread would you like?" Then, eventually they ask what sort of veggies, cheese, and other toppings you'd like. Now, the sandwich is like an Analytic App because you have input into how your sandwich/app is made.

Also, consider that the output of the sandwich could be different depending on the inputs given to the sandwich maker. One person, like my daughter, might request just bread and cheese. However, another person, like my son, could request a mountain of veggies. It's the same process when making an Analytic App—the inputs to the process are different and therefore the end result can be also different.

The Interface tools that we learned about in the last chapter on macros are the same ones we will use to build an Analytic App. The key difference between macros and apps is the fact that we use macros in our workflows, while apps are the final product.

Analytic Apps are best stored on the Alteryx Gallery (Server), where they can be used by as many people as necessary. However, they work great on the desktop, too. Let's walk through how to build your first Analytic App.

Building Your First Analytic App

As always, let's start with simple examples and build from there. I'm going to reuse a workflow we built in Chapter 13, but this time we are going to turn it into an Analytic App (see Figure 14-1). In this example, we will bring in a sample data set, use the Sample tool to choose the first hundred records, and add a Browse tool to see those hundred records. For the Interface tools, we're using the Numeric Up Down tool, connecting it to the Action tool, and having that update the number of records that will be sampled.

The first thing you'll likely notice is that the workflow type is no longer set to Standard Macro, but rather to Analytic App. If you build this workflow from scratch, it should default to Analytic App as the workflow type once the Interface tools are added to the canvas. Once you save this as an Analytic App, you'll also notice that the file extension changes to *.yxwz*.

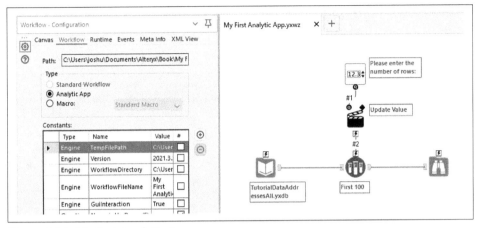

Figure 14-1. My first Analytic App

Now you have built a workflow, you've added the Interface tools, set the workflow to Analytic App, and saved it as a .yxwz file type. Great job! You're probably asking yourself, "How in the heck do I actually use this thing?" Well, it's magic. To be more precise, it's the magic wand. Go ahead and look in the upper-right corner and you'll see that there actually is a magic wand (see Figure 14-2).

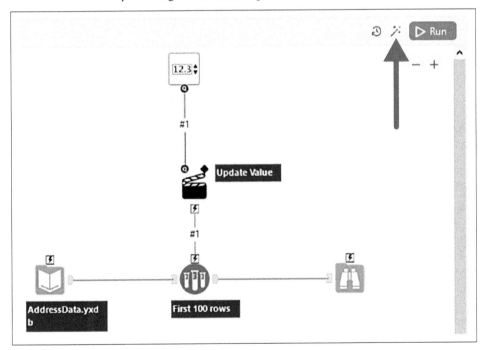

Figure 14-2. The magic wand

By clicking on the magic wand, you will be running this workflow as an Analytic App inside of Alteryx Designer. When that Analytic App opens, you will see something like Figure 14-3.

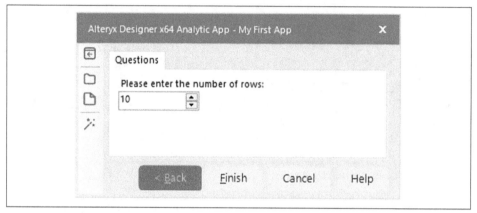

Figure 14-3. The app interface

To use the Analytic App, you need to choose the value you want. In this case, it's the number of rows, which is set by default to 10. Then click Finish to run the workflow. From there, it modifies the configuration (again, in this case, the number 10 replaces the 100 in the configuration of the Sample tool). Lastly, when the workflow is run with that new value of 10, the output of the workflow is affected.

Let's pause here. Imagine the previous example as a workflow. As a workflow, you'd need to open Alteryx Designer and run the workflow, but if you want a different value out of your workflow, you need to change the workflow every time. For our example, we're only talking about one input, but as you build bigger and better workflows you could have upwards of 50 different inputs that need to change based on what the user *might* need.

Imagine if you had to make 50 changes to a workflow every time you received different input. The risk of messing up your workflow alone is high enough to cause you to stop. With Analytic Apps, you build a single workflow and then allow the user to provide input at runtime, instead of making tons of changes to the workflow each time. The best part is if you cut out all the time you'd need to configure and manage the workflow and allow the user to manage any of those different input values (meaning you only make updates to the workflow to improve it or fix a bug), then you become exponentially more productive. The app could be run by any number of people any number of times without you having to do anything! The potential for Analytic Apps to cut out enormous amounts of work and inefficient processes is significant.

Now, when should you *not* use Analytic Apps? That's a question I get all the time. There is no hard-and-fast rule but there are a couple that come close. The first is if the app takes a long time to execute tasks. That just creates a bad user experience. Also, if you have so many inputs in your application that it gets almost impossible to update, the user (think an executive) will be spending a lot of time just trying to go through and enter information. They will eventually not use the app. Spend time trying to understand the user experience so that you can build an amazing app that brings value to your team. Let's jump into some more features that will help you keep building bigger and better apps.

The Interface Designer

You will use the Interface Designer window to customize an app or macro interface. You can also reorder interface questions and actions, add interface elements, test values, and include other content. To open the Interface Designer window, go to View on the menu bar and then click Interface Designer (see Figure 14-4).

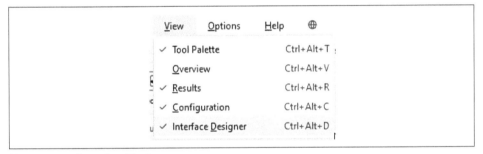

Figure 14-4. Interface Designer

To illustrate the features of Interface Designer, ensure you open the app that we were working on in the previous section. The Interface Designer has four main sections, available via the four icons on the left of the window. The first is the Layout View (see Figure 14-5).

In the Layout View, we can modify the overall layout of interface elements and how they're presented to the user. By simply clicking on the interface element and then using the arrows on the right, we can move them up or down in the interface or to different tabs to fit our needs. In the Add drop-down on the right side (see Figure 14-6) there are four options that you can use to either add interface elements or further organize the layout.

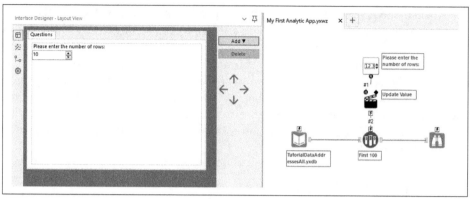

Figure 14-5. The Layout View

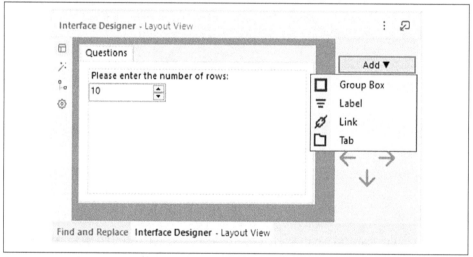

Figure 14-6. The Add drop-down

As you add any of these items to your interface, you will again click the individual item and use the arrows to move them where you want. When you click one of the items, you'll want to have the configuration window open to properly configure their settings (see Figure 14-7).

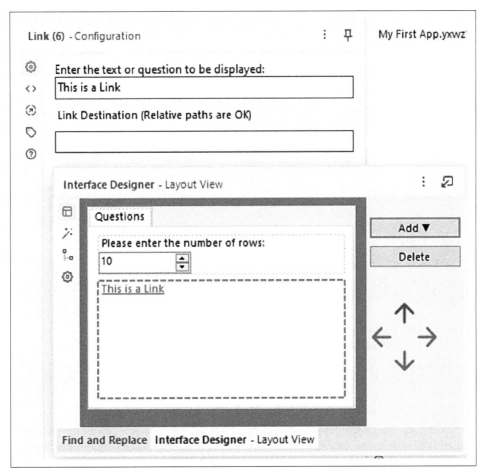

Figure 14-7. Configuration window

The next section is the Test View (see Figure 14-8), which allows you to properly debug your application to ensure that it's working the way you intend. If you look at the App Values on the right side, you will see four buttons: Reset, Open, Save, and View. Reset will set your values back to their original setting. Open will allow you to open what is called a wizard values file with saved values. A wizard values file is just a text file with the saved values you captured. Save will allow you to save your entered values into a wizard values file (*.yxwz*), and View allows you to see what would be saved to the *.yxwz* file. All these options will help you build and test your apps much faster than having to enter the data each and every time.

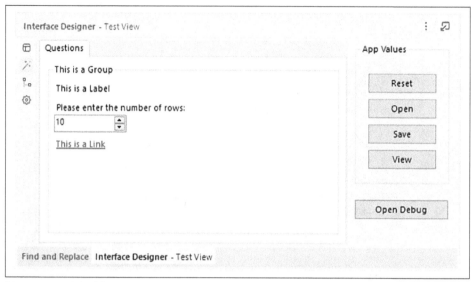

Figure 14-8. The Test View

Since we are in Test View, I want to talk about debugging. It's important you know not only that it exists in Alteryx Designer but also what it is and how to use it.

Debugging Macros and Apps

When you start building macros and apps, it is expected that you will make plenty of mistakes. Understanding how these tools work and how you can build and use them takes time and practice. One of the areas that I found the most helpful was spending time learning how to properly debug macros and apps. I would venture to say that more than half of all Alteryx users don't even know you can debug in Alteryx Designer, but it's the single best way to see exactly how your macro or app is running, end to end. You can always do small tests here and there for an individual tool, but if you want to see how your data flows through an Analytic App, debugging is your new best friend. I really recommend spending some time to get good in this area, as you will be able to fly through not just building apps but ensuring they are working the way you expect.

In the Test View, you can access the Alteryx Designer debugger by first entering values for your inputs (in my example, I changed the value from 10 to 4) and then clicking Open Debug (see Figure 14-8).

A new copy of your app will open, but with a few items that look a little different (see Figure 14-9). What happened here is that the debugger has taken your app and hardcoded the values you inputted, removed the Interface tools, and turned it into a workflow so that it can be run and tested.

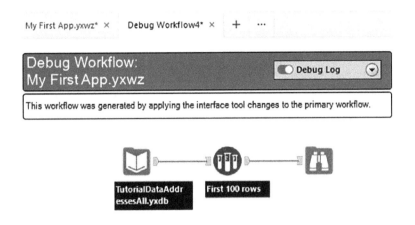

Figure 14-9. Debug workflow

The idea here is that you can run your workflow against a value or set of values from the Interface tools as if it were going to run *.yxwz* a user and see exactly what issues might arise. A good example of this might be where you are expecting a user to select a specific value in a drop-down and maybe they completely miss it or, worse, they enter an input you didn't expect, like letters instead of numbers. With debugging, you can see what would happen when they do.

The third item on the left side of your Interface Designer window is the Tree View (see Figure 14-10), which is quite simple and straightforward. The Tree View displays the hierarchical relationship between questions (which are the questions you are asking to the user via the Interface tools) and actions (via the Action tool you learned about in Chapter 13) in the app or macro. If you want to move things around, you can click on the question that you want to move and use the arrows to move it up or down the list.

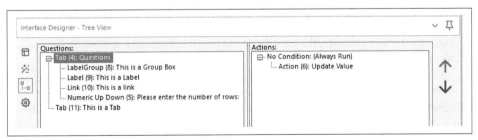

Figure 14-10. The Tree View

The fourth and final section is the Interface Designer Properties (see Figure 14-11). It is important that you spend time here understanding all the different pieces.

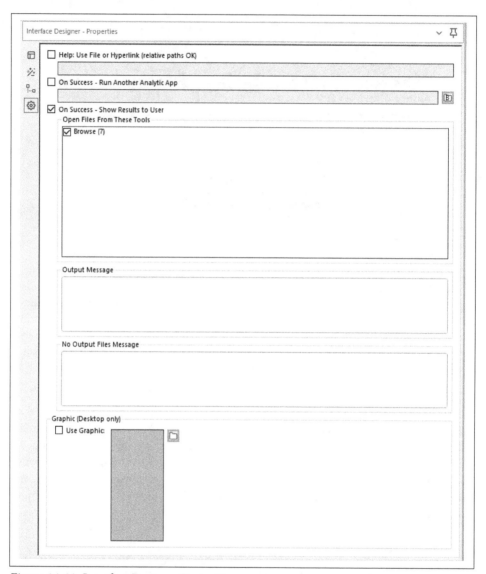

Figure 14-11. Interface Designer Properties

The first option is to set a Help file, which can be a file on your machine or a hyperlink. When a user clicks the ? icon, it allows them to go to where you directed them. The second option is to run another Analytic App on the success of this one. This is used in what we call chained apps, which I will talk about in the next section. The third option is to show all files to a user when a workflow is complete. Any time you add either an Output or a Browse tool, it will show up in this list. If you don't want to provide file output to the user, you could also provide an output message.

Lastly, you can spruce up your Analytic Apps on your desktop by adding a graphic or image.

Chained Apps

Now that you understand how Analytic Apps work and you know how to work with the Interface Designer, it's time to introduce a feature that I think is exciting: chained apps. Chained apps are, on the surface, very easy to understand and conceptualize. However, there are many different use cases that can get quite complex. At their core, they simply allow you to kick off another application once the first one is completed. You can enable this by simply selecting the checkbox in the Interface Designer Properties for "On Success - Run Another Analytic App" and then providing the URL or file location to the additional app (see Figure 14-12). When a user runs the app and clicks Next at the end of the first process, the second app will run and provide those inputs to the user.

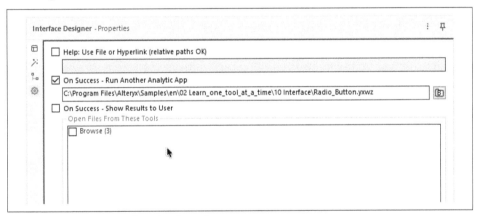

Figure 14-12. Run Another Analytic App

There are a couple of points to consider when using chained apps:

- If you have any one of the apps in the chain running longer than 30 seconds, that chain will break and cause the app chain to fail. If you need to change this, it can be done via a configuration file change. I don't recommend changing this arbitrarily because it can provide a poor experience for the user and present some technical challenges.

- You can pass the values from one app to another by ensuring that the output of files from the first app are the same as the inputs of the second app.

Chained apps can give you dynamic results, but you need to keep an eye on performance and usability. They can take in numerous possible choices and tailor the data and results accordingly. If you are new to chained apps, please don't try to chain four apps together at the start. Start with two and ensure that you feel comfortable with the results. Change the input of the first app in many ways to see and understand how the second app responds. Remember, the key is to output a data set that you will pick up on the next app. That's the handoff that will make them work together.

Conclusion

Analytic Apps are extremely powerful and flexible because they allow the user to drive the results based on the options they choose, rather than relying only on you, the developer, to build out every possible scenario. Though they do require a bit of time to fully understand, it is time well invested. Analytic Apps are very much like macros but are used in a slightly different context in that the UI gets exposed to the user, and not only from within Designer like you see for macros. All the effort that you put in to learn Analytic Apps has direct implications for how you understand macros as there is significant overlap in functionality. If you have executives or other teammates regularly requesting reports or files or other pieces of information that can be automated, using Analytic Apps can turn you into a superhero!

Analytic Apps are primarily intended to be used on the Alteryx Gallery (Server). Whether you use them locally or on the server, remember the importance of debugging your apps. Ensure that you understand all the working mechanisms behind the scenes so that you can build robust apps faster and more efficiently.

We are now going to shift gears and learn about a functionality within Alteryx Designer that has been around since its early days. In the next chapter, I am going to help you unravel the mystery and magic of the Spatial tools!

PART V

Spatial Analytics

CHAPTER 15

Spatial Tools

Alteryx Designer has long offered tools for spatial data and analysis. In 1997, SRC (the initial name of Alteryx) developed the first online data engine for delivering demographic-based mapping and reporting. From there, Alteryx went on to expand into many other areas of analytics but kept in place the foundations it created with spatial analytics.

In this chapter, you are going to learn how to work with spatial data in Designer and understand how you can build workflows that manipulate this type of data in order to get insights from geographical information. You will learn how to work with spatial objects like points, lines, and polygons that represent the forms of a physical location.

When I built my first spatial workflow, I couldn't believe that this type of analysis even existed. I thought it was so cool to be able to calculate things like the distance from a grocery store to 10,000 customers, all in seconds. I loved that I could build drive-time models for how customers might go from one place to another. There is such a wealth of information that spatial analysis can give us. Let's get to it!

Introduction to Spatial Data

At the end of the day, the easiest way to think of spatial data is essentially longitude and latitude values on a map. As you get further into the subject, you'll see it's much more than that but for those just getting started it's easiest to think of it in this way. Many "lat/long" values can then be built up to what are referred to as spatial objects. In Alteryx Designer, there are three types of spatial objects:

Point
> A point is a reference to a single location, usually mapped from single X and Y coordinates.

Line

A line is a representation of two or more points connected in a sequence. This could be a straight line or curved. A curved line is just a collection of very short straight lines, as opposed to an arc.

Polygon

A polygon is the enclosed area of a two-dimensional shape that is created from three or more points.

A trick that I use in many areas of data analysis is to completely visualize what I am trying to understand. If you are standing on a landmark, imagine you are the point spatial object. If you are walking from your favorite restaurant to your house (it helps if you also imagine having fresh blue paint on your shoes), then imagine the line spatial object that you are creating in blue paint. Lastly, imagine if you take a 360-degree walk around your neighborhood (with the same blue paint on your shoes for visual effect). That shape you have created is the polygon. Spatial analysis is visual, and so I recommend thinking of it that way.

What Is Spatial Analysis?

Spatial analysis allows you to analyze locations and relationships in spatial data. If you have a grocery store, for example, and you want to analyze where all your customers are coming from, you will use spatial analysis. Using data visualization, you can see things like the suitability of a new office location because of its proximity to places of interest, where to place a new store based on its proximity to the greatest number of potential customers, and even where to place ads on billboards along the highway to get the highest number of views.

There are many tools that are capable of working with spatial data, but Alteryx allows you to combine spatial and nonspatial data analysis in a single platform. You can not only map out where customers are but also join that with specific details about the customers, like preferences and buying patterns. This is one of the biggest benefits for those who want to conduct spatial analysis using Alteryx.

Let's take a look at some of the different types of spatial analysis.

Types of Spatial Analysis

There are many types of spatial analysis available for you to get your hands dirty. Spatial analysis has a really interesting and rich history, going all the way back to 1400 B.C. in Egypt with the practice of cartography. Spatial analysis is really about studying entities by using their topological, geometric, or geographic properties. The main types of spatial analysis are as follows:

Spatial data analysis
  Relies on getting data, processing it, and adding to it in order to generate valuable outputs according to location-based attributes, properties, or relationships. Through this analysis, you will get access to details like location and distance (to other locations) that would otherwise be difficult to obtain.

Spatial autocorrelation
  Can help you figure out whether multiple data points, which are co-located, are also similar with other attributes. For example, spatial autocorrelation can investigate whether housing with the same features exists in the same area.

Spatial interaction
  Helps you learn more about the interaction between different entities including points, lines, and polygons. For example, you might find store locations that touch, political regions that overlap, or areas with mixed use. This is one of the more common types of spatial analysis you can do in Alteryx Designer.

Simulation and modeling
  Helps you understand geospatial objects and their properties after each iteration of a change to the geospatial model (often thousands of runs or more).

When you start looking at spatial objects as just another type of data object, you can apply your knowledge of Alteryx tools on them. You can summarize and group them, you can join them to other objects with shared attributes. There are so many possibilities to do spatial analysis when you have spatial data, but many users simply shy away from attempting it because either they don't see immediate use cases or they just don't want to tackle another suite of tools. I want to challenge you to learn these tools because you'll be able to do even more amazing things when you are presented with a potential spatial analysis problem. These tools are also on the Advanced and Expert Alteryx Designer Certification exams! Now that you have a better grasp of spatial data and spatial analysis, let's jump right into the Spatial tool palette!

The Spatial Tool Palette

The Spatial tool palette (see Figure 15-1) has one of the larger groups of tools of all the palettes, which stems from it being one of the earliest sets of tools available in Alteryx Designer.

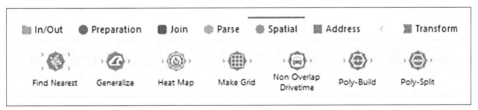

Figure 15-1. The Spatial tool palette

Again, the Spatial tools can be a bit intimidating at first glance but they are powerful and can be used in many different ways!

I've broken this chapter into defined sections to help you build your understanding around each of the tools, while also helping you understand the overall collection of tools and how they can be used together. The first section will focus on those tools that create spatial objects. The second section will focus on the group of tools that are used to modify the spatial objects once they are created. The final section will cover the tools that allow you to interact with or analyze spatial objects.

Building Spatial Objects

These tools help you build spatial objects from underlying lat/long coordinates. Recall the three types of spatial objects that I introduced at the beginning of this chapter: points, lines, and polygons. In this section, you'll learn how to create all three in order to analyze the relationships between them.

Create Points tool

The Create Points tool is one of the more foundational Spatial tools you'll use:

In this example (see Figure 15-2), we have a table of Pet Store data that provides not just the name and phone number of the locations but also the latitude and longitude of the exact store locations as well.

Name	Phone	Lat	Lon
All Creatures Great and Small	(307) 687-0354	44.28167	-105.492272
Animal House	(307) 358-2022	42.759113	-105.385263
Aquatics and Critters	(307) 235-1890	42.845431	-106.26731
Barn	(307) 587-9515	44.533497	-109.03955
Fins and Feathers Pet Shoppe	(307) 856-3333	43.024851	-108.384878
Mutt Hut	(307) 684-8710	44.348153	-106.705347
Pet City	(307) 638-4183	41.160407	-104.807259
Pet Food Outlet	(307) 682-6831	44.268887	-105.50253
Petland	(307) 638-6027	41.140643	-104.763369
Pets-N-Stuff	(307) 674-7387	44.778672	-106.939213
Purr-Fect Pets	(307) 754-9536	44.751645	-108.757799
Summit Pets	(307) 789-0719	41.267252	-110.965114
Summit Pets of Rock Springs	(307) 362-7997	41.583195	-109.253753

Figure 15-2. Latitude and longitude values

If we were to keep this data as is, we run into two main problems. One, we can't easily grasp where these points lie in a visual context. Are some closer to each other than others? Two, it becomes extremely difficult to analyze the data points and answer questions like how many customers are less than 15 miles from one of these stores? Therefore, we need to convert those lat/long values into a spatial object that Alteryx can work with to help us do further analysis and gain a better understanding.

To turn these lat/long values into individual points, we will use the Create Points tool. We will input the data and simply configure the X Field (Longitude) and Y Field (Latitude) values to correspond to the field names we have coming in from the data set (see Figure 15-3).

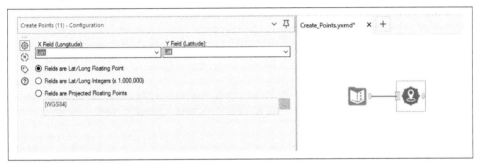

Figure 15-3. Create Points configuration

Once you have that configured and run, you will notice a new field in the output: Centroid. The Centroid field (see Figure 15-4) is the spatial object (in this case, a point) that was just created.

Record	Name	Phone	Lat	Lon	Centroid
1	All Creatures Great and Small	(307) 687-0354	44.28167	-105.492272	Point - View Browse Tool Map Tab
2	Animal House	(307) 358-2022	42.759113	-105.385263	Point - View Browse Tool Map Tab
3	Aquatics and Critters	(307) 235-1890	42.845431	-106.26731	Point - View Browse Tool Map Tab
4	Barn	(307) 587-9515	44.533497	-109.03955	Point - View Browse Tool Map Tab
5	Fins and Feathers Pet Shoppe	(307) 856-3333	43.024851	-108.384878	Point - View Browse Tool Map Tab
6	Mutt Hut	(307) 684-8710	44.348153	-106.705347	Point - View Browse Tool Map Tab
7	Pet City	(307) 638-4183	41.160407	-104.807259	Point - View Browse Tool Map Tab
8	Pet Food Outlet	(307) 682-6831	44.268887	-105.50253	Point - View Browse Tool Map Tab
9	Petland	(307) 638-6027	41.140643	-104.763369	Point - View Browse Tool Map Tab
10	Pets-N-Stuff	(307) 674-7387	44.778672	-106.939213	Point - View Browse Tool Map Tab
11	Purr-Fect Pets	(307) 754-9536	44.751645	-108.757799	Point - View Browse Tool Map Tab
12	Summit Pets	(307) 789-0719	41.267252	-110.965114	Point - View Browse Tool Map Tab
13	Summit Pets of Rock Springs	(307) 362-7997	41.583195	-109.253753	Point - View Browse Tool Map Tab

Figure 15-4. Centroid

Notice it's not a number or string or frankly anything that you can see in plain text, and that's because it's now a representation of a point on a map. The way you will now view all spatial objects is via the Browse tool. By adding a Browse tool and rerunning the workflow, you now can see all these points on a map (see Figure 15-5).

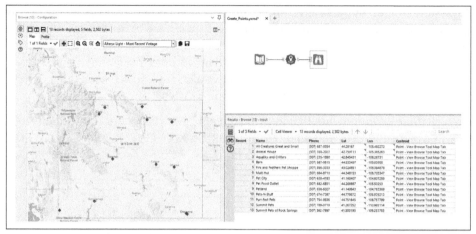

Figure 15-5. Spatial map of points

The first time I saw this in action, I got really excited. This shows us that all those random decimal numbers are not only specific points on a map but specific cities in the state of Wyoming! This gives us a much better understanding of "where" those locations are. You may now have a bunch of questions like "How far away are they from each other?" or "Which ones are the closest to each other?" This is one of those moments where you should let your curiosity fly free.

Now that you know how to convert lat/long values into a spatial point, let's see what we need to do to get many of those points together and create a line (or a polyline) and a polygon.

Poly-Build tool

The Poly-Build tool is used to create a line or polygon based on a set of points. This allows you to take a set of points—say, the four corners of your house or apartment—and connect them into one shape: a polygon:

Think back to your elementary or middle-school math classes and recall that the shortest distance between two points is a straight line. So, let's create that. We'll take two points and create a line using Alteryx and the Poly-Build tool. In this example, we are taking two of those locations we used in the Create Points section (see Figure 15-6) and pushing them into our Poly-Build tool.

Name	Phone	Lat	Lon	Centroid
All Creatures Great and Small	(307) 687-0354	44.28167	-105.492272	Point - View Browse Tool Map Tab
Animal House	(307) 358-2022	42.759113	-105.385263	Point - View Browse Tool Map Tab

Figure 15-6. Two Centroids

We are now going to configure our Poly-Build tool to create the sequence polyline (or, a line). First, select the Build Method, which is basically picking which spatial object you want to create. You can create a convex hull, which is the smallest convex polygon that can be drawn to include a set of points.

 I can hear you thinking, "What's a convex polygon, again?" A polygon is convex if all the interior angles are less than 180 degrees. Think of a stop sign in the US, for example. Also, remember that if it isn't a convex polygon, it would be a concave polygon, like the outline of an arrow.

You can also create a sequence polygon, which is just a polygon of all the points in a sequential order, and lastly you can create a polyline, which simply is a line that connects all the specified points in sequential order. Many times, when you are creating routes of some kind, you'll use polylines because order is important. You'll see in Figure 15-7 that I've chosen to create a sequence polyline. Set your source field to Centroid, which is the field name of the data that contains the point spatial objects. When you've completed the configuration steps, click Run. You'll notice that you get one record with a single value output. The value is the spatial object of a polyline.

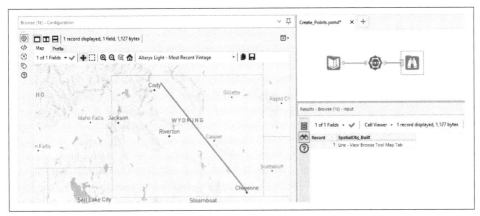

Figure 15-7. A straight line, or sequence polyline

While this particular example shows you two points, which in turn creates a straight line, that doesn't mean you can't have many more. Essentially, you could have as many points as you want, which in turn can create a line as long as you want. The important thing to remember is that when you are configuring the Poly-Build tool, ensure you have a field that dictates the sequential order so that the line is created correctly.

Now that you have built a line based off of two points, let's move on to learn how to build a sequence polygon using the Poly-Build tool. Remember, every time you create a spatial object like a line or a polygon you aren't just getting a line around some shape; you get all the information that comes with that. Think about the distance of the perimeter, the distance from one point to another, and even the area inside the polygon—this can all be really useful information. In Figure 15-8, the data shows a long list of stores. The spatial objects are the radius lines (circles) that are around a store. If you break apart that circle (which, again, is just a curved line), you will also get a group of points and the sequence that those points are in. Notice that each of these circles is currently just a bunch of points plotted on a two-dimensional space. With this example, you want to join all the overlaps of each circle as one unified shape. That way, you can see what the *total* space is that is covered by the multiple circles.

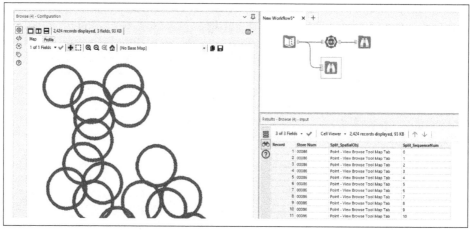

Figure 15-8. Sequence polygon

To do this, we need to essentially bring these shapes together into a polygon. We do this by configuring the Poly-Build tool with the three fields you see in Figure 15-8: Store_Num, Split_SpatialObj, and Split_SequenceNum. Note the Store_Num field is set as the group field so that when the polygons are created, they will be created to represent each individual store. Remember, we want to build our polygons from the data points for that store.

When you get that configured with the correct fields and run it, you will see a circle for each of the 24 stores in the data (see Figure 15-9). So, to reiterate what happened here: we took a list of points that happened to be laid out in the form of a circle (although to Alteryx Designer it wasn't a circle, it was just a group of points.) We used the Poly-Build tool to turn the group of points into a single polygon (now Alteryx Designer sees it as a single unified object). We can do some more geospatial analysis to figure out what the overlap is for each polygon.

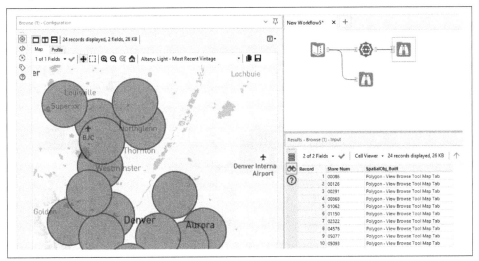

Figure 15-9. Sequence polygon output

 If you have objects that are turning in on themselves because of points that cause sharp angles, you might want to consider using convex hull as an option.

Trade Area tool

The Trade Area tool is a fun tool, as it enables you to draw shapes around a point based on a distance:

Say, for example, we have a single point like a store location and we simply want to know all of our customers within a 5-mile radius. Well, for that we need to create a Trade Area. In the configuration of the tool, we can do this by selecting our store point and radius (in this example, 5.0 represents 5 miles all the way around), and then clicking Run. We then see (as shown in Figure 15-10) that our point now includes a green circle to represent the border of the 5-mile trade area. You can create multiple trade areas around a centroid, which distinguishes the Trade Area tool from the Buffer tool we'll cover in the next section.

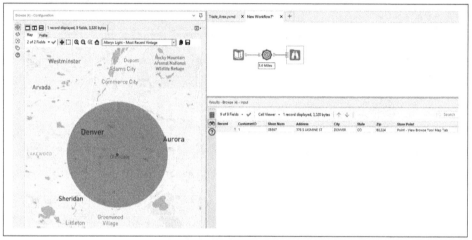

Figure 15-10. Five-mile trade area

This tool can also tap into third-party data. By doing this, we can actually get the drive-time distance around a point, so we could draw a map showing where a customer could drive to in 15 minutes (see Figure 15-11).

A drive-time radius is very different from just a standard radius, as it has to look at roads and traffic data to figure out what a 15-minute drive-time would look like. It produces a very different view, as you can see.

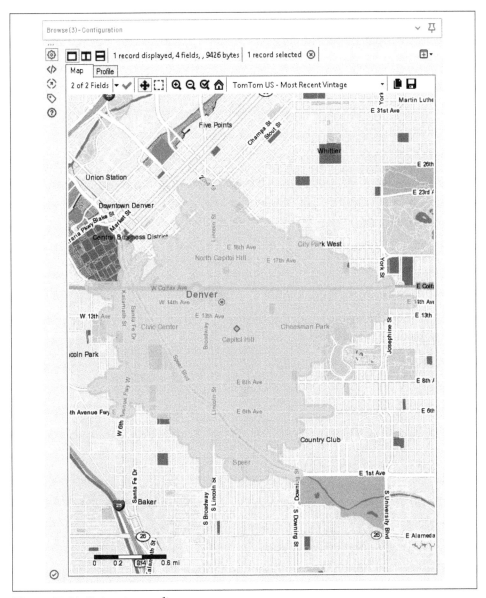

Figure 15-11. Drive-time radius

Spatial Process tool

To fully use the Spatial Process tool, you'll need to understand the creation and use of spatial objects, as its job is to perform operations on spatial objects:

These operations include things like combining two objects, cutting one spatial object from another, intersecting, and creating inverse intersections. This is where you can get pretty creative in the spatial realm. For example, if you have two spatial objects that overlap each other and you want to find the number of square miles that they overlap, you can find this out easily.

In the configuration of the tool, you'll see two spatial field options to choose from. You'll need to ensure that the spatial objects that you're working with are on the same record (row).

You'll also have the following Actions available to you: Combine Objects, Cut 1st From 2nd, Cut 2nd From 1st, Create Intersection Object, and Create Inverse Intersection Object (see Figure 15-12).

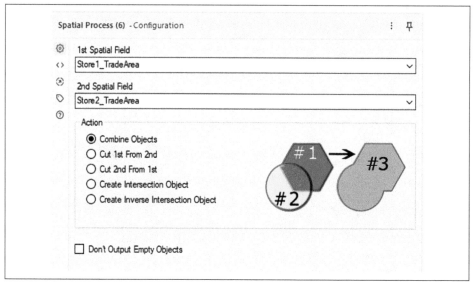

Figure 15-12. Spatial process configuration

Let's look at the Combine Objects action first. If you were to combine two spatial objects, you would go from the diagram on the left side of Figure 15-13 to the diagram on the right. This will allow you to create spatial objects that encompass everything you want versus only the individual objects.

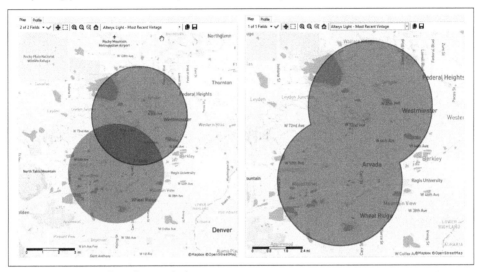

Figure 15-13. Combined spatial objects

You can combine not just two separate objects, but also build some logic into your workflows that only combine objects if they are overlapping or touching each other. If you have two stores with a 10-mile radius, for example, together they cover a certain area and you'd want to know that entire covered area.

The next two actions allow us to cut one object from another. If you select either of those two options in the configurations and run the workflow, then you would see something like Figure 15-14, where Store1_TradeArea is "cut" from Store2_Trade-Area.

Being able to cut spatial objects is critical, especially when you are calculating things like market size, population, land size, and so on. You will find over and over that you will need to cut one object from another. Again, make sure that your data is on the same record.

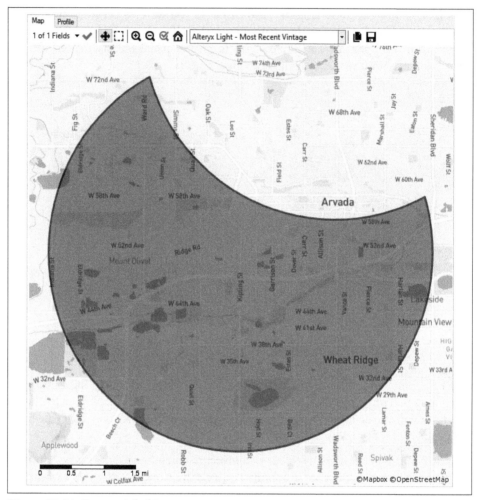

Figure 15-14. Cut spatial objects

You also might need to "intersect" two or more spatial objects by selecting our fourth action—Create Intersection Object—and running your workflow. This is useful when all you really need is the overlap of two objects and not the two original objects you started with. The output of the intersection would look like Figure 15-15. This is useful when you need to better understand where you might have over-coverage or even where competitor areas overlap with yours.

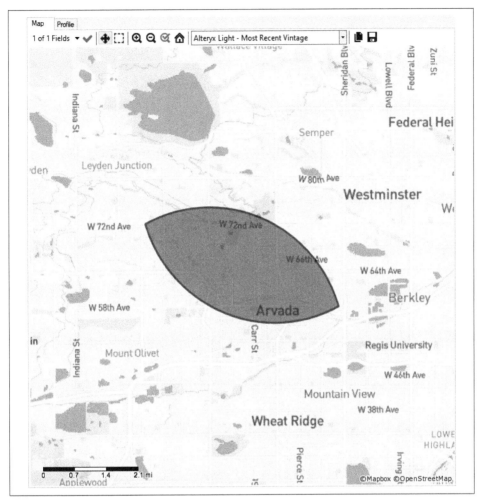

Figure 15-15. Intersection of spatial objects

Remember, if you are interested in calculating the exact overlap of specific objects, then you need to essentially break them apart so that you have an object to calculate on. In "Analyzing Spatial Objects" on page 442, I'll show you easy ways to do this.

Lastly, you can inverse an intersection, so instead of getting just the overlap back, you actually get the two objects *minus* the overlap/intersection. This is useful when you want to calculate the total coverage that is not overlapping. Figure 15-16 shows you what that looks like.

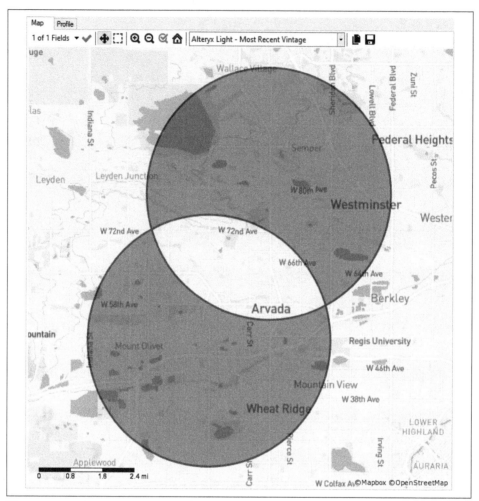

Figure 15-16. Inverse intersection object

As you get deeper into the Spatial toolset, you will realize that many of the tools build off each other or work alongside each other. You might need to learn three, four, or five tools in order to build something you are looking for. In my mind, this is a good thing as it puts the dynamics and power into your hands. While Alteryx Designer is useful, it's not able to make assumptions about what you want to do; it lets you choose what you need. This is true of many of the tools in Alteryx Designer—they encourage control and creativity at the same time.

Before we jump into modifying spatial objects, I want you to take a step back and realize that you now know how to build spatial objects in Alteryx Designer. That's a key milestone in the spatial analytics process. Now we are going to keep pushing forward and discuss how to modify those spatial objects you have created.

Modifying Spatial Objects

Once you have spent a considerable amount of time working with building spatial objects, you'll have a much better appreciation of what it takes to modify them. You'll also understand more about what spatial objects are in the first place. You may see opportunities for modification based on whether objects are overlapping or not. You may see clearer where competitors are encroaching on your territory. You may even see where there are areas you can grow that weren't clear before.

Now let's jump into the tools we can use to modify spatial objects that already exist.

Smooth tool

Besides having quite possibly the coolest name of any tool, the Smooth tool is used to do exactly that: smoothen sharp angles on spatial objects. It does this by adding extra nodes (data points) along the lines that make up the object (therefore giving it a smoother surface):

The Smooth tool, the Generalize tool, and a few others are essentially used in the process of cartographic generalization (*https://oreil.ly/6W48i*). Generalization is about simplifying a great amount of detail into something that is more comprehensible. For example, we might have the outlines of the many curves of a river, but we wish to make a map of the whole state no more than a few inches wide because the whole state is the information that needs to be presented, not all the individual details (such as if the river turns left or right).

This tool takes a rather jagged or sharp-edged polygon (see Figure 15-17) and, using a B-spline smoothing algorithm, makes all the edges smoother by adding points to the polygon (see Figure 15-18).

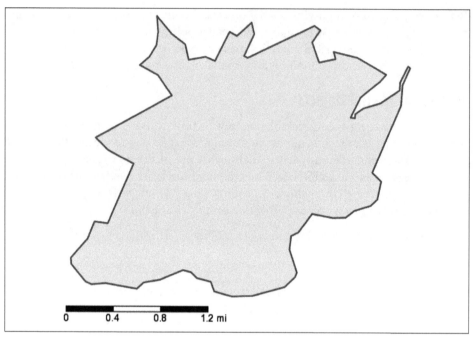

Figure 15-17. A nonsmoothed polygon

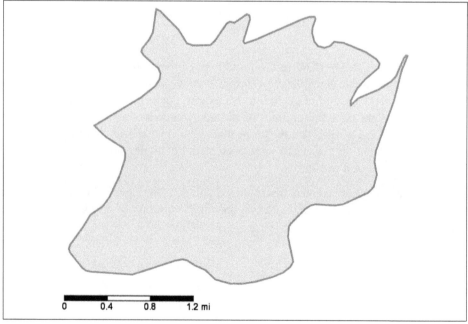

Figure 15-18. A smoothed polygon

To configure the Smooth tool (see Figure 15-19) you must first specify the Spatial Field you want to work with.

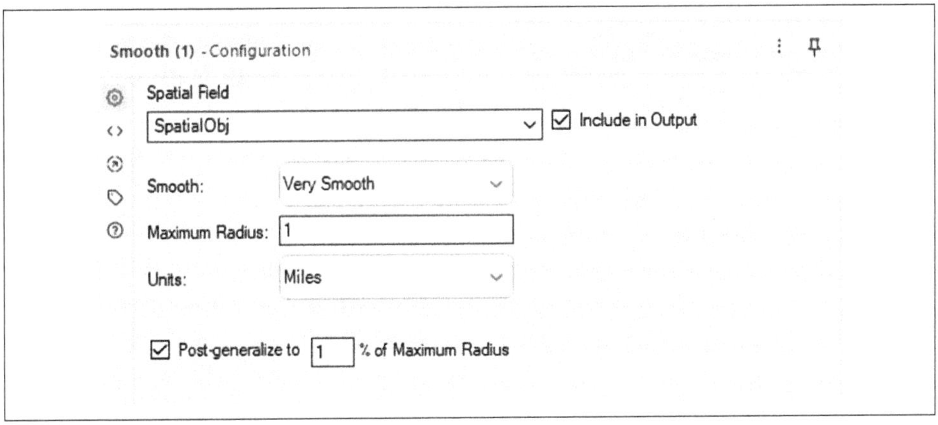

Smooth (1) - Configuration

Spatial Field

SpatialObj   ☑ Include in Output

Smooth: Very Smooth

Maximum Radius: 1

Units: Miles

☑ Post-generalize to 1 % of Maximum Radius

Figure 15-19. Smooth tool configuration

You can then specify the level of smoothness you want to see. There are three levels:

Smooth
> The number of nodes of the original object will be multiplied by 2.

Very Smooth
> The number of nodes of the original object will be multiplied by 4.

Super Smooth
> The number of nodes of the original object will be multiplied by 8.

Once you have the Smooth level set, you can configure the Maximum Radius, which helps dictate how round the curves can be. You can set Units in Miles or Kilometers. For the Post-generalize configuration, the smoothed object will be a simplified collection of nodes and a smaller file size as a result.

Generalize tool

Sometimes having data on every turn or corner of a line or polygon just increases the complexity of analysis and isn't necessary for what you need. The Generalize tool helps to decrease the number of data points (nodes) on every turn or corner of a polygon or polyline, thereby making a simpler spatial object that speeds up and simplifies the analysis:

As a bit of an extreme example, in order to make my point, say you have four points that make up a straight line. All four points are on the same axis. Well, we know that a straight line only really needs two points to be drawn. So, we can remove two of them to "generalize" to that line. Now, when you are working with large polygons with really complex spatial landscapes, you could have quite an impact on the data when using the Generalize tool, so be mindful of what it is that you intend to do.

 The Smooth tool may seem like it's similar to the Generalize tool. In practice, the Smooth and Generalize tools are effectively opposites; however, one cannot directly undo the other. They are opposites because while the Smooth tool adds additional nodes to make the smoothness appear, the Generalize tool is taking away nodes in order to "generalize" a spatial object.

Under the hood, polygons are generalized using the Ramer-Douglas-Peucker algorithm. You can simply configure the Generalize tool (see Figure 15-20) by first setting the Spatial Field, then the Threshold. Every node on the original line is within this specified threshold of the generalized line. Set the Units to Miles or Kilometers and, lastly, confirm whether you want to "Preserve Consistency for Entire Layer" by checking or unchecking the box. By keeping the box checked, you will make sure that line segments that are shared will be handled at the same time. This ensures there are no gaps or overlaps between the objects.

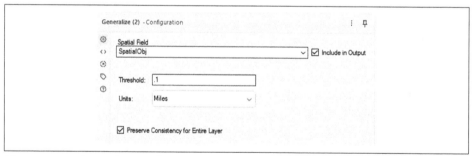

Figure 15-20. Generalize configuration

Figure 15-21 shows a simple example of what it would look like to generalize a polygon.

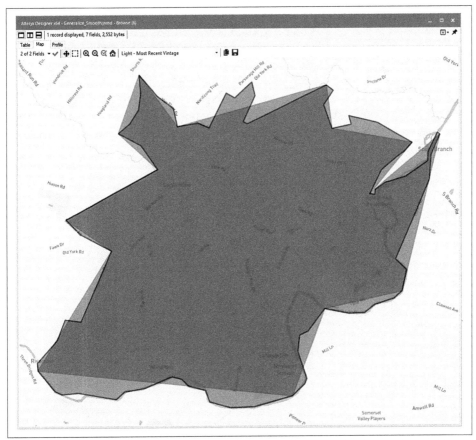

Figure 15-21. Generalized polygon

Poly-Split tool

The Poly-Split tool is used to break a polygon into its points or regions. So, for example, if you have a file where there are 10 countries outlined, but it's all one polygon, you can use this tool to separate those countries:

The configuration for the Poly-Split tool is super simple. You'll need to provide a polygon as the spatial field. You will also need to tell the tool how you want to split the polygon, whether it's split to Points, Regions, or Detailed Regions.

A simple use case for the Poly-Split tool might be to break apart a polygon, filter out what parts of the spatial object you don't want, then use the Poly-Build tool to put the polygon back together. In a very popular Alteryx weekly challenge, there is an example where we have a body of land that we have mapped with a single spatial polygon. There is also a river that goes through this land. If we wanted to identify the river and effectively break that single polygon into three polygons—(1) land left of the river, (2) the river, and (3) land right of the river—then we can use the Poly-Split tool. This is a great example of effectively working with geospatial data (see Figure 15-22).

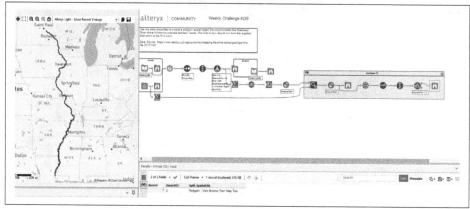

Figure 15-22. Geospatial analytics of a river

Buffer tool

The Buffer tool is quite a significant tool for all its simplicity. The Buffer tool can create a "buffer" around your polygons, meaning an extra space that you decide, whether that's in miles, inches, feet, or any other distance:

For example, the Buffer tool will allow you to calculate a 5-mile border around your location. This is useful because, unlike a Trade Area this is not just a circle or a drive-time border; the Buffer tool can simply add a specified amount to your polygon.

A great use case for this might be where you want to see if your polygon is within five miles of any specific place. You can simply add a 5-mile buffer and then use the Spatial Match tool (which you will learn about in the next section) to see if any other polygon is touching or contained in your polygon. When you are doing spatial analysis, it may sometimes be useful to measure to the edge of a polygon versus measuring to the center of that same polygon. By adding a buffer (see Figure 15-23), you can manipulate that specific calculation. The example in the figure shows a positive buffer of 1 mile and a negative buffer of –1 mile.

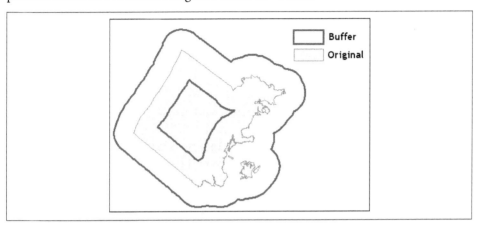

Figure 15-23. Buffer tool example

Configuring the Buffer tool is fairly straightforward, but there are a few options you'll need to pay close attention to (see Figure 15-24).

Figure 15-24. Buffer tool configuration

The first step in configuring the Buffer tool is to select the Spatial Field that you want to buffer. Remember, this could be a polygon or even a line or point. Next, check the two boxes if you want to either keep the spatial field you are passing through included in the output (Include in Output) or if you want to Generalize to 1% of Buffer Size. Checking the Generalize box will optimize speed by cutting down the number of nodes in the buffered object.

The most important part of the configuration is setting your BufferSize. This can be set from a specific flat value you enter, like the 1 you see in Figure 15-24, or you can also drive the buffer from a numerical field. Lastly, you have the option to set Units in Miles or Kilometers.

We've not only covered building spatial objects but also modifying them! Let's now shift gears to learn how to analyze spatial objects to get insights from them.

Analyzing Spatial Objects

The whole point of building spatial objects and modifying them is to use those objects of information to analyze our data in a way that gives us insights to make better decisions. We might want to know if the two areas are touching each other, meaning they are close together, like our store and that of a competitor. Maybe one area overlaps another, meaning that if they were sales areas, we might have two sales reps covering the same space. Keeping your objectives in mind as you do spatial analysis will make it much easier to analyze your data and, in turn, help your team make better decisions.

Spatial Match tool

An easy way to understand the Spatial Match tool is to think about it more like a join tool:

While the way it does the join is quite a bit different, the same idea applies. You would use the Spatial Match tool to establish the spatial relationship between two sets of spatial objects. That spatial relationship is what we're most interested in here.

When you use this tool, the two data sets you're looking to find a spatial relationship between are named "Target" and "Universe." From there, you will choose one of the following options in order to dictate that relationship:

Where Target Intersects Universe
   This matches records where both sets of objects have any area in common. This is used when you want to see when both spaces are shared. A good example is if you want to find out if two stores might be serving the same customer.

Where Target Contains Universe

This matches records where Target objects contain Universe objects in their entirety. This can be used to understand if, for example, the wireless connectivity is covering the entire environment you have.

Where Target Is Within Universe

This matches records where Target objects are entirely within Universe objects. This is really useful if you want to know how many objects (stores, offices, locations) are within a place. It is also a great way to understand how much of a Universe object is covered by your Target.

Where Target Touches Universe

This matches records where Target objects touch the outside boundary of Universe objects. To qualify as touching, neither object can occupy any of the same interior space. This can be used to understand if maybe a 5-mile radius of a river or other waterway is touching an area (meaning you might need to have to follow some government regulations).

Where Target Touches or Intersects Universe

This matches records where Target objects either share interior space with Universe objects or touch the boundary of Universe objects. This is used similarly to Where Target Touches Universe but could also include overlapping polygons.

Bounding Rectangle Overlaps

This matches records where the bounding rectangles of Target objects and Universe objects share interior space. If you put a rectangle around a plot of spatial locations, then you might want to find if that rectangle now covers (or overlaps) some other polygon you've provided.

After making this selection, the configuration is quite easy. You'll have the same functionality as the Select tool (see Figure 15-25), where you can select or deselect columns, reorder, rename, or change their data types.

 When using joins, a little trick to know how many fields you should be expecting is to look at the number of fields in your two data sets. Your output number of fields will always be equal to the number of fields from your Target data set (let's say 9 for this example) and the number of fields from your Universe data set (let's say 3 for this example). If you don't deselect any fields, you would have 12 fields in your new data set. This is a great way to ensure you aren't losing anything by, say, accidentally deselecting a field.

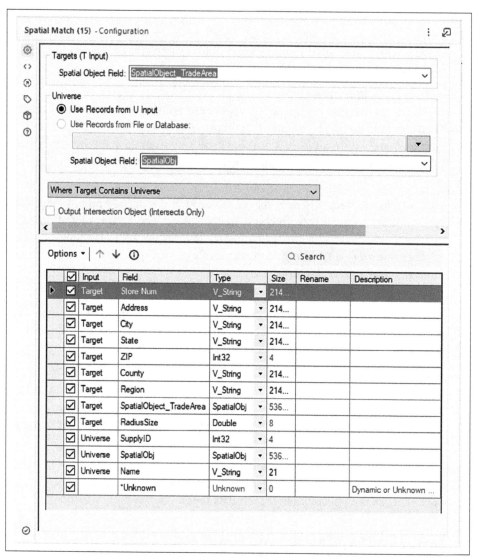

Figure 15-25. Spatial Match configuration

Make Grid tool

The Make Grid tool takes a specified spatial object (point or polygon) and creates a grid based on the spatial object. The resulting grid is either a single grid, bound to the extent of the input spatial objects, or individual grids that dissect each input polygon:

The Make Grid tool allows you to do two important things. First, by providing grids in your row-level data, you can quantify how many units per single grid (think houses, stray animals, new development of apartments). Second, and what many users miss, because you are breaking up your data into grids you can also provide that to tools like Tableau and use it in visualizations as well!

The configuration of the Make Grid tool is quite simple, as you can see in Figure 15-26. We've got a spatial object selected, the grid size noted, and we've also selected how we want to generate the grids.

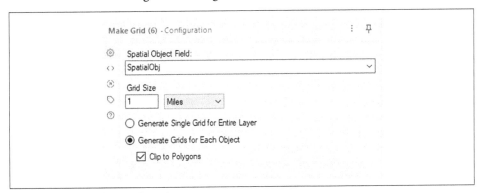

Figure 15-26. Make Grid configuration

The important thing to pay attention to is how you are generating the grids. You can generate a single grid that looks like Figure 15-27.

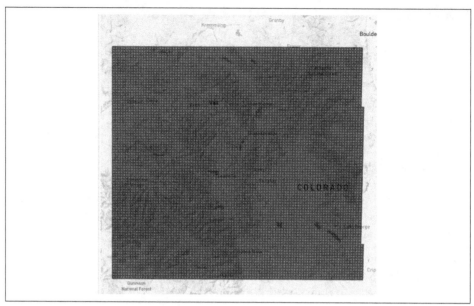

Figure 15-27. Single grid configuration

Notice that it's not form fitting. It is just creating grids up to the point everything is covered, regardless of whether there is one object or many. However, if you generate grids for each object, you can also use the Clip to Polygons checkbox, which fits to the shape (see Figure 15-28).

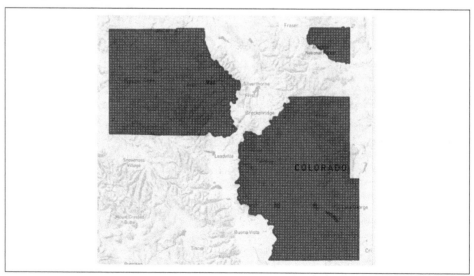

Figure 15-28. Multiple grid configuration

Visually this is interesting, but remember we are working with data. Most of the time, the data is what we want or need, and this is what I like about grids. Each grid becomes a row of data (see Figure 15-29).

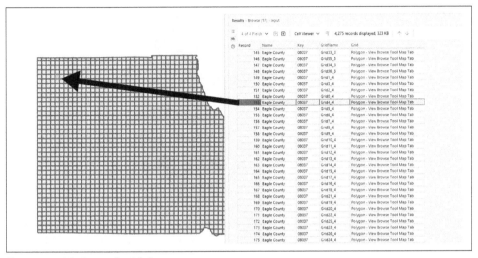

Figure 15-29. Row of grid data

If you want to modify the data in any way, for example to get the border grids of each object in order to determine a set of actions like zoning, then you could. It's really powerful. Remember that you can output this data to Tableau for some amazing mapping visualizations!

Heat Map tool

The Heat Map tool is actually quite cool (pun intended). It generates polygons representing different levels of heat in a given area, which is a useful visual format that makes it easy to understand what is happening:

What I like most about the Heat Map tool is its simplicity. Its whole job is to create the polygons based on the spatial object and data value you present to the configuration. However, if you pair this with another tool, the Report Map tool, you can color the maps that you create (see Figure 15-30).

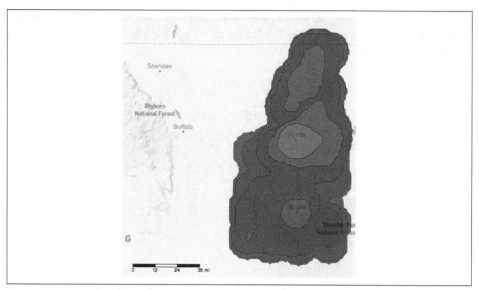

Figure 15-30. Colored heat map

Like many other tools that have a single capability, the true power of the Heat Map tool lies in the data it uses. Different data will produce different results. When you are building your workflows, think about bringing in additional data that might allow you to create or analyze new perspectives.

Find Nearest tool

The Find Nearest tool helps you identify the shortest distance between two or more spatial objects:

To use the Find Nearest tool, you have to bring in two data sets (see Figure 15-31): the Target and the Universe (just like the Spatial Match tool). The Target input is simply the spatial object(s) that you want to measure, and the Universe is simply all of the locations you want to measure the distance of the target to. Let's say you want to measure the distance between your store and your customers. Your store would be the Target and the list of all your customers would be the Universe.

In Alteryx Designer, we are going to tell the Find Nearest tool which data sets we want to use in the initial configuration (see Figure 15-32).

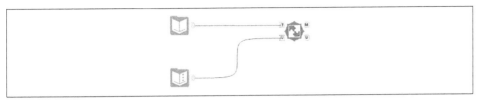

Figure 15-31. Target and Universe inputs

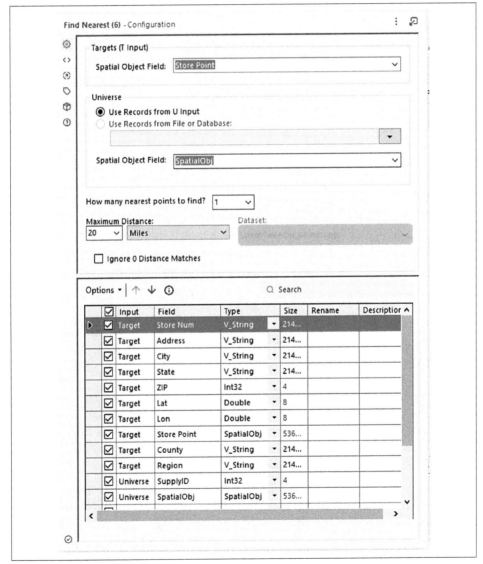

Figure 15-32. Find Nearest tool configuration

You can do this by setting the Spatial Object Field for both the Target and Universe inputs. Next, set how many points you want to find. Sometimes you will only want to find the closest location to your one store. However, this tool is so powerful that it will work even if you have tens of thousands of stores and millions of customers. You can find the top 5, 100, or 1,000 customers at *each* store you have. Once you have that set, enter the maximum distance you want to use to find relationships, and check the box "Ignore 0 Distance Matches" if you want to ignore those that are basically at the same location. Lastly, you'll notice like many other tools you have the option to select, change type, rename, or provide a description for each of your fields.

Once you have fully configured the tool, you can run it and see that the output provides you with three distinct items. The first is FindNearestRank, which is the sort of items from top to bottom for your matches on a specific location (obviously, if you are finding only the single nearest location, then that rank will only be 1). The next item you will notice is the DistanceMiles field, which tells you about the distance between that Target item in the data and the Universe. The two different locations will usually be on the same row of data for reference. Lastly, the Direction is provided, which tells you which direction the Universe is located from the Target.

Distance tool

The Distance tool simply measures from a point or centroid to another point, line, or polygon. However, don't be fooled by its simplicity. This tool can do some seriously powerful things when it's given context like distance between objects, distance to the edge of an object, or even distance from one side of an object to the other:

What makes the Distance tool so interesting is that you can not only measure distance "as the crow flies" (meaning, as if a bird was flying above an object and heading straight to the other object), but you can also measure the driving distance, with all the roads, turns, and freeways accounted for. A great use case for this tool is if you are a grocery store chain and you know your customers are only willing to drive 20 minutes maximum to get their groceries. You might want to know how far, in drive distance, your next store needs to be.

Configuration of the Distance tool is fairly simple (see Figure 15-33). You just need to input the spatial objects you want to measure distance to in the Spatial Objects Fields, and set the "Output Distance" and "When a point is inside a polygon" fields. Setting these options helps Alteryx know where to put the tape measure for measuring. If you are measuring the distance from a point inside the polygon to the edge of that polygon, you have options to decide how to measure the distance.

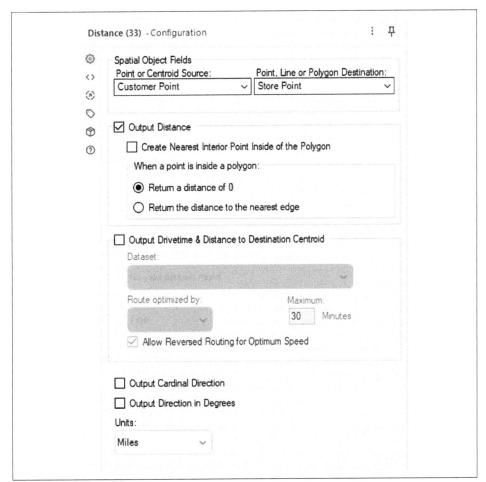

Figure 15-33. Distance tool configuration

If you have access to the third-party data, then configuration is easy as well.

External Data Providers

When it comes to third-party data, Alteryx supports data enrichment through external data providers, allowing users to enrich their existing data with additional attributes and variables for more precise analysis and modeling. One prominent third-party data provider that Alteryx integrates with is Experian, a leading global information services company.

Experian provides comprehensive data sets that encompass various aspects of consumer and business information. Alteryx users can connect to Experian's data services and tap into their collection of data, including demographic data, credit information, geographic data, consumer behavior insights, and more. This wealth of data enables businesses to gain a deeper understanding of their customers, target specific market segments, and make data-driven decisions.

In addition to Experian, Alteryx supports integration with other notable third-party data providers, such as Dun & Bradstreet, Mapbox, and TomTom. This range of available third-party data sources empowers users to explore and leverage diverse data sets within the Alteryx platform, enabling comprehensive analysis, predictive modeling, and decision making based on accurate and up-to-date information.

To dive deeper into this, check out the Alteryx resources (*https://oreil.ly/MfAs1*).

Spatial Info tool

The last tool in this chapter is one that you will likely use quite often if you are doing spatial analysis. The Spatial Info tool simply allows you to extract information about the spatial object(s), such as the area of the polygon, the number of parts, or even the centroid of that object:

There is almost no configuration other than simply selecting what information you want to see (see Figure 15-34).

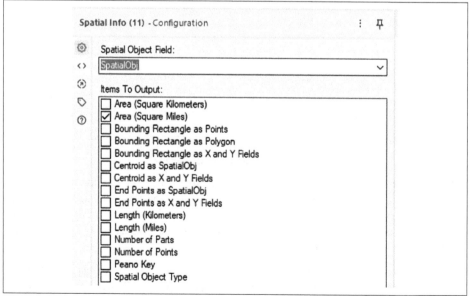

Figure 15-34. Spatial Info tool configuration

Let's say you're doing an analysis where you're using the Spatial Info tool and you cut away a portion of the spatial object from another and now you want to know how many square miles that new object is. You would simply check the box next to Area (Square Miles) and then run the workflow.

With this information, you can make better decisions, but you might be pleased to know that many other tools offer spatial functions within them like the Formula tool.

Spatial Functions in Other Tools

So far, we have covered all the Spatial tools that come out of the box with Alteryx Designer, but we haven't covered all of their capabilities. You can actually do some of the same spatial analysis using any of the tools that allow you to build expressions, like the Formula, Multi-Row Formula, and the Multi-Field Formula tools. There are even spatial operations you can do in the Summarize tool.

I would highly recommend you gain proficiency in using the spatial functions in the original Spatial toolset before you attempt it in the Formula tools, as it's very easy to lose your bearings. Understanding the Spatial tools will help you recognize what is working (or not) in the Formula tool.

Having said that, let's take a look at where you would find the spatial functions within the Formula tool. If you open a clean canvas and add a data input (preferably with a spatial data set configured with it) and then add a Formula tool, you will be able to go to the Formula tool configuration and to the functions menu to see the long list of spatial functions (see Figure 15-35).

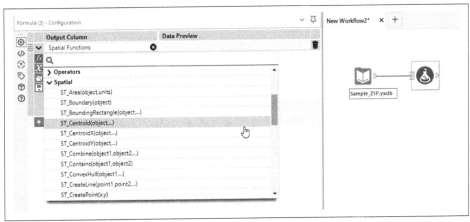

Figure 15-35. Spatial functions within the Formula tool

Everything you can do in the Spatial tools can be done here in the spatial functions of the Formula tool. Think of these as another tool to use however you like. Some users find it easier to write these formulas, as they can easily combine them and not have to use multiple tools to get the job done. It's really just a matter of preference. Some users prefer to use the spatial tools because they are in the mode and building a workflow of geospatial tools. Others want whatever is easiest; both options are fine.

We can also take a look at spatial functions within the Summarize tool. You don't have as many options for spatial analysis with this tool, but you do have a few important ones, like combining spatial objects. You can do the following five things in the Summarize tool for spatial analysis: Combine, Create Intersection, Create Bounding Rect, Create Convex Hull, and Create Centroid (see Figure 15-36).

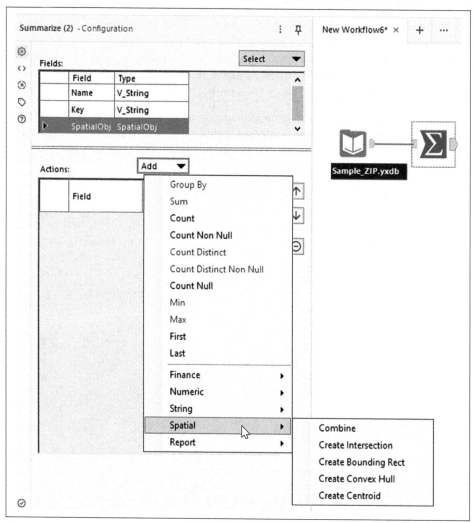

Figure 15-36. Spatial functions in the Summarize tool

Conclusion

The Spatial tools are a powerful suite of capabilities that allow you to work with spatial data. It takes a little time to get familiar with and understand all the components of the Spatial analysis toolset, but you can do it! There are many different use cases for these tools, from site selection to customer retention and many others. Remember to think about the tools in the three focus areas I laid out: building spatial objects, modifying spatial objects, and analyzing spatial objects.

Analysts who can add "spatial analytics" to their repertoire become immensely more valuable as they can think about analyzing 3D spaces instead of just rows and columns of data. When you think "spatially," it's important to visualize what you are trying to look at. Think about two stores being right next to each other, visually picture them and how you would measure how far apart they are. This mindset will help you when your spatial problems become more involved and complex.

In the next chapter, you will learn how to look at address data and the tools you have at your fingertips to help you come up with some key insights.

CHAPTER 16

Address Analysis

In this chapter, we are going to explore an area of analysis in which Alteryx Designer is particularly strong: address analysis. I am going to walk you through address analysis, which involves looking at physical addresses from both an accuracy point of view and a location perspective. As you go through this chapter, start thinking about all the other types of analysis you could do using addresses. Many times, when we are looking to blend data from various sources, we're always looking for a unique identifier and an address is often used as that, but you must make sure that it's accurate. Just because you might not have a specific tool created for it doesn't mean it can't be done. Think about areas of focus in your work today and consider how Alteryx Designer might help you. Ready? Let's get into it!

Introduction to Address Analysis

In the context of Alteryx Designer, address analysis is the examination of physical location addresses that are used to clean and prepare address data for further use in either geospatial or customer use cases. The end goal of doing this analysis is to have a clean data set that contains valid addresses that could be used.

Let's be clear on what constitutes good address data or bad/dirty address data. With bad/dirty address data, you see things like incomplete addresses, ambiguity like missing apartment or unit numbers, inaccurate street spellings, and missing zip codes or postal codes. This data is not valuable. You can't ship to it, you can't use it as a reference in your data, and you can't build further geospatial analysis off bad address data. The more unclear the address, the bigger the uncertainty and therefore the less useful for the purpose of analytics.

Here are two examples that demonstrate the importance of having good address data:

- Imagine you own a chain of restaurants and you have 10,000 customers in a city. If you had the addresses of those customers, you could analyze them geographically and see that you could easily open a new restaurant on the other side of town and ensure that you'd have a large customer base to draw from on the very first day of opening.

- Imagine if you had a team of salespeople who need to drive to multiple customer locations every week within a region, but you also have regions that overlap. Knowing the addresses, you could map out exactly where each salesperson would go that week and ensure they are driving the least number of miles, thus saving gas and overall time on the road.

Address analysis, again, involves looking at physical addresses from both an accuracy point of view as well as a location perspective. Some of you might think that this is just spatial analytics, and you'd be partially correct. Let's dive further into that idea. One area that is important to businesses is to ensure that the addresses they are working with are correct. What does "correct" mean in this context? In most cases, it means a mailable address that, for example, the US Postal Service could deliver a letter to. If the physical address that is used doesn't exist, your letter is going to get returned. Alteryx can tap into the Coding Accuracy Support System (CASS) data set, which we will cover in detail later, to validate that every address is correct (according to a standard list).

Address analysis can also be used for location analysis. When our addresses are correct, we can know not only where our customers are, but we can conduct analytics on the customers with tools like clustering, as well as create projections based on that location data. This type of location analysis relies on the data being correct.

These use cases are low-hanging fruit in the grand scheme of things, just a drop in the ocean compared to what is possible—we haven't even touched on the idea of combining address information with customer information like sales, items purchased, or customer profiles.

For many, conducting analysis against address data is just one part of a broader project, but it can get complex really fast. Alteryx makes processing addresses easy, and it helps to ensure your addresses are accurate and up to date. Think about it— new addresses are popping up everywhere all the time! New houses are being built, new offices, and entire neighborhoods with grocery stores, department stores, and more. All of these spaces need an address, so this data is constantly updated.

Before I jump into the tools to process addresses, I want to ensure you see the use cases and situations that would warrant this sort of analysis. If you haven't done this type of analysis yet, you might think there isn't much to it, but I assure you there is!

The CASS Data Set

Geocoding is a specialization in and of itself. Geocoding refers to the process of associating geographic coordinates (think latitude and longitude values) with input addresses in order to pinpoint locations and carry out geography-based analysis.

In many countries, there is a system that keeps track of all addresses—in the US, that system is called the Coding Accuracy Support System (CASS) (*https://oreil.ly/tmZyk*). CASS was created by the United States Postal Service (USPS) to improve the accuracy of addresses. It incentivizes high-quality address processing in order to reduce undeliverable mail, unsortable mail, and mail that requires extra effort by postal workers to reach the intended address.

The benefits of CASS for the USPS are really clear, as it makes them more efficient, but the exponential payoff has been the fact that software products like Alteryx have benefited greatly by allowing users to conduct analytics against location information that is validated against this unified standard. Nothing is better than verified, accurate, and standardized data—that's exactly what you get with CASS. We'll dig into CASS more shortly.

> Most of the tools for address analysis require a separate installation as part of the core data installation.

The Address Tool Palette

The Address tool palette (see Figure 16-1) will help you not only get your address data parsed and standardized, but it will also help convert it into formats that will be very useful for further analysis (specifically for use in geocoding, which I will explain further). Now, let's get into each of the tools you have available for address analysis, and what they can do for you!

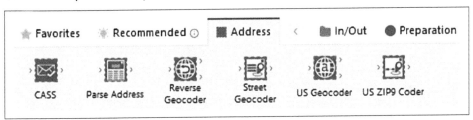

Figure 16-1. The Address tool palette

CASS Tool

If you are working even somewhat consistently with address data, you know it is bound to have issues—either the house or building number is off, maybe the street name is misspelled, or maybe the state is incorrect (believe me, it happens!).

But it's really important that address data be accurate and free from these types of issues. If you are sending products or promotions to an address, don't you want it to arrive? You'd be amazed at how many organizations ship to addresses that don't exist! Using the CASS tool, you can make sure your address data is 100% up to date:

The CASS tool also provides a ton of supplemental information based on your address. For example, maybe you need to know the Carrier Route or Congressional District or even the Zip Code Type—all of this, and more, can be appended to your data set.

To use the CASS tool properly, let's start off with a very simple and straightforward data set that looks something like Figure 16-2.

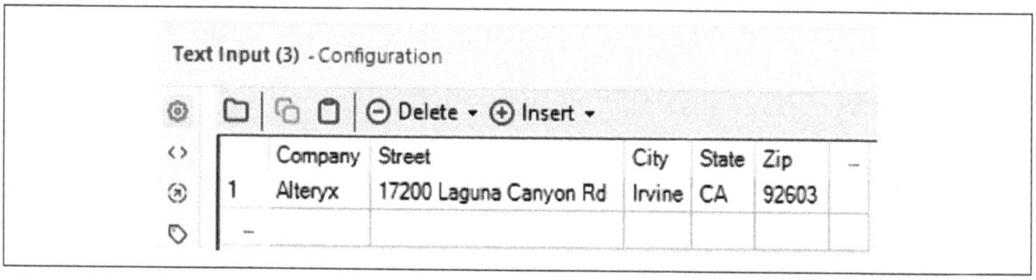

		Company	Street	City	State	Zip	...
	1	Alteryx	17200 Laguna Canyon Rd	Irvine	CA	92603	

Text Input (3) - Configuration

Figure 16-2. Alteryx street address

If we plug that simple text input into the CASS tool (see Figure 16-3), there are numerous options at our disposal.

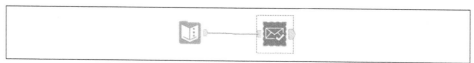

Figure 16-3. Text input to CASS tool

First, we have the configuration of the fields. This is quite a simple task—just map the fields from your data set (in our case, the text input from Figure 16-2) into the fields within the top section of the CASS configuration (see Figure 16-4).

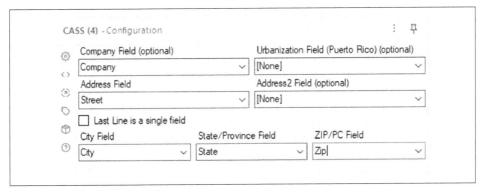

Figure 16-4. CASS tool configuration

Below the mapping of fields, a set of tabs allow you to expand what additional data fields you output. By matching your address data, the CASS tool is going to see all the additional fields that it can offer you. For example, if you have an address and want the time zone or county, CASS can provide it. Just select the appropriate field on the Output Fields tab (see Figure 16-5).

 If you'd like a detailed list of what each CASS field is or what it provides, simply go to the Alteryx help page for the CASS tool (*http://help.alteryx.com*).

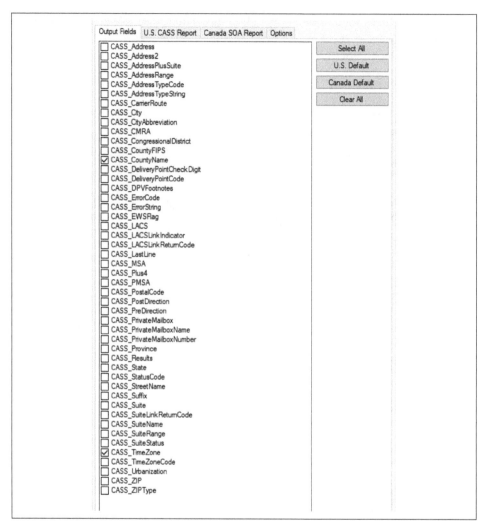

Figure 16-5. CASS Output Fields

When you run this workflow with not only your address fields but the additional CASS_CountyName and CASS_TimeZone fields selected, you'll see those fields in your results (see Figure 16-6).

Figure 16-6. CASS additional fields

When you output any of the "CASS_" listed fields, you are getting the standardized address that the post office uses in its operations. Meaning, you're getting an addressable field that is verified. For example, if you had a street address misspelled or an address street set as "Rd" when it was supposed to be an "Ave," then CASS would give you the correct address. To be clear, CASS output will change the addresses as necessary, but it will also tell you that it did so.

US ZIP9 Coder Tool

The US ZIP9 Coder tool helps you associate geographic coordinates from your input of a ZIP9 (also known as ZIP+4) code in your address data. With this tool, you can conduct geography-based analyses. The US ZIP9 Coder appends latitude and longitude, county and state FIPS (Federal Information Processing System) code, and census tract and block number to your data:

If you want to ensure the zip code values you're inputting are correct, connect the US ZIP9 Coder tool to the CASS tool. You will notice in the configuration all the fields that the tool provides for you (see Figure 16-7).

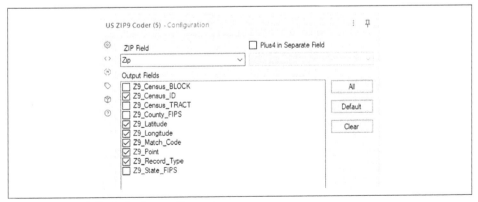

Figure 16-7. US Zip9 Coder configuration

The ZIP9 Coder tool only appends information to existing ZIP9 or ZIP+4 codes. It does not determine the correct ZIP9 or ZIP+4 code for the input address. The input data must already contain the *correct* ZIP9 or ZIP+4 codes.

If you compare this to the CASS tool, all these fields (with the exception of Z9_County_FIPS) are distinct from those in the CASS tool. The most important fields are the Z9_Latitude, Z9_Longitude, and Z9_Point fields. Using the Z9_Point field, we now start to tap into the power of the Spatial tools in Alteryx Designer.

Street Geocoder Tool

The Street Geocoder tool is very much like the US Zip9 Coder tool (it even looks similar) but instead of using the Zip Code to create a geocoded location, it uses...you guessed it...the street address:

The Street Geocoder tool also works a bit differently. Where the output of the Zip9 Coder tool was the census block, the census ID, the census tract, county FIPS codes, latitude, longitude, and match code, the Street Geocoder tool outputs quite a number of valuable variables (see Figure 16-8).

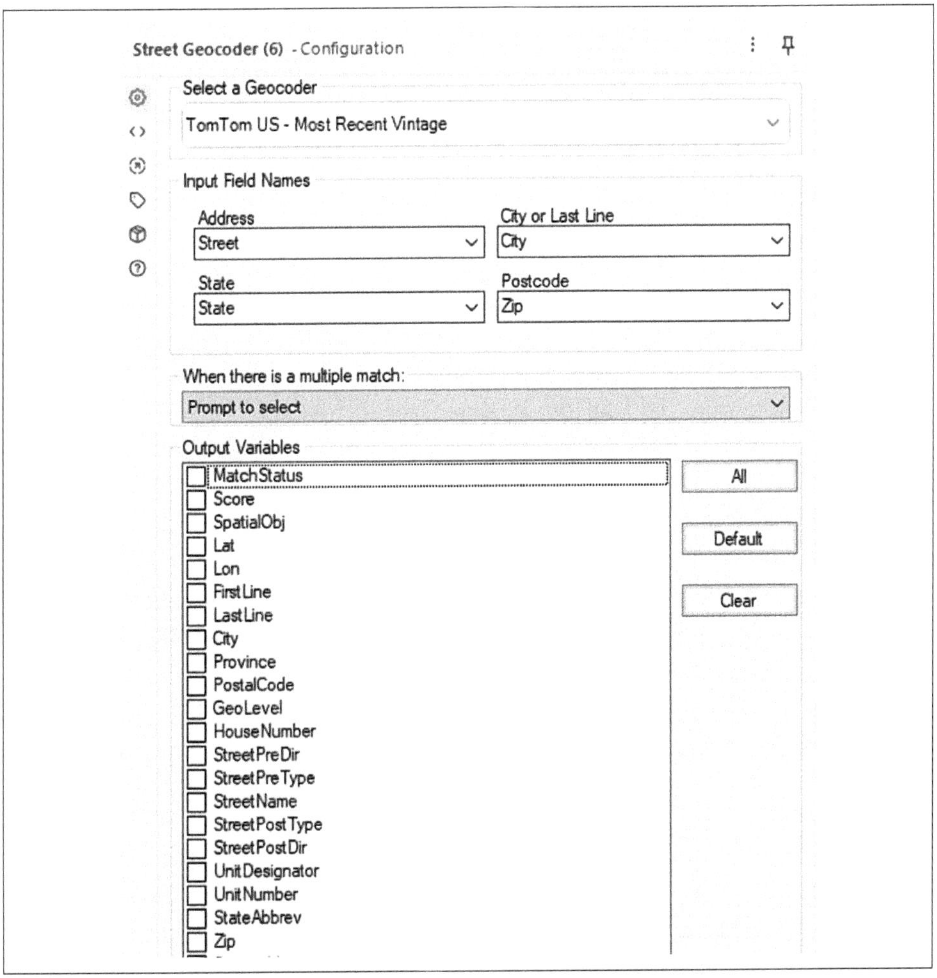

Figure 16-8. Street Geocoder output variables

It's important to pay attention to what happens when there is a multiple match, meaning multiple matches to a street address. The Street Geocoder tool enables you to decide how to handle such cases (see Figure 16-9). One thing to consider is whether you are fully automating this workflow; if you are, then you wouldn't want it to prompt you because no one will be there to run it.

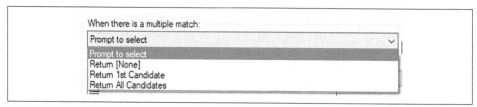

Figure 16-9. What to do when there is a multiple match

Reverse Geocoder Tool

The Reverse Geocoder tool is another tool in the Address arsenal that helps you reverse engineer coordinate latitude and longitude locations. Reverse Geocoder does this by using data from the TomTom Reverse Geocoder API:

The Reverse Geocoder tool helps to format address fields and latitude and longitude coordinates. It also produces a summary output showing a count of records that were successfully and unsuccessfully reverse geocoded.

A great use case for the Reverse Geocoder tool is when you need to assign address data to a spatial object or coordinates, as shown in Figures 16-10 and 16-11. This information can then be used to carry out further geography-based analysis.

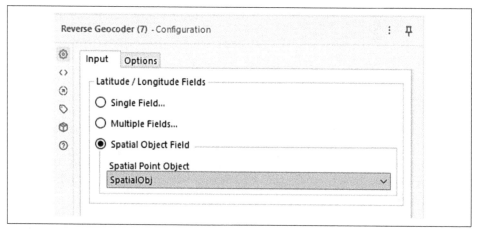

Figure 16-10. Reverse Geocoder input configuration

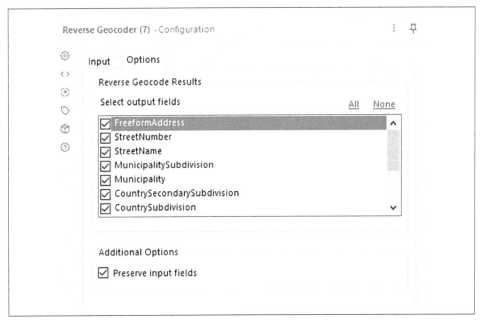

Figure 16-11. Reverse Geocoder options configuration

Parse Address Tool

The Parse Address tool can help you break apart a full address into its parts, such as street number and name, as well as city, state, and zip code:

There is a lot of flexibility in this tool, as address data isn't always formatted in a single line or even two lines. The Parse Address tool allows you to get the standardized address into the format you need. It's an important tool because it leverages the CASS library, a separate data install that is part of the Alteryx Spatial offering.

While the CASS library installation is required, you do not have to run address data through the CASS tool to parse it.

US Geocoder Tool

The US Geocoder tool provides geocoding capabilities for users working with location-based data in the US:

The US Geocoder tool enables users to easily convert addresses into geographic coordinates (latitude and longitude) or vice versa. It uses a robust database of address information to accurately match and assign coordinates to addresses, allowing users to geographically visualize and analyze their data. It uses the CASS tool, Street Geocoder tool, or US ZIP9 Coder tool to geocode a customer file.

You can also use the tool for additional functions such as batch geocoding for large data sets, reverse geocoding to obtain address information from coordinates, and handling various address formats and types. This tool allows you to efficiently leverage location data and unlock valuable insights.

Conclusion

If you have address data, it is critical to ensure that it is correct. Fortunately, there is a standard in most countries for how address data is validated and verified. It is important to use standards like CASS to ensure that your products or mail are delivered to these addresses. This will save you money, time, and effort.

There are many geocoding tools available in the Address tool palette, like the US ZIP9 Coder tool, the Street Geocoder tool, and the US Geocoder tool. It's important that you spend time practicing with these tools to get familiar with their features. Some will offer similar fields, but all of the tools are unique.

We'll switch gears now, moving away from detailed tool walkthroughs, and give you a preview of Alteryx Server.

PART VI

Alteryx Server and Analytics Cloud

CHAPTER 17

Introduction to Alteryx Server

In this chapter, I am going to provide an overview of Alteryx Server. The topic is worthy of another book in and of itself. However, I do want you to get a taste for why it exists and why it's so powerful for automation and collaboration of Alteryx workflows. I also want you to start to see the full analytics process with Alteryx, which isn't only building workflows, but also automating them to gain higher-impact insights, in turn helping your organization become more productive.

Now, consider which of the following scenarios you'd prefer:

1. You go on vacation but each day you must interrupt your beach time by jumping on your laptop to click Run, watch and ensure that your workflow runs successfully, and then send an email stating that it has been completed as expected. This easily eats a couple hours each day out of your well-earned vacation time.

2. You go on vacation and each day—while you are on the beach, playing in the waves, sitting by the pool, drinking your beverages with little colorful umbrellas in them—the Alteryx Server is doing everything that you told it to. It runs the scheduled workflow, it lets your team know the status automatically as it completes, and it sends out a summarized status email to the executives.

Obviously, I'm leading you a bit, but there is so much truth in this thought experiment. You don't need to be handcuffed by your Excel work or manual processes. You should be able to take a "no work" vacation. Your workflows can be 100% automated. They can be scheduled to run at specific times, recurring or static, or even triggered by events, ensuring that data processing and analysis tasks are executed automatically and on a regular basis. This is why Alteryx Server is so powerful.

Let's dig in, starting with what Alteryx Server is.

What Is Alteryx Server?

Alteryx Server (see Figure 17-1) allows organizations to collaborate, share, and scale their analytic workflows across teams and departments. It provides a centralized platform for managing and scheduling workflows that were built using Alteryx Designer.

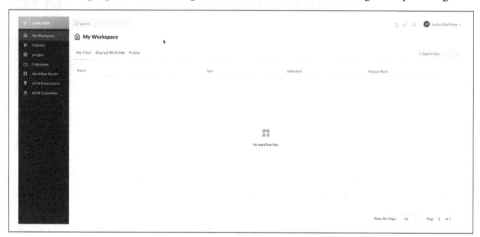

Figure 17-1. Alteryx Server interface

With Alteryx Server, users can publish their analytic workflows created in Alteryx Designer to the server environment. These workflows can be scheduled to run at specific times or triggered by events (such as an API call), allowing data processing and analysis tasks to be executed automatically and efficiently.

The server also enables collaboration by allowing multiple users to access and use workflows simultaneously. It provides version control and a centralized repository for managing workflows, making it easier for teams to collaborate on projects and share insights.

The Main Capabilities of Alteryx Server

Alteryx Server offers several key capabilities that enhance collaboration, scalability, and governance of data analytics workflows:

User and group permissions
> Administrators can set up user and group permissions to control access to workflows and data sources. This ensures that sensitive data and workflows are only accessible to authorized individuals, enhancing data security and compliance.

Monitoring and logging

Alteryx Server offers monitoring and logging capabilities, allowing administrators to track the execution and performance of workflows. This helps in identifying issues, troubleshooting errors, and optimizing workflows for better efficiency.

Scalability and performance

Organizations can scale their data analytics processes by leveraging server resources. Workflows can be executed on the server, which can handle larger data sets and processing requirements, improving performance and reducing the workload on individual machines.

API and web service integration

Alteryx Server supports APIs and web services, allowing integration with other systems and applications. This enables organizations to incorporate Alteryx workflows into their existing workflows, data pipelines, or custom applications.

Data governance and compliance

Alteryx Server provides governance features such as access controls, including telemetry. These features help organizations maintain data integrity, ensure regulatory compliance, and meet data governance requirements.

Scalable Analytic Apps

Alteryx Server enables the creation and deployment of scalable Analytic Apps. These apps can be built using Alteryx Designer and published to the server, allowing users to interact with predefined workflows and models through a user-friendly interface.

I want you to have a robust understanding of each of these components, so let's dive into each one individually. After reading this chapter, you will understand how each component of Alteryx Server amplifies both the value of Alteryx Designer and your potential as an Alteryx Designer user.

Workflow Deployment and Scheduling

Alteryx Server allows users to publish workflows from Alteryx Designer to the server environment. This is an important capability, as it allows for management of workflows in a scalable, collaborative, and always-on environment that anyone with the right permissions can access at any time of the day or night. Management of workflows no longer happens on a laptop that can be turned off, lost, used by only one person, or have limited (not scalable) resources.

This single capability has given thousands of analysts their lives back—including me. Imagine that you decide to take a vacation somewhere hot and sunny, let's say the Virgin Islands. You have a wonderful time but, like many of us, you have a demanding job where nothing can stop running even if you want to use some of that vacation time you have.

Collaboration and Sharing

In organizations that have multiple analysts, it's common for each one to be solely responsible for a portion of the process. This means that no one has full visibility into the entire process. This is not a good place to be in.

From a succession-planning perspective, this is almost as nightmarish as it gets because each analyst is a point of failure in a process. If any one of them leaves the organization, the process fails or Herculean efforts need to be made to keep the process going, putting undue stress on each of the other analysts. We need to spend less time on moving our people around and more time on finding the tools that enable collaboration.

Naturally, there are times when we need help from our colleagues and should have software that helps us to do exactly that. For years, Alteryx Server has helped users like you and I collaborate and share our work—not only to get help during the development process, but also to allow our work to benefit more and more users regardless of department or area of the organization.

One way that Alteryx Server drives collaboration is via version control. If you and I are working on a workflow and I make changes, wouldn't you want those changes to be reflected in a different version than what you're working on? Of course! Alteryx Server provides version control and helps to ensure users are clear about who does what and what exactly got updated, changed, or deleted. It also goes one step further and allows you to easily roll back to another version with one click.

User and Group Permissions

Within Alteryx Server, there are a couple of different areas that you will interact with once you log in. You have Users and Groups (of Users) that you can give permission to use studios and collections. Studios are the individual workspaces that you will work in, and collections are much like a studio that can be shared between you and your team. When you upload a workflow, it will initially go to your personal studio. With the right permissions, you will be able to move it to a collection.

Any type of software environment must be easy for users to sign up and use, and also easy for administrators to manage and maintain. Alteryx Server provides the ability to tie users' access to, say, enterprise systems like Active Directory, while also using SAML or other single sign-on mechanisms. This alleviates a huge burden on IT organizations to manage user access. Alteryx Server also supports groups, which adds another level of access.

Alteryx Server supports DCM so that administrators can ensure the data connections, and the workflows that use those data connections, are secure on the server. Multiple levels of access ensure you're giving the right level of access to the right users.

Fun fact for super users: you can specify a password on a workflow (regardless of whether the user has access on the server). This is extremely useful in the right scenarios, but an absolute mess when it's not required as it creates too much red tape and unnecessary bottlenecks.

Monitoring and Logging

I once had the opportunity to manage and maintain the largest Alteryx Designer and Server deployment in the world. I was therefore passionate about what the monitoring and logging features could do for me.

Alteryx Server helped me understand what was happening with the software at any point in time. If a workflow failed, I could look at the logs to figure out exactly what was happening and fix it. If a node went down, I could dig into it and understand why. This was critical, as having multiple nodes all over the world was not an easy or straightforward task and I sure wasn't going to do it manually! I could build a workflow that worked with the database and pulled out the information I needed. I could look at prebuilt dashboards that would give me all the information I needed to make sound decisions.

Not only can administrators see workflows that are having issues, but they can also see how much value automation brings to those workflows.

Scalability and Performance

By default, Alteryx Server is a single-node installation with a controller node and a worker node on the same server. While this is powerful, it is wholly dependent on the computing power of that single server and it also presents a single point of failure. Alteryx Server offers the option to configure additional worker nodes for more resilience and to expand the computing power to run more jobs in parallel.

A precursor to scaling is analyzing and optimizing the schedule. If you find that there are a lot of jobs queued between 6 a.m. and 8 a.m., but there is lots of white space elsewhere in the schedule, moving jobs around can make a big difference. When users like us get to building bigger and more complex workflows, there is a demand for an environment that can take on the extra workload as well as run workflows faster and under bigger loads of data. Alteryx Server can provide such an environment.

When you are working to automate larger and larger workloads, you want to know what you'll need to scale and you want to ensure the necessary level of performance is achievable. See "Considerations for Scaling Alteryx Server" (*https://oreil.ly/yX2cU*) for more details.

API and Web Service Integration

One of the releases that I was the most excited about, in more than 10 years of working with Alteryx, was the release of the Alteryx V3 APIs that opened up the entire Alteryx Server operations via APIs. This meant that the entire operation and management of an Alteryx Server could not only be scripted, but automated. Workflows could be triggered by other systems within an organization.

For those who haven't needed to work with APIs, it's hard to appreciate the immense value they provide. I didn't fully realize it until I encountered an organization that almost never had to log in to the Alteryx Server environment because they did everything, from user management to workflow execution, via API calls. This means that users didn't have to spend extra time logging in to the Alteryx Server. They didn't have to click the buttons to run a job, and they didn't even need to set a schedule. They could do it directly from whatever app they were using that was integrated with Alteryx Server. It was so magical and I still love seeing it done today. It allows for communication between the most unlikely of systems.

There is a set of Alteryx macros built specifically for using the V3 APIs, which you can see in Figure 17-2.

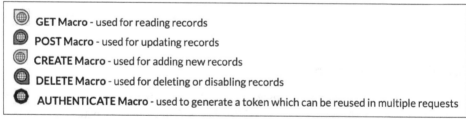

Figure 17-2. Alteryx Server V3 API macros

With those Alteryx V3 macros, you can orchestrate many different jobs that exist on the server.

Data Governance and Compliance

Alteryx Server can be governed with the same standards that many organizations require. Powerful functionality like telemetry is also built into Alteryx Designer. There is also the capability to use what is called "Phone Home" data, or data that comes from each individual user in an organization and can be directed to Alteryx Server's MongoDB.

Scalable Analytic Apps

Analytic Apps, which we discussed in a previous chapter, are by far the most underrated and underutilized functionality in Alteryx Server. They can turn any workflow into a dynamically configurable app with a simple UI. Imagine making that simple app available to every employee in your company. This is self-service analytics in its simplest form, and the value Analytic Apps bring could save or make your organization millions of dollars in time savings or top-line revenue.

These apps are built using Alteryx Designer and published to the server, allowing users to interact with predefined workflows and models through a user-friendly interface. Now, a "user" in this case is someone who only needs to run an application and doesn't need a license. It's free to access Analytic Apps on the Alteryx Gallery. Users can run a workflow with inputs on it that will filter data points like a date, a name from a drop-down, a location, or even a typed value.

 Analytic Apps on Alteryx Server allow anyone to leverage Alteryx. Users of Analytic Apps don't need to know how to build a workflow to get the benefit of the outputs (and they aren't reliant on the developer to produce the output for them).

Imagine you want to build a sales report. You (a single-license user) can build a workflow that automates this process. You then can publish it up to the server and even schedule it. Now, wouldn't it be amazing if you could provide a link to the 2,000 salespeople in your organization and not only allow them to have access (for free!) to run that report but also build it into an app that could take parameters like the region or location of the sales territory, or the sales manager, or even filters like greater or less than an amount. Now, every salesperson can not only get the sales reports but also generate reports that are specific to what matters most to them. This is just scratching the surface of what's possible with Analytic Apps.

Conclusion

The Alteryx Server is a simple concept but can become as complex as needed for your organization. Its features have a direct impact on your productivity and that of your users. It can deploy and schedule workflows to start cutting the hundreds of hours of wasted manual work. It helps to drive collaboration and sharing of workflows and applications all tied together with governance and the ability to manage thousands of users around the world. For administrators, it can not only scale and perform well against even the largest of data sets, but also monitor and log activity to ensure any issues are easily and quickly addressed. Lastly, although Alteryx Server is a separate product and cost, it drives scalable products like Analytic Apps that can impact an entire organization. Now, let's pivot to the Alteryx Analytics Cloud Platform.

CHAPTER 18

Introduction to the Alteryx Analytics Cloud Platform

A couple of years ago, Alteryx could see that the power of cloud computing combined with scalable analytics was a powerful combination. They also saw that customers who had grown to love the simplicity and ease-of-use of Alteryx Designer, but who needed to move to the cloud, weren't being addressed. Out of this observation came the idea for the Alteryx Analytics Cloud Platform.

Alteryx leadership posited that platforms work best and therefore committed to building the Alteryx Analytics Cloud Platform (*https://oreil.ly/L7qx-*). At the time of this writing, the vision that is being worked on is to pair Alteryx Designer and Alteryx Server alongside the Analytics Cloud Portfolio of Apps. Designer and Server are what is called "Cloud Connected Applications," whereas everything else is "Cloud Native Applications." This is useful because, like Amazon AWS or Google Cloud Platform (GCP), having a suite of applications that are built to work closely together and serve the landscape of users and use cases is a more efficient and cost-effective way to deliver technology. I won't dive too deep into this topic here, as this too could be a whole book on its own, but I want to ensure that you have a solid understanding of what's available and how to best use those features.

The fundamental concepts you'll learn about in this chapter include:

- Why platforms are valuable
- The move from all-purpose to purpose-built functionality
- The influence of AI

You'll also get a high-level overview of the current cloud applications available in the Alteryx Analytics Cloud Platform (AACP), including:

- Designer Cloud
- Alteryx Machine Learning
- Auto Insights
- App Builder
- Location Analytics
- Plans

Let's dive in and discuss why platforms are valuable.

Why Platforms Are Valuable

In the last decade or so, with the explosive growth and maturity of cloud providers such as Google Cloud Platform (GCP), Microsoft Azure, and Amazon AWS, more businesses are being influenced and enticed to move their infrastructure and software to the cloud. It could be because of the cost implications, where operating one environment and reducing the number of people that must manage it will cost less, or it could be the idea that many companies have so many different tools in their organization and it is becoming increasingly harder to manage. Then lastly, the capabilities in a cloud platform might just be better or more advanced and more scalable. Cloud platforms are often considered valuable for several reasons:

Integration and compatibility

Platforms provide a common framework and set of tools that allow different software applications to integrate and work together. They enable interoperability between diverse systems and can simplify the process of connecting and exchanging data between applications. This often promotes efficiency, reduces duplication of efforts, and enhances overall productivity.

Customization and flexibility

Platforms are often designed to be flexible and customizable, allowing users to adapt the software to their specific needs. They provide a foundation upon which developers can build applications, extensions, and plug-ins, tailoring the platform to suit their requirements. This flexibility can enable businesses and individuals to create unique solutions that meet their specific objectives.

Ecosystem and collaboration

Platforms often foster vibrant ecosystems of developers, third-party vendors, and users. These communities contribute to the platform by building and sharing add-ons, extensions, and integrations. The collaborative nature of platforms encourages innovation, accelerates development, and expands the capabilities of the software through the contributions of a diverse range of stakeholders.

Scalability and performance

Platforms are designed to handle complex tasks and large-scale operations. They typically offer robust infrastructure, scalability options, and performance optimization, enabling them to handle high volumes of data and user interactions. This scalability helps the software to grow and adapt as the needs of the users or the business evolve.

Cost efficiency

Software platforms often provide a cost-effective solution compared to building custom software from scratch. They offer prebuilt components, tools, and frameworks that can significantly reduce development time and costs. Additionally, platforms often provide maintenance, updates, and support services, reducing the burden on organizations to manage and maintain their software infrastructure independently.

Time to market

Using a software platform can help accelerate the development process. By leveraging existing components and infrastructure, developers can focus on building unique features and functionalities without reinventing the wheel. This allows organizations to bring their products or services to market faster, gaining a competitive edge in their respective industries.

I recognize that this can feel a little fluffy and even a bit salesy, but that is truly not my intention here. I believe it is valuable to understand why cloud computing and especially platforms are useful and a worthy investment of your time. According to IDC, cloud computing has reached over $500 billion in revenue (*https://oreil.ly/e1Jky*). There must be something to it.

It's important to note that not all cloud providers are equal nor do they offer the same functionality across the board. The AACP, for example, is a purpose-built platform that can sit on top of any of the three major cloud providers listed earlier to provide the necessary analytics and data science tools across many users and use cases.

The Move from All-Purpose to Purpose-Built

Alteryx Designer has been developed for more than 25 years with enthusiastic support and input from customers. As you've learned in previous chapters, Alteryx Designer can not only handle basic data preparation and blending but also spatial analytics, building macros and apps, and even predictive and prescriptive analytics. It's known to users as a Swiss Army knife for analytics.

This is great if you have a decently powerful laptop, are not being forced to the cloud, and if there aren't 10,000 other users at your company, as it becomes very difficult to manage and administer—as well as stay well organized—as more and more companies democratize analytics (meaning, have more users do analytical work). But we are in a changing world where AI and globalization require purpose-built software.

Purpose-built software refers to applications or systems that are specifically designed and developed to meet the unique needs and requirements of a particular industry, organization, or user group. Think of Salesforce, as an example. That is what I would call a purpose-built cloud platform, as it is specifically designed to meet the needs of salespeople and those who support sales. Does it do other things? Sure, but its focus is to support the sales process and provide sales information.

Figure 18-1 demonstrates how AACP is an example of a purpose-built platform.

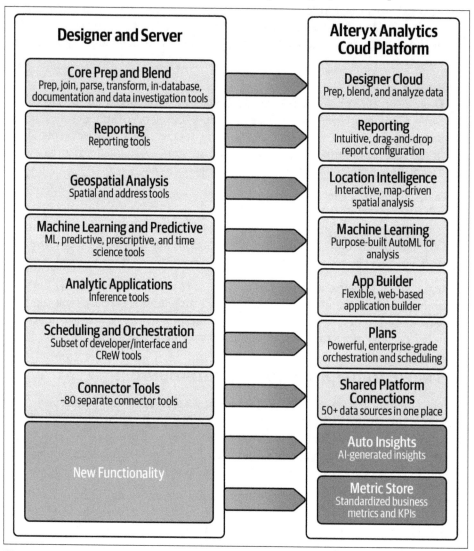

Figure 18-1. Purpose-built capabilities of the AACP

On the left side, you see the high-level capabilities of Alteryx Designer and Alteryx Server. All these features and capabilities are part of only two products. Think of a

Swiss Army knife that is one tool with many different functioning parts. Now, you will notice on the right side the more focused, purpose-built AACP applications that align with each specific capability of Designer and Server.

The Influence of AI

AI has had a significant influence on cloud platforms in general and especially on Alteryx's approach to its own platform. AI is transforming the way data is collected, analyzed, and used. Some of the ways AI has impacted cloud analytics platforms include leveraging machine learning and deep learning techniques to uncover insights from large volumes of data; automating or assisting in data cleansing, transformation, and preparation tasks; AI algorithms that can build predictive models and recommend optimal actions based on historical data; and detecting security threats and anomalies within data.

Overall, it's clear that the integration of AI into cloud analytics platforms has revolutionized data analysis, enabling organizations to extract more value from their data, gain deeper insights, and make data-driven decisions at scale. Let's talk a bit more about the AACP.

The Alteryx Analytics Cloud Platform

The AACP, as of this writing, provides a set of tools and features for data blending, predictive modeling, machine learning, and data visualization. The platform allows users to access, manipulate, and analyze data from various sources in a secure and scalable environment. With its familiar interface and drag-and-drop functionality, users can create workflows, automate processes, and get valuable information from their data. The AACP has tried to enable collaboration, sharing, and scheduling of analytics workflows as well.

Currently, there are six apps available in the AACP. Each has a focused purpose, but all are highly integrated. I'll cover each one at a high level, as it stands today. I won't dig into the details on how to use each one (that is outside the scope of this book), but you can dig into the documentation (*http://help.alteryx.com*) for more details.

Designer Cloud

Alteryx Designer Cloud provides a visual, drag-and-drop interface for users to access and manipulate data from various sources. Designer Cloud incorporates the familiar Designer Desktop UI in a cloud environment that allows you to connect to your cloud data, as well as upload your localized data sources (files on your desktop), and push compute into cloud-based databases. It leverages the power of cloud computing to efficiently process and analyze large-scale data sets. Designer Cloud promotes collaboration and sharing within teams, allowing users to securely publish and share workflows.

Users would use Designer Cloud for data prepping and blending. For more information, check out the help documentation for Designer Cloud (*https://oreil.ly/Ml7cM*).

Alteryx Machine Learning

Alteryx Machine Learning allows users to build and deploy machine learning models. It provides a step-by-step interface for data preparation, feature engineering, model training, and model evaluation. With Alteryx Machine Learning, users can choose from a variety of algorithms and techniques, including regression, classification, and time series. Additionally, Alteryx Machine Learning integrates with other Alteryx tools, enabling users to incorporate machine learning into their end-to-end data workflows.

It's important to point out that Alteryx Machine Learning is simply meant to help build models and does not replace or overlap much with the Alteryx Intelligence Suite, which is used with Alteryx Desktop Designer. The Intelligence Suite has many tools to support capabilities such as text classification, reading PDF documents and images, as well as sentiment analysis. Now, where some users might get a little confused is where the Intelligence Suite has a palette of tools called "Machine Learning," which many refer to as AutoML. These tools in Alteryx Desktop Designer help users build machine learning models within a workflow. Many of these capabilities were improved on and made available in the AACP with Alteryx Machine Learning.

Users would use Alteryx Machine Learning to build a model for understanding whether a person is likely to make their scheduled doctor's appointment. For more information, check out the help documentation for Alteryx Machine Learning (*https://oreil.ly/nT9Dd*).

Auto Insights

Alteryx Auto Insights leverages advanced statistical techniques and algorithms to analyze the data and identify meaningful patterns and trends. With Auto Insights, users can explore and visualize their data without the need for manual coding or extensive data analysis expertise. The tool provides interactive charts, graphs, and summary statistics that facilitate data exploration and communication. It saves users time and effort by automating the process of generating informative visualizations, allowing users to focus on extracting valuable insights from their data.

One of its more recent features is Magic Documents, which creates emails or documents like PowerPoint presentations automatically with the data and analysis done in Auto Insights.

Users would use Auto Insights to automatically analyze a data set and deliver insights that they can drill into further. For more information, check out the help documentation for Alteryx Auto Insights (*https://oreil.ly/WSQOa*).

App Builder

Alteryx App Builder empowers technical users to create custom applications that are used from the browser. It provides a user-friendly interface for designing and building interactive applications that automate data processes. With App Builder, users can create intuitive UIs, define data inputs and outputs, and incorporate advanced features such as decision trees, macros, and analytic models. The tool supports customization options, allowing users to tailor the application's appearance and behavior to meet specific business requirements. App Builder enables users to streamline data workflows and provide self-service analytics capabilities to a wider audience within their organization.

Users would use App Builder to build a simple UI for a group of executives to choose which elements of a report or data set are useful. Then, based on the selections, users can process or manipulate the data in the right manner for the executives. For more information, check out the help documentation for Alteryx App Builder (*https://oreil.ly/uCVvD*).

Location Intelligence

Alteryx Location Intelligence allows technical users to leverage spatial data and perform advanced geographic analysis. It provides a range of tools and capabilities for geocoding, spatial blending, and more. With Location Intelligence, users can integrate location data from various sources, visualize data on maps, and derive insights based on spatial relationships. The tool allows users to unlock the full potential of their data by incorporating location-based context and analysis into their workflows.

Plans

Alteryx Plans lets users orchestrate, operationalize, and automate data workflows. Users can execute their workflows in parallel or based on conditional logic, and set alerts if a process doesn't complete as expected. This functionality empowers users to streamline and automate their data processes, optimizing efficiency and productivity within the Alteryx Designer Cloud environment. Pay close attention to this particular application, as it has the potential to orchestrate an entire department's workload.

Future Applications

Because the AACP is fairly new and growing fast, there will likely be many more applications for Alteryx users. Pay attention to developments in this platform and keep current on what new technologies are soon to be implemented.

Conclusion

In summary, implementing cloud analytics with Alteryx delivers value by providing scalability, flexibility, cost-effectiveness, easy integration, advanced capabilities, and robust security. It enables organizations to leverage data for informed decision-making, driving innovation, and gaining a competitive edge in today's data-driven world. It empowers technical users to efficiently handle large-scale data, collaborate effectively, automate workflows, and leverage cutting-edge analytics tools to drive impactful insights and outcomes. More than all this, in my humble opinion it makes analytics fun!

I want to sincerely thank you for spending your valuable time with me. I truly hope that this book has helped you learn more about Alteryx Designer and has encouraged you to think a bit about the future. Analytics can be fun and enjoyable. I hope you find the same as you figure out new things by analyzing data. I strongly encourage you to stick with learning Alteryx over time. After so many years, I continue to experience little aha moments and I tell new users that I still haven't tapped into the full capabilities of Alteryx Designer.

I have one small but important ask of each of you. If you found a new passion in analytics and data, or you've renewed one, please share your knowledge. It is one of the best parts of the amazing Alteryx Community—the abundance of caring people who share the love of analytics and solving problems, and who gladly give their time and energy to spreading that passion. It is what drives me and, as I often say, we need all the help we can get. So go on and write a blog, record a video, teach a course, or do something really wild like write a book on Alteryx! Always feel free to reach out if I can ever be of help to you on your analytics journey.

Peace, Love, and Silliness,

Joshua Burkhow

joshua@altertricks.com

Index

About the Author

Joshua Burkhow is an Alteryx ACE Emeritus and the chief evangelist at Alteryx, where he focuses on advocating for Alteryx users and sharing his deep knowledge of the Alteryx platform. Previously, he led the global deployment of Alteryx at PwC, supporting over 100,000 users, and consulted on Alteryx-focused initiatives with Nike, Mercedes-Benz, Adidas, Verizon, and many others.

As one of the leading international experts on Alteryx today, Joshua is also an analytics expert and consultant with over 20 years of experience in analytics-based technical leadership roles. For 10 years, he has designed and taught Alteryx training courses to hundreds of companies and thousands of analytics professionals across the United States, from beginners to expert-level Alteryx users.

You can contact Joshua at *joshua@altertricks.com*, on LinkedIn (*https://www.linkedin.com/in/joshuaburkhow*), Twitter (@joshuaburkhow), and Instagram (@joshuaburkhow).

Colophon

The animal on the cover of *Alteryx Designer: The Definitive Guide* is a butterfly agama (*Leiolepis*), also known as a common butterfly lizard. These lizards are native to Southeast Asia.

Butterfly agamas dig burrows underground where they sleep. Their diet consists mostly of insects but can also include fruits and vegetables. In appearance, they typically have a gray or olive-green base with sides of a variety of colors (from yellow to red to black stripes). The young can be distinguished by their reddish tails.

The current conservation status (IUCN) of the butterfly agama is "Least Concern." Many of the animals on O'Reilly covers are endangered; all of them are important to the world.

The cover illustration is by Karen Montgomery, based on an antique line engraving from *English Cyclopedia*. The cover fonts are Gilroy Semibold and Guardian Sans. The text font is Adobe Minion Pro; the heading font is Adobe Myriad Condensed; and the code font is Dalton Maag's Ubuntu Mono.

O'REILLY®

Learn from experts.
Become one yourself.

Books | Live online courses
Instant answers | Virtual events
Videos | Interactive learning

Get started at oreilly.com.

©2023 O'Reilly Media, Inc. O'Reilly is a registered trademark of O'Reilly Media, Inc. 175_7.25.19.7.5

Printed in the USA
CPSIA information can be obtained
at www.ICGtesting.com
JSHW050024090724
66057JS00010B/75

9 781098 107529